BLACK STUDENT POLITICS, HIGHER EDUCATION
AND APARTHEID
FROM SASO TO SANSCO, 1968-1990

BLACK STUDENT POLITICS, HIGHER EDUCATION AND APARTHEID
FROM SASO TO SANSCO, 1968-1990

M. SALEEM BADAT

Human Sciences Research Council
Pretoria
1999

ISBN 0-7969-1896-1

HSRC Cataloguing-in-Publication Data
Badat M. Saleem
    Black student politics, higher education and apartheid : from SASO to SANSCO, 1968-1999 / M. Saleem Badat.–1999.
    402p. – 115 x 210 mm
    Bibliography references
    ISBN 0-7969-7969-1896-1

Cover design: Glenn Basson
Layout and design: Susan Smith

Published by:
HSRC Publishers
Private Bag X41
Pretoria 0001

For
Shireen, Hussein and Faizal
and
in memory of
Harold Wolpe: mentor, colleague, comrade and friend

Preface

I n both scholarly and popular literature, black students in South Africa have tended to be treated in two ways. In accounts of educational conditions they have frequently been characterised simply as victims of apartheid. In writings on political opposition to apartheid, although their campaigns and activities, and their roles as catalysts and detonators of educational and political struggles have been noted frequently, these have seldom been analysed. Few scholars have shown an interest in analysing either the remarkable continuity of student activism and militancy over almost two decades, or the historical development, ideological and political character, role, contribution and significance of the organisations to which black students belonged.

The book aims to rectify this dearth of analysis by examining two black higher education organisations that span the period 1968 to 1990. One is the South African National Students' Congress (SANSCO), which was previously called the Azanian Students' Organisation (AZASO). The other is the South African Students' Organisation (SASO), popularly associated with the person of Steve Biko and Black Consciousness. I analyse the ideological and political orientations and internal organisational features of SASO and SANSCO and their intellectual, political and social determinants. I also analyse their role in the educational, political and other spheres and the factors that shaped their activities. Finally, I assess their salient contributions to the popular struggle against apartheid education and race, class and gender oppression and the extent to which and ways their activities reproduced and/or undermined and/or transformed apartheid and capitalist social relations, institutions and practices.

To these ends I draw on recent social movement theory and the international literature on student politics. I also emphasise the need to analyse SASO and SANSCO in relation to the distinct historical conditions under which they operated, and argue that the character and significance of either organisation cannot be read simply from an examination of their ideological and political dispositions and membership. An analysis of their practices and effect on the terrain in which they moved is also required.

My essential argument is that SASO and SANSCO were revolutionary national student political organisations that constituted black students as an organised social force within the national liberation movement, functioned as catalysts of collective action and schools of political formation, and contributed to the erosion of the apartheid social order, as well as to social transformation in South Africa. Black students were not just victims of apartheid but were also thinkers, conscious actors and historical agents. In the face of an authoritarian political order and intense repression, they displayed bravery and an indomitable spirit of courage and defiance, activated anti-apartheid opposition, and contributed immensely to the struggle for national liberation and transformation of education.

Acknowledgements

I t is a pleasure to acknowledge gratefully all those who made this book possible. My partner, Shireen, and my two boys, Hussein and Faizal, have over many years borne with tremendous patience the demands made by research and writing on my time and energy. I am immensely thankful for the sacrifices they have made, their deep loyalty and their love. Dr Anne Akeroyd provided invaluable support and guidance during my stays in York, England. At different points, I also received helpful comments from Elaine Unterhalter, Harold Wolpe and Philip Altbach. I am especially indebted to Harold Wolpe for his pivotal contribution to my intellectual development and for my commitment to critical scholarship. My close friends Yusuf, Sigamoney and Cathy, other friends, and various colleagues at the University of the Western Cape provided much encouragement and I thank them all for their wonderful friendship and support.

Various people assisted with research materials and facilitated my work. Adam Small made available an impressive collection of SASO documents. Librarians at the universities of Cape Town, the Western Cape, Boston, London and York provided much courteous assistance. Numerous ex-SANSCO activists generously made time available for interviews. My partner, Shireen, spent many backbreaking hours transcribing the interviews with her normal efficiency. Finally, the Sociology Department at the University of York provided an office and facilities, which contributed enormously to my productivity.

Finally, I thank my parents, parents-in-law, and brothers and sisters for their love, friendship, and various kinds of support.

Abbreviations used in the Text

AC	Annual Congress
ANC	African National Congress
ANCYL	African National Congress Youth League
ASA	African Students' Association
ASUSA	African Students' Union of South Africa
AUT	Association of University Teachers
AZAPO	Azanian Peoples' Organisation
AZASM	Azanian Students' Movement
BC	Black Consciousness
BCM	Black Consciousness Movement
BCP	Black Community Programmes
BPC	Black Peoples' Convention
BSM	Black Students' Manifesto
BSS	Black Students' Society
BWP	Black Workers' Project
CATE	College of Advanced Technical Education
CI	Christian Institute
CIIR	Catholic Institute of International Relations
COSAS	Congress of South African Students
COSATU	Congress of South African Trade Unions
CST	Colonialism of a Special Type
DET	Department of Education and Training
EC	Education Charter
ECC	Education Charter Campaign
FOSATU	Federation of South African Trade Unions
FUS	Free University Scheme
GSC	General Students' Council
GST	General Sales Tax
IC	Interim Committee
JMC	Joint Management Committee
MDM	Mass Democratic Movement
MEDUNSA	Medical University of Southern Africa
MK	Mkhonto we Sizwe
NEC	National Executive Committee
NECC	National Education Crisis Committee
NEUSA	National Education Union of South Africa

NIC	Natal Indian Congress
NP	National Party
NSMS	National Security Management System
NUSAS	National Union of South African Students
OFS	Orange Free State
PAC	Pan Africanist Congress
PROBEAT	Promotion of Black Educational Advancement Trust
RAU	Rand Afrikaans University
ROAPE	*Review of African Political Economy*
RSA	Republic of South Africa
SAAWU	South African Allied Workers Union
SACOS	South African Council on Sport
SACP	South African Communist Party
SAIRR	South African Institute of Race Relations
SANSCO	South African National Students' Congress
SAS	South African Statistics
SASCO	South African Students' Congress
SASM	South African Students' Movement
SASO	South African Students' Organisation
SASPU	South African Students' Press Union
SCM	Students' Christian Movement
SOYA	Students of Young Azania
SPM	South African Students' Organisation Policy Manifesto
SRC	Students' Representative Council
SSC	State Security Council
UCM	University Christian Movement
UCT	University of Cape Town
UDF	United Democratic Front
UDUSA	Union of Democratic University Staff Associations
UDW	University of Durban-Westville
UF	Urban Foundation
UFH	University of Fort Hare
UN	University of Natal
UNIN	University of the North
UNISA	University of South Africa
UNITRA	University of Transkei
UNIZUL	University of Zululand
UNMS	University of Natal Medical School
UOFS	University of the Orange Free State
UPE	University of Port Elizabeth
UPRE	University of Pretoria
UPS	University of Potchefstroom
US	University of Stellenbosch
UWC	University of Western Cape
Wits	University of Witwatersrand
WUS	World University Service

Contents

Introduction

I t is generally recognised that mass popular struggles during the 1970s and 1980s played a pivotal role in eroding apartheid and creating the conditions for the transition to democracy in South Africa. However, few works on political resistance to apartheid and capitalism during this period have provided a detailed analysis of a specific movement or organisation – its historical development, social base, ideological and political character, role and contribution, immediate and more long-term significance, the specificity of the particular social sphere and terrain it occupied, and its movement and activities on this terrain.

Even if the movements and organisations of particular social groups like black South African workers and the more nebulous and amorphous "people" have not been extensively analysed, black workers and the "people" have at least featured prominently in narratives of resistance politics. The same, however, cannot be said for other social groups, one of which is students. Of course, in accounts of political opposition to apartheid and capitalism during the late 1970s and 1980s, the campaigns and activities of black secondary and higher education students and their militancy and role as catalysts and detonators of anti-apartheid political struggles has been noted frequently. Yet – despite massive and continuous social conflict around education, the remarkable continuity of student activism and militancy over more than two decades, the persistence of national student organisations through intense repression and their salient contribution to the winning of democracy – student politics in South Africa has been analysed little. Given this, it is not surprising that the analysis of student movements or specific student organisations is also virtually non-existent.

Matona has suggested that one reason that mass organisations have not received much attention is that analyses of political resistance in South

Africa "have over-emphasised the spontaneity of the popular struggles" with the result that formal organisations have been "largely treated as incidental" (1992:1). The purpose of this book is to contribute to rectifying the dearth of analysis of mass democratic anti-apartheid organisations in South Africa by examining two black higher education organisations that span over two decades between 1968 and 1990.

One is the South African National Students' Congress (SANSCO), which between 1979 and 1986 went by the name of the Azanian Student". Organisation (AZASO).[1] Established in 1979 and the largest and most influential of the national organisations representing black higher education students in the 1980s, SANSCO was an important and integral component of the broad mass democratic movement in South Africa. The other is the South African Student". Organisation (SASO), formed in 1968 and popularly associated with the person of Steve Biko. SASO gave birth to the Black Consciousness movement in South Africa, was the leading formation within this movement, and did much to revitalise black opposition politics during the 1970s before it was banned by the apartheid government in 1977.

The focus on SASO and SANSCO is of fivefold importance. First, 1998 represented the thirtieth anniversary of the formation of SASO and the twenty-first anniversary of its banning, while 1999 marks the twentieth anniversary of the formation of SANSCO. This makes it an opportune moment to reflect on the historical contribution of the two organisations. With regard to SASO it is especially crucial to be reminded that the doctrine that it developed, Black Consciousness, was a response to particular institutional conditions and experiences. In the current context of calls to "forget the past and embrace the future" and the rhetoric of democratic South Africa as a "rainbow nation" and non-racial society it is all too easy to neglect to examine the extent to which the previous institutional conditions have indeed been fundamentally transformed. Such an omission could mean failure to grasp the possible relationship between institutional conditions and, if no longer Black Consciousness, the emerging notion of an "African renaissance". In relation to continued debate around issues of "race" and identity, the book hopefully highlights the point that approaches such as Black Consciousness, concerns with identity and certain exclusivist forms of organisation need not be retrogressive. On the contrary, they can be progressive and make an important contribution to true non-racialism and national culture. In today's parlance, to recognise "difference" and attempt to deal with it is not necessarily to elevate and ossify difference. Nor is it to succumb to a "politics of difference" and to turn one's back on a "politics of equal recognition". Indeed, it may be that genuinely "equal recognition" will only be possible when, with great honesty and patience, we learn to work through the issue of "difference".

Second, we live in a period where there is a danger of critical historical and sociological work being obliterated on the altar of "relevance" and "immediatism", of knowledge, techniques and quick-fix solutions to fuel economic growth and accommodate new forms of social regulation. This could have grave consequences for the intellectual life of our country, and a humane, environmentally sustainable social development path for it. Instead, I concur with Tosh who writes that "historical knowledge can have important practical implications [but that] the kind of enquiry whose sole object is to re-create a particular conjuncture in the past remains valid and important in its own right" (1984:128).

Third, despite an authoritarian and repressive political order and an array of coercive and ideological instruments to maintain national oppression and class domination, the apartheid government ultimately failed to eradicate dissent and crush political opposition in South Africa. While not without failings and weaknesses, the mass student organisations and student militants played a vital and dynamic role in the winning of democracy. It is appropriate that, in accounts of popular resistance in South Africa, the contribution of students and their organisations – and their often indomitable spirit and selfless bravery and courage – be recognised and acknowledged.

Fourth, each successive generation of student activists in South Africa appears to be ever more poorly informed about the history of student struggles and activism and the history, role and contribution of its own and other student organisations. While accounts of past organisations, struggles and experiences may not necessarily provide answers to contemporary and immediate questions, for student activists a knowledge of the history of student politics and student organisations is always a useful reminder of their own location in the stream of history and may also be suggestive in other ways. Finally, South Africa is a country with a particularly rich history of student activism and militancy, yet this is hardly obvious when one examines the literature on student activism. Thus, there is a need for research and analysis around student politics, as well as student movements and organisations, and a need to share the South African experience with activists and scholars in other parts of the world.

The aim of this book is not to provide an account of the entire spectrum of black student political activism within South Africa. Neither is it to deliver a comprehensive history of SASO and SANSCO. Rather, its purpose is a sensitive historical sociological analysis of the key national black higher education student political organisations during the period 1968 to 1990. More specifically, the principal aims are to understand

1   the ideological, political and organisational constitution, identity, qualities and features of ASSO and SANSCO, and their intellectual, political and social determinants;

2   the role played by the two organisations in the educational, political and other spheres and the factors that shaped their role; and

3   in relation to the particular structural and conjunctural conditions under which SASO and SANSCO operated, their salient contributions to the popular struggle against apartheid education and race, class and gender oppression, and their significance in the struggle for education transformation, national liberation and democracy in South Africa.

Beyond this, a further aim is to compare and contrast SASO and SANSCO with respect to their character, role and significance and to attempt to account for their similarities and differences.

To interpret and understand the character, role and significance of SASO and SANSCO it is necessary first to establish an appropriate conceptual, empirical and analytical foundation. This entails

1   the development of a conceptual framework to guide analysis and interpretation;

2   an account of the conditions within apartheid society, and especially higher education, that constituted the immediate context in – and terrain on – which SASO and SANSCO operated;

4

3   a description and analysis of the ideological and political orientations of SASO and SANSCO, their goals, principles and policies and the political, economic and social determinants of these;

4   a description and analysis of the mobilisation, organisation and collective-action incidents during the activities of SASO and SANSCO in relation to students and other social groups and with respect to educational, political and other issues; and

5   an assessment of the particular contribution of SASO and SANSCO to political opposition to apartheid and capitalism and to the struggle for democracy in South Africa, and the manner and forms in which – and the extent to which – their activities reproduced and/or undermined and/or transformed social relations, institutions and practices.

Each of these themes, of course, gives rise to a number of empirical and analytical questions, and why these themes are especially pertinent requires some motivation.

My point of departure is a number of assumptions and propositions which, taken together, constitute a conceptual framework which has informed and guided my investigation and shaped the analysis that is advanced. Here I want to make clear some of the key general points of departure of the investigation resulting in this book, leaving a detailed discussion of the more specific assumptions and presuppositions to Chapter 1.

All research is theory-laden and knowledge of the real world is appropriated through concepts and theories that, to a greater or lesser extent, and more or less successfully, illuminate the particular objects of enquiry. Moreover, given that it is impossible to collect and sort through every bit of information and data to do with a particular object of enquiry, it is necessary to be selective and have some way of deciding what data are pertinent and essential to one's enquiry. In other words, once the aims of research have been clearly articulated, investigation, analysis and knowledge production require a conceptual framework to structure and guide data collection and analysis through the posing of issues and questions, some seemingly mundane and obvious, but others, hopefully, refreshingly new and imaginative.

My starting point in the investigation of SASO and SANSCO has been to review three different kinds of literature. First, I have closely examined the limited South African and more extensive international theoretical and empirical literature pertaining to student politics, student movements and organisations, students and social class, and students as intellectuals. In addition, I have selectively read theoretically informed case studies of social movements and the theoretical literature on social movements and I have read around the issue of social structure and agency. Finally, I have reviewed writings on the political economy of South Africa, on education and, more especially, higher education. I have also reviewed literature which debates the appropriate theorisation of the South African social order and the appropriate platforms and strategies for political mobilisation and I have read extensively various accounts of political opposition and resistance.

The aim of this review has not been to lay the basis for intervening in theoretical and conceptual issues, tempting as this is because of the atheoretical, empiricist and conceptually weak nature of much of the literature on student politics. The focus of this book, however, is less theoretical than historical and interpretive. Thus, the literature review has been carried out principally to illuminate, sensitise, guide and suggest – in short, to play a heuristic function – with respect to appropriate methodology, ways of seeing, avenues of analysis and questions to confront. In this regard, there exists a literature on student activism that poses particular questions and needs to be drawn on for analysing SASO and SANSCO. At the same time, I argue that recent advances in the field of social movement theory make it an especially fertile source of important new issues and imaginative questions which help to generate a more extensive and deeper knowledge and understanding of organisations like SASO and SANSCO.

A second assumption of the book is that the character of an organisation and its activities and significance cannot be understood by focusing exclusively on the organisation alone. Individuals, organisations, social movements and political parties operate under definite structural conditions. As Marx puts it,

> [m]en make their own history, but they do not make it just as they
> please; they do not make it under circumstances chosen by

themselves, but under circumstances directly encountered, given and transmitted from the past (quoted in Tosh, 1984:140).

That is to say, humans do "make their own history" and social relations and institutions and practices are ultimately the outcome of the actions of individuals, organisations and movements pursuing particular intentions. However, the variety and conflict of these intentions and the weight of the past in the form of ideas and institutions shaping and setting limits to the possibilities of action ensure that, in practice, history becomes a record of the unintended consequences of the actions of individuals, organisations and movements (Abrams, 1982:34). The two-sided interaction of action and structure means that social relations, institutions and practices are the both the medium and outcome of individual and organisational actions and social struggles. It is thus the dynamic relation between the purposes, intentions and actions of SASO and SANSCO and social structure that must necessarily inform any sensitive and balanced analysis of the two organisations.

In terms of this perspective the book includes specific chapters that discuss the particular structural and conjunctural conditions that characterised the periods during which SASO and SANSCO existed. These chapters serve three functions. First, they illuminate the social relations and immediate conditions in the political and higher education spheres under which SASO and SANSCO operated. Second, they contribute to the understanding of some of the determinants of the character, role and activities of SASO and SANSCO. Third, they facilitate analysis of the extent to which SASO and SANSCO reproduced and/or altered, undermined and transformed social relations and conditions. Overall, the consideration of both social conditions and the ideology, politics, activities and effects of SASO and SANSCO enables a more sensitive and balanced assessment of the significance of the two organisations.

The allocation and attribution of significance and character to an organisation is, of course, not a neutral or innocent act nor is it unaffected by conceptual approach and methodology. Thus, an important task is to decide what approach and criteria should be employed in assessing SASO and SANSCO, and in drawing conclusions about their character, role and significance.

7

One approach to the task of interpretation could be to concede that knowledge around these issues is intrinsic to the actors themselves, and to accept the definitions and conceptions contained in their documents, reports, and statements, as well as in speeches of officials. If this settles the question of how one assesses, it also suggests an answer to the issue of who should assess. However, a point made by Feinberg in relation to historical explanation is pertinent here. He writes:

[i]t is easy to understand why ... scholars might want to take the participant". understanding as the bottom line of historical explanation. It has the appearance of avoiding the elitism of placing the scholar in the role of the expert who understands the acts of people better than the participants themselves. I think that a better way to avoid elitism is to share one's interpretation with others – the participants (or those who identify with them) – and to take their responses seriously. Avoiding elitism, however, should not be thought to require that we shed our own best understanding for the understanding of another (Feinberg, 1981:237).

Feinberg is surely correct, for otherwise the meanings and voices of participants are not only unduly privileged but also treated as unproblematic. There is no critical interrogation of meanings and self-definitions or dialogue with other empirical evidence, which could, indeed, be deemed irrelevant. Such an approach is more accurately described as "propaganda", and characteristic of the "official histories" of some organisations, rather than serious scholarly work.

Another approach to interpretation could be to concentrate on various elements internal to an organisation, such as social class origins and location of membership, ideology, programme and organisational activities. However, as I will argue, membership alone is a poor indicator of political position or character. Furthermore, other elements are also inadequate determinants of role, character and significance if they are not analysed in relation to historical, structural and conjunctural conditions.

A third approach could be to analyse SASO and SANSCO largely in relation to one's theorisation of the South African social order, and normative definition of appropriate resistance ideology, political goals, programmes and strategies. In this case, the extent to which SASO and SANSCO conformed to these would become the crucial determinant of how they were assessed. As will be seen, this has, indeed, been the way that SASO has been assessed by some activist scholars. Such an approach is, however, flawed in at least two respects.

First, there is the problem of arbitrariness in that one's own conception of appropriate ideology, political goals and strategies of political struggle becomes the sole and privileged basis for deriving conclusions about an organisation. The extent to which an organisation conforms with one's normative criteria drives analysis, and different conceptions of the social order and political goals and strategies which may yield alternate interpretations of character, role and significance are summarily precluded. Especially where an organisation that is the object of analysis does have a different view of appropriate political goals, programmes and strategies, a hostility to its conceptions may result in a myopia with respect to its actual contributions and real significance.

Second, such an approach is, in practice, fixated with the internal elements of organisations and is intolerant and voluntarist. The emphasis is very much on whether an organisation has the "correct" goals, strategies, forms of mobilisation and the like. Moreover, such aspects tend to be defined either in isolation from structural and conjunctural conditions or in terms of very optimistic readings of the possibilities afforded by these conditions for collective action and social change. In other words, there is little serious consideration of the constraints on action and the manner in which the internal elements of organisations may themselves be shaped by social conditions.

If one rejects such approaches, how then is the task of interpretation to be approached? First, an organisation's self-definitions and the meanings given by participants need to be duly taken into account but not privileged. Second, internal elements such as ideology and programmes are important but inadequate in themselves. Third, analysis of internal elements in relation to a normative definition of the appropriate processes and goals of political struggle are of some value as long as one acknowledges that there is no single incontestable definition and that alternative definitions exist. Ultimately, however, what is of fundamental importance is a sensitivity to structural and conjunctural conditions, especially in the political and higher education spheres, and how these conditions shaped the responses and activities of SASO and SANSCO, how they established limits and opportunities for action, and were also re-shaped by these organisations.

For various reasons this book has been almost a decade in the making. During this time my focus, analytical framework and, necessarily, analysis and interpretation have all undergone important changes. It is useful to signal the changes and the reasons behind them.

Initially, the book was to focus only on SANSCO. Part of the motivation for investigating SANSCO was my involvement in the organisation, first as vice-president of the University of Cape Town branch of SANSCO, and thereafter as national co-ordinator of the Education Charter campaign (1982-83) and projects officer on the national executive (1983-84). However, while I was deeply committed to the goals and policies of SANSCO and to the project of national liberation, I was not interested in producing an official and sanitised history of the organisation. Instead, I sought to draw on my experience of SANSCO to produce a disinterested critical analysis of the organisation as a contribution to the literature on student politics and to informing and improving the future practices of SANSCO. As Tosh writes, "myth-making about the past, however desirable the end it may serve, is incompatible with *learning* from the past" (1984:17) (author's emphasis).

In the investigation of SANSCO, the analysis of SASO was to be confined to a brief background chapter which would have situated SANSCO in the stream of black higher education student politics and would have also indicated the continuities and discontinuities between SANSCO and SASO. However, as I was reading the available literature on SASO it became clear that there existed multiple and very different interpretations of its character, role and significance. I became keen to understand the reasons for these differing interpretations and to develop my own interpretation of SASO. I thus redefined my focus to include a more detailed investigation of SASO. Since such an investigation would also provide the basis for a more extended and rigorous comparative analysis of SANSCO and SASO, I also made such a comparison an additional aim of my investigation. I reasoned that extending the investigation in this way would reveal more sharply the relationship between historical conditions and the ideology, politics and activities of organisations. The fact that my political commitments and organisational affiliations made me lean towards a generally negative assessment of SASO and the Black Consciousness movement also afforded me the opportunity to analyse the organisation more rigorously and dispassionately.

During the first few years of research and writing, my approach was to treat the ideology, politics and activities of an organisation as the essential markers of its character, role and significance. Increasingly, however, I came to appreciate that it was crucial to be sensitive to the structural and conjunctural conditions under which an organisation operated. This meant that, instead of interpreting organisations largely in relation to their internal elements, it was of vital importance to pay serious attention to their effects on contemporary social relations, institutions, thinking and practices. Later, in the course of other research and teaching I also became exposed to literature dealing with social movements. Here, to my excitement, I discovered a theoretical perspective that was analytically suggestive in numerous ways and enabled me to pose interesting and refreshing new questions. Drawing on the work of key social movement theorists pushed the analysis of SASO and SANSCO in new directions and facilitated a richer understanding of their character, role and significance.

Since I began work on this book after a long period of intense and full-time political activism, during the initial years of research and writing I was not always easily able to make the transition from political writing, in the service of the liberation movement, to disinterested and critical scholarship. It is also possible that my early analysis was affected by political prejudices towards Black Consciousness organisations. However, I am confident that the chapters that follow reflect the kind of disinterest that is vital to good critical scholarship. As a result, the analysis and conclusions of this book are substantially different from what they would have been had the book been completed ten years earlier. One indicator of this is my interpretation of SASO. Whereas my initial evaluation of SASO was extremely negative, the in-depth investigation of SASO, changes in my analytical approach, and my intellectual development have all brought me to appreciate the positive character and role of the organisation and have led me to conclude that it was of crucial significance to the struggle for national liberation. Whereas I previously adhered closely to the

11

negative interpretation of SASO by a particular scholar, I now develop a critique of both his analytical framework and his conclusions.

Finally, the book has also been shaped to an extent by the political changes in South Africa. Prior to 1990, for reasons related to the organisational security of SANSCO and the personal security of its officials, I would have been obliged not to pursue certain lines of analysis. Today, it is, of course, possible to analyse SANSCO openly and fully and I am thus able to comment on issues such as the influence of the ANC on SANSCO, and the role of SANSCO in relation to the ANC.

I have relied principally on documentary research and have drawn extensively on a wide variety of documents. In the case of SANSCO – since a secondary literature does not exist – extensive use has been made of primary documents in the form of articles in commercial, non-profit community and student newspapers and magazines, public speeches of officials, organisational materials in the form of national, regional and local newsletters and pamphlets and official documents relating to national and regional conferences and meetings.

Three points are pertinent with respect to my sources of data. In the first place, articles, reports and interviews with officials both in student newspapers like *SASPU National* and in community newspapers have had to be treated with caution. My post-SANSCO editorship of a community newspaper made me aware that the "alternative press" and popular journalists generally attempted to follow faithfully the Guinea-Bissau revolutionary Amilcar Cabral's dictum, "Tell no lies, claim no easy victories". However, the fact that this press included as its goal the popularisation of anti-apartheid organisations, and acted as a mouthpiece of popular organisations, meant that the internal conflicts, problems and weaknesses of these organisations were not always reported. Moreover, the strength and support base of organisations and the extent to which their mobilisations and collective actions were successful and victorious was also sometimes overstated.

Second, the organisational newsletters, pamphlets and conference minutes that have been drawn on had been part of my personal collection during my involvement in SANSCO, or were collected later for the purposes of this book. Since I am familiar with the form and style of student media I have no doubts about the authenticity of these documents.

Furthermore, my involvement in SANSCO has provided me with privileged access to the real and underlying meaning of certain phrases and terms that are employed in SANSCO media. Finally, SANSCO was generally lax in the recording, production and safe-keeping of minutes of national conferences and meetings. This, together with the seizure of records by the security police on various occasions, has meant that very little survives in the form of official minutes and records. Consequently, much reliance has had to be placed on reports in commercial, student and community newspapers, as well as in organisational newsletters, for information relating to the themes, concerns and outcomes of national conferences.

In the case of SASO a secondary body of literature in the form of academic and activist descriptions and analyses – some penned by contemporary and ex-SASO members themselves – is available and has been drawn on in two ways. First, it has been used to develop an empirical and, to a lesser extent, analytical, foundation for the interpretation of SASO. Second, the various interpretations of SASO that are advanced by this literature have been critically interrogated and have provided a partial basis for my interpretation of SASO.

I have also made extensive use of primary documents in the form of official SASO newsletters, reports and minutes of the proceedings of national conferences, training workshops and executive meetings, much of which was obtained, from a contemporary SASO sympathiser. SASO was considerably more scrupulous than SANSCO with regard to the recording and production of conference and workshop minutes and reports, and these are important sources of empirical data. Numerous sets have survived and I was able to compare the documents that were provided to me with others held in various libraries. Moreover, as a consequence of the 1975-76 court trial involving SASO leaders, SASO documents are also part of public court records. The primary documents enabled me to fill numerous gaps in description and analysis around SASO's organisational infrastructure and structure and especially around SASO activities in relation to higher education. However, their use was also stimulated by my desire to investigate more intensively the format, themes, concerns and discourse of SASO gatherings and to develop a more extensive and comprehensive empirical base for my interpretation of SASO. Interviews by scholars with ex-SASO activists, and critical analyses ex-SASO members and Black Consciousness sympathisers, have been useful in putting aspects of the contents of SASO documents in perspective.

To complement documentary research, interviews were conducted with select persons who held key positions during different periods of SANSCO's existence. The existence of a mutual familiarity between all the interviewees and myself facilitated access, and meant that interviewees were generally at ease, and it also encouraged an openness on their part. The interviews enabled interviewees to share their conceptions of the essential ideological and political orientation of SANSCO and its determinants, and to speak about issues that could not be spoken or written about previously without inviting repression. I was also able to test my understanding of the formation and very early days of SANSCO with one particular interviewee.

I did not conduct any interviews around SASO because a number of ex-SASO activists have penned analytical articles on the organisation and some of the secondary analyses of SASO draw on interviews with various officials. I have been able to make effective use of these and they, together with the primary documents that were available to me, have been more than sufficient for my purposes.

For the investigation of SANSCO I could draw on my involvement in student politics during the late 1970s, in SANSCO during the early 1980s, my editorship of a community newspaper between 1983 and 1986, involvement in the National Education Crisis Committee (NECC) in the late 1980s and on my role as an adviser and consultant to SANSCO activists. While for ideological and political reasons I did not join SANSCO until 1982, I nonetheless observed closely and with considerable interest the formation and early development of the organisation. My official positions in SANSCO involved me in a diverse range of activities. These included attending local, regional and national meetings, workshops and conferences; participating in debates and discussions around questions of ideology, programme, policy, strategy and tactics; speaking on behalf of the organisation at public demonstrations and meetings; visiting campuses to assist in the mobilisation and organisational efforts of local branches; and representing SANSCO at meetings of other popular organisations and movements. All these activities provided valuable first-hand experience and knowledge of SANSCO. However, other occasions such as the time spent with fellow activists during mobilising and organising activities, long road journeys to meetings and informal social gatherings were also fertile periods for learning about SANSCO. On such occasions there were often vigorous individual and small group exchanges around student and national politics and — outside the constraints on discussion imposed by draconian security legislation and security surveillance on official SANSCO meetings — also a more open and uninhibited sharing of ideas and views.

After my involvement in SANSCO, my position as editor of a community newspaper which also covered student politics meant that I was able to continue to observe SANSCO closely. There were also numerous and continuous invitations to address SANSCO meetings and workshops, ongoing contact with contemporaries who were still active in the organisation, and meetings with rank and file activists and officials seeking information, assistance or advice. Finally, there was interaction with SANSCO through my participation in the National Education Crisis Committee (NECC). In all these ways, I continued to be well positioned with respect to knowledge, information and experiences related to SANSCO.

Finally, twenty years of political activism have also afforded me the opportunity and privilege of countless informal discussions with a large number (and generations) of student leaders and activists. These have ranged from former SASO leaders to leaders of the predominantly white National Union of South African Student". (NUSAS), with which SANSCO was to develop a close alliance; from leaders of student organisations at odds with the ideological and political orientation and strategies of SANSCO to leaders of the secondary-school student organisation, the Congress of South African Student". (COSAS), with whom SANSCO was closely allied. The often animated, candid, fascinating, even humorous recollections of, and conversations with, past student activists have been invaluable in numerous ways. For example, they sensitised me to the different political and educational conditions that confronted different generations of student leaders and organisations. They also alerted me to the ideological and political contestations that unfolded in SASO during the mid-1970s, and they revealed tensions in relations between SANSCO and NUSAS at some campuses. Thus, as much insight and understanding has been obtained from informal conversations as from formal interviews.

The book in brief: In Chapter 1, I discuss the perspectives informing the book. Although the concern here is with theoretical and conceptual issues, the object is less the theorisation of student politics than the development of a framework for the analysis and interpretation of SASO and SANSCO. The remainder of the book, bar the Conclusion, has two parts. Each comprises a number of chapters which focus on conditions in the political and higher education spheres, and the analysis and interpretation of the organisations.

In this vein, Part I, comprising Chapters 2, 3 and 4, is primarily devoted to an analysis of SASO. Chapter 2 describes and analyses the particular conditions within society and higher education that confronted black students and SASO, and which constituted the terrain on which it had to move. Apart from a brief sketch of black higher education prior to 1960, the focus is on the period from the banning and exile of the liberation movements in 1960 to the Soweto uprising of 1976/1977. This chapter is crucial in shaping the analysis of the emergence, development and eventual demise of SASO.

Chapter 3 revolves around the emergence of SASO in the late 1960s, and its ideological and political orientations and shifts. Chapter 4 describes and analyses its organisational and mobilisation activities and collective actions, and its position within the BC movement. Finally, in Chapter 5, I critically engage some of the key analyses of SASO and advance my interpretation of its character, role and significance.

Part II consists of Chapters 6 to 10 and has as its primary focus SANSCO. The principal concerns here are the description and analysis of SANSCO, in order to lay the foundation for the interpretation of its character, role and significance.

In Chapter 6, I focus on the social and higher educational conditions of, first, the period after the Soweto uprising until the declaration of a national state of emergency in 1986 and, then, on the harshly repressive period of the state of emergency until De Klerk's liberalisation measures of February 1990. The new political conditions that were a consequence of the Soweto uprising and later the state of emergency are discussed, these constituting the terrain on which SANSCO moved. In addition, I examine higher education, focusing on the different institutions attended by black students, their location and organisation, relations with the state and corporate capital, student enrolments, and the conditions under which students lived and studied. The object is to pinpoint those features of the structure and organisation of the higher education sphere that conditioned student mobilisation, organisation and activity.

Chapter 7 begins with a discussion of the origins and formation of SANSCO in 1979. Thereafter, it discusses SANSCO's initial politics of student vanguardism, its eventual ideological and political re-orientation, the organisation's approach to the question of the nature of the South African social order, and its programme and policies. In Chapter 8 the focus is on internal organisational aspects, including the composition of its membership, its organisational infrastructure on the campuses and activities related to organisational development and reproduction. Also addressed is the impact of the states of emergency between 1986 and 1990 on organisational structures and membership and the implications of SANSCO's proscription in 1988 for its activities.

Chapter 9 is concerned with the form and content of SANSCO's mobilisation of students and other social groups, its collective actions in the educational and political spheres and its relationship with other student and popular organisations. These issues are considered in relation to the period 1979 to mid-1986, which was one of extensive political mobilisation, the mushrooming of popular organisations and intense social and political conflict, and the period mid-1986 to 1990, during which SANSCO and other mass organisations and movements experienced severe state repression. Finally, Chapter 10 presents my interpretation of the character, role and significance of SANSCO.

The Conclusion draws together the interpretative analysis of SASO and SANSCO and advances general arguments with respect to their character, role and significance in relation to their internal characteristics, the South African social order and the particular historical conditions under which they operated. In addition, there is a comparison of the respective contributions and significance of SASO and SANSCO.

17

1
Interpreting the Character, Role and Significance of SASO and SANSCO: A Conceptual Framework

A s I have indicated, the appropriate framework for the analysis of SASO and SANSCO is not a given and by no means obvious. Hence, it is necessary to make explicit the overall framework of assumptions, concepts and specific questions that structure and guide my investigation, analysis and interpretation of SASO and SANSCO. The "framework" is much like what Abrams refers to as a "problematic":

> ... a rudimentary organisation of a field of phenomena which yields problems for investigation. The organisation occurs on the basis of some more or less explicitly theoretical presuppositions – it is an application of assumptions and principles to phenomena in order to constitute a range of enquiry... [O]ne's problematic is the sense of significance and coherence one brings to the world in general in order to make sense of it in particular (1982:xv).

I draw on diverse literature from the fields of social theory, social movement theory, student politics and comparative student activism and South African political economy. The emphasis, though, is less the development of theory in relation to student activism than the elaboration of a framework which plays a heuristic function with respect to the analysis and historical and contextual understanding and interpretation of the character, role and significance of SASO and SANSCO.

Student Politics

Given the concern of this investigation, the clarification of the concept[*] "student politics" is a useful starting point.

Burawoy defines politics as "struggles over or within relations of structured domination, struggles that take as their *objective* the quantitative or qualitative change of those relations" (1985:253). He further argues that [w]e must choose between politics defined as struggles regulated by *specific apparatuses*, politics defined as struggles over *certain relations*, and the combination of the two. In the first, politics would have no fixed objective, and in the second it would have no fixed institutional locus. I have therefore opted for the more restricted third definition, according to which politics refers to struggles within a specific arena aimed at specific sets of relations (*ibid.*:253-54).

This understanding of politics "refuses to accept the reduction of politics to state politics and of state politics to the reproduction of class relations" (*ibid.*:254). The reason why Burawoy refuses to conceive of the state only in relation to class relations is because

[w]hat is distinctive about the state is its global character, its function as the factor of cohesion for the entire social formation. The state not only guarantees the reproduction of certain relations but, more distinctly, it is the apparatus that guarantees all other apparatuses (*ibid.*).

The merit of Burawoy's approach is the space it creates for extending "politics" to diverse social arenas beyond the state – education, health, environment, etc. – and the recognition it gives to the role of the state in the reproduction of other non-class, yet important, social relations having to do with, for example, race or gender. In terms of this one, can conceive of "education politics" and "relations in education", and these being of as much interest to a state as relations of production, the social relations between classes in a social formation. One can also conceive of "curriculum politics" and "governance politics" as subfields of education politics. Finally, one can begin to think about politics also in relation to specific social classes and categories such as workers, women, youth and students.

Burawoy's formulation steers us to conceive of "student politics" as being characterised by the struggles of students "within a specific arena aimed at specific sets of relations". It also helps us recognise that since student struggles occur within a particular institutional setting it means that they will be "regulated" and, necessarily, also structured, conditioned and shaped by the distinct institutional arrangements and organisational matrices of the setting.

Burawoy's definition of politics is immensely useful. However, as Wolpe (1988:55) has argued, it may be "too restrictive". Wolpe acknowledges that the structure of a specific sphere "will condition the form and orientate the content of the struggles, which occur" but rightly points out that the "objectives of struggle" may not be confined to social relations in a particular sphere (*ibid.*). That is to say, the concerns of students and student organisations may extend beyond the educational arena and social relations in education to social relations in the political sphere. This means that the form and content of student struggles may be mediated not only by educational apparatuses but also by the apparatuses of the political sphere.

Student organisation, movement and body

Despite its virtues, the literature on student politics — the involvement of students in particular structural and historical settings in activities aimed at either conserving, reforming or/and fundamentally transforming prevailing social relations, institutions and practices — tends to be conceptually sloppy. Frequently, key concepts such as "student organisation", "student movement" and "student body" are not defined and are conflated, even though they are conceptually distinct. For the purpose of this investigation, it is important to define these terms and to outline their relationship to one another so that there is clarity around what is the essential unit of analysis.

A student organisation is a collective of students whose basis of affiliation to the organisation is either political, cultural, religious, academic and/or social. Various terms such as "council", "club", "society", "association", "union" and even "organisation" itself may be used to designate such a formation. Most student organisations are characterised by a voluntary membership, although some student organisations, for example the student representative councils (SRCs) at black higher education institutions, have automatically incorporated all registered students. A large variety of student organisations have existed at black higher education institutions. The majority has been specific to particular institutions, but some have existed as regional or national organisations. Prominent black national higher education student organisations, despite their names, have been the University Christian Movement, the Azanian Students' Movement and, of course, SASO and SANSCO. The terms and conditions under which organisations have been allowed to operate has, however, frequently been the object of conflict and contestation between students and the authorities of higher education institutions.

The term *student movement* is difficult to define and the following will have to suffice as a working definition:

> The sum total of action and intentions of students individually, collectively and organisationally that are directed for change in the students' own circumstances and for educational and wider social change (Jacks, 1975:13).

Of course, "action and intentions" could also be directed at the preservation of the prevailing student situation and maintenance of the educational and social status quo. Notwithstanding this, the above definition does have certain implications:

1   Not all student organisations are necessarily part of the student movement.

2   The student movement is not reducible to a single organisation and is not an extension of one or even many student organisations, but is a broad entity, which includes individual students who are not formally attached to organisations.

3   A student movement is a dynamic entity whose size and boundaries are likely to vary depending on political conditions, time of academic year and the issues being confronted.

The student movement is, then, to be clearly distinguished from a student organisation. The objects of this investigation are SASO and SANSCO and, since the unit of analysis is student organisation, it is important, to hold on to the distinction between the "student movement" and "student organisation". However, it is often the case that a specific student organisation stands in a particular relationship to the student movement, enjoys a certain status within, and plays a certain role *vis-à-vis*, the student movement. Thus, while the higher education student movement in South Africa is not the concern of this book, it is necessary to analyse the connections and relations between SASO and SANSCO and the student movements of their time since this has a bearing on their character, role and significance.

The term *student body* denotes the collective of individuals who are engaged in academic study and vocational education and training at a particular higher educational institution. While each higher education institution has its own specific student body, the totality of individuals registered at all the higher education institutions collectively constitute the general student body.

The *student body* has been analysed in two ways: in relation to the political participation and to the political affiliation of students. Hamilton, writing about student politics in Venezuela, has defined three categories of students: "militants" who are actively involved in student and national politics; "sympathisers", who, while not consistently active, may or may not support organisations, vote in elections, attend meetings and engage in demonstrations and other activities; and "non-participants", who for a variety of reasons stand aloof from student politics (1968:351-52). Soares comments that "political participation embodies different forms, levels and degrees of intensity". This means that "reading about politics, voting, and stoning embassies are different forms of participation", which are not only "different actions" but also "involve different degrees of intensity" (Soares, 1967:124).

Lenin, on the other hand, focused on political groupings within the student body. Writing in 1903, he identified six groups within the general Russian student body. Three groups, the "liberals", the "social revolutionaries", and the "social democrats", represented particular political positions. Another three stood in a specific relationship to the student movement: the "indifferents" were unresponsive and detached from the student movement, the "reactionaries" opposed it, and the "academics" believed that the student movement should be concerned solely with academic issues. In Lenin's view, the existence of these groups was not accidental, but inevitable. Students as

the most responsive section of the intelligentsia ... most resolutely and most accurately reflect and express the development of class interests and political groupings in society as a whole. The students would not be what they are if their political groupings did not

23

correspond to the political groupings of society as a whole (Lenin, 1961d:44-45).

If the relationship between a student organisation and the student movement is of some concern, so is that between a student organisation and the student body. The student body constitutes a student organisation and is the source of potential members, supporters and sympathisers, as well as antagonists. Moreover, its size, social composition, nature and so on are bound to condition the activities of a student organisation with respect to student mobilisation, organisation and collective action and, thus, the character and role of an organisation.

History, Structure and Conjuncture

I have argued that the analysis of SASO and SANSCO must take into account the historical, structural and conjunctural conditions under which the two organisations operated. The distinction between structural and conjunctural

> refers to the division between elements of a (relatively) permanent and synchronic logic of a given social structure, and elements which emerge as temporary variations of its functioning in a diachronic perspective. The distinction allows one to separate the analysis of the pre-conditions of action from the factors activating specific forms of collective mobilisation (Melucci, 1989:49-50).

For example, until 1990 the denial of full and meaningful political rights to black South Africans was a permanent feature of the South African social order, and the fundamental basis for black social disaffection and political opposition. However, during the apartheid period (1948 to 1990) there were various government initiatives which gave the impression of conceding political rights but fell far short of extending all the rights associated with full citizenship. These initiatives were consistently the trigger for anti-government political protests and mobilisations.

One reason for considering structural conditions is that, as Abrams so cogently puts it,

> [d]oing justice to the reality of history is not a matter of noting the way in which the past provides a background to the present; it is a matter of treating what people do in the present as a struggle to

create a future *out* of the past, of seeing that the past is not just the womb of the present but the only raw material out of which the present can be constructed (1982:8).

Another reason is that "what we choose to do and what we have to do are shaped by the historically given possibilities among which we find ourselves" (*ibid*.:3).

Structure and action

Social structures, institutions and practices condition social activity and struggles. Crucial to the analysis of the outcomes, and success and failure, of organisational initiatives and collective action, and also to understanding the form and content of struggles, is to ask

under what conditions do these struggles occur; what are the conditions which structure them and affect their outcome? Of particular importance in this regard is the question of the form or structure of the political terrain in addition to the question of the form of the state (a distinction which is rarely made in the literature) (Wolpe, 1988:23).

To state that social relations and institutional arrangements "condition" social action is not, however, to argue that they constrain solely as subfields of education politics in the sense of rendering struggles and change impossible and automatically guaranteeing the reproduction of existing social relations. As Wolpe argued, "the formation of structures and relations is always the outcome of struggles between contending groups or classes" (*ibid*.:8). Class and popular struggles can, and do, undermine, modify, and in certain cases even transform social structures and institutions, and the latter are ultimately the outcome of such struggles.

Moreover, in South Africa,

the apparatuses in and through which white domination is maintained may stand not only in a functional, complementary and supportive relationship to one another, but also in relations of contradiction and conflict ... [T]he possibility is opened up that, within certain apparatuses and institutions, white domination may continue to be reproduced, albeit in changing forms, while within others it becomes, at the same time, eroded (*ibid*.:9).

In other words, notwithstanding its generally authoritarian and repressive character, the apartheid state and its myriad apparatuses and institutions cannot be conceived as omnipotent, absolutely monolithic and homogeneous, or as impermeable to political opposition.

The use by Wolpe of the concept of "access" is pertinent here. He argues that

> certain state apparatuses provide the possibility for mass or class struggles and others do not. The difference lies in the type of access which is available in relation to different state apparatuses (Wolpe, 1988:57).

Wolpe suggests that there are at "least two different modes of access to state apparatuses which may have vastly different effects upon the possibilities of class struggles from within these apparatuses" (ibid.). One kind of access leads to the isolation of individuals and to individualised contestation. Another kind, however, which applies to state educational institutions, "provide[s] different conditions for action" (ibid.:58). This is because institutions such as universities "are premised on, and depend on, access of individual subjects ... who are brought into direct relationship with one another" (ibid.). Here "participation" is "a sine qua non of the functioning of the institution and thus establishes an essential condition for the possibility of a politics of participation within such state apparatuses" (ibid.).

> Finally, social analysis, according to Abrams, must recognise the relation of the individual as an agent with purposes, expectations and motives to society as a constraining environment of institutions, values and norms – and that relationship is one which has its real existence ... in the immediate world of history, of sequences of action and reaction in time (1982:7-8).

The relationship between action and structure needs to be "understood as a matter of process in time" (ibid.:xv). Thus, even if the activities of student organisations in South Africa did not constitute an immediate and serious threat to the system of racial and class domination, their struggles might nonetheless weaken the pillars of such domination to the extent that the dominant classes would be impelled to restructure the institutional mechanisms that maintain domination. In this process, new conditions and a significantly altered terrain of struggle could be established which may be more favourable to the efforts of class and popular movements and organisations.

Paying attention to the particular historical conditions under which SASO and SANSCO operated means being sensitive to continuities as well as discontinuities in conditions. This facilitates an understanding of the conditions, problems and challenges that were common to both organisations, and what were distinct to each. Furthermore, it could also contribute to an understanding of the similarities and differences that may have existed between SASO and SANSCO.

Here, the concept of "periodisation" is important

since it signals the possibility that the historical development of a society, or sectors of it such as the economy or polity, may be demarcated by periods which differ in significant respects from one another (Wolpe, 1988:19).

In this book three historical periods, 1960 to 1976/1977, 1976/1977 to mid-1986, and mid-1986 to 1990, are identified, primarily on the basis of the structure of the political terrain. The analysis of SASO and SANSCO is conducted in relation to these historical periods.

Social Movement Theory

Some of the theoretical development in the field of social movements during the past decade has resulted in considerably more interesting and rigorous analysis of collective phenomena such as the civil rights movement in the United States, the environmental movement in Europe and other forms of collective action. It may be objected that a social movement is an altogether different unit of analysis from an organisation and that the theoretical work in the field of social movements cannot legitimately be applied to the analysis of organisations. It is true that a clear distinction has already been made between a student organisation and a student movement. It is also the case that some of the innovations within social movement theory would be especially useful for knowledge production with respect to the student movement and other mass movements in South Africa. Nonetheless, the issue of unit of analysis is not a serious barrier to harnessing some contributions within social movement theory to the analysis of organisations.

Analysing social movements

Alberto Melucci, the prominent Italian theorist, conceptualises social movements as "a form of collective action (a) based on solidarity, (b) carrying on a conflict, (c) breaking the limits of the system in which action occurs" (1985:795). The dimension of solidarity involves "actors' mutual recognition that they are part of a single unit" (Melucci, 1989:29), while that of "conflict presupposes adversaries who struggle for something which they recognise as lying between them" (*ibid.*). Finally, to say that a social movement *"breaks the limits of compatibility of a system"* means that "its actions violate the boundaries or tolerance limits of a system, thereby pushing the system beyond the range of variations that it can tolerate without altering its structure" (*ibid.*, emphasis in original). The characteristics that Melucci attributes to social movements are, of course, also present in other "collective phenomena" such as popular organisations, which have as their objects the transformation of social relations, institutions and practices. However, the justification for critically drawing on social movement theory relates not only to this recognition. It is also motivated by fact that some of this theory is a fertile source for asking new questions about organisations like SASO and SANSCO and for approaching the issues of their character, role and significance in innovative ways.

Melucci's point of departure is unexceptionable. Collective action, he argues, cannot be viewed

> either as an effect of structural conditions or as an expression of values and beliefs. Collective action is rather the product of purposeful orientations developed within a field of opportunities and constraints (Melucci, 1989:25).

Eyerman and Jamison, who are especially interested in the knowledge production moments of social movements, make essentially the same point. Movements are "at once conditioned by the historical contexts in which they emerge, their particular time and place, and, in turn, affect that context through their cognitive and political praxis" (1991:62). A more important contribution of Melucci is to point to the pitfall of the tendency to treat social movements as a "personage" with a *"unitary character"*, and to reify collective action "into an incontrovertible fact, a *given* that does not merit further investigation" (1989:18; emphasis in original). However, rather than assume that social movement has a unitary character and treat collective action as a given, Melucci argues that they should be seen as

action systems operating in a systemic field of possibilities and limits ... Social movements are action *systems* in that they have structures: the unity and continuity of the action would not be possible without integration and interdependence of individuals and groups ... But movements are *action* systems in that their structures are built by aims, beliefs, decisions and exchanges operating in a systemic field (1985:793, emphasis in original).

Keane and Mier elaborate on this theme. They argue that social movements should be conceptualised as

fragile and heterogeneous *social constructions*. Collective action is always "built" by social actors, and thus what needs to be explained in concrete terms is how movements form, that is, how they manage to mobilise individuals and groups within the framework of possibilities and constraints presented them by the institutions of our complex societies. Collective action must be understood in terms of the processes through which individuals communicate, negotiate, produce meanings, and make decisions within a particular social field or environment. They establish relations with other actors within an already structured context, and through these interactions they produce meanings, express their needs and constantly transform their relationships (Keane and Mier, 1989:4; emphasis in original).

The advantage of taking such an approach to student organisations is it enables fruitful lines of enquiry related to questions such as

1   the recruitment networks and processes through which students were drawn into SASO and SANSCO;

2   the basis of appeals for involvement;

3   the processes through which collective actions were constructed by these formations; and

4   the modes by which organisational continuity was maintained in the face of repressive conditions and the transitory status of students.

The perspective of "social construction" also renders problematic the formation of collective identity within an organisation. Now, identity is not something that an organisation begins with but is the outcome of ongoing processes and activities. This means that objectives, strategies and tactics, sites of struggle and organisational processes and forms are not to be regarded as ready at hand or static but as being socially and collectively formed.

The question of the "cognitive identity" as well as the "cognitive praxis" of social movements has been of special interest to Eyerman and Jamison (1991). One criticism they have of writing on social movements is that

[t]he particular historical interests that a movement aims to further are not analyzed in the process of being formed, as a central component of movement praxis. The knowledge interests of a social movement are frozen into static, ready-formed packages, providing the issues or ideologies around which movements mobilise resources or socialise individuals (Eyerman and Jamison, 1991:46).

Their response is to stress the historical and social construction of ideas and the active role social movements play in knowledge production. Cognitive praxis they argue

does not come ready-made to a social movement. It is precisely in the creation, articulation, formulation of new thoughts and ideas – new knowledge – that a social movement defines itself in society (ibid.:55).

Knowledge is the result of social interactions and "a series of social encounters, within movements, between movements, and ... between movements and their established opponents" (ibid.:57). Moreover, knowledge is produced through debates over meeting agendas, the planning of meetings, campaigns and demonstrations and also exchanges over strategies and tactics. It is also generated in interaction with old movements, old traditions, concepts and values and in the recombination and reinterpretation of intellectual roles and practices.

"Cognitive praxis", however, is not just aspects of thought but is also forms of social activity to which there are three dimensions. The first, as noted, has to do with the production of the basic assumptions, world-view and goals of a social movement or organisation. Relevant here is Eyerman and Jamison's notion of "movement intellectuals" – "actors who articulate the collective identity that is fundamental to the making of a social movement", who are central to the production and dissemination of ideology, to the theoretical and empirical definition of the opposition, and to the education of new members (ibid.:114-18). Of course, the historical context is bound to condition the particular types of intellectual produced and their forms and roles. The second dimension of cognitive praxis relates to the issues that are identified for criticism and protest and are the targets of opposition. The final dimension concerns the organisational moment – how knowledge is disseminated, how calls to action are made, modes of planning, vehicles and instruments that are employed and internal practice.

Another important insight of Melucci is the need to avoid conceiving social movements in purely political and instrumental terms, for this misses the cultural, expressive and symbolic moments of these movements. Thus, Melucci argues that although the collective actions of social movements may have visible effects – helping bring about institutional change, serving as recruitment grounds for new elites, and cultural innovation relating to new forms of behaviour, social relationships, customs and dress – much of their activities may be interpreted as taking place on a symbolic plane (Melucci, 1989).

The symbolic challenge of social movements takes three main forms. The first is "prophecy", the proposition that alternative frameworks of meaning, in contrast to those that are dominant, are possible. "Paradox" consists of exemplifying, in exaggerated form, that what is termed "irrational" by dominant groups is actually very true. The final form is "representation", which makes use of the theatre and other visual forms to show contradictions of the social system. All of this helps render "power visible" (Melucci, 1989:76). In this sense, beyond being a challenge to cultural codes, social movements are also laboratories of cultural innovation. Also important, social movements are said to operate as a "sign" or "message" for the rest of society in that they are not just a means to an end. As Melucci puts it, the organizational forms of movements are not just "instrumental" for their goals, they are a goal in themselves. Since collective action focuses on cultural codes, the *form* of the movement is itself a message, a symbolic challenge to the dominant codes (1989:60, emphasis in original).

Thus, he suggests that the continuous rotation of persons in leadership positions and strong emphasis on genuinely participatory forms of democracy in some organisations can be seen as having a deeper significance than was initially thought.

Finally, it is important to comprehend the relationship between the "visible" and "latent" dimensions of collective action. During the latency phase

the potential for resistance or opposition is sewn into the very fabric of daily life. It is located in the molecular experience of the individuals or groups who practice the alternative meanings of everyday life. Within this context, resistance is not expressed in collective forms of conflictual mobilizations. Specific circumstances are necessary for opposition and therefore of mobilizing and making visible this latent potential (*ibid.*:70-71).

Thus, phases of latency, far from being periods of inaction, are crucial to the formation and development of abilities and capacities for mobilisation and struggle. Consequently, they deserve attention and analysis in much the same way as do phases of visible mobilisation.

Comparative Literature

With regard to the comparative and international literature on student politics, what pointers do they provide for the analysis of SASO and SANSCO? Here, I have been guided by the assumption that since SASO and SANSCO formed part of the radical opposition to apartheid, literature on radical student organisations – particularly in social contexts of political authoritarianism – would be most pertinent. This is not to attribute in advance, a radical character to SASO and/or SANSCO. Rather, such a characterisation may be treated as a hypothesis and point of departure for the analysis of the two organisations.

The question of character

Six points can be made about the character of radical student organisations, or with respect to issues that have a bearing on the analysis of their character.

First, regarding the origins of a radical organisation, the comments of Maravall are useful. Writing about student radicalism in Spain under Franco, Maravall states that,

> [b]ecause of the constraints that non-democratic political conditions present, student radicalism often has a minoritarian, elitist origin. In these circumstances, access to available ideological alternatives is restricted and becomes the privilege of a few ... The militant has, then, very distinctive features which make him non-representative of the student population as a whole (1978:119).

The militant politicised student is likely to be the product of a "deviant political socialisation", and/or of contact with surviving "political groups ... not ... totally eradicated by repression" (*ibid.*:166-167).

Second, a radical student organisation is likely to draw attention to the links between education and politics, and emphasise the continuum between student life and life as a member of an (often oppressed) community and between student politics and national politics. *Third*, if one is to distinguish between student organisations in terms of whether they are norm-oriented (taking up immediate and limited issues, and focusing on specific goals) or value-oriented (taking up longer-term issues, linking educational and political issues, and focusing on general social goals), a radical organisation is more often of the latter type. Thus, for black university students in colonial Zimbabwe, student issues "appear[ed] inconsequential" and the target was the state, because at stake was the destiny of Zimbabwe (Cefkin, 1975:146). However, many radical organisations also take up immediate issues and organise around specific goals, but attempt to transcend immediate issues and link specific goals with broader political and organisational goals. Moreover, a relationship of some sort may exist between a radical organisation and norm-orientated organisations, and members of the former may also be members of organisations of the latter kind.

Fourth, a radical student organisation is often a collective of students "inspired by aims set forth in a specific ideological doctrine, usually ... political in nature" (Altbach, 1967:82). *Fifth*, although a radical organisation may have a small membership, its members often display a high level of commitment. In addition, members frequently work in other campus and off-campus organisations. *Finally*, a radical organisation is often influenced by and/or affiliated to off-campus political organisations and parties. National political issues and struggles are brought onto the campuses and the potential of the organisation in certain areas may be harnessed by political organisations. Conversely, political guidance and assistance may be sought by the radical organisation from off-campus political activists and groups.

The issue of role

The comparative literature on the role of student organisations is not only descriptive but, occasionally, also prescriptive. That is, there is both analysis of the role that student organisations and students generally have played in political struggles in both advanced and underdeveloped capitalist countries, and arguments around the role that they ought to play. There is no point in detailing the myriad activities students in various countries have engaged in. Many of these activities are highly specific to conditions in particular social formations and, as Emmerson has argued, it is important to recognise "the vital influence of diverse national conditions on the political roles ... of university students' (1968:391-92). Instead, I will briefly outline the interesting perspectives of Cockburn (1969) and Lenin (1961a-e) on the role radical student organisations ought to play in relation to political and educational struggles, and sketch some of the general roles that have been played by student organisations.

Cockburn argues that the aim of the student movement should be to forge a revolutionary alliance with the working class (1969:15). The role of students is, however, not conceived as external to revolutionary politics – that is, defined only in terms of expressions of solidarity with the working class. Instead, "once the student movement is committed to an alliance with the working class it can begin to explore the specific contribution it can itself make to the general revolutionary cause" (*ibid.*). An important rider to the above is that if the student movement is to make an effective contribution to revolutionary struggle it has to "first be itself" (*ibid.*:16). The implication is that the contribution of the student movement to revolutionary politics will be enhanced if it concentrates on student mobilisation, establishes a strong organisation and defines a distinct role for itself. In this regard, it is asserted that the real power of students resides in the universities and colleges, and means have to be found to challenge the authoritarian structures and undemocratic practices of higher education institutions and to extend and consolidate student power. Thus, educational institutions are defined as important arenas and sites of struggle in the overall battle against bourgeois power. Cockburn wrote in the immediate aftermath of student militancy in France, Britain and elsewhere in 1968, and his conception of the role and tasks of students and their organisations was thus informed by the concrete experiences and lessons of the 1968 student struggles.

Lenin, scornful of "the over-clever contention that bourgeois students cannot become imbued with socialism" (1961d:42), was also of the view that student organisations and students had an important role to play in revolutionary struggles. Writing in mid-1903, Lenin welcomed the "growing revolutionary initiative among the student youth" and called on the Bolshevik party organisation to help the students organise themselves (1961b:471; 1961c:509). However, Lenin argued for a particular approach to the organisation of students. He was in full agreement with an editorial in the September 1903 edition of the *Student*, a revolutionary student newspaper, which argued that "revolutionary sentiments alone cannot bring about ideological unity among the students', but that this "requires a socialist ideal based upon one or another Socialist world outlook" (Lenin, 1961d:43). For Lenin, the editorial represented a break "in principle with ideological indifference ... and ... put the question of the way to revolutionise students on a proper footing" (*ibid.*), since talk about "ideological unity" among students in the context of a heterogeneous student body was absurd. According to Lenin, the phrase "ideological unity" could have only two implications: winning over the mass of students to a particular ideology and politics, and attracting them to off-campus groups with the same ideology.

The task of social-democrat students was not to "gloss over" the differences in the student body "but on the contrary, to explain it as widely as possible and to embody it in a political organisation" (Lenin, 1961d:53). Social-democrat students had to have their own autonomous organisation since

> only on the basis of a perfectly definite programme can and should one work among the widest student circles to broaden their academic outlook and to propagate scientific socialism, i.e. Marxism (ibid.:50).

This insistence on an autonomous social-democratic student organisation and stress on political work on the basis of a "definite programme" does not mean that Lenin rejected general student councils or unions or that he considered academic issues to be unimportant. On the contrary, student unions were seen as important and it was stressed that

> when the Social-Democratic student breaks with the revolutionary and politically-minded people of all the other trends, this by no means implies the break-up of the general student and educational organisations (ibid.).

Although on certain occasions an emphasis on purely academic issues could detract from political issues, and it was then correct to oppose academicism, in general, and especially during periods of political calm, it was imperative to support an academic movement, to work within it, and attempt to transform it into a political movement. During this process, through agitation and active participation, new students could be won over to social-democratic thinking and organisation could be expanded and strengthened.

The above represents the perspectives of a veteran of the 1968 struggles, and those of one of the leading theoreticians and strategists of the 1917 Russian revolution on the role that student organisations ought to play in social struggles. What, however, are some of the roles that student organisations and students have played in political struggles in colonial social formations and in contexts of political authoritarianism?

First, in relation to broader political resistance, students have

> acted as catalysts for the mass movement; more, they acted as initiators of mass action, following up their own demonstrations and activities with a call for a general strike (Woddis, 1972:318).

Thus, they have the potential to ignite a "more general conflagration" (Cockburn, 1969:16), and play a powerful role as "detonator" (Mandel,

1969:52). Second, students have actively assisted in the formation and development of local-level popular organisations (Hamilton, 1968:373-78). Third, they have helped with the propaganda and organisational activities of pamphlet and poster distribution, announcements of meetings, and so on (*ibid.*). Fourth, student organisations have inducted students into a political culture and have provided a training ground for the development of political activists (Myr, 1968:280).

Fifth, they have also served a recruitment function in relation to political and popular organisations (Hobsbawm, 1973:260). Thus, Altbach writing about the Bombay Students' Union has commented: "the students were a valuable source of active cadres in the trade union movement. Students are an active element in the Congress" (quoted in Woddis, 1972:318). Finally, under repressive conditions, student organisations have been outlets for the views of banned organisations, on occasion even speaking for and promoting such organisations (Hamilton, 1968:373-78). It is suggested that such a role was made possible by the greater freedom enjoyed by students relative to other dominated social groupings.

Student organisation: constraints, challenges and possibilities

The extent to which a *student organisation* is able to play all, some, or any, of the various roles outlined above is, of course, conditioned by what Emmerson has called "the vital influence of diverse national conditions" (1968:391) as well as the internal characteristics of an organisation. However, beyond "national conditions" there are also others factors related to the student situation and the educational arena which both challenge and constrain – and also facilitate – student action.

A student organisation's role and character is also conditioned by the manner in which it copes with particular problems related to the student situation, deals with certain practical organisational issues and, by the nature of its relationships, with other class and popular organisations. A major problem facing any student organisation is the transitory status of students, long breaks in the academic year and the demands placed on students by examinations. There is often a near-100 per cent turnover of the student body within a short space of time; breaks in the academic year can have the effects of disrupting ongoing activities; and examination periods may mean a general diminishing of the level of student activity.

This means student organisations may often be "impermanent and discontinuous" (Hobsbawm, 1973:261), finding it difficult to maintain a continuity of activity, organisation and perhaps even of programme and ideology.

A second challenge is that of the recruitment and training of the membership. Where organisations are treated with hostility by educational authorities, recruitment becomes an especially difficult matter. Beyond this, general political conditions within a social formation may inhibit recruitment. Apart from recruitment, the education and training of its membership is especially crucial for an organisation inspired by a radical ideology and a definite political programme.

Finance is a third problem confronting a student organisation. The availability of finances may either facilitate the expansion and activities of an organisation or may constitute a severe impediment to its progress and development. Especially when an organisation operates at a national level, finances may also affect the process of decision making and democratic participation within the organisation. How an organisation addresses these organisational challenges has a bearing on whether it is "impermanent" or more lasting.

Finally, the relationships that a student organisation develops with other non-student class and popular organisations are bound also to condition its activities and role, as well as its character and significance. With reference to the relations between student and worker movements, Hobsbawm has pointed to the need to achieve a confluence, suggesting that if such a confluence is not realised the student movement could well become characterised by "brief brush fires and relapses into passivity by the majority", coupled with student activists engaging in "frenzied ultra-left gestures" (Hobsbawm, 1973:265). Whether, in what ways, and to what extent a confluence was achieved between SASO and SANSCO and popular formations requires analysis.

However, it needs to be kept in mind that various social groupings and organisations are not all capable of orientating themselves equally swiftly, or of organising either with the same rhythm or in parallel. Or, as Hobsbawm puts it with reference to students and workers: "The two groups are evidently not moved in the same way, in the same direction, by the same forces and motives" (ibid.:258). This means that united political action by student, worker and other organisations may not always be possible under all conditions and that tensions could develop between student organisations and others around issues of political strategy, tactics, campaigns, and so on.

With respect to facilitating conditions, the fact that students generally do not have families to support means that they are less tied down and more mobile. Moreover, their congregation, often in large numbers, on campuses makes communication, mobilisation and organisation somewhat easier. Furthermore, higher educational institutions, by virtue of their role in knowledge production and dissemination, may often provide greater political space for militant activities and resistance. Thus, despite the real constraints that student organisations face, there also exist conditions which facilitate mobilisation and organisation and which ensure that students are strategically well placed for political action.

What all of the above point to, then, is the extent to which the role and character of a student organisation are "over-determined" by a large number of elements which are both internal and external to the organisation. Membership, ideology, programme – but equally the student situation, social structure, and the nature of the educational and political terrain – all need to be considered in the analysis of the character and role of a student organisation.

Interpreting Character, Role and Significance

The foregoing discussion on social structure, the contributions of social movement theory and the comparative literature on student politics, has illuminated the themes, issues and questions that are pertinent to the analysis of SASO and SANSCO. What remains to be addressed is the important issue of the specific approach and criteria to be employed in the assessment of SASO and SANSCO.

Beyond class location

One tendency in the literature on student politics is to read off the political character and significance of students and, thus implicitly, of. student organisations, from the location of students in the class structure. The outbreak of militant student resistance in advanced capitalist social formations during the late 1960s led to considerable debate among radical intellectuals around the class location of students and their political significance. On the one hand students, because of their social origins and social destination upon completion of their higher education, were seen as part of the traditional middle class. Theorists of this position argued that students were not an important political force. Essentially middle class, only a few students would be won over to the working class, which was designated as the only politically revolutionary class (Jones, 1969:26-30). On the other hand, a theorist like Mandel, pointing to changes within the capitalist production process, conceptualised students as future "white collar employees of the state or industry, and thus part of the great mass of salaried workers" (1969:49). This led him to argue that "an urgent task is the integration of the students into the workers" movement. Yes, the workers" movement must win back the student movement, particularly in as much as the students are workers" (ibid.:51). Thus, students were seen as part of a vanguard movement for socialist change and accorded considerable political significance.

The fundamental problem of the approaches that conceptualise students as traditional middle class or working class is that they all read off the political character and significance of students from their defined location in the class structure. As a result the political potential of students is either under-emphasised or overstated.

The student situation

More cogent and useful for this investigation is the conceptualisation of students implicit in the work of Poulantzas (1978) on social classes. For Poulantzas, the mental-manual labour division is one of three important distinctions in defining social classes. Professionals, scientists and skilled technicians are seen as constituting the "new petit bourgeoisie", the chief characteristic of this class being the involvement of its members, by and large, on the mental side of the division of labour. Higher education institutions, particular universities, it is suggested, must be located in relation to the mental-manual labour division. The role of these institutions is to socialise, train and distribute agents within the class structure, but is especially crucial in the training of mental labour and the reproduction of the new petit bourgeoisie (Poulantzas, 1978:259). The training of higher education students as mental labour, means that the class trajectory of their education is one that leads them to largely a new petit bourgeois class location. However, since students stand outside production relations (though not outside ideological relations) and experience a social situation different from other members of the new petit bourgeoisie, they can be best treated as a distinct fraction of the new petit bourgeoisie.

If in terms of a structural determination of classes, students constitute a distinct fraction of the new petit bourgeoisie, what of their long-term class-political position? Poulantzas affirms a thesis of most Marxist theorists that the petit bourgeoisie "has no long-run autonomous class political position" (ibid.:297). The class position of the new petit bourgeoisie will be polarised between the class positions of the bourgeoisie and the working class, the balance of class forces between the two fundamental classes playing an important role in determining the political orientation of the new petit bourgeoisie.

In the case of students, their social situation is also likely to be a crucial factor. In this regard, Jones has argued that

any characterisation of students as a social group must simultaneously encompass student *origins*, the student *situation* itself and the social *destination* of students ... These three "moments" are not, however, of interchangeable weight or significance. They form a complex whole, *dominated* by one structure – the student situation (1969:34-35, emphasis in original).

The importance of Jones's argument is the recognition that "from a political perspective, it is ... the student situation itself which has overriding priority" (ibid.:35). The synthesis of the arguments of Poulantzas (1978) and Jones (1969) provides an approach which, although it locates students firmly within the class structure, leaves open-ended the class position and political potential of students. The political position and significance of students in any conjuncture cannot be simply read off from their location in the class structure. Instead, it is a question that can only be settled by the empirical examination of their specific situation within a particular social formation.

The question of political terrain

An important implication of the above argument is that the class location of the membership of an organisation is, on its own, an insufficient indicator of the character of an organisation and its potential significance. This accords well with the important theses advanced by Nolutshungu following his brilliant analysis of the Black Consciousness movement of the 1970s. Nolutshungu argues as follows:

1   The class-relatedness of a political movement (i.e. its role in the class struggle) is not decided by its organisational affiliations, blueprints, or, even, the objective class membership of its empirical representatives.

2   The revolutionary significance of a political movement, whatever its class character, is not determined solely by its own internal characteristics (programmes, ideologies and organisations) but also by the nature of the political terrain and the effects of that terrain on its political practice (1983:200).

Nolutshungu's argument, of course, extends well beyond that of membership. Its strength lies in

1   the emphasis it places on the conditioning of political practice by "terrain"; and

2   the need for the character and significance of an organisation to be interpreted in relation to prevailing structural and conjunctural conditions.

Rootes, in analysing the consequences of student actions, emphasises that the "political significance of student movements varies according to their social and political circumstances" (1980:473). In the context of South Africa, given the historically specific relationship between racism and capitalism, national oppression and class domination, essentially nationalist movements and nationalist struggles can undermine and weaken capitalism. As Nolutshungu notes,

[w]hile nationalist movements are to be distinguished from class movements, they may and often do provide the medium in which class struggles can develop, and can, in their own right, severely

weaken the ideological and political supports of the order of class exploitation (1983:147).

The implication of this is that

a nationalist movement can be revolutionary in a Marxist sense, despite its lack of a revolutionary organisation or, even, ideology. It is revolutionary to the degree that the structures against which it struggles are essential to the survival of the order of class relations ... and to the degree that it is inherently disposed to develop, as the struggle proceeds, in a revolutionary direction (organisationally, ideologically and in point of social composition) (ibid.:199).

Interpretation, then, cannot revolve purely around questions of membership, doctrines and organisation but must also incorporate the educational and political terrain on which SASO and SANSCO operated and their actual effects on this terrain. As Piven and Cloward put it, "what was won must be judged by what was possible" (1979:xiii). Moreover. to paraphrase them, the "relevant question to ask is whether, on balance", SASO and SANSCO "made gains or lost ground; whether they" advanced the interests" of the dominated classes and social groups or "set back those interests" (ibid.).

In summary, it is clear that there is no quick and easy path to interpreting the character, role and significance of SASO and SANSCO. This is, of course, a consequence of the nature of the "problematic" that I have just sketched. Alternative problematics for approaching the principal object of this book are no doubt available. However, although they might offer considerably simpler, faster and straightforward routes to interpretation, they would be likely to result in analysis which is superficial and lacking in rigour and ultimately would produce incorrect assessments.

Answers to the questions on the character, role and significance of SANSCO and SASO entail answers to numerous prior questions. With respect to character, questions are included that relate to the ideological and political orientations of SASO and SANSCO; their conceptions of the South African social order; the programmes, objectives, principles, and policies of these two organisations and the social and political determinants of these; the organisational structure and internal operations of SASO and SANSCO and their relations with other organisations; and their repertoires of collective action.

The issue of the roles of the two student organisations requires analysis of how they conceived their roles and the reasons for their conceptions; the principal themes and issues around which they mobilised and organised and why these themes were accorded priority; how members, supporters and sympathisers were mobilised or/and educated; what was done to ensure organisational continuity, and similar issues. The question of significance involves an examination of the importance of their specific and general activities, and of their effects and consequences; it also involves an analysis of what they achieved, made possible and contributed distinctively. Moreover, key issues are how, in what ways and to what extent did the objectives, principles and policies and practices of SASO and SANSCO contribute to reproducing, undermining or transforming social relations, institutions and practices?

Finally, it has been argued that, ultimately, the character, role and significance of SASO and SANSCO cannot be read off purely from their internal characteristics. That is to say, the meanings to be attached to their character, role and significance must also take into account the real social conditions, the "given and inherited circumstances", under which they were obliged to make history and indeed made history.

Part 1

"Black man, you are on your own": The South African Students' Organisation, 1968 to 1977

2

From Crisis to Stability to Crisis: The Apartheid Social Order and Black Higher Education, 1960 to 1976-1977

This chapter grounds the analysis of the emergence, ideology and politics, organisation and collective actions of SASO which are examined in the next three chapters. The focus here is on the social and higher education structure and conjuncture of the period from the crushing of mass political dissent in the early 1960s to the re-emergence of mass popular action during the early 1970s, which culminated in the Soweto uprising of 1976/1977.

Three issues in relation to black higher education are specifically covered. The first is the description and analysis of the goals and policies that came to be formulated by the Apartheid State during the late 1950s and the economic, political and social determinants of these policies. This analysis is preceded by a brief consideration of the provision of higher education for blacks prior to 1948. The second is an analysis of the organisational features that came to characterise black higher education during the 1960 to 1976/1977 period and the instruments and processes by which these were reproduced. Finally, particular conditions – authoritarian control, the racial composition of administrative and academic staff – internal to black institutions which impinged on students are discussed, so as to better frame the analysis of student action that follows.

Political Economy of Black Higher Education before 1960

Pre-apartheid period

During the early twentieth century, the twin concerns of the South African state were guaranteeing capital accumulation on the basis of cheap unskilled black labour and consolidating the structures of white political domination and privilege. As a result, the education and training of blacks was not a priority. Segregation, institutionalised in the political and social spheres, also constituted a central plank of education policy. In practice this meant limited funding, and inadequate provision of facilities, for black – and especially African – education, as well as an organisational structuring of schooling which took a racial form. The effect of state policies was to ensure that higher education was essentially restricted to certain sections of the white dominant classes.

Prior to 1948, black higher education was largely confined to the universities. There was no provision of advanced technical education, this being a result of the racial division of labour and institutionalised job reservation, which restricted blacks primarily to unskilled occupations. The training of African teachers was conducted mainly by church missions with some financial aid from provincial authorities. While the South African Native College (later Fort Hare) offered a higher teaching diploma, teacher-training was essentially a continuation of secondary education. Teacher-training of Indians and coloureds was carried out by the provincial authorities, and was also largely an extension of secondary education. During 1948 some 6 499 students were enrolled at 39 teacher-training institutions designated for Africans and 1 133 coloured and Indian students attended 16 teacher-training colleges (Union of South Africa, 1961:E7).

By 1948 black university students numbered only 950, a mere 4,6% of total enrolments (Malherbe, 1977:731), reflecting the underdeveloped state of black pre-higher education as a whole. The only institution at which black students were numerically predominant was the South African Native College, established by a church mission society in 1916 and offering post-matric courses from 1919 onwards. Small numbers of black students also attended the white English-language universities of Cape Town (UCT), Witwatersrand (Wits) and Natal (UN). Finally, some students were enrolled at the part-time correspondence institution, the University of South Africa (UNISA). Although the white universities exercised autonomy over whom they taught, "admissions of black students were not, however, encouraged" (WUS/AUT, 1986:5). At Rhodes University, students were often refused registration on the grounds that similar facilities were available at Fort Hare (UFH). At UN, students were enrolled on the basis of segregated academic classes, while at Wits the official policy was one of "academic non-segregation". This meant that outside the academic sphere restrictions were placed on non-racial social activities and, in effect, black students were discriminated against. The white Afrikaans-language universities "rigidly refused to admit black students although none of their charters, except that of Potchefstroom, prevented them from doing so" (WUS/AUT, 1986:5-6).

Elaboration of apartheid education policies, 1948 to 1960

The 1948 elections saw the National Party (NP) emerging triumphant. The NPs' immediate policies were continued capital accumulation on the basis of greater expansion of the manufacturing industry, the mechanisation of agriculture, Afrikaner economic advancement, and apartheid/separate development as the mode of continued white political domination and black subordination. These policies were, in turn, to profoundly shape state policies relating to black higher education – and the organisational structure and mechanisms of administrative control of higher education that were elaborated upon during this period and served as a broad framework until the late 1970s.

The initial position of the apartheid government with regard to the question of black university education was contradictory. In 1949 the creation of a medical school at Natal University to train primarily black doctors, previously approved by the United Party administration, was endorsed. However, a year later, as if to signal a determination to impose apartheid in higher education, it was stipulated that state funding would be made available to the medical school only on the condition that admission was restricted to black students. Although this contravened the university's admissions policy and provoked some opposition, it was on this basis that the school opened in 1951.

The report of the Eiselen Commission (Commission on Native Education, 1949-1951), which powerfully influenced the contents of the Bantu Education Act of 1953, described the key connection between state education policy and political and economic control of the African population. African education was to reflect the dominance of the ideology of white rule and superiority. Moreover, in accordance with the requirements of the "separate development", higher education for blacks was to be planned in conjunction with "development" programmes for the bantustans and to be placed under the direct control of the Department of Native Affairs. The Commission further recommended that the registration of African students at white institutions be restricted to courses that were unavailable at Fort Hare. This was in line with the thrust of state policy on African education:

Native education should be based on the principles of trusteeship, non-equality and segregation; its aims should be to inculcate the white man's view of life, especially that of the Boer, which is the senior trustee (quoted in Brooks and Brickhill, 1980:13).

In 1953, the Holloway Commission (Commission of enquiry on separate training facilities for non-Europeans at universities, 1953-55) was appointed to investigate the practicability and financial implications of providing separate universities for blacks. Holloway rejected the idea on financial grounds, and suggested that segregation of the "races" could be accomplished by locating African and Indian undergraduates at Fort Hare and Natal (where academic classes were segregated) and coloured students and African and Indian postgraduates at those universities prepared to accept them.

Notwithstanding Holloway's recommendation, an inter-departmental committee was set up to investigate the matter further. The committee began, against Holloway's advice, trying to remove the medical school from the control of Natal University, to place it under the academic control of UNISA, and the administrative control of the Department of Native Affairs. Widespread political opposition by black organisations and white liberal groups, and practical issues associated with the operation of a medical school, forced the government to back down.

Despite this setback, the inter-departmental committee's efforts culminated in the passing of the Extension of University Education Act of 1959. This enabled the creation of new racial and ethnic universities, and stipulated that in future black students would be required to obtain ministerial permission to register at institutions reserved for whites. In terms of the Fort Hare Transfer Act of 1959, Fort Hare was to be restricted to Xhosa-speaking Africans and, as with the new universities for Africans, was to be brought under the direct control of the newly created Department of Bantu Education.

In 1959, on the eve of university education being segregated along racial and ethnic lines, and placed under tight state control, student enrolments were as follows (Table 1).

Table 1: **Racial composition and distribution of black students by type of university, 1959**

| Race | Types of university | | | |
	Fort Hare	White	UNISA	Total
African	319	300	1 252	1 871
Coloured	70	541	211	822
Indian	100	815	601	1 516
Total	489	1 656	2 064	4 207
% Distribution	11,6	39,3	49,1	100

(Sources: SAIRR, 1962:252; Malherbe, 1977:311; RSA, 1969:E2/2).

Three points need to be made with regard to Table 1. First, despite Eiselen's recommendations, and in the absence of legislation preventing blacks from enrolling at white universities, throughout the 1950s there was a steady increase in black students at the white English-language universities. Indeed, by 1959 the vast majority of full-time students (77,2%) were enrolled at these institutions. At UCT, black students constituted 12,4% of the total student body; at Natal 21,3%, and at Witwatersrand 5,8% (SAIRR, 1962:252). The figure for Natal is inflated by the attendance of black students at the racially segregated medical school.

It was this process that the legislation of 1959 sought to arrest and reverse.

Second, by 1959 the 4 207 black students constituted a mere 10,7% of total university enrolments (39 390 students) – of whom 4,7% were Africans, 3,9% were Indians and 2,1% were coloureds. University education, then, continued to be concentrated among the white bourgeoisie and petit bourgeoisie. Third, relative to white students, black students were registered predominantly in the humanities and education and were severely under-represented in the scientific and technical fields.

Turning to black teacher-training and technical education, the Bantu Education Act of 1953 stipulated that African teacher-training was to be brought under direct state control. All future training of teachers for state or state-aided schools was to be conducted at departmental institutions. The church missions were given the option of either closing or selling/renting the training schools. Schools deciding to continue operating on a self-financing basis were still obliged to register with the Department of Bantu Education. Crucially, their students were not guaranteed employment in state schools. By 1959 there were 50 small training colleges with 5 656 students (RSA, 1969:12). As in the past, teacher-training continued to be largely an extension of secondary education rather than post-matric training. Coloured and Indian teacher-training was controlled by the provincial administrations. There were 12 colleges for coloureds (1 659 students), and 2 for Indians (536 students).

The provision of higher-level technical education and training, oriented towards skilled and artisan employment in mining and industry, continued to be restricted to whites. Due to the small number of secondary school graduates, as with teacher-training, other vocational courses (social work, nursing, paramedical) also required only a Standard 6 or Junior Certificate.

Structural character of black higher education

Black students at universities are likely to have come mainly from the black petit bourgeoisie and commercial bourgeoisie. The small enrolment (0,32 per 1000 population compared to 12,1 for whites) largely related to the lack of provision of, and the abysmal conditions in, pre-higher education. This is borne out by Senior Certificate (Standard 10) passes: in 1959 only 578 students obtained a pass with matriculation exemption (the entrance requirement for degree courses at universities), while 873 students received school-leaving certificates (necessary for diploma courses) (Malherbe, 1977:724-26).

While this accounts for the limited representation of black students at universities and the low entrance requirements for vocational courses, the structural character of black higher education needs to be explained. First, the racial division of labour as institutionalised by job reservation legislation and enforced by white trade unions was taken as a given. The effect of this was that blacks were excluded from middle and high-level training in scientific and technical fields and higher education was restricted to fields of study (mainly liberal arts) that would not undermine the existing racial division of labour.

Second, the provision of higher education was related to the grand programme of apartheid. A corollary of the 1959 Extension of University Education Act, enabling the establishment of new racial/ethnic universities, was the 1959 Promotion of Bantu Self-Government Act, while the Bantu Authorities Act of 1951 also conditioned higher education. The Bantu Authorities Act sought to replace direct colonial rule in the African reserves with a system of indirect rule through reactionary traditional leaders and collaborationist elements who were to be granted executive and administrative powers. The Promotion of Bantu Self-Government Act took this process further by unfolding the project of geographical segregation and consolidation of ethnically structured territorial units, the bantustans (the previous "reserves"). Beale writes

[t]he political crisis of the 1950s necessitated a revision of the perception of what was needed to enhance the conditions of capital accumulation and secure the prospects of white power and privilege ... By the late 1950s, the Bantustan project was seen as essential for the long-term security of white political and economic control (1991:42-3)

The link between the establishment of the African universities and the launching of the bantustan system was unambiguous. The intention was to restrict the economic advancement, social mobility and political rights of Africans to the bantustans, and it was there that the products of the African universities were expected to exercise their talents.

For Verwoerd (1901-1966), the rationale for the ethnic structuring of universities was "the conviction that the future leader during his ... university training must remain in close touch with the habits, ways of life and views of members of his population group" (Malherbe, 1979:150). The universities were meant to produce the administrative corps for the black separate development bureaucracies and to assist in the class formation of a black petit bourgeoisie that would, it was hoped, collaborate in the project of separate development. The training of blacks for professional occupations (teaching, social work, nursing, medicine, etc.) was to be directed towards meeting the needs of the black population, particularly those in the bantustans – a fact exemplified by the statement of a government minister that the University of Natal's medical school was to be solely "for the training of Non-Europeans ... to meet the health needs of their own people" (quoted in Gordon, 1957:8). However, relating academic opportunities to job reservation and channelling students to the bantustans would also contribute to another objective: that of ensuring that the developing Afrikaner petit bourgeoisie, a crucial support base of the government, did not experience competition in the labour market.

Third, to secure its ideological and political objectives, the National Party brought black education under tight, authoritarian and centralised state control. The criticism of missionary education was that it was

isolated from the life of Bantu society. It prepares them not for life within a Bantu community ... but for a life outside the community and for posts which do not in fact exist (Verwoerd, Minister of Native Education, quoted in Rose and Tunmer (eds), 1975:264).

Consequently, the control of teacher-training by liberal churches and provincial authorities was eliminated. Concomitantly, the "intolerable state of affairs" (Malan, South African Prime Minister, quoted in UNESCO, 1967:84) of black students attending white universities and being exposed to liberal ideas and values was ended. Now, ministerial permission was to be sought by blacks wanting to attend white universities, and the autonomy of these institutions with regard to admission was circumscribed.

Finally, in 1957 a warning had been sounded by Verwoerd that the control of (black universities) by the government is needed as it is necessary to prevent undesirable ideological elements – such as has

[sic] disturbed the non-white institutions not directly under the control of the government (quoted in Beale, 1991:42).

To give effect to this, strict academic and administrative control over staff and students was to be enforced at Fort Hare and at the still to be established ethnic universities.

Political and Social Conditions, 1960 to 1976/1977

To this point my concern has been to explicate the roots and structural features of black higher education. This is because it is important to understand the shaping of black higher education by dynamics within the wider political economy. Moreover, it was during the 1950s that the essential features of black higher education were elaborated, to remain more or less intact for the following two decades. Now, I turn to a description of the social structure and political economy of the 1960 to 1976/1977, period and the conditions that constituted the wider context of student political activity during this period.

Social structure

Throughout this period social relations in South Africa continued to be fundamentally structure along lines of race, class and gender and shaped by the articulation of racism and racialism, capitalism and patriarchy.[2.1] Frequently, apartheid and the national oppression of blacks is explained solely in terms of the ideology of racism or racial prejudice. Yet it is the case, as Davies *et al.* put it,

> that the various changing historical forms of national oppression and racism in South Africa are organically linked with, and have provided the fundamental basis for, the development of a capitalist economy ... The national oppression of black people in South Africa is a product of, and was indeed the necessary historical condition for, the development of capitalism ... [1984] (1988:Vol.1, 2).

Given this, within the radical opposition to apartheid, concepts such as "racial capitalism" and "colonialism of a special type" arose as an attempt to capture, in shorthand, the interrelationship and linkage between racial and class oppression in South Africa.

This is not, however, to suggest that the relationship between racial domination and capitalism has been a necessary one, or that there has been a complete convergence of race and class in South Africa. It is accepted that the relationship between racial domination and capitalism has been historically contingent, and that whether they have been functional to, or in contradiction with, one another can only be answered by concrete analysis. Moreover, there exists also a

> racial division of classes and class division of races ... This means that, on the one hand, cross-class alignments, in which there are differing attachments to the racial order, may co-exist and articulate with cross-race alignments in which attachments to the racial order are subject to dissolution ... [It] is not possible to read off group interests from either "pure" race or class categorisations (Wolpe, 1988:75-76).

Wolpe's signalling of the availability and possibility of cross-race and cross-class alignments is important, and how these alignments were approached by SASO during this period and by SANSCO during the post-1976/1977 period will require analysis.

Patriarchy ensured that women, irrespective of race and class, occupied a subordinate position within South African society, and particularly with respect to equality of access and opportunity in the economic, political and educational spheres. However, the degree of oppression and subordination, as well as access and opportunity, was conditioned by race and class. Thus, whereas white women were denied full equality solely through the operation of patriarchal relations, black women experienced a double oppression on grounds of patriarchy and race, sharing in common with black men a lack of political rights, restrictions on economic and educational opportunities, inferior social services and myriad other disabilities. Black working-class women were subject to the most intense oppression – a triple oppression as a consequence of the articulation of patriarchy, race and class. Subject to low wages, often poor working conditions, long hours of transport to and from work, sexual harassment in the workplace, the effects of the migrant labour system, and primary responsibility for child-care and household duties, the burdens of black working-class women were particularly severe. Finally, African women were also subject to customary law in terms of which they were treated as perpetual minors.

In practice, the apartheid system during this period "secured the interests of the entire capitalist class, enabling all capitalists to intensify the exploitation of African workers and to raise the general rate of profit" (O'Meara, 1983:247). Concomitantly, through institutionalised racialism, it also ensured the maintenance and reproduction of the privileges of whites as a whole.

Political subordination and economic control

White domination and black subordination, established originally by conquest and dispossession, were secured by the exclusion of blacks from the political system and the concomitant denial of full citizenship rights. However, the bantustans (previous "reserves" established in terms of the various native land Acts that legalised dispossession), which constituted 13% of the largely barren surface area of South Africa, were also pivotal to white domination. Long unable to meet the subsistence needs of their inhabitants, during this period the bantustans became less important in relation to their traditional role of subsidising the cost of reproduction of labour-power. Instead, they became a crucial pillar of the separate development project in that it was to these areas that African aspiration and demands for political rights were to be deflected. Moreover, in the context of a well-established system of migrant labour it was in the bantustans that African workers were to be not only located, but also relocated, when superfluous to the needs of the capitalist economy. Indeed, the period from the 1960s to the early 1970s was one of huge population relocation. As a consequence of mechanisation in agriculture, capital-intensive technology in manufacturing, the elimination of African "black spots" within rural "white South Africa", the deproclamation of urban African township and the consolidation of bantustan territories, almost three million people were forcibly uprooted from "white" South Africa and relocated in the bantustans.

Social control over Africans was also maintained through extensive controls over movement, residence and employment. The cynically named Natives (abolition of passes and co-ordination of documents) Act made it compulsory for all Africans from the age of sixteen to carry a reference book ("pass") which had to be produced to an authorised officer on demand. The reference book included a photograph, thumbprint, name and identity number and contained information relating to residential and work rights in an area, employment, payment of taxes, exemptions and so on. Throughout this period, hundreds of thousands were arrested annually and convicted under "offences" relating to the pass laws.

Race and class domination was further underpinned by a virtual white monopoly of land ownership and control of all sectors of the capitalist economy. A period of sustained economic boom between the early 1960s and early 1970s significantly altered the pattern of capital accumulation in South Africa. One result was the emergence of large business corporations and the consolidation of monopoly capitalism in most sectors of the economy. The centralisation of capital and the expansion of monopoly relations meant that a few powerful state corporations, some foreign multinationals, and a handful of private corporations controlled virtually all capitalist production (Davies et al., [1984] (1988); Innes, 1983).

Monopoly capital accumulation, predicated as it was on large investments in new technology and machinery and a rising organic composition of capital, together with the capitalisation of agriculture, had a significant impact on the technical division of labour. The previous unskilled-skilled labour dichotomy now gave way to one that required larger numbers of technicians, supervisory personnel, administrative workers, and semi-skilled labourers. In a context of job-reservation policies, which restricted high-level and many middle-level and technical occupations for whites, the beneficiaries of these jobs were mainly whites, with blacks being employed largely as semi-skilled labourers. However, mechanisation in agriculture and capital-intensive technology in manufacturing also had the effect of extruding hundreds of thousands of mainly black workers from the production process, and contributing to the origin and development of the phenomenon of structural unemployment.

Finally, during this period the battery of laws and practices that institutionalised the segregated and racially discriminatory and unequal provision of educational facilities and opportunities, housing, health care, transport, sports, recreation and leisure amenities, and welfare payments, and which prohibited interracial sport, worship, marriages and sexual relations, was stringently applied and enforced. Indian and coloured South Africans were also subject to the above and, while exempt from the pass laws, they shared in common with Africans the experiences of job-reservation policies, forced removals, and an absence of citizenship and political rights. Legislation and state initiatives were not purely the product of racist attitudes and irrational political practice, as asserted by some liberal writers, but were intrinsic to oppressive and exploitative social relations and the reproduction of class and race domination.

From crisis to stability to crisis

The 1960 to 1976/1977 period both began and ended with the apartheid state in crisis. The crisis of the early 1960s was occasioned by, in response to anti-pass protests called by the Pan Africanist Congress (PAC), the shooting of demonstrators at Sharpeville, the declaration of a state of emergency, the banning in April 1960 of the ANC and PAC, and the turning of the latter to armed struggle and related events. The crisis which led to short-term investor panic and capital flight had been largely dealt with by about 1963, when much of the underground leadership of the ANC was arrested and subsequently imprisoned and hundreds were obliged to flee into exile.

The method of dealing with the political crisis was to set the trend for this period as a whole. Over and above recourse to a state of emergency – during which over 11 000 political activists were detained – raids, arrests, banishment and torture became the norm in dealing with political opposition. Moreover, new instruments were fashioned to suppress political activity – the Unlawful Organisations Act was passed in 1960 and immediately used to ban the ANC and PAC; and the General Laws Amendment Act provided for political detention. The banning of the ANC and PAC continued, on an expanded scale, the process of destruction of the extra-parliamentary terrain, which had begun with the banning of the Communist Party in 1951 and was pursued in relation to various organisations throughout the 1950s (Wolpe, 1988:68). In 1967 the armour of repressive legislation was supplemented by the Terrorism Act, while during this period the Suppression of Communism Act was amended on various occasions (eventually becoming the Internal Security Act in 1976) and the military and police and security apparatuses were restructured and strengthened to attend to internal dissent, as well as to the armed struggle launched by the exiled ANC and PAC during the late 1960s.

The smashing of political opposition and repression created stability and new and extremely favourable conditions for capital accumulation. This, in turn, provided the basis for the sustained economic boom of the 1963-73 period, high rates of return on investment, extensive economic and political restructuring, and the decline in internally based mass political resistance.

However, this period also ended with the apartheid state in crisis: At the economic level a combination of factors led to recessionary conditions and an end to the previous decade of economic boom. Alongside this was the emergence of widespread strikes in 1973 because of low wages and rising prices which, owing to the number of workers involved, their skill levels and other factors, could not be as easily suppressed as previous ones. These strikes, together with the demonstrations and activities of black higher education students – under the influence of Black Consciousness organisations which began to be formed from 1968 onwards – signalled a revival, after a decade of silence, of mass and extraparliamentary action. Organisation was also growing within secondary schools, spearheaded by the South African Students' Movement. Developments in Southern Africa, the defeat of Portuguese colonialism and the success of liberation struggles in Angola and Mozambique and the defeat of the invading South African forces in Angola, all contributed to the militancy and assertiveness of black students. Thus, when the decree that Afrikaans should be the language of instruction for some school subjects was added to the under-funding, overcrowding and generally impoverished conditions of African schooling, students – at least those in Soweto – were ready to take action.

The subsequent events – the protest marches of the students, the police shootings, countrywide student boycotts, parent demonstrations, and stayaways – referred to as the Soweto uprising of 1976/1977 are well known. The state responded, as in the early 1960s, with police and military shootings, mass arrests, detentions, the banning of individuals and the banning, in October 1977, of numerous Black Consciousness and anti-apartheid organisations, including SASO. The uprising was of tremendous political significance. It contributed to the reconstitution of the terrain of mass extraparliamentary politics in South Africa, and helped revitalise the exiled liberation movements. Moreover, it stimulated a re-thinking on the part of capitalists about how best the process of capital accumulation was to be safeguarded in South Africa, and the uprising impelled the state to engage in extensive restructuring of institutions, past policies and practices. In short, the uprising of 1976/1977 produced, as a product of social struggle, new and changed conditions of struggle.

Separate Development and Black Higher Education, 1960 to 1976/1977

If the policy framework for black higher education was elaborated upon during the 1950s, it was the repressive conditions of the 1960s that made it possible to translate policy into institutional form without significant challenge. Following the 1959 Extension of University Education Act, four new racial and ethnic universities were established in 1960 and 1961. The University Colleges of the North (UNIN), Zululand (UNIZUL), the Western Cape (UWC) and Durban – later Durban-Westville (UDW), were to cater for Sotho/Venda/Tsonga-speaking Africans, Zulu/Swazi-speaking Africans, coloureds and Indians, respectively. The University College of Fort Hare was to be restricted to Xhosa-speaking Africans.

The geographic location of these institutions was conditioned by the separate development and bantustan programme of the apartheid state. Verwoerd, in a speech delivered in the Senate in 1954, asserted that

more institutions for advanced education in urban areas are not desired. Deliberate attempts will be made to keep institutions for advanced education away from the urban environment and to establish them as far as possible in the Native areas. It is the policy of my department that education would have its roots entirely in the Native areas ... (quoted in Rose and Tunmer, 1975:265).

The universities designated for Africans were deliberately located not only in impoverished rural areas with limited social infrastructure and amenities, but also in areas far removed from the political militancy and influences of large cities. Thus, the University Colleges of the North and Zululand were built in predominantly African rural areas – the North at Turfloop, near Pietersburg in the northern Transvaal, Zululand at Ngoye in north-eastern Natal. Fort Hare was already located in an area bordering Ciskei. The University Colleges of the Western Cape (in Bellville, Cape

Peninsula) and Durban (in Durban, Natal) were established in areas of greatest concentration of coloureds and Indians respectively.

Student enrolments at universities

Between 1960 and 1976 there was a considerable increase in black student enrolments (see Table 2). Also significant, however, was the change that occurred in the distribution of students between the different types of universities. Thus, while there was little change between 1960 and 1976 in the proportion of correspondence students at UNISA, a tremendous change occurred with respect to enrolments at the white and black universities, so that by 1976 the vast majority of black students were enrolled at the racial and ethnic universities designated for them.

Table 2: **Enrolment of black students and their distribution by type of university, 1960 to 1976**

Year	Type of university					
	African	Coloured	Indian	White	UNISA	Total
1960 %	488	161	-	1 728	2 004	4 381
Distribution	-	14,8	-	39,4	45,8	100,0
1965 %	956	416	1 009	981	2 911	6 273
Distribution	-	38,0	-	15,6	46,4	100,0
1970 %	2 011	936	1 654	1 106	3 704	9 411
Distribution	-	48,9	-	11,8	39,3	100,0
1976 %	5 204	2 438	3 108	1 550	10 609	22 909
Distribution	-	46,9	-	6,8	46,3	100,0

(Sources: SAIRR, 1963:195; 1966:274; 1971:243; 1977:366; Malherbe, 1977:729; RSA, 1987:5.49).

Enrolments at black universities rose by almost 400% between 1960 and 1965, doubled over the next five years and increased more than 100% between 1970 and 1976. Access was facilitated by low fees, state bursaries and loans, and the provision of numerous diploma courses requiring only a senior certificate. This expansion must be related to the massive growth in primary and secondary student enrolments: whereas in 1960 there were 1 452 300 primary and 65 600 secondary students, by 1975 the figures were 3 378 900 and 318 500 respectively (Wolpe, 1988:5). During the same period the number of black students with matriculation exemption passes rose from 637 to 6 212, while those with school-leaving certificates went from 1 025 to 7 457 (RSA, 1983:5.5; Malherbe, 1977:724-26).

The pre-higher education enrolments must themselves be seen in the context of the changes that were occurring in the structure of the economy. The expansion of the manufacturing industry and the service sector, and the introduction of capital-intensive technology, required larger numbers of black workers who were semi-skilled and possessed more than just minimal elementary education. On the one hand, the racial division of labour was modified to accommodate this new reality.[2.2] On the other hand, the provision of education was expanded and adjustments were made to the system of financing of black education. However, although flexibility and adjustments were dictated by economic imperatives, education policy continued to be predicated on the goal of separate development. Thus, the provision of pre-higher education was increasingly and more tightly tied to the bantustan programme and the need for skilled personnel to staff the bantustan civil service as these territories were given self-governing status, including control over education.

An important component of the relocation strategy was also to pressurise African professionals to reside in the bantustans. State bursaries often required students to take up self-employment in the bantustans or to work for state departments. Although after the early 1970s job reservation was eroded in some sectors, it continued to exist. A powerful block was agreements that were negotiated by white trade unions and employers. Consequently, black professionals were restricted to operating in black townships and/or in the service of the growing bureaucracies of the Departments of Bantu Administration and Development, and Coloured and Indian Affairs.

Turning to black enrolments at the white universities, after 1959/1960 there was a decline both in actual numbers at each university, and in overall enrolments. State policy, applied especially strictly in the case of African students, was to direct black students to the ethnic universities or UNISA. However, the situation slowly began to change from the late 1960s. Throughout the 1960s, small numbers of coloured and Indian

63

students were allowed to continue registering for degrees in technical fields such as engineering, architecture and surveying, possibly because of a market in private building and construction among these groups. By contrast, in 1960 the government refused African student applications for engineering degrees on the grounds that there was "no prospect for employment for qualified Bantu engineers" (SAIRR, 1961:230), and it was only after the late 1960s that African students were allowed to register in this field. During 1976, 15 African of the 263 black students (compared to 6 348 white) were registered for an engineering degree; the figures for the architecture/quantity surveying fields were seven African, 79 black, (compared to 2 621 whites). In percentage terms, white students in scientific, engineering and technical fields stood at over 19%, while black students ranged from 11% (African) to 14,7% (Indian), mainly in the natural sciences (RSA, 1983:5.40).

The gradual re-entry of black students into the white universities may be related to three processes. First, some relaxation of the previous strict controls may have been seen as warranted, given the narrow range of courses and fields of study on offer at black universities, the difficulties associated with correspondence study via UNISA, and the consolidation of the ethnic universities. Significant here was the fact that, from the early 1970s, black students began for the first time to be enrolled at an Afrikaans-medium university. However, that no blanket entry of black students was to be permitted is evidenced by a legislative amendment in 1971 which tightened enrolment regulations by restricting registration to the particular course(s) and field of study, and to the specific university for which ministerial permission had been provided. Prior to this, "it had been the practice of students to register for a course unavailable at their "tribal college" and once enrolled to switch to another" (WUS/AUT, 1986:7). Second, the unfolding bantustan programme required, apart from administrative personnel, also skilled technical person-power. Facilities for the training of engineers, architects, quantity surveyors and the like were non-existent at the black universities, and the white colleges of advanced technical education remained closed to blacks.

Finally, the decimation of the national liberation movement in the early 1960s by brutal state repression created favourable conditions for renewed foreign investment and capital accumulation. Rapid economic growth (the average annual growth rate in the gross domestic product was 5,8% in the 1960s and 4,7% between 1970 and 1975) on the basis of capital-intensive technology was placing a strain on the available supply of skilled technical labour. From the mid-1960s, liberal organisations and corporate capital began to argue, on the basis of government and Stellenbosch University Bureau of Economic Research reports, that the unavailability of skilled labour was creating a bottleneck, holding back higher rates of economic growth. By 1974, even the President of the state Atomic Energy Board, Dr A.J.A. Roux, was complaining of a shortfall of 17 000 engineering technicians, the annual output of 3 000 being far short of demand. Noting that "widespread attempts to attract suitable technicians from overseas have borne little fruit", Roux argued "it is evident that South Africa will increasingly have to rely on its own resources ... Two solutions ... were to train Blacks and ... women" (quoted in Malherbe, 1977:197).

In the previous year the *Financial Mail*, a mouthpiece of corporate capital, after listing categories of professional occupations in which there were shortages, had argued that

economic imperatives as well as social justice demand that Africans be trained for and allowed into jobs such as these. ... It is high time it was more widely understood by whites that their own hopes of civilised survival will be enhanced, not diminished, the higher the levels of African education (19 April 1973, p10; quoted in Makalima, 1986:40).

The appeal to whites was directed to the white trade unions that were opposing any relaxation of job reservation, and the white petit bourgeoisie, fearful of competition from black professionals. It is important to note the *Financial Mail's* use of the notion of "social justice": in the aftermath of the large black worker strikes of 1973, sections of corporate capital were already beginning to float the idea of accelerating the development of a black petit bourgeoisie as a "guarantee" against revolution (see Makalima, 1986:34). However, at this juncture this was not a widespread concern. Only in the post-Soweto uprising period would this become a major theme and obsession of corporate capital and the liberal establishment.

Skilled labour shortages and black technical training

The shortages in skilled technical labour alluded to above result in the black education departments attempting to expand the provision of technical education. In 1966 Verwoerd stated that they were

> shifting the emphasis to technical education in order to relieve the pressure on skilled manpower so that non-whites will be able to make a larger contribution to skilled work (quoted in Horrel, 1968:98).

However, given the government's political support base among white trade unions and the white petit bourgeoisie, the state sought to make this shift within the framework of separate development. In terms of the industrial decentralisation strategy, industry – particularly that characterised by a labour-intensive production process – was to be persuaded by attractive financial incentives to locate or re-locate in or near the borders of the bantustans. This strategy was a corollary of stemming the tide of African urbanisation and the forced removal of Africans and their relocation in the bantustans. Trained black technicians were to be employed in establishments in the industrial decentralisation areas or in the bantustans. Furthermore, the emphasis was to be on training lower-level technicians and on diploma courses rather than advanced technical education of engineers and technologists via degree courses.

On the one hand, the apartheid state comprehended the new economic realities and was willing to make certain adjustments to the policy of job reservation. On the other hand, there was antipathy to any erosion of the bantustan strategy since this was a principal tenet of the ideological and political project of Afrikaner nationalism, and change would threaten the vested interests of important sections of the white support base. The response of the state to the demands of corporate capital for skilled technical labour was therefore still constrained by the parameters of the apartheid programme.

However, it is also doubtful, given the poor qualifications of black (especially African) teachers in mathematics and science subjects, whether any quick response to the skilled labour needs of the manufacturing and service sectors could have been forthcoming. Moreover, the restriction of black skilled labour and technicians to the bantustans, or to employment in black urban townships in the service of state departments, coupled with low income, meant that technical education was not particularly attractive.

During this period, then, the provision of and enrolments in higher technical education and training were extremely limited. Advanced technical education for blacks only began in the late 1960s, and by 1976 there were just four institutions offering post-matric training: the Shikoane Matlala (N. Transvaal) and Edendale Technical (Natal midlands) Colleges for African students, and the M.L.Sultan (Durban) and Peninsula (Bellville) Colleges of Advanced Technical Education (CATE), for Indian and coloured students, respectively.

Table 3: **Black student enrolment in technical training in relation to overall enrolment at colleges of advanced technical education, 1969 to 1975**

Year	African*	Indian	Coloured
1969	35 (171)	819 (4 572)	167 (435)
1971	67 (236)	1 181 (5 588)	238 (560)
1973	58 (269)	1 738 (6 978)	367 (734)
1975	70 (373)	2 640 (8 241)	300 (831)

Colleges of advanced technical education, 1969-1975

(Source: Dreijmanis, 1988:113-14).

[Notes: *The figures for African students indicate enrolments in post-matric technical training.]

As is clear from Table 3, only small numbers of black students at CATEs was enrolled in the field of technical training. Moreover, among those enrolled in technical fields, the numbers of students following post-matric technical qualifications were minimal, the figures for African post-matric enrolments being indicative of a general situation. Compared to whites (6 437 out of 36 826 students in technical training at CATEs and technikons during 1975), blacks were severely underrepresented both at CATE and technikon level, and within technical education.

Black teacher-training, 1960 to 1976

As in the case of African teacher-training, during the early 1960s control of coloured and Indian colleges was removed from the provincial administrations. The colleges were now placed, via the departments of coloured and Indian Affairs respectively, under central government academic and administrative control. Throughout this period, as a greater degree of "self-government" was conferred upon the bantustans, teacher-training colleges located in these areas were transferred to the control of bantustan departments of education. As a result, access to these colleges increasingly began to be restricted to particular ethnic groups. Table 4 provides statistics relating to teacher-training during this period.

The fluctuations in the number of colleges for African students, as well as their geographic location, needs some comment. Between 1960 and 1976, numerous institutions situated in "white" areas were closed. Concomitantly, with the redrawing of the boundaries of bantustans as part of territorial consolidation, some colleges now fell within the bantustans and thus came under the control of the bantustan authorities. Finally, new colleges were largely established only in the bantustans. By 1975, only seven colleges with 1 925 students were located in the "white" areas and administered directly by the Department of Bantu Education. The two colleges for Indians were in Durban and Johannesburg. Coloured students also had a college in each of the latter areas, as well as a further twelve in various parts of the Cape Province.

Table 4:   Black teacher-training: Number of colleges and enrolments, 1960 to 1976

Year	African		Coloured		Indian	
	Colleges	Students	Colleges	Students	Colleges	Students
1960	45	4 292	12	1 706	2	554
1965	-	-	13	1 870	2	882
1970	33	7 538	12	2 509	2	885
1975	41	15 563	14	4 995	2	558

(Sources: RSA, 1969:E11/E12; 1975:5.20/5.21; 1979:5.43/5.45).

African teacher-trainees grew in tandem with pre-higher student enrolments. Between 1960 and 1970 their numbers increased steadily and in the following five years more than doubled. Apart from being enrolled at colleges, a further 716 teacher-trainees were registered at universities. A similar trend was evident among coloured students, 268 more being enrolled at universities. Although enrolments at Indian training colleges barely increased after 1965 and in fact declined after 1970, many more students began to attend university for teacher-training, and by 1975 there were 711 such students (RSA, 1983:5.40).

Two points can be made in relation to the above. First, most African and coloured teacher-trainees would not have possessed senior certificate passes. This, combined with schooling in a pseudo-scientific curriculum (Fundamental Pedagogics) with a conservative orientation, and poorly equipped colleges with increasing enrolments, resulted in poorly qualified teachers entering the schools. Second, the student-teachers registered for certificates qualifying them to teach in lower primary schools were predominantly female, while those on route to higher primary and secondary schools – a smaller number – were mostly male. This was a matter of deliberate state policy. Verwoerd had stated in a Senate speech in 1954 that

[s]ince a woman is by nature so much better fitted for handling young children and as the great majority of Bantu pupils are to be found in the lower classes of the primary school, it follows there should be far more female than male teachers in the service. The Department will ... declare the posts of assistants in lower and, perhaps to a certain extent in higher primary schools, to be female teachers posts ... This measure in the course of time will bring about a considerable saving of funds which can be devoted to another purpose, namely, to admit more children to school (quoted in Rose and Tunmer, 1975:265).

Thus, a mixture of gender stereotyping and financial expediency was to give the black teaching force a particular gender character and create within it a distinct gender hierarchy.

Female representation in higher education

While the above illustrates the nature of the incorporation of black females into teacher-training, their overall representation within higher education remains to be addressed.

Throughout the 1960 to 1975 period, black women were under-represented at universities. In 1960 they constituted 11,3% (502) of total black enrolments; in 1970 18,9% (1 580) and in 1975 21,6% (3 928). However, the proportions of women enrolled at the institutions specifically designated for Africans, coloureds and Indians were higher than for the university sector as a whole. Thus, at African universities, for example, female enrolments in 1960 were marginally greater (13,1%) than when considered across the university sector in its entirety (9,2%), and in 1975 considerably larger (31,0%) than the 22,1% for the whole sector (Department of Bantu Education, 1976:118). Nonetheless, from their inception to 1975 the new ethnic universities remained both in relation to students and academic staff, overwhelmingly male institutions. In post-matric technical training, if the 22% representation of African females in 1975 and their concentration in nursing and paramedical courses are used as indicators, it is likely that in general black males predominated and that women were confined to courses leading to the "caring" professions. Only in teacher-training was the position very different, with women constituting 58,6% of enrolments in 1970 and 65,9% in 1975.

Administrative control of higher education

The strong state control that was exercised from the mid-1950s over the teacher-training colleges for blacks was in many ways extended to the black universities. Whereas the white universities, governed by the Universities Act of 1955, enjoyed, despite some limitations, a considerable degree of academic freedom and administrative autonomy and were regulated by the Department of Education, Arts and Science, the black colleges were under the direct control of the Departments of Bantu Education, Coloured Affairs or Indian Affairs. Thus, they were subject to extensive and authoritarian state control with responsible ministers enjoying *de facto* control over both academic and administrative appointments.

Between 1959 and 1969 the following academic and administrative structure of state control was developed. Rectors and vice-chancellors were appointed by the ministers. University councils consisted of the rector, two elected senate members and not less than eight appointees of the State President. Senates were chaired by the rectors, had two elected council members and senior teaching staff. The first rectors appointed were all committed Afrikaner nationalists, while the chairpersons of councils were senior academics of Afrikaans language universities or UNISA. Alongside these structures, Black Advisory Councils and Advisory Senates were set up, the members of the former appointed by the State President, and those of the latter by the university council in collaboration with the ministers. The curricula, examinations and degrees awarded were those of UNISA, a generally conservative institution. The only significant change made to the above structure was in 1969, when the status of the colleges was upgraded to that of fully-fledged universities which allowed them to set their own curricula and examinations and confer their own degrees.

Academic and senior administrative staff appointments and dismissals initially lay with the minister responsible for the various university colleges. Staff could be dismissed upon infringement of any one of seventeen counts, including criticism of the education department or of separate development. According to Beale,

> immediately after the passage of the Fort Hare Transfer Act the Department of Bantu Education began to employ a range of tactics to purge the staff, including direct dismissal, and the introduction of conditions which made remaining on the staff untenable (1991:43).

Liberal senior administrators and academics were fired and repressive measures like a ban on staff engaging in any political activity resulted in resignations. At all the black universities state strategy was "to appoint their own men, some of them recent graduates, invariably from the Afrikaans-medium universities, and promote them rapidly" (Balintulo, 1981:150). Although the logic of the apartheid programme and the bantustan project dictated that black educational institutions should be essentially staffed by blacks, the requirements of ideological and political control necessitated the employment of predominantly Afrikaner nationalists and white conservatives. Concomitantly, liberal opposition to the ethnic universities and the limited availability of black academics also contributed to the patterning of the racial and ideological composition of academic staff.

After 1969, university councils were given control of staff appointments and dismissals. However, the establishment of new posts and confirmation of appointments still required ministerial approval. In 1970, black academics represented only 19,1% (87) of total academic staff at black universities, and in 1974, 28,8% (161). White conservatives dominated top posts. At the African universities, in 1976 only nine out of 105 professors and 14 out of 146 senior lecturers were black. Only at junior lecturer level was there greater parity – 89 white and 73 African lecturers. A similar situation obtained with administrative posts, these also being dominated by white government supporters. Thus, Hill has commented, "the impression of being in a Government department becomes strong when one meets the non-academic staff" (1964:48).

During the 1960 to 1976/1977 period, then, there were severe restrictions on the administrative autonomy of, and academic freedom at, the black universities. This impacted on the black universities in two different, albeit related, ways. It conditioned the racial composition and ideological character of staff at the black universities, and concomitantly profoundly shaped the curriculum content of academic programmes. The racial composition of the staff and the political affiliations of white academics and administrators were to play an important role in structuring the form and content of student struggles during this period.

Conditions at black higher education institutions

Numerous conditions ranging from the governance of institutions, to restrictive rules, to segregated facilities and amenities, aroused student ire. As noted, the councils of universities were dominated by, initially, white supporters of the apartheid government and, later, by those supporters and blacks participating in separate development structures. Both the composition of the council and the policies and rules of the council were objects of resentment. Students resented the control on movement into and out of campus residences, being denied visitors in residences, the general prohibition on alcohol and the lack of social amenities. There were also restrictions on issuing press statements, on student organisations and on student meetings. It is highly likely that the majority of black students would have been in the early to mid-twenties age range and would have also found some of the controls humiliating.[2.3]

The location of the black universities in mainly rural areas, combined with the quality of education and the lack of academic freedom, led to the black institutions being referred to as "bush colleges". Since the universities were designed to serve specific ethnic groups, the architectural design of some institutions incorporated supposedly "traditional" features. Far from comforting students, Hill writes that "it is often said that these features are resented by students" (1964:45). A student at UWC during this period recalled this as a time

... when blacks ... had to suffer gross insults and bitter attacks on their human dignity. When academic discourse and intellectual development were constricted by the most trivial codes of conduct. When the wearing of a tie by male students and a dress by female was exalted as an important precondition for continued academic pursuit. Rules and regulations designed for a place, which was fittingly described as "glorified high school". Where arbitrary suspensions and expulsions were used to lambaste recalcitrant students into line (quoted by Morgan and Hendricks, 1987:11).

To conclude, between 1960 and 1976/1977 an organisational structure was established for black higher education, predicated on strong state control of both the academic and administrative spheres. Considerable expansion of enrolments occurred at both the ethnically structured black universities and UNISA; at the white universities, black enrolments declined, only picking up after the late 1960s, though by 1976 total enrolments had still not reached the 1960 figure. Student numbers at teacher-training colleges also increased, particularly after 1970, and only there were females well represented, although they were being directed towards lower-paying employment in primary schools. African teacher-training was brought under the control of bantustan education departments and began to be ethnically structured, while that for coloureds and Indians came under central government control. Finally, while a beginning was made with higher technical training for blacks, this was extremely limited and framed by the policies of job reservation and separate development.

Despite some calls by corporate capital for greater provision of advanced scientific and technical education for blacks, there was little response from the state; here, however, the existing structure of especially African and coloured primary and secondary education made it impossible for any speedy response to the skilled labour shortages being experienced. Corporate capital itself did not intervene in either the provision of higher educational facilities, nor did it become involved in any large-scale financing of black student bursaries/scholarships. Instead, both the provision of facilities and the financing of students was undertaken by the state, the latter often on the condition that graduates served periods in the bantustans and/or in the employ of state departments.

Some of the adjustments made in the sphere of higher education during this period clearly relate to changing economic conditions. However, developments in this sphere cannot be explained entirely in terms of economic imperatives. The organisational structure that became established and the form that the expansion of black higher education took was also related to struggles both outside and within the state, and to the political objectives of the ruling bloc – itself constituted by an alliance of class forces with differing and occasionally conflicting interests. During this period separate development and the bantustan programme were cemented, and it was this unfolding programme that constituted the context within which higher education developed. Moreover, it was a serious belief in the ability of racially and ethnically structured education to powerfully contribute to the success of the separate development project that partly explains the vigorous state control exercised over higher education.

Social structures and institutions condition social activity and struggles. However, this does not mean that they only constrain or are purely reproductive of, and functional to, existing social relations. Despite authoritarian controls and repressive practices, social institutions may, on occasion, become sites of struggle and generate outcomes, which are contradictory to the interests of the dominant classes. That is to say, class and popular struggles can undermine, modify, and in certain cases even transform social structures (which is, ultimately, the outcome of social struggles). Even when popular struggles do not seriously threaten the reproduction of prevailing racial, class and other inequalities, they may nonetheless impel the dominant classes to restructure the institutional mechanisms that maintain these inequalities. In this process, new conditions are established which could be more favourable to the dominated classes. This is well exemplified in the following chapters, which focus on the South African Students' Organisation (SASO) between 1968 and 1977.

3

SASO: The Ideology and Politics of Black Consciousness

F or white South Africans the late 1960s was a time of political calm, rising living standards, prosperity and sharing in the sustained economic boom of that period. Some blacks shared in the bounty, those for whom the opportunities for the accumulation of wealth, power and privilege through the bantustan and separate development programme proved irresistible. For most blacks, however, it was, in the aftermath of the suppression of the ANC and PAC and the repression of all radical political activity, a period of intensified exploitation, extensive and vigorous social control, demoralisation, fear and enforced and sullen acquiescence. In these conditions it was difficult to see how any serious organised political challenge to white minority domination could be mounted and whence it could come. Any organisation faced the prospect not only of immediate repression, but also the unenviable task of breaking through the demoralisation and fear that were major impediments to organisation building and mobilisation.

As is well known, the South African Students'' Organisation (SASO), formed in 1968, was able to escape immediate repression, to establish itself and develop a mass following on the black campuses, and was to play an important role in reviving black opposition to apartheid. However, it was surprising that the challenge came from where it did. The black racial and ethnic higher educational institutions were not designed to produce dissidents. They had been charged with the responsibility of intellectually and politically winning students to the separate development project and generating the administrative corps for the separate development bureaucracies. That, after all, was the purpose of the strict ideological control of the black institutions, their domination by Afrikaner nationalists and the repressive controls on students.

That the revival of mass political opposition to apartheid emerged from within, and spread outwards from, the black higher education institutions is also understandable. For one, the institutions gathered together students who had survived the rigours and hurdles of black schooling but who, upon graduating from higher education, would still be condemned to a future of limited socio-economic opportunity and inequality. Second, what Beard wrote about an earlier period at Fort Hare, applied to the black institutions of the 1960s:

Most students had common experiences in White South Africa, and there were few who had not encountered directly the humiliation of White superiority attitudes, while all suffered in some degree the effects of legal discrimination. The very fact of their common positions of inferiority in South African society, unameliorated by contact with white students, created a bond which formed a basis for their political mobilisation (Beard, 1972:158).

Thus the institutions provided an ideal environment for the development of shared grievances and aspirations. To the extent that a large number of students lived in residences, this further facilitated communication, mobilisation and organisation.

Finally, Wolpe suggests that

the concentration of ... increasing numbers of students in the recently established black universities provided a site, perhaps the only one in the repressive conditions of the time, in which a radical ideology (black consciousness) could develop. One reason for this was the relatively protected position of the educational institutions (1988:72).

The question of institutional location in relation to the re-emergence of internal opposition to apartheid is an interesting one but is not a major concern of this investigation. I take the black institutions' being the sites of the renewal of political resistance to apartheid as a given, and the issue of institutional location is only of interest in so far as it has a bearing on the principal concerns of this and the following chapter. These are the origins and growth of SASO in the late 1960s, its ideological and political orientations, its initiatives to mobilise and organise students and other constituencies, its relations with other organisations, and the form and content of its collective endeavours. The description and analysis of these issues will lay the basis for the assessment of SASO in Chapter 5.

Student Politics prior to SASO

SASO was not the first manifestation of student politics among black higher education students or at black higher education institutions. Hirson writes that

> [t]hroughout the second world war there were strikes at Fort Hare almost every year ... The precipitating factors were always the atrocious food, unbending discipline, or even physical assaults. But the crucial factor was deeply embedded in the system (1979:34),

and was related to white supremacy and paternalism.

In 1948, a branch of the ANC Youth League (ANCYL) was established at Fort Hare by African students and staff. At about the same time, a branch of the Society of Young Africa, part of the All African Convention which was affiliated to the Non-European Unity Movement, was also formed. These two bodies operated essentially as youth wings of their respective parent political organisations. They competed for membership, politicised students, provided them with a bridgehead to the national political movements and galvanised student support for the numerous political campaigns of the 1950s. The Fort Hare branch of the ANCYL played an active role in the Eastern Cape protests against the introduction of Bantu education and after the mid-1950s was the premier organisation among Fort Hare students. The ANCYL as a whole was pivotal in rejuvenating the ANC and in prodding the ANC towards a more radical African nationalism and more militant and mass-based forms of political struggle against apartheid.

A Student Representative Council (SRC) also existed at Fort Hare, for much of the 1950s under the sway of ANCYL members and in the forefront of student actions.[3.1] The SRC affiliated to the National Union of South African Students' (NUSAS) in 1945, partly on the notion that it was necessary and possible to push NUSAS in a more radical direction. NUSAS had been formed in 1924 as a union of students at the white universities. In 1952, however, the SRC disaffiliated from NUSAS because it was "realised that they had not been too successful in their attempts to radicalise NUSAS. There was also some sensitivity on the part of Fort Harians to alleged racial slights ..." (Burchell, 1986:157). A major obstacle to any radicalisation of NUSAS was that, although the leadership was frequently liberal, and even radical, the mass base of NUSAS tended to be conservative and certainly not ready to support any project of black liberation.

Following the banning of the ANC and PAC in 1960, the African Students' Association (ASA) and the African Students' Union of South Africa (ASUSA) were formed to continue among African students the political traditions of the ANC and PAC respectively. In the Cape and Natal, student organisations were also launched by supporters of the Non-European Unity Movement. According to a SASO publication,

[t]he Durban Students" Union and the Cape Peninsula Student's Union who later merged to form the Progressive National Students Organisation, were fanatically opposed to NUSAS ...and adopted the emotional slogan of the Non-European Unity Movement — "non-co-operation with the collaborators" (SASO, 1972a:1).

ASA was open to both secondary and higher education students, but was strongest at Fort Hare because of the predominant position the ANCYL had enjoyed at this institution. However, a combination of the intense state repression of this time, the small numbers of students enrolled at black secondary and higher education institutions and strong disciplinary controls on student activity meant that both ASA and ASUSA were to have little impact on students.

There is no documented information about the response of the students at the new ethnic and racial campuses to the political events of the early 1960s. Probably, some students would have been connected to ASA and ASUSA, but the small enrolments, the fact that most students were meeting for the first time, the controls and curbs on student activity and the generally repressive conditions could have made collective action difficult. Fort Hare was, of course, an exception. When the institution re-opened in 1960 as an ethnic university, the new administration refused to re-register some students and imposed restrictions on the autonomy of the SRC. As a result, the "next day there was a near-revolt at the college, with protest meetings being held and demonstrations being staged in the dining halls. The students decided to dissolve the SRC ..." (SAIRR, 1961:237).Throughout the 1960s Fort Hare students refused to form an SRC, as an expression of the absence of academic freedom at the institution. They also boycotted graduation and various other official ceremonies. In 1968, on the occasion of the investure of a new rector, political slogans were sprayed on college walls. Seventeen students, identified as student leaders, were held responsible and interrogated by the security police. The student protests that followed led to students being tear-gassed and escorted to the railway station. Subsequently, 21 students, including B. N. Pityana, the first general secretary of SASO, were not re-admitted.

At the other black institutions, student discontent between 1960 and 1968 (when SASO was formed) was mainly expressed around issues relating to autonomous SRCs and affiliation to NUSAS. Students refused to form SRCs at UDW, and, until 1967, at UWC. Students at UWC and at the African universities were forbidden to send delegations to NUSAS conferences or to attend in their personal capacity. Students from these campuses continued, however, to attend NUSAS conferences and participate in its activities. The SRC at the exclusively black University of Natal Medical School (UNMS) was an affiliate of NUSAS, and black students at the white English language universities participated in NUSAS, some holding official positions in NUSAS and on SRCs. In 1967 NUSAS activity was banned on all black campuses. However, well into 1968, the SRC at the University of the North (UNIN) continued to press the university authorities for permission to affiliate to NUSAS.

During the 1950s the Fort Hare SRC had discovered the difficulty of moving NUSAS to adopt a more radical position and to support black liberation, and it had disaffiliated from NUSAS. What, then, was the attraction of NUSAS and why did the SRCs at some of the black institutions insist that they be allowed to join NUSAS?

With the obliteration of the mass extra-parliamentary movements, and in the repressive context of the 1960s, NUSAS provided one of the few avenues for the expression of opposition to apartheid. Beyond this, during the mid-1960s NUSAS was under attack from the government and also right-wing students, being accused of being a "communist" organisation and a front for the banned liberation movements. A number of NUSAS leaders were arrested, banned and deported. This, and the marches and activities sponsored by NUSAS to protest against state repression and interference in higher education, gave the organisation some credibility among black students. Membership of NUSAS also made possible the attempt to influence the organisation to adopt more radical policies and forms of action, something that was also being called for by white radicals in NUSAS. Furthermore, participation afforded black students from the different campuses the opportunity to meet and discuss campus and other developments.

Finally, Hirson suggests that

[i]n seeking affiliation, the black students were demanding the right to associate with organisations of their own choice, and the more intransigent the government showed itself, the more determined the students seemed to become (1979:68).

However, more was at play than the right of black students to freedom of association. In a context where the space for the expression of political dissent was extremely limited, the affiliation issue also provided black students the opportunity to demonstrate their opposition to state ideology and the policy of separate development without expressing open criticism of the state and becoming targets for repression.

To conclude this discussion of pre-SASO student politics: while the ANCYL was, in strict terms, a national youth political organisation, in practice it functioned at Fort Hare as essentially a student political organisation. As such, it was an early indicator of what student politics at a black higher education institution in South Africa under apartheid could involve. The ANCYL at Fort Hare mobilised students around campus conditions, and contested elections to the SRC. It galvanised students to support the struggles of other social groups in the vicinity of Fort Hare, and participated in the education protests of the Eastern Cape. It mobilised students around national political issues and campaigns, and provided a stepping stone to student and post-student involvement in the broader ANCYL and the ANC.

Both the ANCYL and Fort Hare as an institution were also important incubators of black intellectuals and future black political leaders. For example, Robert Sobukwe, who was president of the SRC in 1949 and a member of the Fort Hare ANCYL became, shortly afterwards, national secretary of the ANCYL and, later, a founder of the PAC. Fort Hare, involvement in the SRC and ANCYL, and contact with the Society of Young Africa's ideas of "non-collaboration", provided Sobukwe with the space and environment to develop his own distinct ideas around African nationalism.

Thus, student politics, at least as practised by the ANCYL at Fort Hare, covered education-based and political issues; addressed local, regional and national problems; was characterised by linkages with campus-based and non-campus organisations, including an explicit linkage to a national political formation; and was also defined by the concern of the student activists with questions of political theory and strategy. In contrast to the ANCYL, the ASA and ASUSA were explicitly student organisations. They were also national organisations and exclusively African in membership. To them must be accorded the status of being the first national student organisations among the oppressed population in South Africa. There are no details on their activities, but they did express an unambiguous political alignment with the banned ANC and PAC. Finally, ASA and ASUSA represented a break with multiracial student organisations such as NUSAS. Thus, they constituted a bridge to exclusive national black student organisations, as exemplified by SASO in the late 1960s and 1970s (Brooks and Brickhill, 1980:72). ASA and ASUSA, however, do not appear to have had any major impact on black students or on the political terrain in general. Not the same, as will be seen, can be said for SASO!

Origins of SASO

During the 1960s small numbers of black students continued to participate in NUSAS. However, by the late 1960s many black students increasingly began to feel the frustration and disillusionment similar to that which had led the Fort Hare SRC to disaffiliate from NUSAS in 1952. For some students at the University of Natal Medical School (UNMS) their involvement and experience in NUSAS increasingly suggested that the liberal politics of that union could not serve the immediate or long-term aspirations of black students. Also at issue was the fact that, despite its non-racial membership, NUSAS was essentially dominated and controlled by white students.

Legassick and Shingler have argued this point strongly:

Non-whites, as delegates and office holders, did play a role, but were for the most part overshadowed by their white counterparts, and in some instances were callously used and manipulated as symbols of NUSAS" integrated nonracialism (quoted in Fatton, 1986:55).

It was this kind of situation that Biko had in mind when he expressed in his column, "I write what I like", in the *SASO Newsletter*, his objection to "the intellectual arrogance of white people that makes them believe that white leadership is *a sine qua non* in this country and that whites are divinely appointed pace-setters in progress" (1987:24). Wilson suggests that the superior education of whites and the conduct of meetings in English meant that black students were disadvantaged in participation. This had the potential to appear as if black students lacked intelligence, and to instil feelings of inferiority (Wilson, 1991:23).

In 1967, the University Christian Movement (UCM) was formed as an interdenominational organisation to explore what the church and individuals could do to bring about change in South Africa. More than half of the delegates at the inaugural conference of the UCM were black and the UCM showed a strong interest in the emerging "black theology". By 1968 the UCM claimed to have 25 branches and a membership of 3 000. Despite the name of the organisation, the UCM was not restricted to Christians alone, and students of all faiths – or no faith – were welcome to join (SAIRR, 1968:13; 1969:68).

The growing disaffection of some black student activists with NUSAS,[3.2] and the composition as well as more radical orientation of the UCM gave the latter a greater appeal as a forum for inter-campus contact and discussion. However, black students with experience of NUSAS politics (including Steve Biko, a student at UNMS) who attended the UCM conference in July 1968 discovered that, despite the UCM's political orientation and its majority black membership, leadership of the organisation was concentrated among white members. It is possible that this reinforced the determination of Biko and others, who were increasingly critical of multiracial organisations, to push ahead with the formation of an exclusively black student formation.[3.3] The UCM conference provided those students committed to the idea of a black student organisation the opportunity to convene a caucus of black students. Out of its deliberations came agreement on the need for a new black student organisation and a representative conference of black students. Duly convened at Mariannhill, Natal, in December 1968, and "attended by about thirty members of black university Students' Representative Councils" (Gerhart, 1978:261) the conference gave birth to an exclusively black higher education formation, the South African Students' Organisation (SASO).

The establishment of SASO drew mixed responses. From the side of white liberals, charges of reverse racism were levelled at the new organisation. Biko's response was that

> [n]ot only was the move taken by the non-white students defensible but it was a long overdue step. It seems sometimes that it is a crime for the non-white students to think for themselves ... [w]hat SASO has done is simply to take stock of the present scene in the country and to realise that not unless the non-white students decide to lift themselves from the doldrums will they ever hope to get out of them. What we want is not black visibility but real black participation (1987:4-5).

Apartheid government officials, on the other hand, appear to have gleefully, and mistakenly, hailed it as a vindication of their separate development programme.

Ideology and Politics

Much writing on SASO notes its launch, or its formal inauguration, in July 1969 and the election of Biko as national president, and thereafter plunges into a consideration of the important *SASO Policy manifesto(nd)* which articulates the central tenets of Black Consciousness philosophy. Given that the *Policy Manifesto* was only adopted by SASO two years later, at its Second General Students Council (GSC) in July 1971, the effect is to give the impression that the doctrine of Black Consciousness (BC) was already fully formed at the time of SASO's origin. As a result, the process by which SASO actually moved towards BC is obscured.

The inaugural conference of July 1969

The constitution adopted at the inaugural conference noted, in its preamble, that "it is ideal that any country should have ONE national student organisation, [and] that such an organisation should cater for all the students in the country" (quoted in Nettleton, 1972:130). It observed however that "owing to circumstances beyond their control, students at some non-white centres are unable to participate in the national student organisation of this country", and that "contact amongst non-white students so affected is of paramount importance" (*ibid.*). The objects of SASO are described as:

(a) to promote contact and practical co-operation among students studying at affiliated centres; (b) To represent the non-white students nationally; (c) To bring about contact among South African Students' generally (*ibid.*).

A SASO communiqué released at the end of the inaugural conference reflected the tensions about an all-black organisation. It granted that there was a danger of showing racial division among students; that the formation of a black organisation could be interpreted as the success of apartheid; that separate organisations could heighten division and that this should not be promoted; and that a black organisation could get special attention from the authorities and would perhaps not last long (Nettleton, 1972:128-29). However, the communiqué also stated

[t]hat there is a need for more effective contact is unquestionable, especially in view of the ever-increasing enrolment at the non-white institutions of higher learning ... For all intent and purpose, these students have remained isolated, not only physically but also intellectually (quoted in Buthelezi, 1991:112).

It went on to add that universities sought to breed conformists, a process that had to be stopped by "interfering with the programme of indoctrination and intimidation so effectively applied at all South African universities" (*ibid.*).

Given the criticism of NUSAS, reference to it as "the national student organisation of the country" can only be explained as a strategic move. The formation of SASO did not enjoy unanimous support among black students. Some interpreted it as a defeat for attempts at building a non-racial student culture, while others were suspicious of its aims and concerned that it could be interpreted as an endorsement of separate development. In this context, the priority had to be to win black students over to SASO and any formal and/or frontal attack on, or break with, NUSAS had to be deferred to a more opportune moment.

The stress in the constitution on building student contact may also have been governed by strategic considerations. Fatton interprets this as adopting a "limited student concern, a 'student-as-such' position", as a concern "essentially with their own academic environment and not the problems of the wider society" (1986:67; 158). However, given the repressive educational and broader political environment, the concern might have been to first establish an organisational infrastructure before taking on explicitly political issues.

Critique and the elaboration of black consciousness

At the intellectual level, the two-year period from the inaugural conference to the adoption of the *SASO policy manifesto* (SPM) in 1971 was characterised by the dual activities of critique, deconstruction and rejection, and formulation, construction and elaboration, in conference resolutions, policy papers, open letters, public forums, and articles in SASO publications. As an organisation, and through its leading intellectuals, SASO analysed and condemned multiracial liberal platforms, liberal leadership and policies of assimilation and integration. Concomitantly, and gradually and unevenly, the concept of "Black Consciousness" was formulated and elaborated. Although the critique of SASO members was largely based on the lived experiences of black intellectuals in apartheid South Africa, it was sharpened by the insights offered by Fanon, Nkrumah, Nyerere and various black American "Black Power" activists (Gerhart, 1978:275-76). While the latter were formative influences, on balance the lived experiences were pivotal in the construction and elaboration of an alternative ideology and strategy of liberation in South Africa.

In analysing South African society, SASO viewed "race" as the primary line of cleavage. Class divisions were not seen as important and there was little recognition of gender issues. There was no grappling with the simultaneity of racial and class divisions and the articulation of "race" and class oppression, let alone with the interrelationship of "race", class, and gender factors in the shaping of South Africa's social structure. In fact, it could be argued that until the mid-1970s, "race" and colour were seen as the only significant organising principle of South African society. The experience of racial oppression and the "obviousness" of white domination led SASO to express the beliefs

[t]hat the Whiteman must be made aware that one is either part of the solution or part of the problem, [and] that, in this context, because of the privileges accorded to them by legislation and because of their continual maintenance of an oppressive regime, Whites have defined themselves as part of the problem (SPM, (1971):Appendix 1).

Whites were collectively identified as the "enemy". Political divisions among whites were interpreted as differences over how best to maintain white privilege and political domination. A special target of SASO leaders were white liberals – in the words of Biko, "that curious bunch of non-conformists ... that bunch of do-gooders" (1972:192) who continued to hold out the possibility of integration. For Biko, "the myth of integration as propounded under the banner of liberal ideology must be cracked and killed because it made people believe that something is being done" (*ibid.*:193). Instead, all that white liberal groups and institutions were seeking, ultimately, was merely to relax "certain oppressive legislation and to allow Blacks into a white-type society" (SPM, Appendix 1).

It was not just the goals of white liberals that were rejected. Their role in shaping political strategies, as well as the actual strategies that they advanced, was also called into question. Biko bluntly observed that while one sector of whites "kicked the black", another sector of whites (liberals) "managed to control the responses of the blacks to the provocation" and tutored blacks "how best to respond to the kick" (1987:66). White liberals were accused of creating the

... political dogma that all groups opposing the *status quo* must *necessarily* be non-racial in structure. They maintained that if you stood for a principle of non-racialism you could not in any way adopt what they described as racialist policies (Biko, 1972:193; emphasis in original).

For Biko and SASO, it was the black person's "right and duty to respond to the kick *in the way he sees fit*" (Biko, 1987:6; emphasis in original) and it was crucial that the hold of white liberals over black political thinking be broken. The mechanism for breaking their influence was to be the exclusion of whites from "all matters relating to the struggle" (SPM, Appendix 1). Consequently, contact with whites was discouraged, and multiracial organisation *per se* was rejected.

SASO, however, was not anti-white. It accepted that "South Africa is a country in which both black and white live and shall continue to live together" (SPM, Appendix 1). Indeed, Biko's goal was a

... completely non-racial society [without] ... guarantees for minority rights, be cause guaranteeing minority rights implies the recognition of portions of the community on a race basis. We believe that in our country there shall be no minority; just the people. And those people will have the same status before the law and they will have the same political rights ... (Biko, 1987:149).

What SASO did put at issue was liberal models of assimilation and integration and "value systems" that sought to make a black person "a foreigner in the country of his birth and reduce his basic dignity" (SPM, Appendix 1). Black Consciousness and exclusive black organisation was seen as a strategy:

It's a question of the oppressor and the oppressed, so we had to galvanise ourselves, and that's where we came with the concept of black solidarity: to bargain from a position of strength (Nefolov-hodwe, quoted in Frederikse, 1990:108).

This is underlined by the *SASO policy manifesto* which speaks of an "open society". Such an open society is viewed as depending, ultimately, on the efforts of blacks, and is seen as necessitating an initial withdrawal on their part in order to establish black solidarity and unity and black political goals.

The positive doctrine that SASO proclaimed itself to uphold was "the concept of Black Consciousness" which was defined as "an attitude of mind, a way of life" (SPM, Appendix 1). The key themes of Black Consciousness (BC) as a doctrine of "self-discovery" and self-realisation have been well summarised by Hirson. They included

a liberation from psychological oppression, the building of a new awareness, the establishment of a new basic dignity, the framing of a new attitude of mind, a rediscovery of the history of the people, and a cultural revival (Hirson, 1979:296).

SASO also stressed the need for blacks to develop their own value systems, and to define themselves, rather than be defined by others. The emphasis was on self-reliance: on, as Biko put it, blacks doing "things for themselves and all by themselves" (1987:15). Pityana, addressing a conference on student perspectives on South Africa was even more unequivocal:

Blacks only are qualified to determine the means for change ... The way to the future is not through a directionless and arrogant multiracialism but through a purposeful and positive unilateral approach. Black man, you are on your own (1972:189).

"Black man you are on your own" was to be adopted by SASO as its rallying cry. According to Hirson, "the slogan was an assertion of the right to independent organisation on the campuses and was also a political statement of more general application" (1979:69).

A generally receptive student body and organisational development contributed to a growth in confidence and assertiveness on the part of SASO. In mid-1970, at the first General Students' Council, the previous preamble was amended. It now expressed the beliefs

(i) that Black students in South Africa have unique problems and aspirations pertaining to them; (ii) that it is necessary for black students to consolidate their ranks if their aspirations are to be realised; (iii) that there is a crying need in South Africa for Black students to re-assert their pride and group identity; therefore adopt this constitution in the belief that unity and positive reawakening will result among the Black students of South Africa (quoted in Nettleton, 1972:132)

The new preamble was a far cry from the defensive, and almost apologetic, preamble adopted at the inaugural conference and manifested the new mood of assertiveness within SASO.

At the same time, the previous negative definition of the self as "non-white" gave way to positive identification as "black". An editorial in the *SASO Newsletter* of September 1970 stated the political and strategic rationale for the term "black". It was an attempt to "define one's enemy more clearly and broaden the base from which we are operating. It is a deliberate attempt to counteract the 'divide and rule' attitude of the evildoers" (quoted in Gerhart, 1978:278). A year later, blacks were to be defined as

those who are by law or tradition politically, economically and socially discriminated against as a group in the South African society and identifying themselves as a unit in the struggle towards realisation of their aspirations (SPM, Appendix 1).

However, not all of the nationally oppressed and politically disenfranchised were defined as blacks. Since being black was related to an "attitude of mind" rather than skin colour, the term "non-white" continued to be used in a derogatory sense to designate persons associated with the ethnic political institutions that were a component of the separate development programme. More positively, though not without opposition and considerable debate within SASO, the term "black" became popularised as denoting Africans, Indians and coloureds collectively.

Finally, the new assertiveness led SASO to now state that "in the principles and make-up of NUSAS the black students can never find expression for the aspirations foremost in their minds" (quoted in Nettleton, 1972:133). Consequently, SASO withdrew its recognition of NUSAS as the only legitimate union of students. The break was still not absolute, for the SASO national executive was requested to "continue studying the relevance of the organisation to the black student community and to maintain such contact as is compatible with aims of SASO" (ibid.)

Earlier, I questioned Fatton's argument that SASO began with a "student-as-such" orientation, and I suggested that this was in all likelihood a strategic move. The empirical evidence supports my view. Only months after SASO was inaugurated, Biko, addressing the SASO leadership at the organisation's First National Formation School, said the following:

We have a responsibility not only to ourselves but also to the society from which we spring. No one else will ever take the challenge up until we, of our own accord, accept the inevitable fact that ultimately the leadership of the non-white peoples in this country rests with us (1987:7).

He also included among the aims of SASO the shaping of black political thinking (Biko, 1987:5). By 1971, the SASO constitution began to speak more broadly of the challenges facing blacks, rather than just black students, and committed SASO "to the realisation of the worth of the black man, the assertion of his human dignity and to promoting consciousness and self-reliance of the black community" (SASO Constitution). The aims of SASO now included getting students to "become involved in the political, economic and social development of the Black people" and "to become a platform for expression of Black opinion" (*ibid.*).

Politics, strategy and policies

There is little dispute that SASO's ultimate goal was a non-racial South Africa, although the precise content of the future society was not spelt out in any detail. In any event, SASO's priority was much more the rousing of blacks from a state of apathy, fear and feelings of inferiority to one of active agents of history. As Pityana put it,

> [We] offer no blueprint for a future South Africa. What is required immediately is a complete overhaul of the system. This is necessary for a clearer vision of the future. Only liberated minds are able to shape their future society (1972:189).

> The immediate tasks of SASO were defined by the SPM as being the liberation of the Black man, first from psychological oppression by themselves through inferiority complex, and secondly from the physical one accruing out of living in a White racist society (SPM, Appendix 1).

Liberation appears to have been conceived as involving two stages – an initial stage of "psychological" liberation followed by political liberation. Gerhart suggests that such an approach was shaped by the organisational mistakes of the PAC, the latter's "reckless rush to confrontation at a time when circumstances did not favour a black victory" (1978:284-85). The lesson drawn was that "laying a firm psychological foundation for a time of yet unforeseen circumstances was more important than trying artificially to create a situation of immediate confrontation" (*ibid.*). A SASO leadership training seminar in 1971 defined the practical application of BC in terms of "directive politics, infiltrative politics, orientation projects and self-reliance projects".

The first meant direct political criticism of the regime and its agents and policies. Infiltrative politics...meant entering existing organisations and taking them over or converting them ... "Orientation projects" would "re-examine educational, cultural, religious and economic facilities, needs and aspirations" of Blacks ... Community self-help projects in which Blacks did things for themselves were the fourth leg (Nolutshungu, 1982:171).

The different kinds of "politics" and projects were considered to be vital instruments in the psychological liberation of blacks and in providing the platform for activities around physical liberation.

The avoidance by SASO of detailed engagement around issues of political vision and goals and the strong emphasis on black student solidarity seem to also have been shaped by a particular reading of earlier student politics. A SASO publication suggests that a cause of the lack of student unity and co-ordination on black campuses during the early and mid-1960s was the political rivalry between ASA and ASUSA (SASO, 1972a). Thus, a skirting of political questions, of which most students would have had little awareness, but which were likely to give rise to party political and organisational squabbles made good sense. On the other hand, all attempts to promote BC and black solidarity were to be used. Thus, meetings and newsletters, posters, pamphlets, diaries and T-shirts, and the formation of new organisations and community projects, all became vehicles of political mobilisation and the fostering of Black Consciousness (BC). Even press statements and letters, which were signed off with slogans such as "Power and Solidarity", "Your black brother", and "Breaking the chains", were roped into developing an identity for SASO and for creating a culture of black unity and a concomitant anti-apartheid oppositional culture.

As noted, SASO sought to establish close links with the non-student black population and influence black political thinking. In this regard, the role of black students was to

... take over the responsibility of the people's destiny and devote themselves to the task of eradicating all evils, resolving all problems and generally transforming the spirit of the people. This is the leadership role black students are destined to play towards the development of their people (SASO, 1972a:2).

This clearly established for black higher education students a vanguard role in black political life. However, that SASO's leadership was to be largely at the level of ideas and directed primarily at eliminating "psychological oppression" is well revealed by the statement that with SASO

has come the idealism of the black revolution: a revolution of ideas, of values and standards. .. Community development is the direction black students must take if they are to transform their idealism into stark realism (SASO, 1972a:2-3).

The "ideas" and "values" – embodied in the doctrine of BC – that SASO sought to promote have already been noted. The matter of "community development" and what this entailed in practice will be dealt with in the next chapter. For the moment it is to the "ideas" – the pronouncements – of SASO on more immediate political issues and around education that I wish to confine myself.

SASO's views were publicly disseminated through its various publications, its community projects and cultural initiatives, the commercial media, publications of the Black Community Programmes (BCP) and public meetings. On every issue, the position of SASO was diametrically opposed to that of the apartheid government. Let me take a few examples. With respect to foreign investments, SASO rejected these, seeing them as bolstering the apartheid government. Recognising that sometimes higher wages were paid by foreign multinationals, SASO repudiated this as "conscience-salving". The initiatives of African governments in dialogue with the apartheid government were seen as futile and having no effect on black subordination in South Africa. SASO also expressed support for the struggles of the people of Namibia and criticised the "unwarranted occupation" of Namibia by South Africa (SASO, 1972a:5).

However, it was for separate development – and especially the bantustans, to which SASO was implacably opposed – that the organisation reserved its most bitter attacks. SASO rejected the entire separate development and bantustan policy as divisive, oppressive and designed to retard black political freedom. Separate development political institutions were labelled "dummy platforms" and "phoney telephones". SASO also scorned and criticised the notion of utilising state-created political institutions to challenge and undermine apartheid, a position that was to lead to inevitable conflict with black leaders and members of bantustan governments and political parties involved in the Coloured Representative Council and the South African Indian Council.

While condemning separate development political institutions, SASO did initially have a working relationship with some of the more "progressive" black politicians such as Gatsha Buthelezi, who claimed to be opposed to the bantustans and committed to black political rights in a unitary South Africa. Three developments, however, led in 1972 to a hardening of SASO's position around the issue of working within separate development political structures. First, there was the growing popularity of Buthelezi who was seen as having the potential to seriously confuse blacks about separate development. Second, the Black Peoples Convention (BPC), which SASO had initiated, was about to be formed and there was a need to settle the question of legitimate political platforms. Third, Temba Sono, the third president of SASO (1971-72) had in his presidential speech to the 1972 GSC called for a more practical approach to the liberation struggle, including co-operation with bantustan leaders and the use of separate development platforms. Sono's call was to result in his immediate expulsion from SASO. It also triggered a resolution at the GSC that rejected bantustan leaders, and called on them withdraw from "the system". SASO appealed to them to refrain from being the "ambassadors for black oppression", while the SRCs at UNMS and UNIZUL appealed to them to stop "selling out the black cause".

SASO on education

Until 1972 SASO's engagement with educational issues was extremely limited. At a policy level, separate universities were rejected as an attempt to control the education of blacks. An article in a SASO publication argued that universities were extensions of the apartheid system and had the "effect of creating a black elitist, middle class that is far removed from the true aspirations of the people". The black universities were criticised for being dominated by white staff, for having differential salary and service conditions for white and black staff, and for a curriculum that was "oriented towards white, exploitative norms and values" (SASO, 1971:24).

In its "Declaration of Student Rights" adopted in July 1971, SASO expressed the belief that "institutions of learning and all therein serve in the noble pursuit and unprejudiced acquisition of knowledge" (SASO, 1971:13). Elsewhere, it was stated that the university needed to be recognised as a community in common search for the "truth" – defined in terms of the "needs, goals and aspirations of a people". It was furthermore argued that "the meaning of a university projects the idea of a community", and the challenge for the university was to "bring forth a new humanity with a higher conscience" (SASO, 1972a:2-3). The Declaration of Student Rights also asserted "the right of every person to have free access to education"; and the rights of a student to "free academic pursuit", to "dissent with the instructor" and to "attend the university of his choice" (SASO, 1971:13).

In 1971 an "Education Commission" comprising SASO members, black educationists and "lay men" was established to "explore means of making education relevant to the aspirations of blacks" (SASO, 1971:25). In July 1972, the Education Commission tabled the "Black Student Manifesto" (BSM), for adoption by SASO's third GSC. Through the BSM, SASO members proclaimed that "we are an integral part of the oppressed community before we are Students". They also voiced their rejection of the "whole sphere of racist education", and asserted that "education in South Africa is unashamedly political and therefore ... Black Education is tied to the liberation of the Black people of the world". SASO committed itself to "break away from the traditional order of subordination to whites in education" and to "ensure that our education will further the preservation and promotion of what is treasured in our culture and our historical experience" (SASO, 1972b:24).

In December 1972, a SASO National Formation School on the theme "Towards Black Education" produced a "Charter for a Black University". The Charter was seen as "the foundation of education for liberation, self-reliance and development aimed at a communalistic and egalitarian society". Education was conceived of as being for the benefit of individuals and society, and defined as "a process of inculcating a way of life, of transmitting a cultural heritage, of acquiring knowledge and ideals, and of developing the critical faculties of the individual" (SASO, 1973a:7). The aims of "Black Education" were to foster social change, help realise an "egalitarian and communalistic society", to promote black unity and collective action, and to "inculcate into the Blackman a sense of initiative, enquiry, creativity and self-reliance" (ibid.).

The mission of the black university was to be fivefold. First, it was to "promote the interests and aspirations of the community". Second, it was to inculcate within blacks "pride and confidence in their Blackness, their traditions and their indigenous way of life". As part of this socialisation, the black university was to "discourage elitism and intellectual arrogance which promotes alienation, acquisitiveness and class structures" (SASO, 1973a:8). Third, it was to modernise people, institutions and society – to remove from the community the older epoch of backwardness, dependence and immobility; these must be replaced by one of economic orientations, industrialisation, greater national economy, class mobility and communal solidarity (ibid.).

Fourth, it was to contribute, through the production of knowledge and trained personnel, to economic and social development. Finally, the black university was to contribute to social cohesion and integration; it was to incorporate the entire community more effectively into the structure, values and functions of society; [and also] find foundations for a spiritual awareness, a religious redirection (SASO, 1973a:7-8).

According to the Charter, academic disciplines had to be geared at dynamising the basic perspectives on reality which have usually been of profound pessimism and fatalism, by enabling the student to gain awareness of his capacity to shape his environment, and tools to harness it for his survival (ibid.).

Moreover, the black university had to be especially concerned with "Black Studies" – with Africa, and African thought, history, culture, language and literature, and the "Black experience" (SASO, 1973a:8).

It is evident that prior to 1972 there was no serious and detailed consideration of key education issues such as the goals, structure, organisation and financing of education, curriculum and pedagogy. The criticism of education was in purely political terms and the conception of the university that was posited was thoroughly idealist. During 1972 greater attention began to be devoted to education. However, the BSM too offered little in the way of a substantive critique of South African education and, apart from asserting that "Black education" was linked to liberation, provided no details of the form and content of such an education. Moreover, there was no indication as to how black values, identity and culture were to be promoted through education.

While the "Charter for a Black University" did represent an advance on previous utterances regarding education and the university, it also reflected important silences and contradictory thinking. The SASO activists were well aware of the role of apartheid education in reproducing racial and cultural domination. Influenced by Freire's and Nyerere's notions of education for liberation and education for self-reliance respectively, they conceived of a different role for education – to socialise blacks into new values and conduct, to transfer knowledge of relevance to liberation and to produce critical thinkers. In short, education was to be an important agent in the transformation of blacks and the social order. However, beyond notions of a need to mobilise black teachers and to encourage parents to relate folklore and indigenous stories to children, the Charter offered little in the way of strategy and tactics for contesting apartheid education within the black schools and replacing it with "black education".

In contrast with the earlier monastic, knowledge conception of the university, in the Charter the university was now seen as being involved in "community" service, in conscientisation and identity formation and in the production of trained and skilled personnel and in the fields of economic and social development. However, in defining the role of the "black university" in these fields, the Charter failed to address a number of important issues. First, because of the tendency to treat blacks as a homogeneous group, there was no recognition that, apart from certain common interests and aspirations, very different interests could also be expressed by different sections of the black "community". However, no answer was provided as to how the "black university" would mediate between differing interests and make choices and trade-offs.

Second, as part of SASOs general embrace of "communalism", the "black university" was called on to socialise students so as to counter "acquisitiveness and class structures". However, there was also a call for the "black university" to promote "class mobility". In short, while the university was, at the economic level, called on to promote capitalism and class mobility, at the ideological level it was required to help undo its economic contribution. Finally, while SASO wanted the "black university" to foster black values, identity and culture, it also required the university to be a force of modernisation. Here, it was oblivious to the possibility that modernisation could be accompanied by "Western" values, Eurocentrism, individualism, and the destruction of indigenous culture, the very things that were abhorred by SASO.

It is interesting that following the adoption of the BSM at the 1972 GSC, another resolution rescinded the Declaration of Student Rights. The Declaration was said to "grossly misrepresent the aspirations of the Black Student", and described as "an amorphous instrument paying homage to a utopian situation which bears little relevance to our Black experience" (SASO, 1972b:34). It was also said to be "obsessed with liberal notions of what constitutes the essence of studenthood and the rights accruing thereto" (*ibid.*). Certainly, the Declaration conceived of the university in Universalist and monastic terms, and as a neutral institution that stood above social interests. It was also true that students at black higher education institutions enjoyed few rights and studied under authoritarian conditions. However, the rejection of the assertion of basic student rights, as "liberal notions" is curious. It could be that SASO was disdainful of the notion of struggle around specific rights, seeing this as a characteristic of liberal organisations. Rights, then, were either subsumed under, or counterpoised to, "liberation".

Ideological and political shifts: the question of class

Between 1969 and 1975 SASO was characterised by a large degree of ideological and political homogeneity. The conception of the South African "problem" in terms of racism and racial domination, and the concomitant emphasis on black unity, provided sufficient ideological cement to hold SASO together. After the mid-1970s, however, this cement began to crack and there began to be a more open and public espousal of an analysis that incorporated class and class exploitation as salient features of the South African social order.

How extensive the shift towards a race-class analysis of the South African social order and struggle was within SASO is not clear. That there was a shift is definite. Moreover, the fact that SASO president Diliza Mji was not censured by the eighth GSC of SASO in July 1976 for his presidential address which critiqued the limits of a purely race-based analysis, and advocated a race-class approach to the South African struggle, suggests that there may have been significant support for the new line of thinking. It is pertinent to recall that Sono's call for a major change in policy and strategy, at the 1972 GSC, had led to his ousting. As will become clear, Mji's speech was a radical departure from SASO's doctrine and policy.

The reference to class and capitalism was not entirely new. Whereas the saliency of class and capitalism had been either rejected or was given little currency by Biko, Pityana and the early SASO leaders, resolutions at the fifth GSC in 1974 had begun to refer to the "white racist capitalist regime", and to "black skinned agents of white racism and capitalism" (SASO, 1974a). An article in a *SASO Newsletter* of late 1975, using the vocabulary of dependency and underdevelopment theory, stated that "there will be no end to exploitation and underdevelopment within the framework of the imperialist's system" (5(3)), 1975:5). Another article in a 1976 *SASO Newsletter* (6(1)), after linking the bantustans to white political domination, now also tied them to capitalist exploitation:

They are there to maintain the capitalist system of this country by keeping the black man starving and ignorant so that he can continue being a tool in the white man's farm, mine or industry for the production of wealth for the exclusive benefit of the white imperialist (quoted in Fatton, 1986:93).

There was also an attempt to understand black collaboration with the separate development project of the apartheid government in class terms.

It is the elitist class that is sowing the seeds of confusion and division amongst our people. It is the elitist class, created by the very oppressor that has joined hands with the oppressor in suppressing the legitimate aspirations of the masses...(*ibid.*).

However, the most categorical and significant expression of the ideological and political shift that was taking place within SASO was represented by Mji's address to the eighth GSC in July 1976. Mji argued that the state was promoting the development of a black middle class that would have a vested interest in maintaining the apartheid social order, and that this class was already revealing its eagerness to join the system of capitalist exploitation. Moreover, according to Mji, the black middle class aligned "itself with imperialism, the highest form of capitalism". There was a need

> ... therefore to look at our struggle not only in terms of colour interests but also in terms of class interests... Apartheid as an exploitative system is part of a bigger whole, capitalism. There are a lot of institutions and practices even amongst ourselves that are part of the general strategy of oppression (*SASO Bulletin*, 1,1, 1977).

Mji warned that students could "be the oppressors of the people if not armed with a clear analysis and strategy, and an accurate perception of who the enemy is and in what forms he is capable of presenting himself" (*ibid.*). The survival of BC and its ability "to articulate the aspirations of the masses of the people" depended on "interpreting our situation from an economic and class point of view" (*ibid.*) This would help reveal that the South African struggle was

> ... part of a bigger struggle of the third world that wants to shake off the yoke of imperialism and replace it with socialistic governments in which power is wielded not by a few wealthy families but by the people (*ibid.*).

With respect to strategy, Mji emphasised developing strong relations with workers and the need "to be more organised than before" (*ibid.*).

It is clear that Mji's analysis and interpretation of the South African social order and struggle was a radical departure from the prevailing SASO and BC approach. The latter viewed "race" and racism as the essential fault line of the South African social order, saw little use in Marxism and in giving consideration to questions of class and capitalism. Against white racism was posited black solidarity and a radical black nationalism which was considered to be unaffected by class interests within the black oppressed, and which implicitly assumed a leading role for black intellectuals and students. In contrast, Mji's presidential address to the SASO GSC, as Nolutshungu puts it

> ...strongly reflected the trend towards Marxism. ... [was] a sharp attack against capitalism, imperialism [in the Marxist sense] and bourgeois nationalism,... reject[ed] the middle class accommodation

the regime might envisage, [and] called on students to align themselves with the working people (1982:164, footnote 15).

The difference between Mji's perspectives and the prevailing SASO-BC approach is also commented upon by Marx who writes that Mji "directly contradicted BC's basic assumption of unity among all black victims of oppression" (1992:77). He suggests, moreover, that the issue of class was also introduced for strategic and practical reasons — "in order to reduce the preoccupation with shaping racial identity and to encourage active mass organisation" (ibid.).

Various factors appear to have contributed to the shift in analysis and thinking. For one, the attempt to use a BC framework to pose questions about black agents of oppression and repression yielded unsatisfactory answers. Second, individual members of SASO were beginning to come into contact with the ANC via its underground literature, its Radio Freedom and underground membership, and also through official contact, during 1973, with the ANC in exile. Indeed, elements within the SASO leadership were won over to the ANC's race-class analysis and policies, and recruited into the ANC. Ex-SASO activists have written that

the 1976 General Student Council saw a sizeable shift in BC ranks to the ANC. This was particularly strong among [UNMS] students, some of whom had recently visited Swaziland where contact was made with the ANC (Mokoape et al., 1991:140).

Third, the Natal workers' strikes of 1973 had begun to suggest the potential power of workers and that students, while they were an important part of the anti-apartheid struggle, were not necessarily the most important constituency. Finally, the new ideas within SASO were attributed to developments in Southern Africa. According to Mji,

developments in Mozambique and Angola also had an effect on SASO with resolutions passed supporting the MPLA and FRELIMO ... Slowly people started learning what these movements were all about and learning from their theories and practices ... The ideas of liberation movements like FRELIMO fighting the system of capitalist exploitation and not Portuguese people, as such, and ideas of class struggle filtered through and were giving us light in understanding why Blacks like Matanzima were selling out (quoted in AZASO National Newsletter, November 1983).

He argues that the eighth GSC of SASO brought them ultimately into facing the question of the theory of our struggle squarely and the inadequacy of our approach was realised by many people. For the first time papers dealing with the question of class struggle and the role of imperialism in our struggle were discussed (*ibid.*).

These new ideas were not accepted by all, and "did not go unchallenged" (*ibid.*). There were allegations that SASO "was turning red", and tensions developed between those beginning to subscribe to a class or race-class analysis and gravitate towards socialism and others in SASO and the Black Peoples Convention (BPC) who were comfortable with the emphasis on race and a new social order of "Black communalism" (*ibid.*). The "black communalism" formulation had emerged out of a BPC-organised conference and was meant to represent a third way between "capitalism and communism". According to the BPC president, "Black Consciousness abhors and detests both capitalism and communism with equal contempt", favouring instead "Black communalism", a "modified version of the traditional African economic life-style... geared to meet the demands of a highly industrialised and modern economy" (quoted in Hirson, 1979:300-301). Despite its close working relationship with the BPC (which had been formed, at the initiative of SASO, as an umbrella body of various black organisations), SASO was not consulted about the "black communalism" formulation, and raised objections to it.

It is clear that by the mid-1970s a new strand of thinking was beginning to emerge within SASO. The new line of thinking was important for two reasons. First, an important feature of black opposition politics after the Soweto uprising of 1976-1977 would be a contestation between this new line of thinking and more traditional BC ideas. Second, it prefigured in many ways what were to become the dominant ideological and political ideas of the 1980s, and many of the proponents of this line of thinking would become important cadres of the mass movements that would be the carriers of these ideas.

4

"SASO on the Attack"[4.1]: Organisation, Mobilisation and Collective Action

I now turn to examine select aspects of SASO's organisation and its activities related to student and popular mobilisation and collective action. However, there are no hard and fast boundaries between many of the activities. Thus, SASO's initiatives around publishing, which I deal with in the first section, can be considered to be equally a form of collective action like the education protests and political mobilisation that I describe in the later section. Conversely, the community development and other projects of SASO that I cover under "mobilisation and collective action" can well be seen as aspects of overall organisational activity.

Similarly, although I separate activities in terms of the "education struggle", political initiatives related to the building of the Black Consciousness movement, and "political mobilisation and struggle", in reality it is not possible to make any clear-cut distinction between them. Indeed, all can be considered "political" activities of different forms. Moreover, since the principal objective of SASO was to politically galvanise students and the black oppressed against apartheid, what is treated as organisational initiatives – for example publishing and leadership training – can also be regarded as essentially "political" activities. In short, the mode of presentation should not obscure the connections and relations between the various activities in which SASO was engaged. Finally, while there is some analysis and assessment of SASO's organisation and activities, this is fairly specific and limited in nature. A more detailed and general assessment of the character and role and significance of SASO is left to the following chapter.

Organisation: Membership, Structure and Process

SASO condemned both ethnic political and education institutions. However, an important distinction was made between participation in political and education institutions. Participation by blacks in separate development political institutions was seen as optional, whereas for purposes of schooling blacks were obliged to attend ethnic institutions of learning. Moreover, SASO's view was that ethnic political platforms were inappropriate and dangerous vehicles for any project of national liberation. Education institutions, on the other hand, despite severe constraints, afforded the opportunity and space for black student mobilisation and organisation into radical organisations.

Membership and infrastructure

While activist black students felt the need for an exclusive black student formation that would connect the black campuses and promote student contact, and proceeded to launch SASO, there was little certainty that the various campus authorities or the government would permit SASO to operate, and little guarantee that the organisation would gain a mass following. The repressive political conditions bred fear and acquiescence, and campus authorities maintained strong control over student activities. During 1969 SRCs existed at the University of Natal Medical School (UNMS), and at the universities of Zululand (UNIZUL), the North (UNIN) and Western Cape (UWC). However, only two months prior to the formal launch of SASO in July 1969, UNIN students were still protesting against the refusal of the campus authorities to allow the SRC to affiliate to NUSAS. They also objected to the banning of the UCM and the lack of powers enjoyed by the SRC (SAIRR, 1970:224). Thus, both support for NUSAS and curbs on free activity would condition the development of SASO. At Durban-Westville (UDW) and Fort Hare (UFH) no SRCs existed, students remaining in a deadlock with the authorities over the powers to be accorded to the SRCs.

However, there were also facilitating conditions. The conditions on campuses and within the broader society that were noted in Chapter 2 meant there was much that aroused student anger, resentment and disaffection. The banning of NUSAS at the black campuses potentially left the field clear for SASO. Moreover, SASO began by adopting a strategic approach with respect to both NUSAS and its own objects. Finally, and crucially, the scope for SASO to grow and implant itself on the black campuses was provided by two unexpected sources – government and the campus administrations.

According to Pityana, the first general secretary and second national president of SASO, "the government was at first ambivalent about SASO. The new student organisation attacked the liberal establishment ... and seemed, superficially at least, to echo some apartheid principles" (1991a:205). To the apartheid government's way of thinking, any organisation that attacked white liberals, and especially NUSAS, the bane of Afrikaner nationalists, and emphasised exclusive black organisation, was a potential ally and new recruit to the programme of separate development. There is also evidence that independent black organisation was encouraged by some of the Afrikaner nationalist rectors of the black campuses. Wolfson states that at UNIN two former rectors encouraged students to "shake off the yoke of NUSAS and to establish their own ... organisations" (1976:12). The UWC rector was reported as saying, "I don't want them affiliating to NUSAS ... They must stand on their own feet and learn to do things for themselves ..." (SAIRR, 1968:288). However, consistent with the ideology of separate development and measures to prevent united action by all oppressed national groups, the government departments responsible for UDW and UWC were to prohibit Indian and coloured students from joining SASO.

During 1969 and 1970, SASO's constituency was defined as black students "of institutions of higher learning". By 1971 membership was declared to "be open to all black students" and, under certain conditions, even non-students. Employing language typical of BC, "studentship" was defined by one SASO national president, as "a state of mind, a particular ambition, a particular awareness of one's social role" (quoted by Kotze, 1975:115). Four modes of membership were provided for: "an SRC affiliating on behalf of the student body"; " a majority student body decision for affiliation", especially where there was no SRC at an institution; branch affiliation through ten or more individuals constituting a branch; and individual affiliation through the SASO executive. The predominant forms through which students became members of SASO

107

were student body affiliation via the SRC, and branch affiliation. In reality, SASO's membership was essentially university students, enrolled primarily at the black universities and UNMS, a small number of students at religious seminaries, and a tiny number at teacher-training institutions.

Between 1969 and early 1972, SASO adopted a low-key approach and concentrated on establishing an organisational infrastructure, expanding membership, and formulating and elaborating BC ideas and disseminating these among students. This work was rewarded by *en masse* affiliations, via SRCs, at UNIN, UNIZUL and UNMS. At universities where the authorities either prohibited formal affiliation to SASO (UWC and UDW), or where there was conflict between students and authorities over the role and powers of the SRC (UFH), SASO enjoyed a presence through the formation of local branches. Since nothing precluded SASO activists from standing for elections to SRCs, SASO also began to be the hegemonic force within SRCs. Thus, in the 1972 SRC elections at UWC, eight out of 11 elected candidates were SASO members (Lewis, 1987:278).

Outside the universities, branches were established at the Federal Theological Seminary (FTS), adjacent to Fort Hare, and the Lutheran Theological College, as well as at the Transvaal College of Education, an Indian teacher-training institution. An interesting innovation was SASO "locals", branches which catered for UNISA correspondence students and, in some cases, also ex-students. By early 1972 there were locals in Durban, Johannesburg and Pretoria. At this point SASO claimed a national membership of 4 000 and predicted that membership would reach 7 000 by the end of 1972 (SASO 1972a:3).

In 1973 membership was reported as over 6 000, with locals showing especial growth. New branches were established in Lenasia, Springs, Krugersdorp, Middelburg, Mafeking, Kimberley, Bloemfontein, Maphumulo, and Umlazi and a second branch was formed in Durban. Locals were also said to be in the process of formation in various other towns and cities, including Pietermaritzburg, Port Elizabeth, East London, King Williamstown and Umtata. In addition, a branch was established at the Hewat college, a coloured teacher training institution in Athlone, near Cape Town (SASO, 1973a:21; SASO, 1973d:2; SASO, 1973f:4).

According to SASO, the locals in cities and towns arose "from a need to foster communication between the correspondence student and the full-time student" (SASO, 1973a:21). However, in the aftermath of the mid-1972 mass student protests co-ordinated by SASO, and the repression of SASO on some campuses (see below), there was also a strategic rationale to the locals. They were a creative organisational measure for it was realised that this kind of branch became instrumental in side-stepping the vicious action of the university authorities who have banned SASO on the campus. Many off-campus branches are now catering for students at full-time universities (*ibid.*).

Still, despite their innovativeness, the "locals" held the twin dangers of SASO activists becoming isolated from rank-and-file students on the campuses, and of the campuses being surrendered as the primary terrain of mobilisation and struggle.

Structure and organisational culture

While the affiliated SRCs, campus branches and city and town locals constituted the infrastructure and operational field units of SASO, inter-unit contact and co-ordination and overall organisational coherence and direction was achieved through a number of national and regional structures. The highest policy and decision-making body was the General Students Council (GSC) which met annually. The GSC consisted of the elected national executive of SASO and delegates representing the various affiliated SRCs, branches and locals. The national executive itself was a five-person committee elected by the GSC. It consisted of the president, vice-president, general secretary, "permanent organiser" and publications director, and was responsible for the day-to-day affairs of SASO. The general secretary and permanent organiser (responsible for liaison between the executive, the various affiliated SRCs, branches and "locals", and for research and co-ordinating certain projects) were full-time employees whose appointments were on a three-year basis, to be ratified annually by the GSC. In between the annual GSCs, an executive council made up of the national executive and chairpersons of affiliated SRCs, branches and locals met biannually. At the regional level, regional councils existed to promote SASO and co-ordinate the activities of affiliates within a region (SASO, 1973a:12-13).

The GSCs appear to have been lively occasions, and organised so as to deal not only with policy and organisational matters but to also provide space for exploring particular themes and cultural pursuits. Much time at GSCs was given over to small working commissions – on education, culture, community development, external relations and so forth, possibly to enable issues to be explored in depth and to facilitate participation. Themes such as "separate development", "creativity and black development" and "black theology" were the subject of symposia featuring invited speakers from various organisations and within SASO. There were poetry readings, drama, music and art exhibitions by emerging BC artists and the GSCs, as well as other SASO forums, provided artists with a platform for cultural expression and a means of becoming known nationally (SASO, 1971; SASO, 1972b).

A significant feature of the SASO national organisation was the continuous turnover of key elected officials. Indeed, each annual GSC saw the election of a new president and vice-president. Initially, this was a matter of conscious choice as SASO sought to develop a broad leadership corps. Later, the turnover of leading officials became an effect of the continuous banning of SASO leaders by the state. Previous officials, however, continued to play important roles in other portfolios and as advisers. Moreover, the full-time general secretaries and permanent organisers who were elected for three-year periods provided continuity.

Continuity and organisational integrity was also facilitated by employing staff and field-workers for various SASO projects and initiatives and for day to day administration, leading one commentator to state that "SASO is the best-staffed Black political organisation in the country" (Kotze, 1975:106). A SASO head office operated from Durban, and there were branch offices with full-time regional secretaries in Cape Town, Johannesburg and King Williamstown, with proposals to establish more (SASO, 1972b:21; 1973d:27). Compared to many anti-apartheid organisations, an impressive feature of SASO was its written output in the form of reports to meetings, reports and minutes of meetings, information publications and newsletters.

Offices, staff, and organisational activities, however, cost money. Branch contributions of between 50 cents and R1 (1972) per member brought in some money, but were an insufficient and irregular source of income. Instead, many of SASO's operations were made possible by overseas funding from European church and student organisations, agencies in the United States and organisations like the World University Service and the International University Exchange Fund. Locally, the Christian Institute and other organisations provided some financial and material support.

Organisational culture: Key features

Five features of SASO's organisational culture deserve special mention. First, with the advent of SASO there also emerged a semi-public space for intellectual and political discussion and debate. Institutionally, this semi-public space took the form of on and off-campus social gatherings that were informal and vibrant in nature, and which stood on their own or were attached to SASO conferences, meetings and events. These gatherings assembled black intellectuals, professionals and activists across occupational, geographical, and organisational boundaries, and provided a medium for the testing of ideas, for the circulation of political tracts, and for conversation around literature. Issues and ideas raised at these gatherings would later crystallise in articles, conference resolutions and projects (see Wilson, 1991:30-31).

Second, with SASO came

a particular style of leadership which recognised the enormous advantage of widespread consultation. This did not only mean consultation to win over a proposal but the creation of an atmosphere where individual opinions were considered and taken seriously. They were valued equally (Wilson, 1991:27).

One practical manifestation of this was Biko's use at UNMS of student groups of different ideological and political persuasions as a sounding board for his ideas. Another example was the establishment by SASO of the "Advisory Panel". At each GSC, "distinguished Black persons" from different parts of the country were elected to advise SASO on student politics, regional, legal and financial matters.

Third, SASO provided considerable leeway for individual members to express views and opinions, and much scope for independent initiative by members operating under the auspices of various working commissions. The formulation of policy documents and statements appears to have been often entrusted to commissions (education, culture, etc.), and responsibility to implement conference resolutions was also decentralised to the commissions. SASO publications like "Creativity and Black Development" (Langa, 1973) reflected the intense debates around culture while the *SASO Newsletter* encouraged, within the overall doctrine of BC, a diversity of views.

The only, and dramatic, exception, was Sono's call at the 1972 GSC for a different approach to bantustans and even to the security police. However, even this case reveals the extent to which some leading members of SASO sought to ensure latitude of expression. Biko's response to Sono's speech had been to sponsor a resolution that censured Sono for views that were "contradictory to either SASO policy or to the spirit of the policy", and to confine the rebuke to the GSC's, dissociating itself from Sono's views (SASO, 1972b:6). The more stringent resolution calling on Sono to recuse him from the chair; to resign as president, and to leave the conference was adopted later, in Biko's absence. The wording of this resolution was particularly harsh. It stated that "the dangerous and horrifying references to security police" and Bantustans smack of sell-out tendencies", that Sono was a "security risk to our organisation and black community" and it labelled his views as his "personal "non-white" stand" (*ibid.*:8). It is possible that members, already angry with the content of Sono's speech, became more hostile on learning that Sono had also violated traditional procedure and the consultative approach that SASO had sought to cultivate by not attending the executive meeting immediately prior to the GSC, and not testing his views with other executive members.

Fourth, as the slogans and discourse of SASO ("Black man, you are on your own"; the "Black man", "Your black brother") reveal, its organisational culture was highly masculine, male-dominated, and even sexist. Ramphele's observation that in UNMS "student politics on campus at that time were dominated by male students" (1991b:214) was also true for all the black campuses and SASO. There were three women at the launch of SASO in 1969, and at the 1972 GSC only nine out of the 68 participants were women (SASO, 1972b:3-4). The priority of BC was national liberation and "women were thus involved in the movement because they were black. Gender as a political issue was not raised at all" (Ramphele, 1991b:215). The responsibility for domestic chores at conferences, seminars and formation schools fell on women and in "general, sexist practices and division of labour along gender lines were never systematically challenged ... " (ibid.:219).

If there were more progressive positions among some activists, the general environment of sexism curbed women from playing as full a role as men and also made difficult addressing sexism at a mass level. Those women who displayed a determination to challenge their subordination were granted the status of "honorary men". As Ramphele puts it, "We had, after all, entered the domain generally regarded as the preserve of men and were treated accordingly" (ibid.:220). The new status provided benefits such as fuller participation in meetings, greater involvement in social activities and various other advantages.

Finally, although there was little concern to address and undermine gender inequities and sexism, considerable attention was given to the political and organisational development of current and future student leaders and activists. The primary instruments for the training of cadres were national and regional "formation schools" and leadership seminars. A number of SASO leaders attended a leadership-training course, which covered issues such as social analysis, organisational dynamics and administration, and public speaking (Ramphele, 1991a:163). Such leaders then acted as trainers for local, regional and national leadership seminars for SASO members.

Buthelezi gives an indication of the focus of some of the early formation schools and their nature.

In order to clarify among themselves the kind of language of liberation they sought to popularise, student leaders had to acquaint themselves with the history of the liberation movement in South Africa. This education process was embarked upon at "formation schools" as well as leadership-training seminars organised in 1970 and 1971. These sessions normally lasted four days and involved in-depth discussions on many topics. Participation at the seminars and formation schools was limited to the core cadres from centres and branches; these were locally selected in consultation with the SASO national executive (1991:118-19).

Apart from studying topics and issues deemed crucial for the ideological and political development of SASO cadres and SASO as an organisation, formation schools and leadership seminars also examined in greater depth issues that were to be discussed at GSCs. In addition, they were concerned with questions of strategy and tactics, and skills related to leadership, and organisational management and administration (SASO, 1973a:24; SASO, 1973c).

A SASO "fact paper" entitled *The politics of protest for Black students* gives an inkling of the content of activist training. Participants were introduced to the context of and impediments to protest, such as apathy, fear, lack of unity and repression, and it was argued that "educated leadership and the creation of the right political climate among Blacks [was] a *sine qua non* for effective protest" (Kotze, 1975:183). Political work was said to entail the representation of student grievances and needs, the education of students and the development of their political awareness and confidence, promoting black unity and BC, and developing self-reliance. The conditions for protest activities are seen as including initiatives promoting black solidarity, the "co-ordination of all Black activities", black self-pride and black theology (*ibid.*). Finally, channels for protest were said to include the issuing of statements, boycotts and meetings (*ibid.*).

Organisational and ideological diffusion

The fact that one of the five national executive members was director of publications, and that from 1970 an editor of SASO publications was also appointed, signalled the importance that SASO attached to media. Numerous occasional publications, bulletins and pamphlets were produced, as well as a fairly regular newsletter (the *SASO Newsletter*). By 1972, circulation of the *SASO Newsletter* reached 4 000 copies (Gerhart, 1978:270). The newsletter and publications were crucial instruments of ideological and organisational diffusion. First, they helped to propagate and popularise SASO's ideas and views, and its leadership. Second, they disseminated news and information about SASO initiatives, activities and organisational matters. Third, through articles on events such as the anti-pass demonstrations and the massacre at Sharpeville in 1960, they played an education function. Fourth, they mobilised support for SASO, helped build membership and, through diaries, T-shirts and the like gave SASO an organisational presence.

Finally, newsletters and publications also served as forums for the exchange of ideas and debates. The production and dissemination of media, as organisational activities, also enhanced solidarity among members and loyalty to SASO. SASO publications were not confined to the black campuses but made their way into other institutions and organisations, and to the youth and student groupings that began to emerge in the black townships during this period.

Notwithstanding the problems of male domination and sexism, the organisational achievements of SASO were impressive. In 1969, Biko had seen SASO as "a challenge to test the independence of the non-white students leaders ... organisationally" (1987:7). Without doubt, the black student activists of SASO met the challenge and, as Ramphele puts it,

> The initiative taken in launching a new student organisation, training leadership, and formulating and enunciating the Black Consciousness philosophy, was living testimony that self-reliance was a feasible strategy and objective (1991a:169).

SASO had also sought to "boost the morale" of black students and "heighten their own confidence in themselves" (Biko, 1987:5). Again, there is ample evidence that that active within SASO developed, through practice and training, a range of skills and considerable organisational expertise, and became confident, assertive and articulate activists.

In a letter sent to various student and other organisations in early 1970, Biko had asserted "The blacks are tired of standing at the touchlines to witness a game that they should be playing. They want to do things for themselves and all by themselves" (1987:7, 15). SASO also enabled this to become a reality. Through the day-to-day tasks of maintaining an organisational infrastructure and structure, the production and dissemination of publications, the formation schools and seminars, and various other organisational initiatives, numerous black students were able to become active participants and agents in the building and development of SASO, in the shaping of BC thinking and activities, and in the manifestation, popularisation and spread of BC. SASO ensured that black students committed to social change and political liberation would no longer be mere spectators, but would have the opportunity "to do things for themselves and all by themselves".

Mobilisation and Collective Action

The education struggle

Conditions at black institutions engendered in student's feelings of isolation, frustration and alienation. Rules and regulations were authoritarian and oppressive. There was a strong resentment of curricula, especially in the social sciences; and, generally, there were poor relations and little communication between white administrators and academic staff and black students (Buthelezi, 1991:112-113). Still, as SASO recognised, the black universities exposed the "naked hell" with little of the "blurring" provided by the white liberal institutions; and it was asserted that " ... these dungeons of oppression can be used to unite the artificially created divisions amongst us" (SASO, 1972a:6). The conditions at, and racial constitution of, the black institutions in many ways shaped the content of student demands and protests.

Prior to May 1972, when SASO called for countrywide student protests, the focus of SASO activities was primarily on the low-key recruitment of members, the mobilisation of students through meetings and publications, the establishment of an organisational infrastructure and structure, and the elaboration and dissemination of the doctrine of BC. There were no initiatives directed towards co-ordinated national mass action. What student action did take place was of a local nature, involved meetings, sit-ins and marches, and demanded, in the main, greater autonomy and powers for SRCs. At UNIN, in 1971, there was a student boycott of celebrations to mark the institution's attainment of full university status. In March 1972, there was a further confrontation between the university administration and the SRC when the latter rejected an administration demand to remove the SASO Policy Manifesto from the official student diary, and students instead made a bonfire with the official diaries (SAIRR, 1970:223; 1971:246; 1972:291, 1973:387).

The trigger of the 1972 student protests that SASO co-ordinated was the expulsion from UNIN of Onkgopotse Tiro, a former SRC president, for a graduation ceremony speech that attacked segregated education and white domination of black institutions, and called on students to be active participants in the liberation struggle (BCP, 1973:174-75). A student meeting called by the SASO-affiliated SRC resolved to boycott classes until Tiro was reinstated. The UNIN administration responded by suspending the SRC and banning all meetings. Thereafter, the administration tried to get students either to sign declaration forms promising orderly behaviour or to leave the campus. When this met with no success, the 1 146 students were informed that they were expelled and the police were summoned. However, only after essential services were cut off did students leave the campus.

Parent delegations that resulted from meetings of parents and students, and other black organisations, including SASO, failed to get the UNIN administration to lift the expulsions on Tiro and the other students.[4.2] instead, students were required to apply individually for readmission, sign an acceptance of the expulsion of Tiro, the suspension of the SRC, and the suspension of all student groups, including SASO. The students were advised by SASO to return to UNIN "to continue their fight for education justice", without respecting the conditions of their re-admission. On returning, students discovered that a number of SRC and SASO members had not been readmitted, and this led to a walk-off of 500-700 students, while the remainder resumed lectures under police monitoring (SAIRR, 1973: 388-89).

The Tiro and UNIN student expulsions led to solidarity boycotts, and also served as a catalyst for student protests at UNMS, UWC, UNIZUL, UDW, UFH, some teacher-training and advanced technical education colleges and the Federal Theological Seminary. Initially, only UNMS and UWC embarked on solidarity boycotts. A few weeks later, however, all the black universities and a number of other black higher education institutions were in the throes of conflict. The pattern of the conflict at UNIN was more or less repeated at these institutions. First, there was student expression of solidarity with UNIN students" or/and demands related to conditions at the particular campus. Then, there was student action and counter-action and reprisals by the administration, and harassment and questioning of student activists by the security police. This led to parents" attempts to mediate the conflict. Eventually, there was a return of most students to lectures. Frequently, the return of students was accompanied, or followed, by reprisals against students which took the form of suspensions, expulsions, loss of bursaries, and a ban on SASO.

SASO was instrumental in extending the student protests countrywide to almost all the black campuses. Shortly after the UNIN expulsions a pre-arranged SASO National Formation School issued what became known as the "Alice Declaration" (after the town Alice, near Fort Hare). The Alice Declaration stated that, given the "oppressive atmosphere in the black institutions", passivity in the light of the UNIN expulsions would be a "betrayal of the black man's struggle". It added that

the black community is anxiously and eagerly waiting to learn and hear of the stand taken by black students on the other campuses who invariably are subjected to the same atrocities and injustices (BCPs, 1973:176).

The Declaration then went on to state that SASO believed that the UNIN incident could "be escalated into a major confrontation with the authorities". It therefore called on all black students to "force the institutions/universities to close down by boycotting lectures" on a particular day (ibid.:176-77).

The Declaration, publicised through the commercial media, was well heeded, and resulted in the largest, most widespread and sustained protests yet by black higher education students. If SASO extended the terrain of the conflict, the SRCs, SASO branches, or ad hoc student groups at individual campuses themselves expanded the scope of the protests beyond that of the expulsion of the UNIN students and Tiro. At UDW, the SRC constitution was put at issue, and at UFH an end to police activity on campus and the "dictatorial attitude" of the rector was demanded. At UNMS, students demanded that a black person be appointed as the superintendent of residences, while UWC students sought the appoint-ment of a black rector. The reasoning advanced was that "it is an undisputed fact that the rector at a Black university has supreme power ... to manipulate and gear the situation into whichever direction he desires". A meeting of student leaders from black institutions collated the demands of students from the different campuses into a single document, the *minimum student demands*. One general demand was for black university councils and senates and freedom of organisation on campuses (SAIRR, 1973:389; 391; 388).

Importance of the 1972 protests

The 1972 student protests were important for a number of reasons. First, the display of student solidarity, and unity across ethnic and racial lines, showed those BC ideas were having an impact. Second, the heeding of the SASO call for countrywide protests and the extension of the boycott from UNIN to other campuses confirmed SASO's support among students and its organisational strength. Third, there was some attempt on the part of the government to meet student demands – especially those related to the calls for black rectors and council members (Laurence, 1979:60). For example, although not quite what SASO had intended, two members of the Coloured Representative Council were appointed to the UWC Council. Fourth, the protests catalysed SASO's efforts to investigate the role of education in South African society and to elaborate in greater detail its views on the role that education and universities ought to play. Fifth, and in relation to its ideas on university education, the protests also led SASO to develop the "free university" scheme. Finally, the mass student actions gave rise to an important debate around future strategy. SASO's ideas around education, prior to the May 1972 protests, and after, have already been discussed in the previous chapter. The Free University Scheme (FUS) and the debate around strategy merit greater attention.

The FUS was conceived in the aftermath of the protests, initially to provide financial and academic support to students refused registration at black institutions. Such students were meant to register at UNISA, and the FUS was to arrange tutorials related to UNISA curricula, as well as additional seminars concerned with "black studies". Thereafter, the idea was for the FUS to be expanded into an institution that would be based in various centres, and which would service students registered for correspondence courses with overseas institutions, and offer a curriculum "meaningful to the Black student" (SASO, 1973a:22). The FUS, however, was not much of a success. At the GSC in 1973 it was noted that 64 loans had been provided under the FUS, but that three attempts to hold Free University seminars failed to materialise, and that in one case no students turned up (SASO, 1973f). There was a complaint that students granted loans under the FUS were generally not attending Free University seminars, and a resolution was adopted to make compulsory attendance a condition of the loan (SASO, 1973d:13). A year later it was reported that funding was a problem, and that there were initiatives underway to make the FUS an independent entity.

Another education initiative was the Promotion of Black Education Advancement Trust (PROBEAT). This project sought to raise over R100 000 to provide financial support to needy students at black institutions. However, since its aim was the "inculcation of education for self-reliance", PROBEAT sought to link recipients student loans to a "student voluntary service" that would provide services to black schools. PROBEAT also aimed to involve students in setting up soup kitchens near black schools and establishing an inter-university system of providing text books on loan to needy students. However, PROBEAT also struggled to raise funds and was unsuccessful.

A final consequence of the 1972 student protests was the debate that was provoked around SASO strategy. At the July 1972 GSC there was a motion that SASO members withdraw from "non-white institutions of higher learning", and that the GSC formulate an "action programme". The motion appealed to the spirit of the Fort Hare Students Manifesto, which had called on students "to leave this tribal university of Fort Hare" (SASO, 1972b:22) and signalled, in the aftermath of the student protests and the harsh response of the campus authorities, the beginning among some SASO members of an impatience with activities centred around psychological liberation and a desire for more confrontational and militant action.

Those proposing the withdrawal of activist students from black institutions, in effect, no longer sought to make any distinction between separate development political and education institutions, but sought to elevate the education boycott from a tactic to a principle. Biko, who strongly opposed the motion, raised four questions.

As SASO, were they, in fact, operating within government institutions? Was there much to be achieved by students if they were not to be registered at universities? Would SASO be able to sustain political activity with a large number of students outside the campuses? What would happen to the remainder of students still at these universities? (cited by Wilson, 1991:32).

These were, of course, all pertinent questions. To make no distinction between political and education institutions was to condemn black students to no schooling at all. Whatever the limitations and frustrations of black institutions, they did – as SASO showed – provide a space for the mobilisation and organisation of students into a progressive formation. For activists to withdraw would mean not only losing an important organisational base, but also leaving the field open for reactionary political forces.

However, the fundamental difference between those calling for the withdrawal and Biko and his supporters centred around the meaning given to the 1972 protests. Whereas the former interpreted the protests as signalling the need to move to a new phase of struggle, the view of the Biko group was that SASO was still at an early and preparatory stage of its liberation efforts and could not lose the base that the black higher education institutions provided. While the motion was eventually defeated 29 to 15, with seven abstentions, it highlighted how a particular event, and its implications for strategy, was interpreted in different ways by activists with similar commitments. The debate around strategy was also a harbinger of differences that, as was noted, arose after 1975 around strategy, but was linked on this occasion to questions of ideology and politics.

Post-1972 student education protests

After 1972, and until the banning of SASO in 1977, there were no further nationally co-ordinated struggles. On many campuses, SRCs and SASO branches were engaged in rearguard actions in the face of the increasing hostility and repression of campus authorities, and there were ongoing skirmishes around the autonomy and powers of SRCs, the suspension and expulsion of students, and police action on campuses. There were also protests around the quality of education and food in the residences.

In 1973, at the UFH an unpopular hostel warden was attacked and his home damaged. The police were summoned and 159 students rusticated, only to be reinstated after the threat of a mass student walk-off. Nearby Federal Theological Seminary students engaged in a sympathy boycott with the UFH students (SASO, 1974a). The main flash point was the UWC. There, issues "such as the oppressive rules and regulations, the preponderance of white teaching staff and unequal pay for equal work, and poor lecturer-student relations" and security police raids on campus residences were a focal point of student grievances (SAIRR, 1974:336). Students, led by SASO, also demanded that the white rector, a Broederbond member, resign. A deadlock led to the closing of the UWC.

The students received considerable support from the UWC Black Staff Association and the coloured community. A mass meeting of 12 000 people addressed by, amongst others, Gatsha Buthelezi and Sonny Leon, both participants in separate development political institutions, helped secure the readmission of students. In the subsequent ongoing contestations a number of students were suspended and a few hundred students left UWC with the effect of considerably weakening SASO. With respect to the demand for a black rector, the student campaign was "victorious". R. E. van der Ross, a coloured educationist, was appointed the new rector. The irony was that van der Ross had described the student position as a "large dose of Black Power with political overtones"[4.3] (*Cape Times*, 10 July 19973)

Political initiatives: building the Black Consciousness Movement (BCM)

From the outset, Biko had stressed that SASO had a "responsibility" to the black "community" and that the "leadership of the non-white peoples" and the shaping of black political thinking rested with SASO (Biko, 987:5;7). In line with this, the SASO constitution committed it "to the realisation of the worth of the black man, the assertion of his human dignity and to promoting consciousness and self-reliance of the black community". The Black Student Manifesto set the challenge of the "assertion, manifestation and development of a sense of awareness politically, socially and economically among the Black community" (SASO, 1972b:24). Finally, the SASO Policy Manifesto emphasised "group cohesion and solidarity" as "important facets of Black Consciousness", the need for "the totality of involvement of the oppressed people" and for BC "to be spread to reach all sections of the Black Community" (Appendix 1, SPM).

To give expression to its commitments and objectives, a host of initiatives related to "community development", literacy and education, media, culture, sport, "black theology", worker organisation, the establishment of secondary school student and youth formations and a political organisation, were launched. As a result of these initiatives, BC ideas were diffused beyond SASO's student base; relationships were established with a range of black secular and religious bodies, some of whom were won over to BC; new BC formations came into being; and there was a revitalisation of black cultural and political life. The BCM of the pre-1977 period was largely the achievement of SASO. The essential and core ideas of BC emerged from SASO, BCM intellectuals by and large cut their political teeth within SASO, and for much of its existence SASO, ideologically, politically and organisationally, stood at the head of the BCM.

Community development projects

SASO's community development projects were influenced by Nyerere's notion of self-reliance and "ujaama" and the Freire approach to developing political awareness among oppressed groups. The objective was to assist black communities to determine and realise their own needs. SASO did not seek to be a welfare organisation and community projects were seen not as ends in themselves but rather as a means to win the trust and confidence of people and provide a platform for their education and mobilisation (Dlamini, cited by Fatton, 1986:98). Projects were meant to instil in students and communities the self-reliance that was seen as a prerequisite for self-emancipation. They were attractive to SASO because they provided the opportunity for students to use their skills for community development, instilled the notion of service to the community and enabled black students to give expression to the claim that they were "black" before being students (SASO, 1972b:29; Ramphele, 1991a:154; 156).

Community development projects began with the involvement of the SASO branch at the University of Natal Medical School, attempting to address the needs of squatter and poor communities near Durban for clean water, shelter and health services. Once taken up by other SASO branches and SASO nationally, these projects were meant to include the building of small dams, the construction of school buildings and community centres, a rehabilitation scheme for people uprooted and relocated at Winterveld, near Pretoria, health and preventive medicine projects, soup kitchens, and assistance to a relocated community in the north-western Cape (SASO, 1974a 3). Initially, responsibility for many of the national initiatives lay with the permanent organiser. However, given the numerous duties attached to this official's portfolio, in 1973 SASO decided to appoint a full-time director of community development (SASO, 1973d:14).

Overall, the track record of SASO's community development initiatives was poor. Apart from the construction of some dams, school buildings and a community centre, few projects were fully implemented or satisfactorily operated, serviced and concluded (SASO, 1973f:15; SASO, 1974b). Problems cited included poor planning, the lack of funds and transport, and police harassment. According to Ramphele, who was involved in various SASO projects, there was also a lack of continuity, time and advisory and material support as well as problems related to consulting adequately. Moreover, the assumption of community unity also proved to be an obstacle. However, work of the kind that was conducted at Winterveld represented a "valuable education opportunity" (Ramphele, 1991a:157-59). It revealed the enormity of the economic and social problems of the poor, the extent of poverty of relocated people and put "paid to the romanticism we as students had about poverty and people's responses to it" (ibid.).

As part of community development, SASO was also involved in literacy programmes and a "Home Education Scheme". The literacy project was taken over from the University Christian Movement in 1972. Literacy was seen as playing an important role in "bringing the black community closer to liberation" and in contributing to "political, economic and social awareness and consciousness by permitting wider communication and conscientisation". A director of literacy was appointed to "plan, execute and set up literacy classes throughout the country" and students were urged to "play their role in the sensitising of our community". The Home Education Scheme was also established in 1972 and was meant to be a "natural follow-up of the literacy project". It was intended to provide adult education for the newly literate and tuition for correspondence school students by running classes near universities and vacation schools in select centres (SASO, 1972b:27; SASO, 1973a:15-16).

A number of seminars were organised in different parts of the country to train both students and other interested people as literacy co-ordinators, and literacy work was conducted by some of the SASO branches with various groups, including domestic and campus workers. However, in 1973, the director of literacy was banned. There was also a complaint from the national executive that many people trained as literacy co-ordinators showed no drive and dedication and that, as a result, literacy programmes had not taken off (SASO, 1973f:21). A year later, various SASO branches made much the same complaint, some adding that there was a general reluctance on the part of members to become involved in community development initiatives (SASO, 1974b). In July 1974 it was stated that there had been no major literacy undertakings in the previous six months and plans were underway to decentralise the literacy project and hand it over "to the community" (SASO, 1974c:15). The Home Education Scheme appears to have been even less of a success and to have suffered from a similar person-power problem.

In SASO's view, the essential problem of the community development initiatives was the lack of interest on the part of students, and their low level of participation. In 1974 the SASO national executive had to acknowledge that

> to a very small scale we did live up to our ideals but somehow things took a new turn and students shied away from projects. Lack of funds cannot be used as an excuse, lack of initiative and dedication is our strongest drawback (SASO, 1974c:12).

At the same time, community development was emphasised even more strongly. It was argued that SASO had achieved its goal of making BC "a fact in the community", but that

> the community is tired of listening to speeches, all people want is some tangible manifestations of self-reliance and self-determination. Community Development work offers us this chance and we need to snap it up without much waste of time (ibid.).

However, there is little evidence that after 1974 community development work was "snapped up" by students, or that community projects were in any healthier state.

I noted earlier that for SASO publications were a vital means of disseminating BC ideas. SASO also understood the role of the commercial media in shaping black opinion, recognised the need to develop "good relations with the press", and welcomed coverage given to events like GSCs. However, relations with the commercial media were generally strained. The control of much of the media by white-owned companies, the media's hostility to, or lack of support of, SASO, its failure to be "truly objective" and its tendency to refer to blacks as "non-whites" were all strongly resented (SASO, 1972b; 1973d:6). At the 1972 GSC a resolution, noting that the "white press" was "completely irrelevant" to black "needs and aspirations", and that it was "determined to misrepresent and misdirect the black community", called for the establishment of an "independent black press". The secretary-general was instructed to make contact with black journalists, business people and organisations, to arrange a seminar on the "the role of the Black press" in South Africa and to set up a "Black Press Commission" (SASO, 1972b:20).

The seminar was held and instituted the Black Press Commission. The Commission was to form a private company whose objects were to be to establish a monthly newspaper, and a publishing and printing house. There were, however, no tangible results. The banning of key SASO officials stalled the activities of the commission, and while reference was made in 1974 to the floating of a company it was admitted that little progress had been made. One indirect outcome of this initiative, however, was the formation of the Union of Black Journalists by some of the Transvaal participants (SASO, 1973f:24).

Two of the fields in which SASO had considerably greater impact and success were culture and "black theology". At the 1971 GSC a lengthy resolution was adopted which defined culture as "a dynamic phenomenon involving all activities of a people", and asserted that BC was "a supremely cultural fact". The resolution called for a "cultural orientation" that made blacks realise that they were united by a common experience of political and economic oppression and "insult to human dignity", and for the appointment of an organiser who would be responsible for organising and promoting black cultural activities and disseminating literature (SASO, 1971:22-24). The following year, in lieu of an organiser, a Cultural Commission was established to promote and disseminate black cultural production. Black parents were to be encouraged to give black names to children and to teach folklore, and initiatives were called for to promote black values among children.

SASO and BC played a major role in stimulating and facilitating black cultural production during the 1970s. The 1972 GSC included an art exhibition, poetry reading, and a drama and music festival, and cultural activities were to become an ongoing and vibrant feature of SASO national and local meetings and events, and of campus life. SASO forums provided platforms for BC cultural production and exposure for emerging black artists, while SASO publications carried numerous articles on culture, and also featured black poetry. SASO members were instrumental in establishing a number of cultural formations, played an active role in various theatre, art and music bodies, and a number of them were to go on to establish national and international reputations as novelists, poets and playwrights.

Mzamane has argued that BC

realised ... the essentially political importance of the cultural struggle. It was active in all the arts, but in none more effectively than theatre, which included poetry performances. Black Consciousness emphasised the education function of cultural and artistic activity and exploited the political resources of art, theatre, music, dance and culture in general (1991:185).

The character, form and content of poetry, drama, art and music influenced by BC was strongly conditioned by the audience that it sought to communicate with – primarily the black oppressed, rather than white cultural consumers or any other social group.

While not all of SASO's members were Christian or even religiously inclined, as an organisation SASO understood the importance of religion, and especially Christianity, in the lives of the black population. It promoted "black theology" and achieved some success in popularising it among black theologians, clergy, students at seminaries and members of black Christian student formations. A 1971 resolution defined black theology:

Black theology is not a theology of absolutes, but grapples with existential situations ... .Is not a theology of theory but that of action and development. It is ... an authentic and positive

127

articulation of the Black Christian's reflection on God in the light of their Black experience (SASO, 1971:21).

Christ's liberation was understood as freedom not only from "internal bondage" but also "from circumstances of external enslavement", and therefore black theology meant

taking resolute and decisive steps to free Black people not only from estrangement to God but also from slave mentality, inferiority complex, distrust of themselves and continued dependence on others culminating in self-hate (ibid.).

Black clergy were seen as crucial to the spread of BC ideas and liberation and a commission including other "relevant" religious bodies was established to "study, direct and popularise" black theology. However, another resolution that "black Christians within the white-dominated churches should be encouraged to break-away and form their own independent churches" was resoundingly defeated (SASO, 1971:22). It was probably realised that any break-away call would have little success and would lead SASO into a headlong confrontation with many of the religious bodies with whom it was associated.

The BC ideas and black theology enjoyed strong support among theological students who were active in SASO branches at the Federal Theological Seminary and the Lutheran Theological College, and via them reached sections of the broader black population. Black theology also had adherents within the Students Christian Movement (SCM), and on some campuses there was a close working relationship between SASO and SCM branches. Finally, it had a resonance within the Inter-denominational Association of African Ministers of Religion (IDAMASA), and some support from sections of the Christian Council of South Africa, which consisted of most of the major churches and various religious organisations. One indication of the spread of BC and black theology among committed and more activist black Christian students is provided by the disbanding of the non-racial UCM in 1972. The dissolution of the UCM, according to its president, was the result of the "growth of Black Consciousness among the Black members" (quoted in Hirson, 1979:83).

Organisational relations

SASO's projects and its various activities brought it into contact with a range of organisations. Relations with organisations were generally governed by three considerations. First, relations with certain organisations were necessitated by practical considerations, although the general policy was to avoid contact with these organisations. Essentially liberal and white organisations like NUSAS and the Christian Institute (CI) fell into this category. Even though SASO was generally hostile towards NUSAS, and had, in 1973, secured its expulsion from the Southern African Students' Movement conference, the way was always left open for the SASO national executive to liaise with NUSAS around minor practical matters, and there was some contact around these matters. In the case of the CI, formed by white ex-Dutch Reformed Church clergy like Beyers Naude, although it gave some attention to black theology, SASO drew on it essentially for financial and material support.

Second, relations with a number of black organisations were based on co-operation around practical issues and areas of shared concerns and thinking. SASO saw it as fruitful and strategic to have relations with such organisations and to attempt to influence them to embrace BC. Many of the religious organisations with which SASO had relations, as well as the numerous organisations that attended the meetings to explore the formation of the Black Peoples Convention (BPC) (see below) are cases in point. The initial relations with some bantustan leaders, including Buthelezi, had also been governed by such a strategic consideration.

Finally, there were a number of organisations with which SASO had a close relationship based on shared goals and strategies and common commitment to BC. Some of these organisations were initiated by SASO; in other cases, SASO had played a key role in their formation and development. Collectively, these organisations and SASO represented the core of the BCM. The prime example of an organisation initiated by SASO was the BPC. In April 1971 SASO convened a meeting of some church groups and an education organisation to discuss co-ordination of activities. Two further meetings, during which the number and range of organisations grew to cover the welfare, sport and youth fields, brought participants to the choice of forming an umbrella national cultural or political organisation. Some SASO members favoured the formation of a political organisation; others, including Biko, preferred a cultural organisation on the grounds that more time was required for activities related to psychological liberation (Buthelezi, 1991:125).

Those favouring a political organisation carried the day, and in 1972 BPC was formally launched. Its aims included the liberation of blacks from "physical and psychological oppression", and they were to "formulate, apply and implement the principles and philosophies of Black Conscious-ness and Black Communalism" (Hirson, 1979:83). BPC sought to establish a countrywide network of branches and sign up a million members in three years. However, few of its organisational or political objectives were achieved and, according to Buthelezi, BPC "continued to operate in the shadow of the more highly organised SASO and relied on SASO for both resources and political direction" (*ibid.*:126).

As a result of a decision at the 1972 GSC, SASO also played a key role in promoting and establishing a number of local and regional youth organisations and in running leadership training seminars for youth (SASO, 1972b:16). The following year, at a joint SASO and BPC seminar for regional youth organisations, the National Youth Organisation (NAYO) was formed. While not directly involved in the formation of various local and regional student organisations, SASO undoubtedly created the political climate for the emergence of these organisations, maintained relations with them and also sought to link them into a single national formation (SASO, 1973d:9). By 1973, however, there was a move towards handing over various support activities for youth to the black community programmes (BCPs) which had been formed in 1971. SASO had close relations with BCPs, and provided political direction and advice around projects and person-power for the BCPs' initiatives, like the journal *Black Review*.

Worker organisation

Not all initiatives to draw new social groups into the BC fold and expand the base of the BCMs were successful. In 1971 a project called "EDUPLOY" – Education by Employment – was launched. The idea was to put students into employment to experience working conditions so that they could better advise workers around their problems. A year later, a decision was taken to establish a Black Workers Council as a co-ordinating body to unite black workers and serve their needs and aspirations, to "conscientise them about their role" and to "run clinics for leadership" (SASO, 1972b:17). The initiative arose out of a recognition that "black workers are a massive force", that existing legislation and repression had served to circumscribe "effective bargaining by black workers", and from a criticism of current trade unionism which was seen as seeking to produce "a contented worker" (ibid.). To give effect to this decision, the Black Workers' Project (BWP) was founded as a joint initiative with the BCPs, and full-time organisers were appointed.

Poor planning was blamed for the failure to implement EDUPLOY during the 1971-72 summer vacation. Thereafter, there was a complaint that there was a lack of participation by students, and by 1974 EDUPLOY was considered to be a "closed book", due to poor student response (SASO, 1973f:15; 1974c). Despite widespread worker strikes during 1973, the BWP also failed to take-off. The pre-emption of the Black Workers Council by the launch of the Black and Allied Workers Union (BAWU) by a BC notable, a lack of experience and state repression all contributed to the BWP's lack of progress. However, the fact that BAWU itself made little headway among black workers suggests that the philosophical themes and intellectual approach of BC failed to attract workers. Meetings were held between BAWU and the the BWP to look at collaboration, but these did little to enhance worker organisation.

Political mobilisation and struggle

One effective way in which SASO mobilised students and non-students was through its publications that were disseminated on campuses and beyond. Another mode of mobilisation was through mass meetings, demonstrations and protest marches on campuses, and public rallies in the cities and black townships, often hosted jointly with the BPC, to commemorate particular events and focus on select issues. "SASO days", which branches were expected to organise, included 21 March, termed "Heroes Day", in memory of the shooting of anti-pass demonstrators at Sharpeville; 10 May, which was billed as "SASO Day" to celebrate the establishment of SASO; and August 17, which was meant to be for "mourning ... assaults on the Black man's dignity" (SASO, 1972a:8).

Other mobilisations were triggered by events such as the killing of Tiro, a leading SASO activist in exile in Botswana, by a parcel bomb, the shooting of workers at Carltonville in 1973, and the detention and banning of SASO and other BC leaders. At UNIZUL, there were meetings and demonstrations in 1976 at the award of an honorary doctorate to Buthelezi (Brooks and Brickhill, 1980:130). Meetings were usually advertised through the regular SASO publications, commercial media, as well as special posters and pamphlets, and featured SASO and BPC's leaders and other BC notables.

The only national political campaign organised by SASO involved the "Viva FRELIMO" rallies, which it organised jointly with the BPCs in 1974, to celebrate FRELIMO's ascension to power in Mozambique, and Mozambican independence. The campaign propelled SASO into head-long confrontation with the state. Twenty four hours prior to the rallies being held, the state banned all BPC-SASO gatherings to celebrate Mozambican independence. In Durban, a combination of the late notification, and defiance, of the banning, resulted in a large crowd congregating for the rally. At UNIN, since the celebration was organised by the SRC, it was understood to be exempt from the ban which referred to the SASO-BPC meetings. In any event, both in Durban and at UNIN, police intervened, with a number of people being injured and arrested. The arrests at UNIN were to result in a class boycott, and a protest march to, and picket of, a nearby police station. Thereafter, police raided the offices of SASO and BPC and arrested numerous officials. Following on this, a number of BC activists were charged under the Terrorism Act Number 83 of 1967 and after a two-year trial for "endangering the maintenance of law and order", six BC leaders, including three SASO national executive members, were jailed.

State Repression and the Decline and Demise of SASO

Initially, SASO was viewed favourably by the state and it was hoped that, because of its rejection of multiracial organisation, it could be persuaded to accept separate development. This attitude provided SASO with the space to operate on the campuses and root itself among students. However, the increasingly public attack by SASO of apartheid, bantustans and segregated education, and especially its leadership of the mass student protests during 1972 ended any hopes that the state may have entertained about SASO as a potentially compliant and pro-separate development organisation.

In 1972, two SASO members were served with banning orders (SASO, 1972b:35). Thereafter, in March 1973, the SASO president, general secretary, permanent organiser and editor of publications, and three other leading members, including Biko, were served with five-year banning orders by the government. The 1973 GSC elected a new leadership. However, during the following six months, nine more leading officials were banned. The banning orders, which restricted the SASO leaders to their hometowns, had the effect of dispersing them all over the country. By mid-1975, 29 leading officials of SASO had been banned (BCP, 1975:113). During 1975-76, the entire SASO national executive was detained at one point or another, the same fate being experienced by the 1976-77 national executive members. Throughout the 1973 to 1977 period, numerous SASO activists were forced into exile to escape repression.

From 1972 onwards, SASO was also under continuous attack from campus administrations. During 1972, SASO was banned at UWC and UDW, and suspended at UNIN on the grounds of being responsible for the mass student protests. At UFH the administration precluded the SASO branch from using its funds for affiliation to SASO. The reasoning of the UFH rector was that

[u]nder normal circumstances I feel this part of the allocation may be used to pay affiliation fees. However, while SASO could have wonderful work at University level on the black campuses, in my opinion they have failed miserably. Its present leaders have by far overstepped the limits of tolerance (quoted in SASO, 1973f:12).

In 1973 the organisation was banned at UFH, and in 1975 at UNIN. At UNIZUL there were various initiatives to undermine SASO and frighten students away from the organisation. However, although formally banned at many institutions and some branches became defunct or moribund, SASO continued to operate through other organisations and the locals.

The bannings, detentions, arrests and trial and flight of members into exile had numerous effects on SASO. First, as a consequence of state repression early 1973 represented the peak of SASO's membership and organisation and thereafter SASO went into a decline, from which it was not able to fully recover. At the fourth GSC in July 1973 the acting president complained that "activity at branch and local level has left much to be desired. Volunteers for our physical projects have not been coming forward" (SASO, 1973g:5). Almost a year later, in May 1974, the permanent organiser stated

[w]hereas in the past we have progressed very fast and with lesser difficulties the year 1974 has presented us with challenges and even threatened our continued existence. Both in terms of membership and leadership our resources have waned terribly (SASO, 1974b).

This admission came after the special GSC in January 1974 to replace banned leaders had mandated the permanent organiser to concentrate on re-establishing branches at various institutions.

At the same time, however, the permanent organiser was requested to discourage central affiliation through SRCs (SASO, 1974a:2-3). With a sharpening of the conflict between SASO and the state, student leaders appear to have become impatient with what they termed "passengers" – students who were members of SASO by virtue of central affiliation through SRCs. The feeling was that branches provided a base of more committed members. Moreover,

[c]entre affiliation has the one disadvantage that many things may not get done because students mandate is lacking. In terms of propaganda it is all very well to boast of 20,000 students whereas there are 20 followers. Therefore, it is high time we become realistic and fight with our real members (SASO, 1974c:6).

SASO was then proclaimed to be an organisation that was "no more a membership-conscious organisation but a more expansion-conscious organisation, in that we shall not count people in terms of numbers but in terms of work"(ibid.:4).

However, it seems that the repressive measures of the state and campus administrations also began to deter students from being active in SASO. During a tour of campuses in early 1974, the SASO president found that, even at an institution like UNMS, there was "difficulty in harnessing the students' co-operation" (SASO, 1974b:1). The UNMS SRC president's own opinion was that the UNMS "student populace had been presenting a false image of itself during the past years and that this had now become difficult to circumvent" (ibid.). The reference to "false image" hints at the frustration that probably began to be felt by some activists. While the conditions of repression were interpreted by activists as requiring more committed and greater student activism, the repression, of course, also raised the stakes of participation and held back student involvement in SASO. This, coupled with the emphasis on quality of membership rather than quantity, meant that after 1973 SASO began to become a smaller, more selective and exclusive organisation.

A second effect of the repression was the lack of experienced and competent leadership cadres. The SASO permanent organiser's complaint at the waning of "leadership resources" was noted earlier. The problem of lack of leadership, and its effect, was confirmed by a representative of the Transvaal SASO locals.

One snag with these branches is that people who have no clear conception and understanding of the struggle are being chosen into positions of leadership and thus contributing to the general lethargy of members (SASO, 1974b).

The problem was said to exist not only at the level of branches: the SASO head office, too, was accused of displaying a lack of direction and initiative and there was a call for leadership training (ibid.). The focus of a SASO formation school in May 1974 was, however, on youth (SASO, 1974c), and while a regional formation school in late 1974 was devoted to political education, and some branches used certain commemoration days for leadership seminars, there is little evidence of any major initiative around leadership training.

Third, the crisis in the organisation and the removal of important leadership figures appears to have contributed to discipline problems. A SASO official claimed with respect to a seminar on strategy held in April 1973 that

[i]t was not as fulfilling owing to certain things that need not be repeated anywhere. There was singular lack of self-discipline and motivation from a number of participants (SASO, 1973f:18).

Some branches complained of "idlers" who frequented SASO offices and used organisational resources such as telephones without becoming formal members or participating in SASO activities. As a result, in 1974 a resolution was adopted to draw up a code of ethics that would be binding on SASO members (SASO, 1974a:4).

Fourth, the government declaration of SASO as an "affected" organisation under the Affected Organisation's Act Number 31 of 1974 meant that SASO could no longer receive funds from overseas sources. At the same time, funds were increasingly having to be diverted towards the support of banned officials, families of detainees and for court trials. As a result, SASO came under severe financial pressures which hampered its activities and the running of the organisation.

Fifth, as a combined effect of the removal of leading officials, financial pressures and the harassment of SASO's printers by the security police, SASO publications began to be produced only intermittently. In mid-1973 it was reported that the circulation of the *SASO Newsletter* had not risen above 4 000 copies, and it is likely that this represented its peak (SASO, 1973f:21). A year later it was stated that the "least said about our publications department would be the best thing" (SASO, 1974c:21). The *SASO Newsletter* was not produced for almost two years between mid-1973 and mid-1975, and after a brief revival, disappeared after early 1976. Despite good sales being reported for publications that introduced students to SASO, these also no longer appeared, and were said to be one of the reasons for SASO's membership problems. The inability to produce publications deprived SASO of a crucial instrument of ideological and organisational diffusion.

According to a journalist who observed the rise and demise of SASO, "from 1973 to its banning in October 1977 SASO went through one crisis after another as it battled to survive in the face of counter-action by the Government" (Laurence, 1979:61) Laurence also writes that "by mid-1974 SASO began to take up a defiant and even provocative stand towards the authorities, in spite of the battering it had taken the previous year" (*ibid.*), and suggests that continuous repression and harassment of SASO, as well as the killing of Tiro by a parcel-bomb in early 1974, "helped to produce a reckless, almost desperado anger" (*ibid.*). The FRELIMO rallies are then interpreted by Laurence as representing a trial of strength between the SASO-BPC and the state.

Certainly, state repression appears to have seriously hamstrung SASO. By mid-1974, one SASO official even stated, "I am sure that some organisations think we are no more. We are actively campaigning to crush that image. SASO is and will be for a long time to come" (SASO, 1974b). Yet, interestingly, key officials blamed SASO's membership, infrastructure and organisational problems principally on internal weaknesses rather than repression. For example, for Myeza, the underlying problem was

an inherent tendency of exclusiveness among the SASO members which develops to the formation of what could be called cliques. This gives the impression that SASO belongs to a chosen few and is therefore "underground". This deters potential SASO members terribly (SASO, 1974b:3).

It was also alleged that SASO activists were tending to "to compromise on their principles and adopt a defensive role" which limited the spread of BC ideas and activities (ibid.). A third problem was said to be leadership: "Campus leadership leaves much to be desired and the leadership training must be intensified greatly" (ibid.). Finally, it was suggested that a lack of organisational activities meant that new students were poorly informed about SASO.

The attribution of all SASO's organisational weaknesses to internal subjective factors with no consideration of the effects of changed objective conditions, and the concomitant prescription of deeper commitment, a redoubling of activist effort, more open organisational activity and greater leadership training is voluntarist in the extreme. Indeed, I will argue later that SASO was characterised by a distinct voluntarism and a tendency to underestimate the ruthlessness of the apartheid state, and it is perhaps to this that Laurence refers to when he speaks of a "reckless anger" on the part of SASO.

Yet, it was probably only such a voluntarist stance that enabled SASO to survive until its banning in October 1977. After 1973, there was some revitalisation in particular areas of the organisation. During 1974 branches at UWC and UNIN were revived – at the latter the SASO branch president also captured the SRC presidency (SASO, 1974c:5). Furthermore, during 1975 there was also a revival of the publication of the *SASO*

Newsletter, and a *SASO Bulletin* was published in mid-1977. In general, SASO continued to have a presence, in one form or another, on most black campuses. Notwithstanding state repression, SASO GSCs also continued to be held. The sheer commitment, bravery, courage and fighting spirit of numerous student activists meant that SASO survived as an organisation and never totally collapsed.

Still, after 1973 the decline in membership and organisation was real and never completely reversed. The intense and continuous repression, the arrests of leading officials in the aftermath of the pro-FRELIMO rallies, the long and debilitating court trial and imprisonment of key officials all meant that on the eve of the 1976-77 Soweto uprising SASO was in a severely weakened state. As a result, as far as the uprising is concerned, apart from the roles played by individual members and the initiatives of branches on some campuses, as a national organisation SASO was not much in evidence and its contribution to the trajectory and course of the actual uprising was minimal.

5

The Character, Role and Significance of SASO

I n this chapter I now interpret the character, role and significance of
SASO. To this end, I draw on the analysis of the previous two
chapters, the chapters that analysed conditions in the political and
higher education spheres during SASO's existence, as well as the
conceptual framework elaborated in Chapter 1. Moreover, I also draw on
the key literature that analyses in some detail SASO or, more generally,
the Black Consciousness (BC) movement of the 1968 to 1977 period.[5.1]

Such literature is limited. Indeed, only four examples can be cited: a
chapter of Gerhart's *Black Power in South Africa* (1978); Hirson's *Year of
Fire, Year of Ash* (1979), which is primarily concerned with the 1976
Soweto uprising; the final section of Nolutshungu's *Changing South Africa:
Political Considerations* (1982), and Fatton's *Black Consciousness in South
Africa: The Dialectics of Ideological Resistance to White Supremacy* (1986).
Other literature advances arguments around SASO and the BC movement
in the context of more general analyses of black politics (Lodge, 1983),
enquiries into the post-1976 political terrain and resistance (Price, 1991;
Marx, 1992), analyses of the Soweto uprising (Brooks and Brickhill, 1980),
investigations of one or other aspect of BC (Pityana, *et al.*, 1991) and
studies of particular political themes such as the "national question" (No
Sizwe, 1979). Since some of this literature provides certain useful insights
and advances interesting views about SASO, I also draw on it.

Of the four key investigations of SASO and the BC movement, those
of Nolutshungu, Gerhart and Fatton assess SASO in generally positive
terms, and only Hirson's tends towards a strongly negative interpretation.

As will be noted, I largely agree with both the framework of analysis employed by Nolutshungu and his assessment of SASO's character, role and significance. Concomitantly, I strongly disagree with Hirson's interpretation of SASO. Since evaluations are conditioned by frameworks of assumptions and/or a particular mode of analysis, as part of my disagreement with Hirson I also critique the "problematic" that he employs for interpreting SASO.

Character of SASO

According to Nolutshungu, "SASO ... was not a political party, had no well-defined ideology, programme of action or code of internal discipline ... It was primarily a students' organisation" (1982:149, 193). It was "led by intellectual, "middle-class" youth, and spoke to people very like themselves, most of the time, and ... had only limited and intermittent organisational contact with workers" (Nolutshungu, 1982:161). However, although essentially composed of university students and not a "political party", SASO attempted to transform prevailing social relations in the education and political spheres and its goals were clearly political. Thus, using Burawoy's definition of politics, it is best understood as a student *political* organisation.

Gerhart locates SASO within the "school of African nationalist thought in South Africa" which "emphasised racially exclusive strategies for the overthrow of white domination" (1978:3). Its precursors are considered to be the "Africanist" factions within the ANC during the 1940s and 1950s and the Pan Africanist Congress (PAC). She recognises that an important difference between SASO and the Africanists, however, was that SASO did not exclude Indians and Coloureds but defined them as part of the oppressed and, thus, as also "black".

Fatton argues that SASO reflected a rupture with liberalism and white values and norms. It also signalled the emergence of a new philosophy, Black Consciousness, which embodied four key elements: an ideology capable of ending mental subordination to white values; a critique of liberalism which included an attack on its cultural, moral and other norms; the definition of all blacks as oppressed; and black solidarity as the basis of ending oppression. For Fatton, the doctrine of BC was a seminal contribution of SASO because political struggle requires not only organisation, but also the formulation and diffusion of an ideology to displace that of the ruling class. SASO's virtue was to give considerable attention to consciousness, and it understood that " ... every revolution has been preceded by an intense labour of social criticism, of cultural penetration and diffusion" (Gramsci, cited by Fatton, 1986:61).

SASO "inherited from ASA and ASUSA a sense of the essential unity of the black student movement with the cause of national liberation in general" (Brooks and Brickhill, 1980:73). However, unlike ASA and ASUSA, SASO was not the student wing of the ANC, PAC or any political organisation. It was, politically and organisationally, an independent national student political formation. Any alignment with the banned liberation movements would, of course, have been the death-knell of SASO. However, the avoidance of the political partisanship associated with ASA and ASUSA related essentially to the desire to be inclusive of the vast majority of black students. Biko had sought that "differences of approach should not cloud the issue" (1987:7) and thus an organisational culture was created that enabled different political loyalties to co-exist, but also be relatively submerged, within SASO.

If one innovative feature of SASO was the creation of an inclusive political culture, another was its organisational form and strategy. With respect to this there had been the important questions of whether a commitment to a future non-racial society necessarily entailed conducting the struggle through non-racial organisation and structured contact with white or multiracial organisations and, second, whether organisational composition and strategy should be determined entirely by principles and goals or also by structural and political conditions. The view of SASO's founders was that the different lived experiences of black and white students generated very different, and even contradictory, interests. Moreover, white leadership and organisational domination of multiracial organisations was seen as an obstacle to the active and meaningful participation of blacks in the liberation struggle. These realities then dictated the need for exclusive black organisation and, by severing the ostensibly indissoluble link between goals and strategy, SASO set an important example for the generation of student organisations that were to follow. Of course, it does not follow that exclusive black organisation logically entails a ban on all structured contact with white or multiracial organisations. That it did in the case of SASO was the result of the conflation of multiracial and white organisation with liberal organisation, something that would be avoided by SANSCO.

One of the issues of especial concern to Nolutshungu is the political character of SASO. Did SASO essentially advance petit bourgeois interests in opposition to specifically worker interests? Put another way, did the quest for black solidarity and unity without an appreciation of the different and contradictory class interests among blacks in effect make SASO a petit bourgeois reformist organisation that served middle-class interests alone. Nolutshungu's view is that BC doctrine was "instrumental and secondary to the opposition it sought to mobilise – at the level of consciousness – against attempts to consolidate and "modernise" white racialist rule" (1982:193). What were crucial, ultimately, was not SASO's formal theses, policy statements and utterances, but what the doctrine of BC "made possible".

If the BC movement represented the interest of the "petit bourgeoisie as a whole in the reordering of the South African political system ... that in itself, and in context, was not contradictory to the interests of other classes of blacks" (Nolutshungu, 1982:196). Granted, the black population was not homogeneous and there were different social classes and class interests. However, it

> does not follow that the area of common opposition to the state form may not produce a struggle that is revolutionary – undermining the existing political and ideological supports of capitalism without being able to establish alternative ones ... (ibid.:198-199).

In South Africa this possibility was enhanced by the myriad economic and social disabilities experienced by the black petit bourgeoisie and the lack of political rights and oppression that it suffered in common with black workers. A struggle led by the black petit bourgeoisie against solely racial and national domination could also win rights and opportunities for the working-class and create the political space and conditions for the erosion of capitalism.

For Nolutshungu, nationalist movements can, in certain contexts and circumstances, be revolutionary. He advances the important argument that is not necessary to

142

decide whether black consciousness was revolutionary or not in a Marxist sense by reference to its organisation and doctrines, or the empirical characteristics of its leaders, in the first place. Far more decisive are the necessary implications of its objective political situation and practice; in short, the form of the political terrain and how it was bound to move on that terrain (Nolutshungu, 1982:199).

SASO "was a product of revolutionary circumstances which was itself driven to a profoundly subversive political role" (ibid.:201). It helped ignite, in the form of the Soweto uprising, a political conflagration that reshaped political relations in South Africa. In so doing, it hardly promoted purely middle-class interests at the expense of worker interests. Thus, " ... there cannot be much difficulty in recognising the black consciousness movement as having been revolutionary" (ibid.:200).

SASO's organisation of the pro-FRELIMO rallies and its support of the school-student demonstration that sparked the Soweto uprising illustrated the impact of changing circumstances. SASO generally did not favour ""demonstrations after the fact" which changed nothing" (ibid.:185). A speech in 1973 by the SASO president, Henry Isaacs, exemplified this position very well, if it also revealed the sheer idealism and illusions of some SASO leaders. Isaacs argued that the oppressive system in South Africa would "only be changed by a demonstration of solidarity and faith in ourselves as Blacks" (SASO 1973g:3-4). While justifiably sceptical of appeals to morality and deputations and petitions, he also asserted that "protests in such a society are meaningless" (ibid.). All that he was then able to offer was that "Our only hope lies in our solidarity and Black Consciousness is a strong foundation for this" (ibid.). SASO, however, organised the pro-FRELIMO rallies and supported the 1976 school student demonstration because "passions had been aroused among members, and the desire for action was widely and acutely felt" (Nolutshungu, 1982:185). Moreover, the banning of SASO leaders and pressure "from the state was a taunt and a goad to action" (ibid.). Thus, despite the idealism of leaders like Isaacs, SASO " ... showed in its own development a tendency towards social radicalism that reflected both the political and economic circumstances in which it arose" (ibid.:147).

Nolutshungu's characterisation of SASO as a *revolutionary nationalist* student political organisation would not find favour with Hirson (1979). He contends that, although SASO activists and black students were deeply angry and frustrated with the social system, "nonetheless their petit bourgeois aspirations coloured their entire outlook" (Hirson, 1979:284). He criticises the student activists because "they looked inwards to their own problems. They sought "awareness", "self-identity", "liberation from psychological oppression", and some mythical "black value-system" (*ibid.*). He is also critical of their failure to establish contact with workers and become involved in worker struggles, and alleges that "they were curiously insensitive to the broader struggles around them" (*ibid.*:283).

Hirson accuses SASO activists of "obscurantist" statements, "unreal" notions and "unrealistic" views in relation to political goals, strategy and conduct. He lambastes them for making people "dream dreams" without a realistic assessment of the strength of the state and of popular forces, without adequate preparation for struggle and defence in the face of repressive actions and for failing to comprehend the "logistics of the political struggle in South Africa" (*ibid.*:110-12). Finally, he criticises them for failing to give leadership to the school students during the Soweto uprising, for the "absence of organisation, ideology or strategy", for there being "no plans, no ideas on what should be done" (*ibid.*: 9). Hirson does acknowledge that SASO contributed to the political awakening of students and sections of the youth and to the mood that resulted in the Soweto uprising. He also recognises that "the young leaders of SASO ... were inexperienced" (*ibid.*). Nonetheless, his overall characterisation of SASO is that it was an essentially reformist organisation, and a purveyor of petit bourgeois politics based on a petit bourgeois ideology.[5.2] Moreover, not only was SASO not radical, but "... in all its outpourings, the Black Consciousness Movement was apolitical" (*ibid.*:297).[5.3]

Hirson confesses that his book "is by no means impartial", that he writes as one committed to the "South African revolution", and says his intention is to "help the forces of socialism and liberation" to realise a free South Africa (*ibid.*:2). Much as I identify with his commitments, I strongly disagree with his interpretation of SASO. His appraisal is, ultimately, the result of certain assumptions and a particular mode of analysis and thus it is important to engage with them.

First, although Hirson seemingly is aware that "race" is an important dimension of social relations in South Africa, his preoccupation with social class means that "race" is essentially subsumed under class, and racialism is treated simply as an epiphenomenon of class relations. The effect is that racialism is accorded little significance as an independent material reality and there is little appreciation of the way it may shape and structure the responses of dominated classes and groups.

SASO activists witnessed all around them white power, domination, and privilege, and the essential unity of whites of all classes in the defence of white supremacy, and concomitant black subordination and impoverishment, and fear, apathy, and resignation. Confronted by these experiences, it is understandable that they concluded that "race" was the primary line of cleavage and that they counterpoised black solidarity and unity in opposition to white power. If SASO activists attacked the white staff at higher education institutions, the white press and white liberals, these targets were defined by their lived experiences. Moreover, the ideological postulates of BC, black assertiveness and pride, and non-Eurocentrism were

an inevitable and historically progressive by-product of the anti-colonialist and anti-imperialist struggles of the 20th century. It is the revenge of the slave on the master and, for the present, it wants to negate whatever is associated with the master (No Sizwe, 1979:122).

The lived experience of apartheid was, however, not the only factor that structured the response of the SASO activists and, here, Hirson does not fully appreciate the historical conditions under which SASO arose and operated. The SASO activists were a generation, born largely in the decade after 1945, that was too young to have been involved in, or to have paid close attention to, the mass political struggles of the 1950s, the suppression of the liberation organisations and the harsh repression of the early 1960s. As Brooks and Brickhill put it, the activists of SASO

grew up largely immobilised, unsupported and uneducated by ongoing, day to day struggles of the sort which had previously carried the South African liberation movement into the vanguard of anti-colonialism and anti-imperialism (1980:69).

In conditions of strong repression of dissent and an extensive apartheid security apparatus, black youth seeking solutions to the obvious injustice of white supremacy would have been mostly counselled by their elders to leave politics well alone. Hence, the SASO activists also constituted "a generation which ... had to make its own way in the world" (Brooks and Brickhill, 1980:70).

This insight is confirmed by two SASO leaders. Mji refers to the BC period as one "in which there was a disconnection between the historical evolution of the struggle" (quoted in Frederikse, 1990:117). Lekota states:

I regard my days in SASO as my formative years, politically ... We were deprived of the wealth of the heritage of struggle which others who had gone before us had already amassed. We moved into this as virgins, completely (quoted in Frederikse, 1990:133).

Lekota is also candid about the inexperience and limitations of SASO activists and about SASO being an elementary school of politics. In the light of the above, Hirson is much too harsh in his scathing criticism of SASO, and especially in regard to its "failure to work out a strategy by means of which the apartheid system could be undermined and then destroyed" (Hirson, 1979:119). Implicit in Hirson's analysis is the belief that things could have been different. His expectations of SASO are, however, highly unrealistic and, especially in relation to the Soweto uprising, he demands of it, decimated as it was by repression, the kind of leadership that could only have been provided by mature, experienced and practised revolutionaries.

Hirson also claims that SASO activists "seemed to respond with the heart rather than the mind" (1979:9), while Frankel asserts that BC was characterised by "an emphasis on the primacy of experience which seems to make concrete rationalisation and expression not only unnecessary but positively untoward" (quoted in Kotze, 1975:79). Certainly, "lived experience" was important in shaping SASO activists – but to conclude, as Frankel seems to, that SASO was irrational or anti-intellectual is to fail to understand its real nature and the influence of historical conditions. If SASO cadres did tend to "respond with the heart", it was because they were isolated and had to make their "own way in the world". If they sensed which values, beliefs, relations and social behaviour they rejected, they were not necessarily able to "name", systematically comprehend, and draw connections between, these. If their

> ideas were seldom put forward in fully developed arguments they
> signified a groping by young students, often with inadequate
> equipment, for intellectual support for what they believed they felt
> and knew, ultimately — independently of theories (Nolutshungu,
> 1982:157).

Ultimately, SASO cadres had to fashion their views and conduct from what was available in terms of literature and ideas, and whatever their illusions and naiveté, at least the ideological and political battle against white supremacy had been joined.

Mji has made the point that "you must remember that our political development was not from a textbook: it was from participating in events that were happening at the time ..." (quoted in Frederikse, 1990:117-18). This leads to my third criticism of Hirson: that his approach to SASO's doctrine and strategy is rather static and pays little attention to unfolding processes and the overall path of their development. Hirson is aware that by the mid-1970s there began to be some questioning of a solely "race" based analysis of the South African social order. Early SASO leaders had refused to attach any importance to "class" and had rejected class analysis. This was not surprising since the "class analysis" that they had been exposed to treated race as an epiphenomenon of class. Now, however, under the influence of the revolutions in Mozambique and Angola and contact with the ANC, the saliency of class began to be posed, a Marxist-inspired critique of capitalism and imperialism began to emerge and political and organisational strategies also began to be called into question. These developments were nipped by the Soweto uprising and subsequent repression but not completely erased, and debates around these issues continued after the banning of SASO in October 1977.

At the same time, following contact with the exiled liberation movements, there was greater discussion around the issue of a transition from efforts around "psychological liberation" towards those of "physical liberation" and around the question of armed struggle. The point is that, *contra* Hirson, the character and identity of SASO and its role was not permanently settled or fixed by its doctrinal statements. It is also not at all evident that student struggles under SASO were about black students securing "positions of (comparative) affluence after graduation" (Hirson, 1979:69). SASO's ideological, political and strategic dispositions were not static, and throughout its existence SASO reflected a dynamism and openness to new ideas. Indeed, whatever its limitations, and there were many, the history of SASO shows a disposition towards developing ideologically, politically and organisationally in a more radical direction.[5.4]

Finally, Hirson appears to reserve the term "revolutionary" exclusively for formations adhering to Marxism, and committed to class analysis and the struggle for socialism. However, in a context where racial and national oppression nourished capitalism, it is incorrect to designate as "revolutionary" only organisations committed to socialism and to characterise nationalist formations like SASO as petit bourgeois and reformist. Nolutshungu correctly argues that while nationalist movements which challenge national and racial domination

are to be distinguished from class movements, they may and often do provide the medium in which class struggles can develop, and can, in their own right, severely weaken the ideological and political supports of the order of class exploitation (1982:147).

He adds that

[i]t is in this sense that a nationalist movement can be revolutionary in a Marxist sense, despite its lack of a revolutionary organisation or, even, ideology. It is revolutionary to the degree that the structures against which it struggles are essential to the survival of the order of class relations ... (ibid.:199).

Thus, even if "there was little that was specifically radical" (Hirson, 1979:109) in the ideas or projects of SASO, its character is not a question of just doctrine and organisation but also of its effects on the political terrain. What is important, following Poulantzas (1978), is the political position of SASO in the conjuncture rather than a reading off of its character from simply its class composition or policy statements (see Chapter 1). In these terms, as will be underlined by the consideration of its role and significance, there can be no doubt that SASO was, if nationalist, also a revolutionary formation.

Turning to the internal organisational character of SASO, within SASO there were informal modes of working, much was left to individual initiative, action and spontaneity was encouraged and considerable latitude was allowed for "individual expression and spontaneity" (Nolutshungu, 1982:151). Concomitantly, the leadership displayed a willingness to canvass ideas and views around important political, organisational and strategic issues with one another, and with other members and political figures. The boundaries of thought and action were "defined as much by a spontaneous community of outlook as by the written principles of SASO" (ibid.:173). The element of spontaneity shaped SASO's relation to the state in two differing ways. On the one hand, there was a refusal to consider the state as omnipotent and all vigilant and thus a unwillingness to accommodate to the "system", and indeed, an attitude of defiance towards everything associated with the state. On the other hand, spontaneity also meant being "less conscious of tactical and strategic subtleties and, therefore, also less conscious of security risks" (ibid.).

The features of spontaneity and defiance that characterised SASO deserve greater emphasis and comment. SASO was characterised by tremendous initiative and an almost uncompromising militancy. At a time when fear, apathy and resignation to white domination reigned, the SASO activists not only "believed that radical political activity could still be undertaken within the constraints of the legal and political structures of apartheid", but indeed pushed "to the limit the bounds of possibility ... in order to confront and undermine the system" (Pityana, 1991a:202). Using the limited political space provided by the black universities, the founders of SASO carved for themselves an organisational niche and formulated, elaborated, and diffused the doctrine of BC outward and upward towards black professionals and intellectuals, and downward towards black school students and youth. In a number of arenas – educational, cultural, political – "current and former SASO members were well to the fore in the years leading up to the 1976 uprising – energetic, creative and uninhibitedly militant" (Brooks and Brickhill, 1980:74). Not surprisingly, SASO was the indisputable organisational and intellectual vanguard of the BC movement.

However, considerably more than just spontaneity and initiative characterised SASO. Overall, it was also characterised by a distinct and strong voluntarism. This was manifested in SASO's tendency to "underestimate the power of the state and its willingness to use force ruthlessly to suppress opposition" (Nolutshungu, 1982:174). In the previous chapter I also noted the tendency of SASO leaders to underplay the impact of the repression and to blame membership and infrastructural weaknesses on purely subjective and internal factors. The strong voluntarism was, however, especially evident in relation to SASO's projects and community development initiatives, the vast majority of which arose during a one-year period between mid-1971 and mid-1972. A SASO publication triumphantly proclaimed that "for SASO the year 1972 must be regarded as the most productive and historic of her existence. It was in this year that many of her plans were put into effect" (SASO, 1973a:5). Community development initiatives are described as being "methodically brought into operation". Indeed, "so much progress was made" by community projects that "it became necessary for SASO to increase her staff". Moreover,

> Publications, Literacy and Community Development Programmes
> ensured that SASO was reaching out to the millennium of Black
> people. High school students, varsity students, social clubs,
> organisations, sport groups − all of them began to join the
> mainstream of Black endeavour and self-assertion (ibid.).

State repression from early 1973 onwards seriously undermined disrupted and impeded SASO's projects. The national executive, however, blamed internal subjective factors:

> We have as yet not "arrived" and to be able to attain greater
> heights we need to have a close look at ourselves and ask ourselves
> whether or not we are really committed to change ... So many of
> our projects do not come off because we do not apply ourselves
> wholeheartedly with determination and genuine resolve (SASO,
> 1973f:20).

Since this view was expressed after just the first state action against SASO, greater culpability could possibly be placed on subjective problems such as the lack of membership commitment and participation. Still, the central question is whether the alleged lack of "determination" "whole heartedness", and "resolve" on the part of SASO members is sufficient to explain why many of SASO's projects failed to take off or achieve much success. That is to say, apart from the real and "objective" problem of repression, were there other "subjective" problems that also accounted for the poor performance of many SASO initiatives?

A study of the minutes of the various SASO GSCs and other meetings, but especially the 1971 and 1972 GSCs, reveals that there was no shortage of ideas and, going by the language of the proposals, passion for projects and new initiatives. The practice was to adopt and acclaim all proposals. No doubt there was a deeply felt need for each and every project that SASO resolved to establish. Yet, and as indicator of its voluntarism, there appears to have been no concern with or appreciation of the sheer scale of financial, material and person-power resources that was required by some of the projects, such as literacy, the Home Education Scheme and the Free University Scheme, if they were to meet all the objectives defined for them.

This mode of operation is perfectly illustrated by a report from the Natal region tabled in mid-1974. The report first laments that conditions "left a dark cloud that was constantly threatening the existence of the organisation", but draws inspiration that "ours is the truth and the truth will always triumph"! It then mentions a decision taken by a recent Free University Seminar for the

> [e]stablishment of a Legal Aid Scheme to assist people who are victims of the nefarious influx control laws, pass laws and a host of other dehumanising laws. One Free university member has been assigned the task of seeing this Scheme off. With dedication and co-operation with the local attorneys, a scheme of this nature is bound to be a success (SASO, 1974b).

Not just ideas for projects, but projects themselves, emanated from all kinds of forums; and the triumph of truth and the success of a considerable undertaking was simply a matter of "dedication and co-operation"!

SASO recognised that the political mobilisation of black communities required different strategies and tactics from those who had enabled it to mobilise students so successfully. Community development projects were defined as the entry points for political work in black communities and were also a means of attempting to ensure that black students did not turn their backs on the oppressed communities from which they originated. However, the success of projects necessitated strong student participation. It is probable that SASO took confidence from the ease with which it mobilised black student support and considered that this would guarantee the success of its various projects. However, as Gerhart has commented,

"... recognising the problem of student detachment and prescribing the solution of grassroots involvement were not the same as actually achieving that solution in practice" (Gerhart, 1978:291).

Although 6 000 students were counted as SASO members in early 1973, only a small number made themselves available for community projects. Thus, SASO was obliged to conclude :

Very few field projects do attract the amount of man-power that is urgently needed ... Black students usually shun these projects and even those who do go there sometimes display an abject lack of urgency and proper motivation (SASO, 1973f:15).

It is certain that the vast majority of the 6 000 members were "supporters" and "sympathisers" who – while they identified with SASO, read its literature, and participated in campus meetings and actions – were unlikely to participate in SASO activities on any continuous and sustained basis. The community development projects were of the kind that required ongoing and sustained commitment and would, thus, have had to be serviced by SASO's core and deeply committed activists.

Such activists, however, were only numbered in the hundreds. They were responsible for maintaining the SASO infrastructure on campuses, its central organisation, and were increasingly the targets of state repression and counteraction on the part of campus authorities. The removal from circulation of key activists deprived SASO of a wealth of day to day, immediately on hand, political and organisational expertise and skills, which were not easily replaced. With all the commitment and will in the world, the solid core of SASO cadres would have found it impossible to service the myriad initiatives that were launched. There is also some evidence that certain members, while proclaiming that "We are tired of talking, we want action, baby, action!", had in mind militant political action rather than the kind provided by community development initiatives (SASO, 1974b).

Given that SASO's community development initiatives aroused little interest among the mass of students, it was unrealistic to expect the committed core of activists to shoulder every project and futile to accuse them, as the national executive committee does, of lack of "determination and genuine resolve" (SASO, 1973f:20). The fundamental problem was threefold. First, project after project was adopted willy-nilly without any attempt at prioritisation in relation to political objectives and strategy and resources. Second, SASO was completely unrealistic about its ability to successfully implement and realise the aims of some of its projects. Third, it also seriously underestimated what the projects would in practice entail. Thus, both in terms of actual practice and overall conception and strategy, the claim that "community development projects were methodically brought into operation" generally has to be regarded as far-fetched. Moreover, the suggestion that "progress" dictated the employment of staff, cannot be accepted as accurate for all projects. It is inconceivable that any progress could have been achieved around the aims set for literacy or some of the other community development activities without the employment of full-time staff. In any event the full-time staff were, on their own, to also prove inadequate.

The voluntarism that was an indelible feature of SASO arose from a number of sources. The SASO generation was not only angered by white prosperity and black deprivation, but also frustrated and impatient with black apathy and acquiescence. There was a strong feeling that something had to be done. They were especially scornful of the illusions fomented among blacks by white liberals lacking the political power to effect change. Freed from the counsel of white liberals, SASO activists were "much freer to express, with the daring of youth and inexperience, the native anarchy of dissent, the recklessness of the oppressed" (Nolut-shungu, 1982:175). The SASO generation had also not witnessed the harsh repression of the early 1960s and the suppression of the ANC and PAC. "Not having seen it, they could not anticipate its brutal re-enactment" (ibid.), and this meant that they were not in complete awe of the state. Moreover, "by defining state power as white power they subordinated its reality to ideology, making it too, subjective, and subjectively everything seemed possible" (ibid.:178). Finally, this was the first student generation that was subjected to Bantu education whose aim was to secure their acceptance of the status quo and their subordinate place in the apartheid social order. Yet, in this respect, Bantu education failed, and this seemed to instil in this generation a strong belief in them and hope.

For Biko, there had to "be some type of agitation. It doesn't matter if the agitation doesn't take a fully directed form immediately, or a fully supported form" (quoted in Gerhart, 1978:288-89). Action, rather than sophisticated theory and detailed social analysis of the kind sought by Hirson, was more urgent and important. In the political vacuum created by the banning of the ANC and PAC and the general quiet in the country, it was, understandably, difficult for the SASO activists to see from where else, apart from themselves, the lead for action could come. Without waiting for any exiled liberation movement to play its professed leadership role, or for the working class to take its position as the supposed vanguard of the South African struggle, SASO and students took it upon themselves to use the space provided by the black campuses to reactivate black political opposition as best they could.

The actions of SASO were also born more out of hope than despair. Hobsbawm has argued that in addition to an oppressive, exploitative and unjust society it is also the belief that "the relatively modest expectations of everyday life ... cannot be achieved without revolution" that turns individuals into revolutionaries (Hobsbawm, 1973:247). Certainly, the limited position within South African society to which black students could aspire was a revolutionising factor. However, Hobsbawm also adds that when all doors to social change are closed the tendency is not to batter in the doors, but first to explore other options. Only when these other options are seen as not viable, and there is the belief that the doors can indeed be battered open, will this more drastic approach be used. In other words, "becoming a revolutionary implies not only a measure of despair, but also some hope" (ibid.:248).

The argument that spontaneity and voluntarism characterised SASO is implicitly challenged by Gerhart who writes that, in SASO, the PAC's "exaggerated faith in the spontaneous revolutionary disposition of the masses was largely abandoned in favour of a more hard-headed emphasis on patient organisation" (1978:301). The lesson from the PAC's history "was clear: patience was more important than heroics" (ibid.:285). Gerhart's focus is largely on the early years of SASO (1968 to 1972) and on its ideology and political perspectives, and little attention is given to issues of organisation and to SASO's various projects and initiatives. Had she broadened her focus she might have changed or qualified the view that SASO was characterised by a "hard-headed emphasis on patient organisation".

Certainly, there was a strand within SASO and the BC movement, associated with Biko, that stressed careful, patient, and sustained work around the psychological liberation of people and the need to avoid unnecessary confrontations with the state. Indeed, a SASO editorial had asserted that it

is very important to rid ourselves of impatience which yields disillusionment in the face of lack of success. The road will be long and hard, the rewards few and sporadic (*SASO Newsletter*, June 1970).

Yet, after the 1972 student protests the stress on "patient organisation" was challenged by cadres who sought more militant, and potentially confrontational, action. The initial demand, at SASO's 1972 GSC, for more militant forms of actions was rejected by the majority of delegates. However, in the years to come, and especially as the state's response to SASO grew more repressive, the impatience with activities centred around "patient organisation" grew. One manifestation was the poor participation by members in community development projects; another was the organisation of the pro-FRELIMO rallies and support given to the 1976 demonstration that triggered the Soweto uprising.

Spontaneous initiatives can, of course, be followed by patient organisation. In SASO's case the reflex and almost frenzied approach to educationand community development projects and the lack of sober, meticulous, diligent and patient planning and organisation meant that spontaneity was in intractable tension with "patient organisation". As a result projects were mostly unsuccessful in achieving their immediate objectives and providing a platform for mass mobilisation and organisation. According to Mji,

in implementing ... projects, it was quite clear we were only reaching a few selected groups of people, and not in any systematic way. It was quite clear that we were not making any impact outside the student movement (quoted in Frederikse, 1990:117).

The priest, Smangaliso Mkhatshwa, echoed this: "SASO only reached the educated and sophisticated segment of the population. Through its projects it is now gradually moving towards the grassroots" (quoted in Hirson, 1979:107). Mkhatshwa was writing in 1975. By then, far from any accelerated thrust towards the grassroots, SASO projects were already in a weakened state. Thus, at the organisational level there was no significant and extensive move "towards the grassroots" or "reaching out to the millennium [sic] of Black people" as was claimed (SASO, 1973a:5).

The voluntarism of SASO, and the notion that commitment and will alone were sufficient to overcome all obstacles, straight-jacketed it into a "more of the same" approach. More importantly, it potentially also retarded the search for new organisational strategies and tactics for survival and optimum effectiveness under the post-1972 conditions of state repression. However, SASO's voluntarism also contributed to its survival and to the tenacity to its cadres. Although SASO activists were bloodied by their battles with the state and campus authorities, they continued to act with courage and bravery and defiance, and to maintain a militant and uncompromising attitude towards their antagonists. As Pityana puts it,

they refused to be defeated; instead they continued to live and work as fully as they dared, despite the legal constraints; testing, challenging ... Many of those who were banned were never idle. They generally defied the banning orders or continued the principle of testing the limits of possibility (1991a:206).

This indomitable spirit of courage and defiance enabled SASO, damaged and depleted, to survive without being totally destroyed – a remarkable achievement considering the repression that it suffered. It was this spirit that SASO contributed to the student and youth that confronted the police and army during the Soweto uprising. Finally, it was also this spirit that SASO activists carried into the exiled liberation organisations that they joined, and into the internal post-Soweto formations such as the United Democratic Front and the National Forum.

For all its initiative and innovative character, however, one field in which SASO displayed a distinct lack of these attributes was that of gender relations. During its existence, women university students constituted between 12% and 25% of total university students; at the teacher-training colleges, where SASO's organisational presence was insignificant, women represented the bulk of students. There is no evidence that SASO made any special efforts to mobilise women students, that there was any focus specifically on "women's issues" or that there was any conscious initiative to ensure that women students were represented at all levels of the organisation and in all activities. Only a very small number of women actively participated in SASO, and only one woman appears to have been elected to national office.

Moodley writes that

despite the designation of the black world as "communalistic" as opposed to the "individualistic" orientation of the white world, the sexual division of labour within the black Consciousness Movement closely resembled that of white society. Women were for the most part relegated to traditional women's domestic roles ... (Moodley, 1991:147).

Ramphele, as noted in the previous chapter, has confirmed that this was so and that women were only able to claim full participation as "honorary men". However, she also makes the important point that freeing women students from feelings of inferiority related to being black did provide a platform for their liberation as women (Ramphele, 1991b:217). This would have especially been the case for the small number of women who were active SASO members and participated in the formation schools and leadership-training seminars. Moreover, one effect of the sexist world of the male-dominated universities and SASO was that it made women who sought meaningful involvement in SASO become "tough, insistent, persistent" and "assertive" (*ibid.*:219).

No doubt, even had the inclinations of male SASO leaders and SASO as an organisation been otherwise, the sexist culture of the universities and society would have put a major brake on the full and equal participation of women within SASO. Structural factors would also have kept some women from joining and actively participating in SASO. Feminism was yet to influence South African student politics and would only become influential after the late 1970s. For all its voluntarism, when it came to attacking gender oppression SASO was very much a creature of its time. Thus, whatever else SASO may have been, it was also a predominantly male organisation with a discourse and language that was unabashedly male-centred.

Role of SASO

In the context of the political conditions of the late 1960s and early 1970s, the launch of SASO was an important and progressive step and the organisation performed a number of historically specific and valuable functions.

SASO was instrumental in re-kindling a new era of black political activism and mass popular resistance. Its formation ruptured the silence and despair that characterised the early and mid-1960s. It activated "sentiments and ideas" that responded "cognitively and operationally, in militant ways towards certain objects – in this case the state, its functionaries and the doctrines and structures of its legitimation" (Nolutshungu, 1982:148). By seceding from, deconstructing, and challenging multiracial and liberal politics SASO played a vital role in reconstructing and recreating black politics and political action. Once again, national and racial oppression was made the focus of struggle, the apartheid programme was challenged, and a forum was created for organised opposition to apartheid.

Through the doctrine of Black Consciousness, SASO attempted "to rebuild and recondition the mind of the oppressed in such a way that eventually they would be ready forcefully to demand what was rightfully theirs" (Gerhart, 1978: 286-87). Its essential focus was "consciousness", and through its activities it sought to develop the self-esteem, pride, confidence and solidarity of black students and the black oppressed and contribute to their "psychological liberation". This approach was shaped by the conjunctural conditions of the late 1960s and early 1970s, a period during which the apartheid regime seemed to be so firmly entrenched as to be immovable and black responses were a mixture of fear, apathy, resignation, defeat, sullen acquiescence and accommodation to separate development. In concentrating on "psychological liberation", SASO saw its role as complementing that of the ANC and PAC, whom it regarded as the authentic spokespersons of the people, and had no notion of competing with the exiled liberation movements. Other aspects of liberation, for example the "physical liberation" that was spoken about and which implied armed struggle, it sought to leave to the liberation movements even though most SASO leaders were not opposed to the armed struggle; and there was some contact with the liberation movements around this (Nolutshungu, 1982:160, 171-72, 179-85).

SASO also had no notion of incorporating non-students, or of itself becoming a political organisation with an orientation towards one or other liberation movement. It attempted to avoid being paralysed by ideological divisions of the kind that had weakened the black student body during the time of ASA and ASUSA and aimed to forge a broad unity of all the oppressed. To this end, outside of the education sphere, it played a key role in the launching of other anti-apartheid formations, such as the Black People's Convention, encouraged the formation of youth and cultural organisations, and lent support to the Black Community Programmes. Here too, it promoted black unity and solidarity as the basis for effective struggle against white power. SASO's role within the overall BC movement that it helped to create is well captured by Nolutshungu: "At the centre of the movement, giving leadership, was SASO" (Nolutshungu, 1982:149). However, there were limits to the extent to which SASO was prepared to submerge political differences in the quest for black unity. After initial relations with some of the ostensibly more progressive bantustan leaders, black organisations and individuals participating in separate development structures were condemned and attacked since there was a concern that fear and passivity could lead to black accommodation with separate development.

SASO provided black higher education students a political home and avenue for political activity outside the black political parties involved in separate development institutions. Many, like Masterpiece Gumede, were inducted into progressive politics through SASO. As Gumede says, "When we came to Ngoye we were immediately grabbed by SASO ... I only got into politics through the student movement at university" (quoted in Frederikse, 1990:110). By being an exclusively black organisation, SASO made it possible for black students to no longer stand "at the touchlines", and to "do things for themselves and all by themselves" (Biko, 1987:15). It helped to engender a culture of black pride and assertiveness. It provided political education and organisational training and the "experience of leadership, planning, strategising and mobilising ..." (Pityana, 1991b:255). With respect to its community development initiatives, Ramphele adds that there was

> success in empowering activists in its ranks at all levels. Most of these individuals attained total psychological liberation and realised the meaning of being active agents in history. The impact of this

success had a multiplier effect on the wider black community (1991a:173).

Thus, SASO members would take into post-Soweto popular organisations considerable political and organisations skills and expertise.

In a context where politics was generally regarded as the preserve of adults, SASO also constituted students as an independent political and organisational force. Beginning with SASO and whether palatable to adults and political organisations or not, organised students become a permanent and irrevocable feature of South African politics, and a vital sector of the national liberation struggle. Through its various projects and initiatives, meetings, statements and publications, SASO diffused ideas and a mood that aroused both anger and hope and a spirit of resistance among students. The diffusion of ideas and mood was given impetus by the student boycotts of 1972, which also contributed to school-student and youth political awakening and organisation. Even the court trial of 1975-76 was used

to restate the nationalist viewpoint, and [the accused] took every opportunity to symbolise their defiance of the state by singing freedom songs and raising clenched fists in the courtroom. Thus, instead of contributing to the suppression of Black Consciousness ideology, the trial, by giving the accused a continuous public platform through the press, merely disseminated that ideology even more widely, and held up to the youth once again a model of "rebel" courage (Gerhart, 1978:298-99).

Through its contribution to the Soweto uprising, and the subsequent flow of students and youth into exile, SASO also gave

to the ANC oxygen and new life, which the movement desperately needed — youth of the South African people, tempered in defiance in action (Mongane Wally Serote, cited by Pityana *et al.*, 1991:10).

Thus, in various ways, SASO mobilised opposition to white minority rule and contributed to interrupting the previously untrammelled reproduction of apartheid power and domination.

Significance of SASO

Within higher education, SASO began the tradition of the racial and ethnic campuses being sites of activism and struggle. The formation of

SASO gave a more political character and hue to the overall black higher education student movement. Prior to SASO, students tended to be elected to the SRC on a parochial or faculty loyalty basis. With the emergence of SASO the political affiliations, positions, abilities and experience of candidates became considerations for the electorate (Buthelezi, 1991:112). These considerations also influenced elections to positions within the student religious, cultural and sport organisations. SASO members were often also members of such student formations, contested elections to leadership positions within them, and/or sought to develop close relations with their officials. Of course, not all student organisations necessarily supported SASO or even sought political involvement. SASO, however, strongly impacted on the overall black higher education student movement, stood at its head, and generally provided its political direction.

SASO's mobilisation of students around campus conditions, the racial composition of staff and governance structures, and the powers of SRCs forced the state to establish various "commissions of enquiry" to investigate student grievances and demands. The recommendations of commissions tended to be double-edged. On the one hand, the "Africanisation" calls by SASO – for black rectors and black members of governance structures – tended to be easily incorporated without any significant change in power relations between students and the campus authorities. On the other hand, the recommendations sometimes contributed to the restructuring of the education terrain on campuses in a way that opened up new spaces for mobilisation and organisation.

SASO's call for black rectors was controversial, with Alexander, a leading black South African Marxist intellectual and activist, for one denouncing it as an "attempt to dignify sectarian institutions of education". He claims that this was to accept

the idea of working the administrative apparatus of apartheid. There is no difference between administering a "Coloured University" and administering a "Coloured Representative Council" (Alexander, 1991:250-51).

Certainly, SASO activists seem to have harboured some illusions about the difference that a black rector would make to an institution and about the willingness of the state to install as rectors the kind of black intellectuals that SASO probably had in mind. Nonetheless, the organisation did draw an important distinction between apartheid political and education institutions, and was unlikely to accept the suggestion that "there is no difference between administering a "coloured university" and administering a "coloured Representative Council". To the extent that black universities were viewed not only as arenas of struggle but also seen as the stakes of such struggles, SASO could have argued that it was both legitimate and strategic for it to advance demands around all aspects of an education institution.

Although SASO failed to organise concerted campaigns and struggles around relations in education to do with the curriculum, texts, and the learning-teaching process, its media did attempt to expose the academic inadequacies of black institutions and seek to encourage a critical attitude towards the form and content of education. It is likely that at an intellectual level apartheid ideas were largely rejected. What must remain uncertain, however, was the extent to which students were able to penetrate, challenge and transcend the conservative and/or liberal social theories that would have been hegemonic among the academic staff of the black institutions.

For activists, participation in SASO and involvement in knowledge production, debates, formation schools and leadership-training seminars, media production, and other organisational activities, would have constituted a rich and powerful education experience. The "non-formal" and "informal" education and "on the job" training provided by organisations like SASO should not be underestimated. Indeed, for many activists, and especially those who were "organisation intellectuals", the knowledge and skills that they learned within SASO and through political involvement were likely to have been more stimulating, enriching, enlightening and rewarding than anything that their higher education provided.

Finally, through the black universities the apartheid state had sought to win black higher education students to the programme of separate development and to generate the intellectual, professional and administrative corps for the separate development bureaucracies. SASO, however, within and outside the black campuses, renewed and reinvigorated the historical opposition to bantustans that had begun in the 1950s. It denounced separate development, attacked bantustan leaders, and mobilised students around an ideology of a united and common South Africa. In doing this, SASO was generally successful in preventing the state from winning over black students and graduates, intellectually and politically, even though black graduates would have in some cases been obliged to seek employment in the separate development bureaucracies.

The political significance of SASO is a matter of some debate. Fatton's thesis is that ideology and the changing of consciousness is crucial in bringing about revolutionary change. Consequently, his consideration of SASO is shaped by its performance in

> effecting what Antonio Gramsci described as an intellectual and moral reform. This reform is a profound cultural transformation which changes the masses" conception of life, politics and economics. Accordingly, it ushers in a new social and moral vision and it restructures the role and place of the hitherto subordinate and dominant classes (Fatton, 1986:57).

Fatton argues that because of repressive conditions it was difficult for SASO to openly state its views and goals. He is, however, in no doubt that it was "animated by a revolutionary will and vision" (ibid.:126) and was tremendously successful in effecting an "intellectual and moral reform". BC helped blacks to develop their own sense of being and humanity, to move out of a state of apathy and passivity, and it eroded the ideological hegemony of the apartheid state. It also united Africans, Indians and coloureds and developed black solidarity. Its overall achievements were to liberate people from mental enslavement, to clarify the targets of ideological and political struggle and to prepare people for their historical role (ibid.). Moreover, through ideology, SASO contributed to the Soweto uprising and post-Soweto politics and was thus of considerable historical significance.

There is no denying some of the achievements that Fatton attributes to SASO. Yet, using his own yardstick, I am not convinced that such an enthusiastic and glowing appraisal of SASO is merited. A major problem is that Fatton attaches great weight to the doctrinal utterances of the BC movement and gives scant attention to its concrete initiatives and practices. As a consequence, he grossly overstates the extent to which the BC movement did produce a "cultural transformation" and generate a revolutionary consciousness at a mass level. He also tends to gives BC an ideological and political coherence which is not borne out by the empirical data, and which did not really exist. Finally, he especially overplays the extent to which there existed a class analysis and socialist commitment within the key BC organisations of the 1968 to 1977 period.

As Ramphele notes, the BC tendency to view blacks as a homogeneous group meant that there was a concomitant blindness to the stratification within black "communities" (1991a:171). "Such naiveté", she argues, "was in a sense an inevitable consequence of the very analysis underpinning the BC philosophy". As a result, SASO

failed to comprehend, analyse and tackle the contradictions resulting from internal differences amongst blacks that occurred along the lines of class, gender, age and geographic location. Instead, Black Consciousness exponents opted for the simplistic excommunication of those blacks who failed to act for the common good in solidarity with others – they were banished to the realm of "non-whites". A deeper examination of the limitation of their philosophical stand-point was not undertaken (ibid.:171-72).

If there were criticisms of the black bourgeoisie and merchants and traders and attacks on class privileges, this had its basis more in the aloofness of these groups from BC and their political acquiescence than in any rigorous class analysis (Nolutshungu, 1982:155).

Gerhart argues that SASO's significance was its work among "black university students – a significant percentage of the African intelligentsia and middle-class-to-be of the 1970s and beyond", which resulted in "a level of political education and ideological diffusion never before achieved by any black political organisation" (1978:270). Also of significance was SASO's impact on school students and youth. Gerhart acknowledges that

the BC movement was clearly more successful in communicating the subtler nuances of its message inside the walls of academic and religious institutions than beyond them in black society at large (ibid.: 295).

She argues that this should, however, not detract from its creation of a mood and stirring in black townships. The accomplishment of SASO and the BC movement was to bring about a "mental revolution among black youth", to hand over a new generation of young people that were "proud, self-reliant, determined"; and a major achievement was "an urban African population psychologically prepared for confrontation with white South Africa" (ibid.:2, 315). Like Fatton, Gerhart then regards SASO as making a positive contribution to the cause of black liberation in South Africa. Unlike Fatton, she correctly finds in SASO and the BC movement no Marxist or socialist ideological orientation, and is more realistic about the extent of its penetration beyond student, youth and certain middle-class circles.

For Nolutshungu, SASO, together with the BC movement, was important "because of the questions it posed about the nature of oppositional politics in South Africa and its relation to the nature of South African society" (1982:147-48). Beyond this, it was also significant "because of the forces of protest and rebellion it was to prove itself capable of unleashing", and "the real contribution of black consciousness to the revolt was in the demon it had roused: the defiant attitude among the youth in the face of police violence" (ibid.:185). Finally, SASO and the BC movement undermined the reproduction and restructuring of capitalism and apartheid and produced cadres to augment the ranks of those "committed to the revolutionary overthrow of the entire order of exploitation and domination" (ibid.:201).

Hirson, however, is sceptical about SASO's political significance. He recognises that "the establishment of a group with a political orientation was no mean feat in the 1970s in South Africa" (Hirson, 1979:292), and acknowledges that SASO "provided the leading cadres for the BPC, and helped create the atmosphere which led to the 1976 confrontation in Soweto" (ibid.:8). He also grants that "through their language, songs, meetings and writings" SASO and the BC movement "generated a corporate spirit", and that "in the words of Fanon ... they made "the people dream dreams'" (ibid.:292-93). However, seemingly reluctant to overstate SASO's achievement, Hirson immediately qualifies this state-ment. Instead, they were able to reach "groups of people who were seeking a political message and were already dreaming dreams" (ibid.). Moreover, although "intellectually the black university students took the cause of national liberation to be their goal ... in practice they tended to concentrate on their own problems on the campus" (ibid.:283) and, despite SASO's aspirations, "in the final analysis ... there was no campaigning and no direction. In place of real political activity, there were just words (*ibid.*:113). In Hirson's view, SASO lacked a theoretically coherent ideology, effective political strategy and extensive organisation, its influence was limited to "the elite circles the students frequented" and its significance was essentially to create the atmosphere for the Soweto uprising.

I reject this appraisal of SASO's significance. Nolutshungu usefully cautions against attaching too much importance to SASO's statements since they were "primarily instrumental than theoretical", and because BC "may have been important less for what it literally said that for what it made possible" (1982:162). Pityana, one of SASO's founders, makes a similar point: BC, "as such, was not a political philosophy or ideology but a strategy for action" (1991a:212). Still, he acknowledges that SASO and the BC movement "displayed a naiveté and innocence born out of an inadequate theoretical basis for [their] political activities" (*ibid.*:212). Similarly, Brooks and Brickhill have noted the following:

If one turns to the literature of the movement itself, one enters a world of eloquent and deeply felt rhetoric, full of spirit and boldness, unmistakably committed to black liberation. Yet one searches in vain for a definitive programme, for a clear strategy, or for discussion about methods of struggle (1980:76-77).

Certainly, there were many failings and BC did not make any real inroads, politically and organisationally, among urban, rural and bantustan workers and the unemployed. Still, there is a world of difference between pointing to the very real limitations of SASO and Hirson's claims that SASO defined itself out of the realm of struggle and was even "apolitical".

Here, it is useful to draw on Melucci's distinction between the "visible" and "latent" dimensions of collective action and their relationship. The danger of focusing only on the "visible" dimension of collective action – campaigns, mass action and physical engagements between organisations and the state – is that latent dimensions of collective action tend to be ignored. However, activities related to the latency phase of an organisation – recruitment and induction of members into the organisation or movement, political formation and training, building of inter-personal bonds of solidarity, diffusion of ideology and the influencing of new individuals and groups – are crucial. They are vital to the formation and development of the propensity, abilities and capacities for opposition and struggle, for sewing "the potential for resistance or opposition ... into the very fabric of daily life" (Melucci, 1989:70-71).

Lodge makes the important point that SASO members, supporters and sympathisers "were to become school teachers, priests and journalists", and that BC's "basic themes were taken up in the popular press, in township cultural events" and elsewhere (1983:324). Notwithstanding that these themes were unlikely to find a strong resonance among workers, he argues that even

if its influence was limited to the urban intelligentsia this would have guaranteed its imprint on almost any African political assertion of the time. Distilled to a basic set of catchphrases Black Consciousness percolated down to a much broader and socially amorphous group than African intellectuals (*ibid*.:325).

He also takes issue with the contentions of Hirson and Brooks and Brickhill that SASO and BC ideas had little impact on school students .The problem with their position is that "they tend to estimate the influence of ideas in terms of formal organisational structures and affiliations" (*ibid*.). In reality, the Johannesburg office of SASO was a meeting point for not only SASO activists but also school students and youth, and SASO members like Tiro taught for a period in Soweto (Buthelezi, 1991:115). Johnson, on the basis of interviews with secondary school student activists who were active in the Soweto uprising, has noted that

[i]n the absence of adult-led black resistance, Montsisi's generation seized upon the message of black student leaders at the universities. Impromptu political discussions took place in and out of the schools, the text for debate often being the SASO Bulletin, the Black Consciousness journal (1988:101).

Lewis, in his history of coloured politics, claims that BC spread rapidly among coloured youth and that during "the 1976 unrest, it proved to be the decisive mobilising ideology for united black action on the university and school campuses" (1987:278). Thus, given that black higher education students, teachers and priests "were an important reference group" for school students it also "would surely have been a little surprising if sentiments inspired from [BC] were not found in school children" (Lodge, 1983:332-33.).

An analysis of the "latent" dimension of SASO's collective action reveals, then, more clearly the real spread of SASO's influence and the connections it, and its individual members, had with township student and youth. If not the central medium of the Soweto uprising, SASO was one of the vital catalysts. The uprising, in turn, profoundly altered political relations in South Africa by exposing the vulnerability of white rule and stimulating the generalisation of resistance organisations and political struggle in later years. Given this, and *contra* Hirson, it is, as Lodge notes, "difficult to see how its achievement could have been more significant" (1983:336).

SASO was also of political significance in other ways. An important contribution was the definition of "black" to encompass not just Africans but also coloureds and Indians. Admittedly, "black" unity did not extend beyond professional, intellectual, and urban student and youth circles. SASO, however, both renewed and gave new form to the tradition of joint action initiated in the 1950s by organisations representing these national groups, and also set an example for post-Soweto resistance. This was no small achievement in a society in which Africans, coloureds and Indians lived in geographically segregated areas and where differences, real or otherwise, and prejudice hindered contact and unity. Moreover, there was also an important indirect consequence of the emergence of SASO as an exclusively black organisation. In time, NUSAS was to shift its policy to accept that the primary responsibility of students was to work for change in South Africa . Beyond this, more radical white students turned towards involvement in the fields of worker support and eventual worker organisation. These efforts were to be important in the emergence of the non-racial trade union movement during the late 1970s.

There has been an unfortunate silence around the important feature of the "cognitive praxis" and knowledge production of SASO intellectuals. Social relations in South Africa ensured that knowledge production was principally an activity engaged in by whites, and especially white males. There were very few black academics, and they published little. On the other hand, the liberation movements and organisations had long been key arenas of knowledge production by blacks. SASO was no exception and the knowledge production of its "organisation intellectuals", to paraphrase Eyerman and Jamison, the social movement theorists discussed in Chapter 1, was of great significance given that it helped spawn an entire social movement network in the form of BC. In the South African context it was, however, doubly significant for it was also knowledge production by blacks, and at that by young blacks whom Bantu education failed to render intellectually sterile.

In Chapter 3 I criticised the tendency to write on BC doctrine to give the impression that the doctrine emerged with SASO's launch, and to obscure the fact that it was actually formulated over a two-year period. I now want to argue, following Eyerman and Jamison, that this also obfuscates the "cognitive praxis" that produced BC as a doctrine. BC did not drop from heaven as a ready-made package. The world-view, goals, oppositional targets and strategies of SASO were socially constructed by its "organisation intellectuals" – pre-eminently Biko – but also Pityana and many others. The act of construction was, moreover, *contra* Hirson, not a one-off event but a process.

The views, beliefs, ideas, and objects of opposition of BC were produced by "organisation intellectuals" in historical time and space. They were generated through the mutual interaction of "organisation intellectuals", their personal and collective confrontation with NUSAS and other organisations, their encounter with the available "relevant" literature, their contacts with white liberals and radicals, and through acquaintance with blacks who supported different liberation movements. The ideas of the "organisation intellectuals" were embodied in speeches, in articles penned for conferences and workshops, and for the *SASO Newsletter* and other SASO publications, and in manifestos, declarations and resolutions. The knowledge production of the "organisation intellectuals" – the BC doctrine – gave SASO its distinct "cognitive identity", while organisational activities and SASO media ensured that the ideas constituting this identity were disseminated outwards onto the campuses and beyond.

Finally, the literature on SASO generally tends to view it in purely political and instrumental terms. As a result, the cultural, expressive, and symbolic moments of the organisation are ignored (Melucci, 1989). At the level of cultural innovation, with SASO and the BC movement came a number of developments all connected in some way to enhancing black pride, assertiveness and solidarity. One was the slogan "black is beautiful" and an attack on hair-straightening and skin-lightening cosmetics. Another was the "Afro" hairstyle and dress of a more African nature. Yet another was the clenched fist salute embodying opposition to white domination and black solidarity. There were also the various slogans and songs that emphasised black self-reliance, expressed defiance to the existing social order and voiced the hope of a better future. Finally, there was the cultural production inspired by BC such as poetry and drama – what Melucci calls "representation" – which was important in critiquing the social order and stirring black audiences to action.

Symbolically, SASO played a vital "prophetic" function in repudiating white liberal notions of black assimilation into the existing white and Eurocentric culture and in asserting that a future non-racial society would need to be the product of all national groups and to reflect the diversity of all cultures. In repudiating the term "non-white" and claiming they were "black", the SASO activists rejected being identified in the negative, sought to escape the categories and language of the dominant group and asserted their own identity and the right to "name" themselves. Their attempts to expound on the concept "black", or on "black values" or the concept of a "black university" may have been somewhat inchoate, and even incoherent. But, to their credit, they refused to accommodate to white conservative and liberal conceptions of the world, and of behaviour and conduct. And they pointed, as best as they could, to the possibility of radically different conceptions. Moreover, through their organisation they illustrated that black students need not depend on whites for their thinking and organisational activities. In summary, SASO both challenged the dominant culture and attempted to innovate intellectually and culturally.

Curiously, in the context of the authoritarian political order under which they existed, it is difficult to discover any references by SASO or its intellectuals to "democracy" and to the human and civil rights associated with democracy. It is possible that some intellectuals were scornful of these notions, and counterpoised them to freedom and liberation. Still, even if SASO did not talk in terms of democracy, its organisational culture and internal working was fundamentally democratic and, to a large degree, characterised by freedom of expression, the right to dissent, a consultative style of leadership, an adherence to rules and norms established by its constitution, regular elections, continuous turnover and rotation of leading officials and the avoidance of a leadership cult. On the one hand this mode of operation was shaped by the need to ensure that there was a rapid production of leadership for expanding the BC movement and withstanding state repression. On the other hand, and complementing its "prophetic" role, the organisational form was a conscious challenge to the dominant cultural codes and a "sign" or "message" for other organisations and institutions of an alternative and considerably more democratic form of organisational practice. However, the organisational form and the practices associated with it were not simply a means to an end; to paraphrase Melucci, they were not just "instrumental" for SASO's goals, but a goal in themselves.

Without doubt, a number of criticisms can be levelled against SASO and various weaknesses can be pointed to in its doctrine of BC, its analysis of the South African social formation, its political strategies, and in its organisation. There were also silences and omissions on its part. None of this is to be denied. However, there are good grounds for some of the criticisms of SASO to be tempered, and for a greater indulgence and understanding of the organisation's weaknesses and limitations. The evaluation of SASO on the basis of essentially its ideas and doctrines, and a mode of analysis that lacks sensitivity to historical conditions in South Africa, as carried out by Hirson, is simply inadequate for any balanced assessment of the organisation. Any rigorous appraisal of SASO must also take into account unfolding processes, and the latent dimensions of collective action. It must extend beyond the political to also incorporate the cultural and symbolic aspects, and not conceive all thought and practice in purely instrumental terms. Most crucially, and ultimately, any assessment of SASO must be not only in relation to its own internal characteristics, but also with reference to the South African social order, the particular historical conditions under which it operated, and its effects on those conditions.

In these terms, there can be no question about the revolutionary nationalist and highly innovative character of SASO. Despite being primarily a student organisation, forced by historical circumstances to play the leading political role in pre-Soweto South Africa, SASO took on the responsibility and rekindled black intellectual and political opposition to white domination. Through the "cognitive praxis" of its organisation intellectuals", it provided a framework for opposition to racial and national oppression. Through its "latent" activities it helped sew the "the potential for resistance or opposition ... into the very fabric of daily life" and there is no disputing the bravery and courage, and defiant and indomitable spirit, of its cadres, and the example this set for school students and youth. Finally, as a catalyst of the conflagration that was the Soweto uprising, and in also creating the conditions for the generalisation of political resistance and organisation post-Soweto, SASO ensured that it was of tremendous historical significance in the struggle for national liberation in South Africa.

Part 2
"The Freedom Charter is our beacon": The South African National Students' Congress, 1979 to 1990

6

Reform, Repression and Mass Resistance: South Africa, 1976/1977 to 1990

The uprising of 1976/1977 marked a watershed in political relations between the apartheid state and the dominated social groups. Henceforth, a combination of state restructuring of the previous terms of domination of the black population, economic recession, the political offensive of the nationally oppressed and the failure of the state to crush the extra-parliamentary mass opposition to apartheid would ensure that white minority rule, shaken, but still secure in 1976/1977, would begin to be negotiated out of existence during and after 1990.

This chapter analyses the political, socio-economic and higher education conditions of, first, the period post the Soweto uprising until the declaration of a countrywide state of emergency in June 1986 and, then, the harshly repressive period of the state of emergency until De Klerk's liberalisation measures of February 1990. The purpose is to highlight the terrain on which SANSCO moved and the conditions that shaped student mobilisation, organisation and activity. The focus is on all sectors of higher education – universities, technikons and teacher-training colleges – because from its inception SANSCO defined its constituency as all black higher students. Moreover, the concern is not just with black student representation in higher education but also with its gender composition. This is to lay the basis for an analysis of the representation of women in SANSCO and its relationship to women students.

"Organic Crisis" and the Demise of Apartheid, 1976/1977 to 1990

From Soweto to the state of emergency, 1976/1977 to 1986

After the mid-1970s, the apartheid state was mired in a profound crisis – conceptualised by Saul and Gelb as an "organic crisis" because of the existence of "incurable structural contradictions" of an ideological, political and economic nature (1986:11; 57). With respect to the economic dimension of the crisis two general points can be made. First, there was a crisis of capital accumulation which was related to crisis conditions in the world capitalist economy and South Africa's location therein: its reliance on the export of minerals, particularly gold and agricultural commodities, and dependence on imported capital goods and technology. Second, the racial structure of South African capitalism (narrow home consumer market, skill shortages and so on), specific government policies, and the political offensive of the dominated social classes and groups contributed to exacerbating the economic crisis.

During the 1980s, the economic crisis continued and deepened. Whatever indices are used – economic output, unemployment, foreign debt, balance of payments, inflation and bankruptcies – the picture was one of severe economic problems. Output in almost half of the industrial sectors declined by 30%. As a result thousands of workers were retrenched during the 1980s and this, coupled with a tremendous increase in compulsory liquidations and insolvencies, added to the level of unemployment. Unemployment, structural in nature but increased by the recession, reached over two million, with 25% of the potentially economically active Africans being unemployed.

Balance of payments problems and efforts to promote economic growth saw foreign debt increase from $ 16 billion in 1979 to $ 23,7 billion in late 1985, and from some 8,4% of GDP in 1980 to 26,8% of GDP in 1984. A concomitant sharp decrease in the value of the South African currency meant that there were problems with the repayment and servicing of foreign debt. With the international anti-apartheid movement intensifying the sanctions and disinvestment campaign, and foreign banks beginning to call in the greater part of South Africa's foreign debt, far-reaching measures had to be introduced to prevent the further collapse of an already ailing economy.

An additional feature of the South African economy during the 1980s was high rates of inflation. Already 14% in 1980, inflation spiralled to 20% in 1985. The adoption of monetarist policies by the government to check inflation intensified the recession. Not only did unemployment increase, but monetarist policies placed increasing burdens on black workers and the poor in general. Throughout the 1980s the cost of basic foods increased as subsidies were cut back. Living standards were further assaulted when a General Sales Tax (GST) was introduced on most commodities and reached 12% in 1985. To decrease government expenditure the funding of black local government was cut back, with the result that local officials attempted to increase revenues through increased rental and service charges. This conjuncture of retrenchments, rising unemployment, inflation, increased rentals and service charges, and increased transport costs all combined to financially squeeze black workers and the poor and created the conditions for the worker and popular mass struggles of the 1980s.

The political dimension of the organic crisis was even clearer. For my purposes, a detailed analysis of the political terrain is not necessary. Instead, I will confine myself to outlining some of the important developments within anti-apartheid politics and a number of key features of political resistance during the 1980s.

(1) The Soweto uprising and banning of SASO and other Black Consciousness (BC) organisations led anti-apartheid activists to debate the ideology, politics, strategy and tactics appropriate for the further prosecution of the anti-apartheid struggle. Ironically, the opportunity for leading political activists to debate political issues was unwittingly provided by their detention at prisons like Modder B in the Transvaal. According to Diliza Mji, a past president of SASO, "opposing views which had been developing within the [BC] organisations crystallised within the cells of Modder B" (AZASO National Newsletter, November 1983). This was to result in a major bifurcation, in terms of ideology, political orientation and strategy and tactics, within radical anti-apartheid forces between those oriented towards Black Consciousness, the Azanian Peoples' Organisation, the National Forum and the Azanian Manifesto,

and others supportive of the non-racial tradition of the ANC and Congress movement, the United Democratic Front and the Freedom Charter.

In May 1978 the Azanian Peoples Organisation (AZAPO) was established. AZAPO saw itself as a "bulwark against sectionalism by creating a united front" (SAIRR, 1980:50), and aimed to "conscientise and mobilise black workers through Black Consciousness" and to "expose the exploitative and oppressive apartheid system" (Davies et al., 1984: Vol. 2:308). According to Curtis Nkondo, the first president, the essential problem in South Africa was

> not necessarily a racial one but an economic one ... Words like race and colour have been used as an excuse to oppress and exploit the people ... We have to shift from the idea that race is the main issue. Race is used as an instrument of economic exploitation (Sisuly, 1979).

This thesis led to the formulation that "the worker is the vanguard of the organisation" (ibid.). The category "worker" was, however, not defined in classical Marxist terms. Rather, a

> worker is a Black man and no White man is a worker. Blacks are workers because they are voiceless, exploited with no opportunity for advancement, and do not own the means of production and distribution (ibid.).

While all whites were "part and parcel of the evil system, blacks are not", an exception was made for black bantustan leaders and collaborators who were classified as part of the "evil system" (ibid.).

These formulations were not dissimilar to the SASO categories of "black" and "non-white", though by incorporating the economic dimension they represented an attempt to generate a more rigorous analysis of South African realities. However, in terms of providing clear political direction they was bound to run into difficulties. Moreover, the affirmation of non-negotiation with state bodies and officials as a principle had serious implications for mass mobilisation around immediate issues and the potential to remove AZAPO from the terrain of local-level community politics and organisation building.

If AZAPO represented one of the "opposing views" crystallising within progressive opposition politics, the other "view" gravitated towards the kind of politics that was represented by the Natal Indian Congress (NIC). The NIC had been part of the South African Indian Congress which, in the 1950s, had been an affiliate of the Congress Alliance spearheaded by the ANC. Especially active in the NIC were a new generation of young activists who had cut their teeth on the student politics of the 1970s. Espousing a race-class analysis, they argued that South Africa was characterised by both national and racial oppression and class exploitation. Drawing on the traditions of the Congress movement, they called for mass mobilisation and mass organisation and for a non-racial multi-class alliance under working class leadership. The political manifesto advanced was the Congress movement's Freedom Charter, which had been adopted, at the Congress of the People in 1955. By 1979, the analytical framework and political and strategic goals and commitments of the NIC began to be shared by an increasing number of new organisations. The Congress of South African Students' (COSAS), formed in May 1979, was from its inception guided by this approach. So too was the South African Allied Workers Union (SAAWU) which coupled a commitment to non-racialism in practice, with an emphasis on worker-controlled trade unions and the leading role of the working class in the national liberation struggle. At the same time, local and regional-level community organisations orientated to mass mobilisation and struggle around immediate issues such as housing, rents, electricity, and transport began to emerge in various areas under the leadership of Congress movement activists.

During the late 1970s, the divide between the BC and Congress movements was not wide or rigid. Many individuals and organisations straddled the divide and only in later years would conflicts around principles and strategies cement and harden. However, during the 1980s the BC movement came to be considerably over-shadowed by the Congress movement as its member organisations mounted impressive political and popular campaigns and resistance. These included the Release Mandela campaign of 1980, the anti-Republic Day movement of early

1981, the anti-South African Indian Council campaign of late 1981, and various local and regional-level struggles around civic and education issues.

* (2) Crucially important, the mobilisations and struggles of the early 1980s around political, education, and civic issues were frequently translated into enduring organisation. Spurred on by the experience of struggles and facilitated by regionally-based community newspapers and local community newsletters which promoted grassroots mobilisation, education, and organisation, permanent local-level organisations in the form of civic, youth, students, women's, and progressive religious organisations began to mushroom. Increasingly, local organisations representing specific constituencies coalesced to form regional structures such as the United Women's Organisation in the Western Cape and the Port Elizabeth Youth Congress.

(3) During 1982-1983 the government introduced new constitutional proposals which sought to incorporate Indians and coloureds as junior partners in political decision-making. In addition, two Bills were produced which "proposed new measures to control and regulate the presence of Africans in cities" (Lodge, 1992:35), and the Black Local Authorities Act of 1982 was passed which "gave the highly unpopular and frequently corrupt township governments a range of new powers and responsibilities" (ibid.).

In order to protest and frustrate these new state initiatives, anti-apartheid organisations launched two national formations in 1983. One was the Congress-movement-oriented United Democratic Front (UDF), comprising over 500 decentralised, local and regional civic, youth, women's, political and religious anti-apartheid organisations, together with national student organisations and trade unions. The other was the smaller National Forum, a loose association of some 200 BC-oriented organisations and small left-wing groups. From 1983 onwards the UDF, as a popular, non-racial, multi-class alliance, was to be at the forefront of resistance to apartheid. UDF campaigns stimulated the formation of hundreds of new organisations, especially, and significantly, in the rural areas. Lodge captures well the character and significance of the UDF.

The formation of the United Democratic Front (UDF) in 1983 was a turning point in this shift in the balance of power between the South African government and the black opposition. The UDF inspired an insurrectionary movement that was without precedent in its geographical spread, in its combative militancy, in the burden it imposed on government resources, and in the degree to which it internationalised hostility toward apartheid. The movement that the UDF headed was profoundly popular, infused "from below" by the beliefs and emotions of "ordinary people". In contrast to earlier phases of black opposition, a class-conscious ideology was the essential motivating force among a large number of its rank-and-file activists. In this sense, it was a much more radical movement than any that had preceded it.

While at the moment of its birth the UDF undoubtedly borrowed from the traditions, symbols, iconography, and ideology of the ANC, it expressed them with greater force and resonance (1992:29-30).

(4) The 1980s saw the continued growth of powerful trade unions among black workers. The economic conditions coupled with the work of trade union activists provoked hundreds of work stoppages and strikes. This facilitated the unionisation of black workers and helped strengthen the progressive union movement. Two strikes, that of members of the Food and Canning Workers Union employed at the Fattis and Monis company in Cape Town, and that of the Ford workers in Port Elizabeth, were particularly significant. The former resulted in a fairly successful national consumer boycott of Fattis and Monis products, while both strikes generated strong support among other organised workers, black students, youth and township residents. The strikes and the worker-support campaigns built links between worker, student, youth and civic organisations, contributed to the growth and strengthening of organisations and ushered in a tradition of worker-student-community action and alliance. Also crucial during this period was the formation, in April 1979, of the Federation of South African Trade Unions (FOSATU) which linked together fourteen progressive trade unions.

During the early 1980s the policies of the unions towards participation in political campaigns differed. Some unions identified themselves as part of the Congress movement, drew explicit linkages between economic and political issues, and workplace and township-based struggles, and participated in various political and community campaigns. Others, after an initial period of participation in political campaigns, held back for strategic reasons, while the FOSATU unions refrained from any participation in political campaigns. Although many of the unions did not fully subscribe to the ideology and politics of the Congress movement, there were important areas of shared commitment and concern. Many of the unions endorsed non-racialism in practice and stressed, as a complement to township and education-based organisation, the building of strong workplace organisation under workers" control. The parallel, if uneven, development of the democratic union movement and the Congress movement was ultimately mutually reinforcing and at the same time the movements apart from the BC movement.

In any event, by the time of the township uprisings of 1984 in the Transvaal against rent increases and corrupt local government, even the FOSATU unions began to be involved in joint actions with student organisations and civic formations. By late 1985, the Congress-oriented unions, those that had held back political involvement for strategic reasons as well as the FOSATU unions, joined together to form the half-a-million-strong Congress of South African Trade Unions (COSATU). The alliance of COSATU and the UDF was to have a major impact on the direction and content of anti-apartheid politics.

(5) Lastly, if significant developments were taking place within internal radical opposition politics (as contrasted with external exile-politics), the ANC was not entirely incidental to this process. Invigorated by recruits from the uprising of 1976/1977, and subsequent struggles, the ANC began to develop "a strong clandestine organisation in the country" (Stadler, 1987:160). ANC members played an important role in the orientation of activists away from BC and in the formation of a number of internal mass organisations. From 1980 onwards, support for the ANC began to be openly expressed at mass public meetings, commemoration services, funerals, marches and demonstrations. Especially during the 1984-86 period when mass resistance reached insurrectionary proportions and a peak, support for the ANC was widely and openly expressed. ANC leaders in prison and in exile enjoyed considerable popularity, and the organisation could legitimately claim a mass following.

The "armed propaganda" activities of the ANC's military wing, Umkhonto we Sizwe (MK), in the form of attacks on military facilities and apartheid establishments also contributed to enhancing its image, especially among students and the youth. From 13 attacks in 1979, MK attacks increased to 136 in 1985, and 281 in 1989. (Lodge, 1992:178). After 1985 MK also sought to root itself more firmly within South Africa, to train and arm local people and to give leadership and content to the ANC call to render South Africa "ungovernable".

Having sketched some of the developments within radical opposition politics, I want to now identify some key features of political resistance during the 1980s.

1   Tom Lodge, writing in 1983, concluded as follows after a brief analysis of the post-1976 political developments:

> It should be evident that a qualitative transformation has taken place in African political life. The complex combination of social forces present in black resistance have succeeded in igniting a conflagration which no amount of repression will succeed in extinguishing (1983:356).

Given the developments that occurred after 1983, this statement is almost prophetic. Certainly a "qualitative transformation" did occur in opposition politics, as should be evident from the points made above, and as will be emphasised by the points below.

2   Since the mid-1970s, "the period of recuperation required before people returned to political struggles has shortened" (Stadler, 1987:1). Moreover,

> despite the massive scale of state repression, oppositional activities generated and maintained a momentum entirely at variance with the pattern exhibited during earlier periods of intense conflict (ibid.).

Indeed, for much of the 1980s, economic and social conditions and unpopular state initiatives and diverse forms and levels of increasingly combative and confident popular organisation combined to produce, as almost a permanent feature of the political terrain, myriad struggles distinguished by differing content, form, duration, geographical and institutional location and spread, and the involvement of differing constituencies. State repression in the form of detentions, banning, restrictions on individuals and organisations,

183

assassinations, declarations of partial and total states of emergency (1985 and 1986 to 1990) and naked violence proved unable to dampen resistance for any extended period or to destroy the mass base of the democratic movement.

3   Political opposition during the 1980s was not confined to the urban centres but extended, significantly, into rural towns and the bantustans. Particularly oppressive conditions in rural areas failed to prevent the development and spread of mass organisations and the radicalisation of entire communities, and throughout the mid-1980s remarkably strong and resilient organisations emerged in rural towns and villages of the Orange Free State, northern and eastern Transvaal, and eastern, northern and southern Cape. The formation of organisations in the bantustans and opposition to bantustan independence drew the bantustan regimes into the wider political conflict.

4   The focus of activism was the activation of popular grievances and mass mobilisation leading to mass organisation. Learning from the progressive trade unions, popular organisations emphasised demo-cratic participation, decision-making and control. Attempts were made to create structured and effective links and co-ordinated and concerted action between local-level student, teacher, civic, youth, women's, religious and other organisations and trade unions. Such initiatives sought to activate and implement rent strikes, consumer boycotts, stayaways and other forms of action and, during the 1984-86 period, to establish organs of popular power in those instances where local state bodies had collapsed in the face of popular opposition. Interlocking action, or what Price calls

> this insurrectionary process of catalysing, interacting and reinforcing forms of resistance emerged fully in the Transvaal during September-October 1984, and set a pattern which was to be repeated over and over again across South Africa in the subsequent twenty-two months (1991:195).

5   Constructive – if heated – debates, the formation of COSATU, and the political offensive of the mid-1980s contributed to a reduction in tensions between so-called "workerists" and "populists". Saul and

Gelb suggested in 1981 that the simultaneity within the anti-apartheid struggle of popular democratic and proletarian moments could result in these two moments being "complementary rather than contradictory, each drawing out the progressive potential of the other" (1986:241). Indeed, the 1980s revealed the complementary nature of popular democratic and proletarian politics; the two

tended to reinforce each other, the strength of popular democratic assertions helping further to politicise the trade unions ... the growing assertiveness of the working class helping further to deepen the saliency of class considerations and socialist preoccupations within the broader movement (Saul, 1986:241).

6   During the 1980s there was also a growth of anti-capitalist sentiment and increasing support – especially among workers, students and youth – for socialism. While an emphasis on the leading role of the working class in the South African national liberation struggle and a stress on the development of worker leadership within multi-class organisations was a common feature of many popular organisations, an explicit orientation towards some kind of socialist future became increasingly evident from the mid-1980s onwards. Moreover, the flags and symbols of the South African Communist Party (SACP) began to be openly displayed at political rallies, demonstrations and funerals of activists.

State strategy in the 1980s

An "organic crisis" is normally resolved either through social revolution from below or "formative action" on the part of the ruling class (Saul and Gelb, 1986:211). "Formative action" for the preservation of ruling class hegemony entails more than merely defensive initiatives and involves considerable economic, political and ideological restructuring. The attempts of a ruling class to resolve an organic crisis, its " ... incessant and persistent efforts ... form the terrain of the conjunctural and it is upon this terrain that the forces of opposition organise" (ibid.:57). Thus the conjuncture – the immediate terrain of struggle – is shaped not only by structural conditions, but also the various initiatives of capital and the state.

Although the apartheid state's restructuring had important implications for the form and content of opposition politics, it was less than fundamental in nature. Three broad aspects of the reform process can be identified. First, the reforms continued the old policy of divide and rule. A new constitutional structure, the tricameral parliament, which was racially divided and excluded Africans was to be the instrument for the incorporation (and co-option) of Indians and coloureds into the political process. With respect to Africans, the aim was to establish a divide along urban-rural lines. Urban residents were to be provided certain concessions – an end to job reservation, greater opportunities for education and training, long-term housing leases – and politically incorporated through local government structures. Those designated as rural were to be stripped of South African citizenship and incorporated into bantustan political processes.

Second, the division of the African population along geographical lines was to be supplemented by initiatives to promote class divisions, and an explicit effort was to be made to foster the development of an African petit bourgeoisie. Obstacles to training opportunities were to be removed, small businesses promoted and assisted, better housing built and petit discrimination eliminated. Considerable significance was attached to higher education in the creation of a black petit bourgeoisie. The aim was to produce a class of blacks who would have a stake in political stability and would "find their interests best served by an alliance with capitalism" (*Financial Mail*, quoted in Davies *et al.*, 1984: Vol. 1, 39). Finally, the right of black workers to democratic trade unions was recognised, although at the same time legislation sought, through the institutionalisation of unions, to have greater control over them and prevent their involvement in political issues.

These attempts to

remodel political institutions, increase economic and education opportunities for blacks, and institutionalise relations between capital and labour in order to generate some legitimacy for the social order (Stadler, 1987:161)

were double-edged. On the one hand, the reforms refined and reinforced controls in some areas and over certain categories of people, while concomitantly granting concessions to and attempting to co-opt others.

On the other hand, state restructuring was dictated not just by economic imperatives but also by the political resistance of the dominated classes and groups. If the reforms were "formative", they were nevertheless being undertaken in areas and on terrain where the authority and hegemony of capital and the state was already contested and challenged. Thus, the outcome of the "incessant and persistent efforts" would be determined by the balance of political forces at both the general level and within specific arenas which were the object of restructuring. That is to say, the ability of state reforms to resolve contradictions, and their success in "controlling, containing, diverting and redirecting the pressures from below" (*ibid.*:7-8) was by no means guaranteed. Given the gulf between the reform initiatives and the demands of the political opposition, state restructuring more often than not sharpened contradictions between the regime and the dominated classes and gave impetus to anti-regime political mobilisation. Indeed, as Lodge has written with respect to the economic recession and state restructuring of the 1980s, "the contradictions and tensions flowing from the interaction of these two forces helped to generate the black rebellion of the 1980s" (1992:30).

The post-Soweto period however was not simply characterised by state reforms. An important plank of the state's post-1976 "total strategy" was also repression of forces threatening white supremacy. Consequently, during this period there was an increasing centralisation and militarisation of the state, and a significant shift in power from the legislature to the executive, with tremendous power and authority located in the hands of the State President. Executive power revealed itself in the form of numerous cabinet committees, the State Security Council (SSC), and the National Security Management System (NSMS) with its regional joint management committees (JMCs) and local level mini-JMCs.

The state of emergency, 1986 to 1990

The SSC, NSMS and JMCs came to the fore during the mid-1980s as the government moved to systematically repress organisations and individuals deemed to be behind the popular insurrection. According to Price,

[u]nder conditions of widespread mass insurrection ... the commitment to heightened repression was folded into a broad and systematically conceived counterrevolutionary "security re-

gime" ... The SSC was the "brain" of the counterrevolutionary security regime, and its operational arms constituted the other basic elements of the NSMS ... The far-flung network of ... JMCs, each headed by a military or police officer, were the "line organisations" of the counterrevolution – they were to adapt counterrevolutionary doctrine to particular local conditions and integrate repressive, socio-economic, psychological and ideological policies "on the ground"(1991:252-253).

Under cover of a state of emergency declared in June 1986 and renewed annually until June 1990, areas of militant political opposition were occupied by the military, over 29 000 people were detained, 32 organisations, including the UDF, were, in February 1988, placed under restrictions that prohibited them from being involved in almost any activities, and numerous activists were arrested and charged with treason for establishing organs of popular power in townships. In addition, anti-apartheid organisations and activists were subjected to physical attack from state-sponsored vigilante groups that engaged in murder, assassinations and the torching of offices and homes.

If the repression succeeded in ending the insurrection of the mid-1980s and dampening overt opposition, it failed in its objectives of "winning the hearts and minds of people", addressing socio-economic problems confronting black communities and creating viable counter-organisations to those of the radical opposition. In any event, control over the opposition was less than complete. Workers in COSATU continued to strike around a range of issues and engage in stayaways, township residents continued to engage in rent strikes, consumer boycotts and to boycott local authority elections, and students continued to boycott classes around education-related demands. By 1989, despite the restrictions imposed on them the UDF and allied formations were once again spearheading mass campaigns and demonstrations.

The failure of reforms and repression, the continued vigour of political opposition and widespread support for anti-apartheid organisations and the liberation movements, and severe international isolation and little improvement in the economic situation all combined to provide the impetus for the South African government's announcement of 2 February

1990 which set into motion political negotiations for a non-racial democracy.

Black higher education: Expansion, reform and contradiction

Having outlined the conditions in the economic and political spheres which constituted the broader terrain of SANSCO's own initiatives, I want to now examine conditions within higher education and the processes that shaped this sector during the 1976/1977 to 1990 period. The discussion centres around the expansion of black higher education after 1976 in the context of the concerns of corporate capital and sections of the state around skills shortages and the contradictions between reformist initiatives and conditions within higher education institutions.

The economics and politics of school expansion

Between 1977 and 1985, African secondary school enrolments more than doubled while those of coloured and Indian schools rose by 50%. Concomitantly, African students with matriculation exemption and school-leaving certificates increased by over 400%, coloured students by over 90% and Indian by more than 100%, all these students being qualified to enter higher institutions for degree or/and diploma courses. The figures for the 1985 to 1990 period, while not as spectacular as those for the 1977-85 period, are still dramatic. Clearly, the impetus for expanding higher education enrolments was rooted in the massive growth of primary and secondary schooling. However, the developments in higher education cannot be accounted for in terms of processes internal to education alone; that is, the growth in pre-higher enrolments itself needs to be explained.

Bundy has argued that the

spectacular growth in black schooling has two distinct causes. There has, first, been an explicit attempt since Soweto to upgrade education so as to stave off school-based rebellion. Government departments and big business alike have pumped very large funds into black education. This has been a crucial component of the strategy of fostering and coopting a black middle class (1986:54).

However, as he acknowledges,

secondly, education was already showing mass growth before Soweto. The impetus at this point was economic. The growth of the South African economy through the 1960s and into the early 1970s ... brought about major structural changes in production and employment. A perceived "skills shortage" was the topic of much reformist concern before and after Soweto (*ibid.*).

Bundy's thesis that economic and political imperatives explain the expanded school enrolments is a starting point. However, there is a need to investigate to what extent this holds specifically for black higher education, and to explore the relationship between the political and economic pressures. Moreover, it is also necessary to consider the initiatives of capital and/or the state within black higher education in attempting to secure their economic, political and ideological objectives.

Corporate capital, the state and skill shortages

During this period a constant theme in statements by corporate capital and sections of the state was a lamentation about the shortages of skilled professionals and technicians and a call for the training of blacks in these occupations (Swainson, 1991; Kraak, 1989). The following comment was made 1982:

> From the Urban Foundation to Manpower 2000, from Anglo-American to Barlow Rand, the argument has consistently been made that unless South Africa's education system is restructured, "economic growth" will not be maintained (Anon, *Work in Progress*, 21, 1982:35).

Pressure for more skilled personnel also came from state departments like the health and postal services, stimulating a change in attitude to the training of blacks (Hartshone, 1986:121). In 1980, the government-appointed National Manpower Commission stated that economic development could not be achieved by the recruitment of solely white high-level labour-power and that "high priority would have to be given to increasing the participation of Africans" (quoted in SAIRR, 1982:366). Although the government accepted this recommendation it reaffirmed that training of blacks would continue to take place at segregated institutions. From 1977 there was a considerable expansion in enrolments at black higher education institutions.

Capital's theme of skills shortages cannot be accepted at face value. Meth, for one, has questioned the extent of such shortages arguing that while shortfalls in scientific workers and engineers were serious during the boom years of 1979-81, in absolute terms numbers were small and the level of vacancies for managerial personnel low. The emphasis on training Africans betokened a political agenda, as the supply of skilled white women, coloureds and Indians had not been exhausted (Meth, 1983:196). Elsewhere Meth has observed about the theme of skill shortages:

It is obvious that ... a persistent belief that there is such a thing, particularly a belief that such shortages are widespread, is likely ultimately to have important political consequences (quoted by Anon, *Work in Progress*, 21, 1982:35).

Chisholm has argued that "the skills shortage is ... partly a metaphor through which consent to restructuring is won" (1984a:405). Restructuring in the form of the elimination of job reservation threatened the interests of white workers and the white petit bourgeoisie and, according to her, the theme of skill shortage

appears to be used as a rationale for bringing about changes which cannot be brought about directly since various class interests are thereby threatened. These changes are nevertheless essential in securing the support of certain categories of blacks (1984a:406).

It is clear that the theme of skills shortage incorporated the political aim of creating a black, and especially, African petit bourgeoisie. Even prior to the Soweto uprising sections of corporate capital and the liberal establishment were already asserting the need to develop a black middle class. Although at that time this was a minority opinion, post-Soweto "the notion of solving South Africa's problems through the creation of the "black middle class" gained popularity (Makalima, 1986:41). By the late 1970s the interests of corporate capital and the state increasingly coincided on this. As Makalima puts it,

[w]hat started as an economic imperative to incorporate an increasing number of blacks into new petit bourgeois occupational positions ... became a widely accelerated political imperative of capitalist reproduction linked to the prospect of creating a supportive urban black petit bourgeoisie (1986:38).

Statements on the theme of developing a black petit bourgeoisie abound. Dennis Etheridge, a previous executive director of Anglo-American and president of the Chamber of Mines, attempted to link the economic and ideological necessities. He argued, first, that in periods of economic upturn the absence of a pool of skilled personnel would force up salaries. Moreover, "Blacks in senior positions" were better equipped "in dealing with the Black consumer" (Etheridge, 1986:138). Given the analysis of the skills shortage this reasoning is not entirely convincing. Etheridge's second point is more pertinent. Noting "that the free enterprise system ... is looked upon with great suspicion and even hostility by many Blacks [and] ... is in danger of rejection in favour of something socialist", the lack of blacks in senior positions within business corporations meant that corporate capital was seen as "linked inexorably with the political system of apartheid" (ibid.). In this analysis the movement of blacks into high-level jobs was crucial for ideological and political reasons.

The argument for training and employing blacks as middle and high-level labour was made in many other ways. "Educated and experienced blacks" were reckoned to be important as intermediaries between capital and labour (Timber Manpower Representative, 1981; cited by Christie, 1985:209). Judge Steyn of the Urban Foundation (UF) appealed for the involvement of capital in the UF saying

> I cannot see any thinking businessman declining to participate in South Africa's future through the Urban Foundation. His dividend will be the emergence of a black middle-class ... the maintenance of the free enterprise system ... [and] the survival of everything we hold dear (Financial Mail, 11 March 1977; quoted in Frederikse, 1986:59).

For government minister Piet Koornhof, "the level of progress of Africans in a free enterprise system should be so advantageous [and] revolution would hold such risks that Africans would fight against it" (quoted in Makalima, 1986:60). These examples illustrate the reformist thrust of corporate capital and sections of the state. Black embourgeoise-ment was seen as important in fracturing black inter-class solidarity, widening the social base of adherents to capitalism and in creating an ideological and political buffer between the black working class and the ruling class.

One means of expanding the "traditional" fraction of the black petit bourgeoisie was to remove obstacles in the path of trading and capital accumulation and to provide financial assistance to these sectors . However, the fostering of the "new" petit bourgeoisie – trained professionals such as doctors, engineers, accountants, lawyers, teachers, and the like – was almost entirely dependent on higher education, and on expanded employment opportunities within state departments and large business corporations. The imperative to expand the new petit bourgeoisie was thrust onto the agenda of capital and the state by the struggles of students and the dominated classes between 1973 and 1976/1977. This hastened the growth in black higher education that took place after 1977.

State and capital initiatives in expanding black higher education

Between 1976 and 1990 the state created numerous new higher education institutions, and also supported new faculties and departments at established universities. In 1976 MEDUNSA began to operate at Garankuwa, near Pretoria. Seven years later, VISTA University opened. VISTA comprised a complex of campuses, which were located in various urban African townships but administered from Pretoria. The significance of MEDUNSA and VISTA was that they were urban campuses, and signalled the acceptance by the state of a permanent urban African population in the "white" areas. However, they could also be seen as part of state strategy to enforce a divide between urban African residents and rural and bantustan African residents. Between 1977 and 1983 campuses in the bantustans, initially developed as satellites of existing African universities, were transformed into independent institutions resulting in the universities of Transkei (1977), Bophuthatswana (1979), Venda (1983), and QwaQwa (1983).

Higher technical education also expanded. In 1979, the Mangosuthu Technikon opened at Umlazi, near Durban. The following year the Mabopane East Technikon began functioning near Pretoria. Both institutions were restricted to African students. Concomitantly, the Colleges of Advanced Technical Education (CATEs) for coloureds and

Indians were upgraded to technikons. Again, significantly, the new technikons for African students were located in the "white" areas. Finally, a couple of new teacher-training colleges for Africans were built in the urban areas.

From 1977, increasing numbers of black students at universities, technikons and teacher-training colleges received state bursaries and loans. In 1977, 8 278 black students at universities and teacher-training colleges received state bursaries, which meant that 67% of all coloured students and 86% of Indian students at teacher-training colleges were funded by the state (calculated from SAIRR, 1978:464-65). By 1982/1983 the total number of black students receiving state bursaries rose substantially: 4 560 state-funded bursaries were awarded to African university students, 2 880 bursaries to Africans at teacher-training colleges, 3 573 awards were made to coloured students and 2 271 to Indian teacher-trainees. State bursaries to Africans alone in 1982 amounted to R4,6 million (SAIRR, 1983:421-22). In 1989 state funding for bursaries for Africans at higher education institutions reached R15 million, while an additional R14 million was spent on bursaries for coloureds and Indians (SAIRR, 1988/89).

Corporate capital (including foreign-owned multinationals) also began to intervene in, and make large donations to, black higher education after 1977. This was largely a new phenomenon and took three different forms. First, pressure was applied on the state, either directly or via organisations like the Urban Foundation and the South African Institute of Race Relations (SAIRR), to modify policies on black higher education. Calls were made for all universities to be placed under a single state department, for greater autonomy to be granted to black institutions, for admissions policies to be determined by education institutions alone, and for greater provision to be made for black technical education and the upgrading of teacher qualifications (SAIRR, 1980-1985).

Second, corporate capital entered into a partnership with the state, largely on the latter's terms, to provide more facilities at higher education institutions. Notable examples were the Soweto Teachers Training College, which opened in 1977, and the Mangosuthu Technikon, both financed by the Anglo-American Corporation and De Beers Chairman's Fund but run by state departments. Large donations were made to already-established institutions to facilitate black student access and promote particular subjects like business management. For example, in 1985 corporations gave substantial support to the University of Cape Town (UCT) for the establishment of the Centre for African Management to train and develop black managers (RSA, 1985:814). In 1986 the Gold Fields Foundation provided R1 million to Stellenbosch University for hostel accommodation for black students (RSA, 1986:159), and in 1990 low-interest loans for hostel accommodation were made available to Peninsula Technikon and the University of the Western Cape (UWC) by a mining corporation.

Third, corporate initiatives to provide bursaries for black students expanded and increasing amounts of money were allocated for scholarships administered either by business corporations directly or by higher education institutions and bodies like the SAIRR. Programmes offering black students scholarships at overseas universities were also initiated or expanded. For example, in 1979, United States business corporations established the South African Education Program, which made available scholarships tenable at American institutions. Considerable donations were made by foreign-based multinationals in the late 1980s. Mobil made annual grants of R1 million, from 1987, for scholarships to black university and technikon students. In 1987 the US-based Kellogg Foundation gave R2 million for bursaries to black undergraduates at universities (RSA, 1987a:10). The Ford Foundation made annual grants, from the late 1980s, to black post-graduate students who were employed as research assistants.

For much of the 1980s, then, the vast majority of black students at teacher-training colleges, large numbers of teacher-trainees at universities, and considerable numbers of university and technikon students received either state or private bursaries. In detailing the reformist interventions of corporate capital and the state within higher education it is not taken as a given that these initiatives necessarily succeeded. Restructuring is neither automatic nor unproblematic, and is the object of struggles both within the dominant classes, and between the dominant and dominated classes. Restructuring frequently generates contradictions, new conflicts, and new spaces for mobilisation and political activity which opposition organisations can harness in constructing an alternative hegemonic project to that of the ruling class. The terrain on which capital and the state intervene may also be occupied by progressive forces and organisations.

Indeed, after 1977 a number of local progressive student organisations, as well as SANSCO, were active on higher education campuses and could have mediated the interventions of corporate capital and the state. Although black higher students constituted a social category rather different from the mass of the black population who were predominantly workers or unemployed, they shared with other black dominated classes a common experience of national oppression. Of course, individual black students experienced the effects of political oppression and capitalist exploitation differentially, the extent and intensity of their experiences being related to their social class origins and position within South Africa's system of racial classification.

After 1976 the number of first-generation students from working class families began to expand tremendously; for example, by the early 1980s some 90% of students at UWC were from such families (*Times Higher Education Supplement*, 16 November, 1986:10). For students from working class backgrounds, low wages for parents, unemployment, inadequate housing, poor transport services and poverty were lived experiences. African students were not exempt from influx control legislation and pass-book harassment, or unaffected by forced removals and the stripping of South African citizenship from those deemed to be citizens of "independent" bantustans. These realities have a bearing on the form and content of student actions, particularly when combined with conjunctural struggles on the political terrain and in the factories, townships, and schools.

Black enrolments at universities

As Table 1 indicates, during the period 1977 to 1990 the numbers of black university students increased tremendously.

Between 1977 and 1985 total enrolments more than tripled, and then increased by some 77% between 1985 and 1990. Student numbers at all the black universities rose rapidly, though at African institutions growth was particularly spectacular: between 1977-1985 enrolments increased fivefold and then almost doubled again between 1985 and 1990. However, one institution, VISTA, accounted for 45% of the enrolments in 1985 and 58% of those in 1990. Many of the students at VISTA were teachers registered part-time for secondary teacher diploma and certificate courses. A notable shift began to occur in the distribution of students between the different types of universities with, in proportional terms, a pronounced move of students from the distance institution UNISA to residential institutions in the bantustans, as well as to the other black and white universities.

Finally, an important new, and primarily post-1985, phenomenon was the increasing entry of African students into universities previously reserved for coloureds and Indians. By 1990, barring the African residential universities, UWC and UDW had the largest enrolments of African students. At UWC, African students constituted almost 28% of the student body (UWC, 1990). A reverse movement of coloured and Indian students to African campuses was virtually non-existent. Significant was the decline among Indian students of enrolments at UDW and their marked movement into the white universities. A similar pattern of movement to the white universities, although with no decline in enrolments at UWC, was also evident among coloured students.

Since SANSCO operated at the white English-language universities there is a need to examine more closely the representation of black students at these universities. Moreover, to determine whether the attitude of the state to the entry of black, and especially African, students changed over this period it is also necessary to analyse the "racial" composition of black students. Numerically, black student representation at the white English-language universities more than tripled between 1977 and 1985, from 1 968 students to 7 412, and then almost doubled during the following five years to reach 13 847. At each of these universities, black students began to constitute a sizeable sector of the general student body – between 13% and 25% in 1985, and between 22% and 36% by 1990. This meant they had the potential to assert pressure on university administrations and shape the form and content of education and political struggles on these campuses.

Although African student numbers increased and began to constitute a larger percentage of the total black student population at the white English-medium institutions, for much of this period Indian students continued to predominate at these institutions. The reason for this is partly historical: previously entrance controls to the white universities were more stringently applied against African than Indian or coloured students. Thus,

African student representation at these universities began from a much smaller base. As fees at these institutions are considerably higher than at the black universities, the greater numbers of Indian students may also be related to the class and income structure of that "racial" group.

Table 1: "Racial" composition and distribution of students by type of university, 1977 to 1990

Yr.	Race	Afr.	Col.	Ind.	Bstn.	Whi.	UNISA	Tot.
1	Afr.	4 422	0	1	279	494	6 320	11 516
9	Col.	0	2 598	39	0	720	2 000	5 357
7	Ind.	0	146	3 482	0	1 126	3 477	8 231
7	Tot.	4 422	2 744	3 522	279	2 340	11 797	25 104
	% Dis.	-	42,6	-	1,1	9,3	47,0	100
1	Afr.	6 592	18	13	1 512	1 040	11 366	20 541
9	Col.	4	3 615	36	8	1 562	3 131	8 378
8	Ind.	0	144	4 838	5	1 882	6 869	13 738
1	Tot.	6 618	3 777	4 887	1 525	4 484	21 366	42 657
	% Dis.	-	35,8	-	3,6	10,5	50,1	100
1	Afr.	21 923	308	145	na	2 894	17 556	-
9	Col.	68	6 527	150	na	2 316	3 872	-
8	Ind.	24	332	5 925	na	3 218	8 210	-
5	Tot.	22 015	7 167	6 220	5769	8 428	29 638	79 237
	% Dis.	-	44,7	-	7,3	10,6	37,4	100
1	Afr.	42 206*	3 425	2 637	na	7 311	40 899	-
9	Col.	317*	8 322	154	na	4 484	4 370	-
9	Ind.	166*	474	4 474	na	5 018	8 695	-
0	Tot.	42 689*	12 221	7 265	7652#	16 813	53 964	140 604
	% Dis.	-	44,4–	-	5,4	11,9	38,3	100

(Sources: Collated and compiled from SAIRR 1978:522; 1980:54; 1982:507; 1986:400-01; 1992:222-23). [Notes: *Excluding Fort Hare; # excluding Venda}. [Abbreviations: Afr. = African; Bstn. = Bantustan; Col. = coloured; Dis. = Distribution; Ind. = Indian; Tot. = Total; Whi. = White; Yr. = Year.]

However, most important is the manner in which the state continued to deal with African student applications for permission to study at the white English-language universities. Whereas in 1981 92,2% (1 126 of 1 221) of coloured and 88,1% (924 of 1 049) of Indian students received permission to enrol, only 48,0% (667 of 1 391) African students were allowed entrance. In 1983 the rejection rate of Africans became even greater: only 36,6% (954 of 2 605) of applications were approved while the consent rates for coloureds and Indians were 91,5% (1 255 of 1 371) and 78,8% (1 323 of 1 679) respectively (SAIRR, 1984:461). It is possible that the greater approval rate of coloured and Indian student applications was related to the new constitutional dispensation which sought to co-opt these groups.

Finally, there was a gradual enrolment of small numbers of black students at the Afrikaans-language universities and at the dual-medium University of Port Elizabeth (UPE). In 1977 some nine black students were registered at Potchefstroom and Orange Free State for post-graduate and theology courses. However, during the 1980s, both numerically and in percentage terms, the representation of black students at the Afrikaans-language universities and at UPE was minute. By 1990, the vast majority were concentrated at just three institutions: at UPE – 675 students or 13,9% of the student body; at Stellenbosch – 755 students or 5,3% of the student body; and at the Rand Afrikaans University – 564 students or 6,2% of total students. It was at these institutions, and especially at UPE, that black students could possibly have constituted a viable political force. However, creating this would have been immensely difficult given the conservative disposition of most white students at these universities.

Black technical training

A similar pattern is shown in relation to enrolments of black students at technical training institutions (Table 2).

Four notable developments occurred during the 1985-90 period. First, there was a large increase in black student enrolments at the black residential technikons. Second, black students began to enter technikons previously reserved for whites. Thus, by 1990, 3 822 black students (1 616 African, 1 583 coloured, and 623 Indian students) were enrolled at white residential technikons. Third, the pattern of considerable African University enrolments at UWC and UDW was repeated at the technikons previously designated for coloureds and Indians. By 1990, African students comprised 23% of the student body at Peninsula Technikon and 19% at ML Sultan. Finally, large numbers (by 1990, some 7 900) of African students began to enrol for technikon courses through distance education (SAIRR, 1988:463, 1992:218).

Table 2 : Student enrolments at black residential technikons and white technikons, 1977 to 1990

Technikons	1977		1981		1985		1990	
	Inst.	Enrol.	Inst.	Enrol.	Inst.	Enrol.	Inst.	Enrol.
African	2	480	4	762	3	1 604	4	4 985
Coloured	1	1 038	1	2 120	1	2 396	1	4 906*
Indian	1	na	1	4 217	1	3 680	1	5 951#
White**	6	40 829	7	39 790	7	51 069	7	53 818
Total	10	42 347	13	46 889	12	58 749	13	69 660

Sources: Republic of South Africa (1987) 1986:5.67-5.72; SAIRR, 1988:463; 1992:218). [Notes: * Includes 1 149 African students; # includes 1 144 African students; ** includes distance education students.] [Abbreviations: Inst. = Institutions; Enrol. = Enrolments.]

Despite increasing black enrolments, advanced technical training continued to be concentrated among whites. During 1981 white students comprised 85% of all technikon students. By 1990, if black distance education enrolments are taken into account, white students constituted 64,5% of total technikon enrolments. As in the case of the poor representation of black students in science and technical fields at universities, the major problem was the poor quality of mathematics and science education within black schools. In addition, because of the previous job reservation policy of the state, higher technical training was severely undeveloped and only expanded during this period. Consequently, black student numbers began to rise from a very small base. Apart from offering commercial, secretarial, paramedic, surveying, science, and engineering courses, the technikons also began to train technical teachers for secondary schools.

Black teacher-training

Between 1977 and 1990 the trend was towards a considerable expansion in the numbers of Africans and coloureds at teacher-training colleges.

Amongst all groups there was also a shift towards registrations at universities for teacher qualifications. Thus, enrolments at UDW rose from 813 in 1978 to 1 225 in 1983, and among African students university-based teacher-training enrolments expanded from 559 in 1978 to 2 925 in 1983 (SAIRR, 1980:505-507; 518; 1985:667-68; 679). The expansion of teacher-trainees at universities was most likely related to the demands of both corporate capital and school students for better qualified secondary school teachers. Although throughout this period both teacher-training colleges and students continued to be predominantly located in the bantustans, the provision of new facilities in the "white" areas meant that an increasing number and percentage of students began to be located at colleges in the urban African townships.

The representation of black women in higher education

Historically, black women were poorly represented at universities and technical colleges and were concentrated in teacher-training and paramedic courses. This trend continued in the 1980s, except at universities like VISTA which, by offering part-time education degrees, attracted a large number of women teachers. Table 3 shows, however, that the numbers of black women at universities increased both absolutely and proportionally over this period. The numbers of women at teacher-training colleges also increased, especially among Africans. While the proportion of African women teacher-trainees increased slightly over the 1977 to 1990 period, the proportion of coloured and Indian women teachers declined. The numbers of black women at technikons increased tremendously, although women continued to be considerably underrepresented within this sector. Moreover, women tended to be concentrated in particular fields. In 1982, 61% of the coloured female students and 57% of the Indian women were registered for secretarial and commerce courses. At technikons 75% of the African women were registered for secretarial courses or health sciences.

In summary, the statistics in this chapter show the extent of the expansion in enrolments at higher education institutions. This quantitative increase was a key part of the state and capital's reformist strategy to create a black middle class. But implementing this strategy was a more complex matter than merely expanding enrolments. Expansion, as will be seen, was accompanied by contradictions and contestations around the control and administration of universities, student conditions, and political issues.

Table 3: Enrolments of black women in higher education by "race", and their representation as a proportion of their "racial" group, 1997 to 1990

Sect.	Race	Year			
		1977	1981	1985	1990
Univ.	Afr.	2 902 (26,7%)	8 131 (39,9%)	19 025 (44,1%)	na
	Col.	1 060 (22,3%)	2 523 (30,9%)	4 721 (36,5%)	na
	Ind.	1 819 (25,6%)	3 942 (33,7%)	7 236 (41,8%)	na
Tech.	Afr.	na	200 (17,5%)*	609 (22,6%)	5 318 (36,7%)
	Col.	na	522 (23,9%)*	na	2 232 (39,1%)
	Ind.	na	902 (29,5%)*	939 (30,7%)	2 305 (43,3%)
Tetr.	Afr.#	10 388 (63,4%)	9 213 (64,2%)	10 335 (55,3%)	22 987 (64,2%)
	Col.	3 154 (72,0%)	2 546 (61,6%)	2 939 (52,1%)	4 780 (60,1%)
	Ind.	547 (61,8%)	861 (60,7%)	910 (61,7%)	1 012 (58,6%)

(Sources: Dreijmanis, 1988:113-19; RSA, 1987:5.63; 5.70-5.72; RSA, 1993:5.46). [Notes: #: African teacher-training enrolments for 1977 exclude Transkei; for 1981, Transkei, Bophuthatswana and Venda; and for 1985 and 1990 all the "independent" bantustans. * Technikon figures are for 1982]. [Abbreviations: Afr. = African; Col. = coloured; Ind. = Indian; Tech. = Technikons; Tetr. = Teacher-training; Sect. = Sector; Univ. = Universities.]

The administrative control of black institutions

After 1977 the structure of administrative control of higher education became extremely complex. Universities and teacher-training colleges in the "independent" bantustans fell under the control of bantustan state structures. Universities located in non-independent bantustans, and universities, technikons, and teacher-training colleges for Africans in the "white" areas were administered by the Department of Education and Training (DET). Education departments of non-independent bantustans controlled all teacher-training colleges in their territories, as well as technikons and technical colleges. The only exception was the Shikoane Matlala Technical College which, while located in Lebowa, was administered by the DET. Higher education institutions designated for Indian and coloured students fell under the Departments of Indian and coloured Affairs respectively. After the establishment of the segregated tricameral parliament in 1984 these institutions fell under the Department of Education and Culture of the House of Representatives (for coloureds) and the Department of Education and Culture of the House of Delegates (for Indians).

Turning to the internal organisation of the black institutions, until the mid-1970s university councils were dominated by white representatives of the state, and senates were controlled by white staff. During this period, partly as a result of previous student demands for Africanisation, and partly to link universities more closely to bantustan and collaborationist coloured and Indian political structures, there were changes in the representation and the powers of councils. Black Advisory Councils, which had no power, were abolished. Convocations were established at all black universities. At the same time, the government began to place blacks, on a racial and ethnic basis, on the councils of the various universities. In 1977, the number of state appointees on councils was reduced from eight to four, senate representatives on council increased from two to three, and provision was made for a member of the convocation, and representatives of bantustan and coloured or Indian collaborationist administrations. Councils now had the power, albeit with the concurrence of the minister, to appoint the rector of the institution, to admit students other than those for whom the university was "racially" reserved, and to determine staff establishment. After 1975 black rectors began to be elected or appointed at some universities and technikons.

During the late 1980s, as a result of a combination of student and progressive staff struggles within institutions and mass struggles outside, progressive black rectors were elected at some of the black universities. Thus, although there was no change to the structure of the councils at these institutions, the political orientation of the councils was not pre-given. Councils were themselves sites of struggle and the mass struggles of the 1980s impacted upon them. The changes that followed the appointment of progressive rectors, the most dramatic being at UWC, which sought to become the "intellectual home of the left", created a new terrain for student organisation and the form and content of student actions. At Fort Hare, space for change was created by the coup in Ciskei during 1990. Students, academic staff and workers used this space to eject the previous conservative administration from office. A new university council was ushered in and, according to the Democratic Staff Association at Fort Hare, its main task was to

> continue to transform the decision-making processes of the university – for instance challenging the composition of university committees. The committees still reflect the racial composition of the Senate where only four out of 48 members are black (*UDUSA News*, September 1990:2).

As will be seen below, the predominance of white academics was not unique to Fort Hare.

Conditions at black higher education institutions

M.O. Nkomo has noted that

> the institutional/administrative, physical, social and academic environments within a university constitute or produce an empirical reality that influences student attitudes and behaviours (Nkomo, 1984:3).

Thus, it is necessary also to focus on the lived conditions of students within their immediate institutional settings, since these conditions contributed to shaping the form and content of student activities, struggles and demands.

From 1977 the state made physical improvements to black universities and instituted new academic faculties and departments. However, many of the long-established inadequacies of black higher education institutions altered little. Students compared the academic facilities, range of degrees and courses offered, quality and content of teaching, student facilities and other features of black institutions with those for whites and found theirs to be generally wanting.

A simple examination of library facilities is revealing. A valid comparison can be made between the black universities established in 1960-61, and the Rand Afrikaans University (RAU) established in 1968. One would expect the former to be better stocked, being older institutions. However, by the mid-1970s RAU's library contained 195 000 volumes, while the libraries of the black universities each held between 67 000 and 84 000 books (Human Sciences Research Council, 1976: 277-87). The position changed little during this period. Marcum writes of the University of North library that "of its approximately one hundred thousand volumes, many are obsolete or, otherwise useless – including dated and poor quality rejects from other libraries" (1982:42). His comment on Zululand University library in relation to that of RAU is even more illuminating:

[A]fter more than twenty years, its library contains less than one hundred thousand volumes in contrast to the three-hundred-thousand-volume, automated library of the much newer Rand Afrikaans university (ibid.).

After 1982, decreasing government expenditure on universities meant that the book-buying capacity of universities was reduced and these initial inequalities were not rectified (WUS, 1989).

At black universities, academic staff were predominantly white. In 1985, only 99 academics (31%) at UWC, 366 (32%) at African universities, and 147 (41%) at UDW were black. (SAIRR, 1986:400). In 1986, whites comprised 87% of staff at MEDUNSA, 82% at VISTA, 65% at Fort Hare and 51% at UNIN (File, 1990:10). At the African technikons over 90% of posts were occupied by whites, while at teacher-training colleges under the DET and the non-independent bantustans 52% of teaching staff were white (DET Annual Report, 1982:130, 1983:253; 1984:235). Black staff tended to be concentrated on the lower rungs of the staff hierarchy. Since senates of universities comprised largely senior staff, white staff dominated academic decision-making. I highlight the racial composition of staff since, in the context of racial oppression and privilege, the dominance of white personnel may become an issue of conflict, particularly if such personnel support the existing social order.

From their inception, for reasons related to the separate development programme of the National Party and strong state control, black higher education institutions tended to be staffed by Afrikaner nationalists and white conservatives. This continued to be a feature of these institutions during this period. For example, it was reported that at UNIN

approximately 65% of the white academic and administrative staff support the Herstigte Nasionale Party ... [and] ... Conservative Party. The university's academic registrar is ... a Broederbond member ... and a member of the education committee of the South African Bureau of Racial Affairs (*SASPU Focus*, July 1982).

Even the Black Academic Staff Association at UNIN, by no means a radical body, felt obliged on one occasion to comment that the registrar's attitude "consistently reflected his arrogance and impatience which borders on contempt and lack of respect for blacks" (*ibid.*).

An additional problem was the content of many of the arts and social science courses offered at black universities. With few exceptions, the dominant orientation was conservative or, at best, liberal. Radical social theories and writing were largely ignored. The generally conservative course content was related to the fact that academic staff were predominantly graduates of the University of South Africa and Afrikaans-medium universities, both known for their conservative orientation. Thus, critical investigation and discussion was non-existent and academic freedom was extremely limited. Liberal UNIN staff complained that there were "considerable controls on teaching. The use of enlightened methods and course content is met with strong opposition from those who effectively control the campus" (*SASPU Focus*, July 1982). Such controls often led to frustration and the resignation of liberal and radical academics. Given such conditions, and the racial structuring of higher education, it was not surprising that black students continued to refer to the black universities by the derogatory phrase "bush colleges". However, by the end of the decade, through student and staff struggles, the influence of more progressive administrations, and the entry of progressive academics, some changes in teaching and course content were evident at certain black institutions.

Conditions in the majority of teacher-training colleges however altered less dramatically. The poor facilities and poorly qualified staff of Bophuthatswana colleges during the late 1970s may be taken as an indication of a general phenomenon (de Clerq, 1984:37). Conditions were little better by the end of the decade (Nkomo, 1991). Finally, although African technikons were newly built, Chisholm has suggested that they were poorly staffed and had limited facilities (1984b:15). These conditions generated many student grievances. To add combustion, expanding university enrolments strained existing facilities at some institutions resulting in large classes and limitations being imposed on course options.

There were also problems with student accommodation and transport at some institutions. At many institutions the quality of catering and food in hostels was a widespread grievance.

On top of poor material conditions, institutions were characterised by authoritarian control and lack of student representation. When SANSCO was formed in 1979, only one SRC, with limited autonomy, existed on a black campus. At most black universities, and particularly at technikons, teacher-training colleges, and bantustan-based institutions, the democratic right of students to autonomous SRCs and independent student organisation continued to be denied. At VISTA University, no student organisation could be formed without the permission of the University Council. Students were barred from contacting or joining any organisation not recognised by the council, and prior approval had to be obtained to distribute any publications (World University Service, 1986:8).

The repressive conditions on many campuses were underlined by security guards policing entrances to universities. Such security often harassed student activists and interfered with student activities. At the University of Transkei, student and lecturer allegations of harassment were corroborated when the director and deputy-director of security services acknowledged that they were "involved in surveillance and harassment of students and lecturers" (UDUSA News, September 1990:1). They also admitted that they had strong links with the South African police and Transkei security forces.

Many university and college administrations frequently summoned the riot police at the slightest sign of student opposition, and throughout the 1980s students were whipped, baton-charged and tear-gassed by police on campus. Between 1986 and 1989 the University of the North came under military occupation by the South African Defence Force. A curfew was imposed, soldiers invigilated exams, and raids on student residences were common (WUS, 1989). In 1989, three students were killed by the army during a protest against the continued military occupation of their campus. It was under such conditions that progressive democratic student structures had to be established and had to survive.

Very different conditions obtained at the white English-language universities. Liberal administrations meant that student structures (NUSAS, SRCs, student newspapers) enjoyed greater space for their activities. Apart from NUSAS and some SRCs playing a progressive political role, left-wing groups like the Wages Commissions, Students Action Movement (Wits), Students for Social Democracy (UCT), and women's movements were also active. On some campuses small numbers of black students' participated in such groups, and/or conducted their activities through black students' societies. There, then, conditions were more conducive to black student organisation and to student action.

As a consequence of the reformist objectives of corporate capital and the apartheid state, and particularly the goal of creating a black middle class, black higher education expanded tremendously during the 1976/1977 to 1990 period. New institutions were established and the numbers of black students in higher education increased dramatically. However, the poor conditions on many black campuses, authoritarian controls, the repressive measures of administrations and security forces and the broader political context contributed to a general disaffection among black students. This created fertile conditions for student formations like SANSCO to mediate the initiatives of capital and the state, project alternative agendas and to raise alternative demands. Of course, not all students at black higher-education institutions were politicised and took part in anti-apartheid struggles. Contradictory forces continued to work on students. One such force was SANSCO, and it is to its initiatives and actions, its impact on students, and to its character, role and significance that I now turn in the following four chapters.

7

SANSCO: The Ideology and Politics of Non-Racialism, the Freedom Charter and National Liberation

My concerns in this chapter are twofold. The first is to sketch the formation of SANSCO in late 1979. The second is to analyse SANSCO's ideology and politics. With respect to the latter, I show how SANSCO initially adopted the doctrine of Black Consciousness (BC) and sought to essentially continue the tradition established by SASO. Thereafter, I track its shift away from BC and its re-orientation towards the Congress movement, and also account for this development which was formalised by SANSCO's first national congress in July 1981. Finally, I describe and analyse the themes, beliefs, views and approaches that constituted SANSCO ideologically and politically.

The Formation of SANSCO

The banning of SASO in October 1977 deprived black higher education students of a national political student organisation. However, there were ongoing skirmishes between students and university authorities on some campuses. At UNIZUL in 1978, 400 – mainly women – students boycotted classes in protest against the expulsion of a pregnant student. Thereafter, there were student protests around conditions in the science faculty which resulted in seven SRC members being expelled, a number of students being refused re-registration, and some 200 students not returning to campus. During 1979, UNIN was the focal point of student-administration conflict. There, student protests occurred around the expulsion of students for organising a Sharpeville commemoration meeting, and around plans to hold a beauty contest on June 16, the anniversary of the Soweto uprising. In addition, the question of an autonomous SRC continued to be a flashpoint. Finally, there was a march by some 100 students through a nearby township protesting against the forced removal and relocation of the Makgatho community. At Fort Hare students demonstrated against the killing by campus security of a student for alleged burglary. At UWC there was a food boycott around the quality of food in the residences. Western Cape higher education students also pledged their support for striking workers at a local spaghetti and pasta manufacturer as well as for a consumer boycott of the manufacturer's products. At the University of Natal (Pietermaritzburg) black students went on a canteen boycott for alleged racist remarks by the manager of food services (SAIRR, 1980:52, 293, 549-53).

The University of Natal boycott was, significantly, spearheaded by the Black Students' Society, a campus-level exclusively black formation that was to be a feature of most of the white English-language universities after 1977. However, the initiative for the formation of a national student structure to replace SASO did not come from black campus-level organisations. Instead, in a reversal of the SASO-BPC genesis and relationship, it came from an Azanian Peoples' Organisation (AZAPO) conference of September 1979. Here, students elected an Interim Committee (IC) whose task was to prepare the ground for the launch of a national student organisation. The consultative process around the formation of a new national student organisation was however extremely limited and inadequate. As a result, although some 100 students from six campuses attended the inaugural conference, most did so in their individual capacities. Mandated delegates were present from just two institutions – the universities of Fort Hare and the North.

The inaugural conference, held on 23 November 1979 at the Edendale Ecumenical Lay Centre near Pietermaritzburg, nonetheless established a new national student organisation called the "Azanian Students' Organisation" It also adopted a Preamble to serve as the new organisations' guiding principles, and elected a new interim committee. The adoption of a constitution and policy document was deferred to a future conference, which could be more representative of black higher education students. The organisation (renamed SANSCO in 1986) was to become the dominant force in black student life until 1991 when it amalgamated with NUSAS.

Ideology and politics, 1979 to 1981

The commitment to Black Consciousness

The Preamble of SANSCO expressed four basic points. First, it accepted Black Consciousness (BC) as "a philosophy of life". Second, it declared "we are members of the oppressed black community before we are students". Third, it noted that black students were the conscience of the community and the need "to maintain the traditional role of black students in the community". Finally, the preamble emphasised the necessity to "promote the role of the black student as a vanguard in the struggle for liberation".

The name of the new organisation – "*Azanian* Students' Organisation" – and its adherence to BC doctrine reflected the process of its birth. According to Nkoane, who was elected interim president,

[t]he whole process was left to AZAPO to organise. Invites, delegates to come to the conference ... they paid for everything ... After the formation of AZASO we were given an office, one of the offices belonging to AZAPO, so we were effectively in the same office with AZAPO (Interview, 1995).

While sponsored by AZAPO and ostensibly BC in orientation, SANSCO was far from politically homogeneous. At the inaugural conference there was much contestation around a preamble produced by AZAPO, with a clause that AZASO recognised AZAPO "as the only legitimate political organisation in the country" being especially contentious (Interview with Nkoane, 1995).

According to Nkoane, himself an adherent of the Congress movement, the party political allegiances of participants attending the conference were unclear since "around the time that the organisation was formed the lines were not clearly drawn" (*ibid.*). However, it was evident that there was not unanimous support for AZAPO and that many were disposed towards the Congress movement. Those supportive of the Congress movement argued for, and won, the removal of the clause that gave sole

211

recognition to AZAPO on the grounds that the new student organisation had to cater for students with differing political allegiances. However, in the interest of ensuring that the conference did launch an organisation, Congress movement supporters compromised around other contentious issues:

Now we did not want the situation where we would come out of there without having formed an organisation ... So we felt, okay, on some of the issues we are going to compromise. We are going to let the preamble go on as it is and we will take the responsibility of correcting this as time goes on (Interview with Nkoane, 1995).

The elections to the Interim Committee produced an interesting outcome in that Congress movement supporters were elected to key positions, including the portfolios of president and general secretary, and now required to spearhead an organisation that was formally committed to BC.

SANSCO's discourse was strongly influenced by that of SASO, a point confirmed by Nkoane:

Well, most of us were influenced by black consciousness and SASO particularly. When we came into the political scene there was SASO and therefore our thinking was along those lines (Interview with Nkoane, 1995).

The student's declaration that their oppression as blacks took priority over their status as students had been a central assertion of SASO. Furthermore, as with SASO, the term "black" continued to be applied to all the politically oppressed national groups. The notion of preserving the "traditional role of black students" also suggested that SANSCO conceived its role as essentially replicating that played earlier by SASO.

The impact of political developments during 1980

Although SANSCO was initially committed to BC, a number of developments during 1980 moved sections of SANSCO's membership, and particularly its elected officials, to sever their links with AZAPO, to reassess SANSCO's ideological and political orientation, and to align it with the Congress movement.

First, tension emerged between SANSCO and AZAPO after the suspension of the AZAPO president, Curtis Nkondo, for alleged "violation of policy and protocol". SANSCO hinted that there were manoeuvrings within AZAPO to oust Nkondo, while in some quarters it was suggested that Nkondo's alleged misconduct was an excuse for his removal since he was perceived as being too close to the Congress movement (Phaala, 1983b:3). The details of this controversy are less important than the effects. SANSCO challenged the suspension and demanded the immediate reinstatement of Nkondo. Significantly, it also asserted that it was not a student wing of AZAPO but an independent organisation. The suspension was also challenged by the Congress of South African Students' (COSAS), a national secondary student organisation. The latter had, from its inception in May 1979, committed itself to the principles and programme of the Congress movement and also maintained a close relationship with Nkondo. Notwithstanding the political differences between SANSCO and COSAS, there was a working relationship between the two organisations. If Nkondo's suspension strained relations between AZAPO and SANSCO, it established further common ground between the latter and COSAS and contributed to SANSCO's gradual shift towards the Congress movement.

A second development that stimulated a re-thinking within SANSCO was the education protests of early and mid-1980. Beginning among secondary school students in the Western Cape, the protests spread to some other areas and also encompassed a number of higher education institutions. SANSCO was not involved in the Western Cape protests and was largely peripheral even to the actions at most higher education campuses. Nonetheless, the Western Cape protests, and especially the ideological and political sophistication displayed by the Committee of 81 – the forum of representatives from schools, colleges and universities that co-ordinated the student boycott – did not leave SANSCO's thinking unaffected. Since the positions of the Committee of 81 powerfully shaped the future ideological direction of student politics in South Africa they merit some attention.

The perspectives of the Committee of 81 were set out in pamphlets that were widely disseminated among students. In a pamphlet, *From the schools to the people*, education and schooling were related to the political and economic order and the nature of the state. Black education and conditions within black schooling were said to be "the outcome of the whole system of racist oppression and capitalist exploitation" (Committee of 81, 1980a:1). The "system", in turn, it was argued, was maintained and reproduced by ideological and repressive state apparatuses, black collaborators within separate development institutions and the acquiescence of black workers. The students were of the view that black workers occupied a position in the social order, which made them a potentially powerful political force, whereas the power of students was more limited:

If the workers could be put in a position where they could say for a few weeks: WE WILL NOT WORK TO MAINTAIN APART-HEID AND CAPITALIST EXPLOITATION, the present loud-mouthed kragdadige government would be shaken to its very foundations. *Our parents, the workers are therefore strong.* They have power. We, the students cannot shake the government in the same way: we can only warn them: we can serve notice on them that the youth will not tolerate the old order (*ibid.*, emphasis in original).

The Committee of 81 argued that it was crucial to get black workers and parents on the side of the students. It invoked the worker slogan of the 1950s, "An injury to one is an injury to all", and called on students to contact church and civic organisations to win support for their actions and to "explain to them our struggle and how we see it linked up with the whole struggle for national liberation" (*ibid.*). At the same time, teachers were urged to also "stand up and be counted" and to begin to provide students with "real knowledge". It was argued that the struggles of students and workers had to be conjoined and students and workers had to jointly "work out a new future. A future where there will be no racism or exploitation, no apartheid, no inequality of class or sex" (*ibid.*).

The overall strategy had to be

to reject, to challenge and replace this system ... with a democratic system of free, compulsory non-racial education in a single democratic, free and united Azania (Committee of 81, 1980b:1-2).

Student leaders emphasised that the school boycott was "not an end in itself" and would not "transform South African society overnight" (*ibid.*). A boycott of formal schooling, it was stressed, was simply one tactic of struggle, and a planned political act, which is designed to achieve specific short-term victories within a given space of time, and also to raise the general political consciousness of broad layers of students (*ibid.*).

Limited struggles, with definite objectives, had the potential to "give students confidence in themselves, teach them through political experience the basic lessons of organisation and create the climate wherein political consciousness can flourish" (*ibid.*).

These statements of the Committee of 81 were not just so much rhetoric as much as a guide to political and organisational practice during the education school boycott and protests. Short-term education grievances were put forward and linked to long-term education and political demands. Awareness programmes were organised around political and education issues. Teacher support was sought and a Teachers Action Committee was established. Furthermore, students aligned themselves with and participated in various contemporaneous civic and worker campaigns and struggles. They galvanised support for a red meat boycott called to express solidarity with dismissed striking workers belonging to the non-racial and democratic General Workers Union. They popularised and helped implement a bus boycott in protest against fare increases and organised commemoration services in remembrance of those killed in 1976. They also arranged rallies demanding the release of Mandela and all political prisoners. As the education protests and other struggles meshed and began to assume the form of mass popular resistance, and as police responded with killings, attacks and harassment, they formed parent-student committees to co-ordinate mass action.

The Committee of 81 has interpreted the principal gains of the education boycott as

political and organisational. The degree of unity is almost unprecedented. A base has been created upon which lasting buildings of the future can be created (quoted in Christie, 1985:249).

Indeed, the interlocking factory, education and township struggles of 1980 created the conditions for, and spurred the emergence of, numerous local and regional umbrella civic, youth and women's organisations. They also provided fertile ground for the formation of SRCs and COSAS branches at schools, for the revival of the SRC at UWC, and for the establishment of SANSCO branches at universities and colleges.

The appeal of the ideological and political thrust of the Committee of 81 was however not the only factor that contributed to SANSCO's theoretical and political re-orientation. Also decisive in its gravitation towards the Congress movement was the increasing visibility of literature and icons associated with the ANC, heightened activity by the ANC's military wing (MK), and the growing presence and influence of the Congress movement. A spectacular attack by MK on the SASOL oil-from-coal refinery enhanced the reputation of the ANC and generated considerable excitement among students. However, especially important was the national "Release Mandela" campaign spearheaded by the Release Mandela Committee and various Congress movement student and community groups.

The campaign popularised Mandela and the imprisoned leadership of the ANC and awakened an interest in the history of the Congress movement and the struggles of the 1950s, and in the programme and policies of the ANC. The campaign also re-introduced the Freedom Charter into political discourse by presenting it as the basis for the fundamental transformation of apartheid society in the direction of a non-racial democracy. The *Sunday Post's* lead in 1980 in publishing the Freedom Charter in full, and in also carrying an article on the history of the Freedom Charter, was soon followed by student groups. In this way, the programme and policies of the Congress movement began to be popularised at a mass level and this, combined with the building of mass popular organisations, contributed to the growing hegemony of the Congress movement within radical opposition politics. At a "Release Mandela" meeting at UWC, ANC flags were unfurled, beginning a trend that was repeated in other parts of the country.

Shifts in political orientation and activities

All these developments and influences, and especially the unmistakable support that was expressed during 1980 by its constituency on the campuses for Mandela and the Freedom Charter and the impressive mobilising capacity of the Congress movement, could not, and did not, leave SANSCO unaffected. The first sign of a shift in political re-orientation came in September 1980 on the occasion of the funeral of Reverend "Castro" Mayathula, a prominent Soweto political figure. COSAS and SANSCO

issued a joint pamphlet in which they paid tribute to Mr. Mayathula. The pamphlet said that as a guide to the political direction of the future, Mr. Mayathula had referred to the Freedom Charter as the most democratic document detailing the demands of the people.

Since this was a joint pamphlet with COSAS, and the latter had during "1980 declared its support for the Freedom Charter" (Davies *et al.,* 1984:Vol. 2, 371), one cannot be certain that the views expressed in the pamphlet necessarily reflected the views of the entire leadership of SANSCO, or/and the entire membership. Indeed, the first congress of SANSCO in July 1981 would demonstrate that there was by no means unanimous support among members for the Freedom Charter.

What is clear, however, is that the political developments discussed above resulted in SANSCO members "reassessing the political content" of the organisation, and re-aligning their political positions (Phaala, 1983b:3). The process of reassessment was extended to incorporate the views of student activists outside of SANSCO. According to Phaala, "at the end of '80, a number of people were invited by the people charged with the duty of organising AZASO to come and share ideas about the direction" of the organisation (*ibid.*). Those invited were student leaders who were politically influential and occupied key organisational positions on various campuses and were in the main adherents of the Congress movement. Among them was Joe Phaala, the immediate future president of SANSCO.

The reasons advanced by Phaala for initially staying aloof from SANSCO were generally representative of most Congress student activists. He states

[f]rom 1979 ... I was one of those people who strongly opposed the idea of an organisation like AZASO forming, at the level of tactics and strategy realising that what needs to be done is not just to duplicate what was done before. And also there was the political content of such an organisation (Phaala, 1983b:3).

It was not the case that Congress student activists from the various campuses were a unified force linked by formal structures or in regular contact, or even strongly familiar with one another. Indeed, contact between these activists only began to occur during 1980-81 through national and regional political and popular campaigns and events and informal networks. Thus, there was no national decision among Congress activists to remain outside SANSCO. There were, however, common concerns.

In the first place, Congress student activists were uncertain about or opposed to a national student organisation. The immediate repressive actions of the state against the first AZAPO leadership raised questions about the advisability of a national formation without a strong grassroots base. Consequently, they preferred to concentrate on campus-level political mobilisation and organisation-building and to allow the formation of a national structure to be a more organic process. Second, like Phaala, "at the level of tactics and strategy" many activists refused to countenance, under the new conditions of the late 1970s, SANSCO simply replicating the role previously played by SASO. A University of Durban-Westville SRC conference around sport on campuses well revealed the strategic concerns of the Congress students. While they expressed their support for the anti-apartheid South African Council on Sports (SACOS), they took issue with the SACOS ban on organised sport on campuses and called for a change in tactics. The UDW SRC president argued that campus sport had to be looked at in relation to mass mobilisation and organisation and political consciousness-raising around the immediate interests of students. A member of the Black Students' Society at Natal University stressed that strategies and tactics could not be solely determined by principles, but had to take into consideration concrete conditions, including the level of consciousness of the black oppressed. This view was supported by the Wits Black Students Society which emphasised the need for a mass approach and mass-based organisation. The essential argument was that people had to be mobilised and organised around all issues affecting them and on all fronts.

Finally, there was the all-important question of "political content". For the Congress students, adherence to BC represented stagnation in ideology and politics. They had embraced a class or race-class analysis of South African realities and were also committed to a non-racial approach to political struggle. Given this attitude, SANSCO had little or no presence on a number of campuses where Congress movement students were hegemonic, and had no influence in structures such as the Committee of 81 and the Natal Schools Action Committee that emerged to co-ordinate the 1980 boycotts. It also meant that the platforms of the Release Mandela Committee, which attracted thousands of students, were largely closed for the popularisation of SANSCO.

Further, and more decisive, public evidence of the shift of SANSCO towards the Congress movement was provided by the anti-Republic Day protests of early 1981. To oppose the celebration of the twenty-first anniversary of the white republic and also politically mobilise against apartheid, a loose alliance of national, regional and local political, community and student organisations and trade unions formed the anti-Republic Day movement. The theme of "nothing to celebrate" under apartheid was coupled to that of "forward to a people's republic", with the Freedom Charter advanced as the basis for the "people's republic". Anti-Republic Day activities occurred at almost all the black and white English-language universities, with mass meetings being coupled with limited class boycotts. On many campuses, South African flags were publicly burnt, an offence carrying the charge of treason. Charney observed that there was also

> an unmistakable mushrooming of support for the non-racial ANC on the campuses, with slogans, flags and speakers associated with the organisation much in evidence at the recent protest meetings.

The student organisations within the anti-Republic Day movement included COSAS, SANSCO and, significantly, the predominantly white National Union of South African Students' (NUSAS), which in the late 1970s came under a radical leadership that aligned itself with the Congress movement. At a Wits anti-Republic day meeting Reveal Nkondo, the SANSCO organising secretary, noted the audacity of the apartheid government in expecting blacks, "suffering from the ravages of colonialism, imperialism and from capitalist exploitation", to celebrate the anniversary of the Republic, and ended his speech with "Mayibuye", a slogan associated with the Congress movement (quoted in Frederikse, 1986:40). However, what was most crucial was not so much the content of Nkondo's speech, which reflected the growing anti-capitalist thrust of

219

1980s black student politics, as his presence at a meeting that was chaired by the white president of the Wits SRC.

"Such a scene", as Charney has written with regard to another anti-Republic Day meeting where "the platform where Mr. Boraine [president of NUSAS] spoke also held representatives of the black Congress of South African Students' and the Azanian Students Organisation", was "impossible not long ago". As far as student politics was concerned, the significance of the SANSCO participation in the anti-Republic day activities was fourfold. First, in sharing a platform with NUSAS and white representatives of the democratic trade unions, SANSCO broke with the SASO strategy of conducting the political struggle on a racially exclusive basis. Second, for the first time in over a decade national black and white student organisations joined together in common opposition to apartheid. Third, the joint action with NUSAS was to be the harbinger of the emergence of a non-racial higher education student alliance committed to the Freedom Charter. Finally, the SANSCO involvement in the anti-Republic Day movement clearly signalled the break of its leadership from BC and its new alignment with the Congress movement.

SANSCO's sharing of platforms with white radicals drew a hostile reception from AZAPO, and the two organisations publicly clashed at a meeting to commemorate the fifth anniversary of the June 1976 uprising. An AZAPO speaker rejected white radicals as liberals, and criticised black students for being "duped" by their "rhetoric colour-blind, orthodox Marxist language". The criticism provoked a bitter counter-attack from SANSCO and COSAS. BC members were described as "black liberals", and BC organisations were accused of being "reactionary" and of having links with the American Central Intelligence Agency. AZAPO was criticised as a practitioner of "cheap politics", and for forgetting that "the struggle continues all the time", for an irregular public profile and for avoiding day-to-day mobilisation and organisation building. This public clash between SANSCO and COSAS and AZAPO reflected a sharpening of the ideological and political differences between the Congress and BC movements, and contributed to their wider and deeper estrangement. In the case of SANSCO, the clash severed virtually all the links between the SANSCO leadership and AZAPO, and accelerated the movement of SANSCO into the Congress fold.

The First National Congress, July 1981

It was against this backdrop that the first national congress of SANSCO was convened at Wilgespruit, near Johannesburg, on 24-26 July 1981. The 30 delegates and 70 invited observers included a number of Congress student activists, although the political loyalties of the delegates were unclear. While the SANSCO leadership had taken the organisation down a path of public alignment with the Congress movement, it was uncertain whether the delegates would endorse this. Those Congress activists who had remained outside SANSCO attended the SANSCO congress with no preconceived objective or strategy of taking control of the organisation from SANSCO. Indeed, all attended as observers, having been invited, as student leaders, to debate the political direction of SANSCO.

The fact that SANSCO had, during the eighteen months of its existence, generally failed to mobilise students and root itself organisationally among black higher education students was beyond dispute. What was the subject of great controversy and debate, however, was the future political direction of the organisation. Congress activists argued that the failures of SANSCO were the result of limitations of BC philosophy, and the reduction of this philosophy by opportunists to a "mere rejection of whites rather than a positive assertion by the oppressed to free themselves from both racist oppression and exploitation". Their attitude was that BC "has served its purpose. We must move on". They further asserted that SANSCO "had to adopt a broader but clearer approach defining the issues at stake". The criticism of BC was challenged by AZAPO supporters and the questions of "issues at stake" and "approach" stimulated considerable debate.

In the heated arguments and exchanges that ensued, there was a walkout of some AZAPO supporters although most adherents of BC stayed the duration of the congress. To their surprise, the Congress activists discovered that although some delegates had concerns or reservations about the Congress movement, they were not implacably wedded to BC either. Such delegates were also open to re-orientating SANSCO along a different path if that had the potential to contribute to its development. Many of these delegates, as well as some BC adherents were eventually won over to supporting the formal re-orientation of

SANSCO's ideology and politics. When it came to elections, delegates voted to eliminate the distinction between student delegates and observers. In the resulting elections, many of the previous critics of SANSCO were persuaded to accept nominations to key leadership positions, were duly elected and now became its inheritors. As a result, "with near unanimity among the 30 delegates ... and overwhelming support from the 70 invited observers, AZASO was able to change direction without a BC breakaway". SANSCO, then, was spared intractable disputes and battles and any resultant major organisational cleavage and paralysis. Indeed, it took, as the *Sunday Tribune* put it, "no more than a gentle nudge of a toecap to ease the political philosophy which did much to rekindle black political activism in the seventies, out of its prime position".

The first congress drafted a constitution with a new preamble, and adopted a Policy Document (Appendix 2, hereto). The aims defined for SANSCO were sevenfold. The first three aims concerned SANSCO's relationship to its defined constituency. Thus, the organisation proclaimed itself open to "all students in institutions of higher learning and training", committed itself to "unite" and to take up the "demands of students", and to be the "national and international voice" of black higher education students. Another three aims related to relations with other social groups and formations. In this regard, SANSCO undertook to "forge links" with progressive organisations committed to national liberation; to identify with the "liberation of the black worker", and to "strive for the eradication of exploitation". A final aim specified SANSCO's intention to work for a "relevant and non-racial education". The purpose of organising students was defined in terms of enabling them to "take up their demands for a relevant role in society", and to play a "more meaningful role in the community in general" (see Appendix 2).

Significantly, in the opening key sections of the constitution covering the "preamble", "membership" and "aims and objectives", there was no explicit or specific reference to the organisation being restricted to black students. The opening line of the preamble to the constitution did refer to " ... we the Black students of South Africa", but this in itself did not necessarily preclude SANSCO from organising white students, since this merely reflected the reality that SANSCO had indeed been founded only by black students. At first glance, then, nothing in the constitution appeared to prohibit SANSCO, were it so inclined, to organise, and extend membership to white students. Curiously, only in the penultimate section of the constitution, under "definitions" was it made explicit that "students shall denote any *black* person who is registered as a student at any institution of higher learning or training ... "(emphasis added, AZASO, 1983a).

The lack of emphasis on "race" (indeed, in the entire constitution the term "black" only appeared three times) was a conscious attempt on the part of SANSCO's activists to move away from a preoccupation with "race" and colour. In line with their ideological and political orientation, they sought to stress that the experience of being oppressed and exploited in South Africa related not just to "race" but to prevailing economic and political structures, and that the struggle was not simply "between black power and white power" but "between the power of exploiter's and people's power" (see below and Appendix 2). It was also an attempt to reflect a commitment not just to a future non-racial democracy in South Africa, but also to non-racialism in practice.

Still, SANSCO organised and was open only to black students and was thus an exclusively black formation, a seeming contradiction to its commitment to non-racialism in practice. SANSCO activists, however, saw no contradiction between a commitment to non-racialism and the organisation restricting itself to black students. In their view, political and organisational strategies were not shaped exclusively by ideological and political commitments but also material conditions. The reality of racial and national oppression, the vastly different conditions on black and white campuses, and the particular problems experienced by black students on white campuses justified the existence of a separate and exclusively black organisation. Furthermore, although SANSCO did consider the organisation of white students, and whites in general, into progressive formations as an important moment of the democratic struggle in South Africa, it was felt that this was a task best left to NUSAS.

In the arguments around the future direction of SANSCO the Congress students had emphasised the need to view class exploitation as a key feature of black oppression. According to Phaala, the first national president of SANSCO, the congress was of the view that racism was ... a secondary problem which had been introduced to facilitate exploitation of the majority ... What is important is that we do not only struggle against racism but see beyond it and recognise ... the primary problem – exploitation of person by person.

The first part of Phaala's statement tends to rather crudely posit a simple functional relationship between capitalism and racism, and to reduce racism to an epiphenomenon of capitalism. Nonetheless, what was significant about it was the attempt to link racial and national oppression and capitalist exploitation, and especially the view that it was insufficient to simply oppose racism without also challenging capitalist relations of production in South Africa.

This analysis was the determinant of a crucial resolution that was to serve as the bedrock of SANSCO's policy document. The resolution stated that what SANSCO learnt from an examination of "the struggle of oppressed people in the world against oppression, pertinently in Angola, Mozambique and Zimbabwe", was that "they fought against the system and not individual Portuguese colonialists or white Rhodesians" (Appendix 2). The resolution furthermore noted and reproduced a long statement of Samora Machel, the important lines of which are :

We always say that we are struggling against the exploitation of man by man ... There are nationalists ... who think that the purpose of our struggle should be to establish black power instead of white power ... Their ultimate aim is to "Africanise" exploitation. For them our struggle should be a struggle between black power and white power, whereas for us the struggle is between the power of exploiters and people's power (See Appendix 2 for the full quote).

Finally, the resolution sought to

dispel the myth that all blacks are workers, whilst we confirm that black workers in South Africa are the most exploited and therefore the vanguard in the national struggle for democracy (Appendix 2).

The resolution, and the policy document in general, was a clear signal of SANSCO's ideological and political commitments. As will become evident, because of the repressive condition phrases like "people's power" and "true democracy" were really euphemisms for socialism.

In a direct rebuttal of the AZAPO thesis that all blacks were workers, SANSCO also acknowledged the existence of class divisions among blacks and asserted the primacy of black workers "in the national struggle for democracy". The accordance of a vanguard role to black workers was a clear refutation of the previous SANSCO position that black students were a "vanguard" of the national liberation struggle. The need for links with worker struggles conducted by progressive trade unions was emphasised, as were links with organisations that generally shared SANSCO's views. Finally, priority was accorded to the tasks of building mass organisations among oppressed and exploited social groups and to building the unity of all the oppressed since, in SANSCO's view, a crucial determinant of the success of the political struggle would be mass mobilisation and mass organisation.

Ideology and Politics: Race, Class and National Liberation

The policy document adopted at the first congress in July 1981 provided one, and early, indication of SANSCO's new ideological and political orientation. Various speeches of SANSCO leaders, interviews with the progressive media, and the newsletters and pamphlets of the organisation in the years that followed make it possible to identify in greater detail the ideology and politics of SANSCO. In this section my object is to examine SANSCO's analysis of the South African social formation, its principles and programme, its analysis of education and the role of students, and its general strategy. In other words, the core components of what SANSCO members came to commonly refer to as the "SANSCO approach".

Conceptualising South African society

In an attempt to capture the importance of "race" and class, and racial and national oppression and class domination in South Africa, the ANC conceptualised South Africa as a "colonialism of a special type" (CST) (Davies et al., 1984, Vol. 2:289). However, despite its political affinity with the ANC, during the early 1980s SANSCO's characterisation of South Africa was not identical to that of the ANC. Indeed, on only one occasion during this period was South Africa conceptualised by a SANSCO leader in terms that approximated to those of the ANC. This was at the 1982

NUSAS July festival, when Phaala argued that in South Africa "the political and social system resembles that of colonialism except for the fact that there is no specific metropolitan state to which the dominant white group owes allegiance" (1982:35). On the one hand, to conceptualise South Africa in terms of CST would have been a brazen act that would have attracted unnecessary attention from state security agencies. On the other hand, even though ANC literature was more widely available, the formulation of CST was not generally well known. Furthermore, the conception that was already popular within the Congress movement was that of "racial capitalism".

Consequently, at all other times and until the mid-1980s, the South African social formation was characterised as a system of "racial capitalism", both by SANSCO leaders and members themselves, and by political, trade union and civic leaders invited to address SANSCO workshops and national conferences. While the formulation "racial capitalism" was regarded as not totally adequate, it was viewed as a useful way of capturing the simultaneity of racial and national oppression and capitalist exploitation in South Africa. SANSCO activists who were familiar with and loyal to the CST thesis neither challenged nor rejected the racial capitalism formulation, and until the mid-1980s there was also not much debate, public or private, as to which of the two formulations was most appropriate. Over and above the question of security, there were three reasons for this. First, within SANSCO there was a general attitude that, while theory was important, to the extent that there was general consensus about the goals and political direction of SANSCO the more crucial object was to build a mass organisation and to mobilise students in education and political struggles. Second, while among political tendencies critical of the ANC the racial capitalism formulation was advanced in opposition to CST and linked to a project of immediate socialism, the manner in which the thesis of racial capitalism was presented in SANSCO did not contradict that of CST. Moreover, while, as will be seen, SANSCO was committed to a socialist future, it also had as its goal national liberation, and had a particular conception of the relationship between national liberation and socialism.

Finally, there was general agreement that, rather than become fixated on shorthand descriptions, the more important object was to give due recognition to the elements of both racism and capitalism, and their interrelation, in the shaping of South African society and the implications of this for political struggle. In this regard, SANSCO argued that there was a close interrelationship between racial and national oppression and capitalism in South Africa, and that the former facilitated and reinforced the latter. While capitalism was identified as the "primary problem" and racism regarded as a "secondary problem", racism and national oppression were not reduced to epiphenomena of capitalism but were recognised as important and real material factors and objects of struggle.

This analysis led SANSCO to identify two broad and oppositional political camps in South Africa. On the one hand there was a "people's" camp consisting of black workers, large sections of the black petit bourgeoisie, other classes, strata and categories among the black oppressed, and white democrats. On the other hand, there was an "enemy" camp comprising the capitalist class, the white petit bourgeoisie, white working class, and sections of the black petit bourgeoisie. As can be seen, the demarcation of the "people" and the "enemy" was not strictly in terms of "race" or class. There was a strong politico-strategic element to the definition of the two blocs. Two issues were emphasised. First, the dividing line between the two camps was not, and ought not to be conceived of as, static. The line was subject to change with the ebb and tide of political struggle, and it was the task of concrete analysis to determine the precise constituents of, and correlation of forces between, the two camps. Second, it was also stressed that political work among those constituting the "enemy" camp had the potential to corrode the apartheid social base and broaden the "people's" camp. In other words, flexibility of tactics was encouraged. The apartheid state was perceived as safeguarding capitalism and white privilege, as representing the general interests of the "enemy" camp, and as attempting to co-opt sections of the "people" so as to extend the social base of the ruling bloc.

SANSCO: Political principles

SANSCO espoused four political principles, derived from its analysis of South African society as well as from its ideological and political goals. The first principle was that of non-racialism in practice. Phaala stated that "because of our emphasis on exploitation as the main problem we are non-racial in our approach to our problem". Thus, conceiving of the essential "problem" as a particular social structure meant that the political target was identified primarily in systemic terms rather than in terms of social groups and "race". Political commitment rather than social origins or "race" was to be the determinant of inclusion or exclusion in the political struggle. For this reason SANSCO accepted "anyone, irrespective of colour who commits himself or herself to the struggle against exploitation as an ally". If, for strategic reasons, SANSCO shared with the BC organisations a racially exclusive membership, it was its commitment to non-racialism *in practice*, as contrasted with non-racialism *purely as a goal* that was one of the key features that distinguished it from BC organisations. The adherence to non-racialism in practice provided the basis for an alliance with NUSAS and other progressive non-racial organisations.

A second principle espoused by SANSCO was that of democratic practice. It was argued that "democracy becomes real and relevant for us only if students participate in decision-making", and in this regard a strategic objective was to "ensure that democratically elected, representative bodies (SRCs or AZASO branches) exist at all campuses" (*AZASO National Newsletter*, June 1983:5). A third principle was unity and struggle, these moments being regarded as "essential for victory" (*ibid.*:4). However, two differing bases for unity were suggested. One was programmatic, in terms of which it was frequently asserted that "all democratic forces in South Africa should be united in the struggle and that the basis of the unity should be ... the Freedom Charter" (*ibid.*). Occasionally, the insistence on a programmatic unity gave way to a call for the "unity of all progressives" – lending consistency to the statement that "despite the differences between us and AZAPO we still hope to work with them in any progressive campaign which they may support". While an emphasis on programmatic unity does not in itself preclude a concomitant commitment to broader strategic and tactical alliances, under certain circumstances it can breed a sectarian approach to political struggle. How SANSCO fared in this regard is an issue that will be examined in a later chapter.

The final principle of SANSCO was that of working class leadership of the liberation struggle. A race-class analysis of South Africa and its ideological commitments had led SANSCO to reject the "Africanisation" of exploitation. Instead, "people's power" was asserted as SANSCO's immediate political goal, and SANSCO proclaimed that "black workers are ... the vanguard in the national struggle for democracy" (Appendix 2). The necessity to develop and assert working class leadership within the liberation struggle was consistently emphasised by SANSCO's leaders and intellectuals, in education workshops and forums, and in SANSCO's mass media (Phaala, 1981:10; 1982:40; *AZASO National Newsletter*, June 1983:4).

In adhering to the above principles, the leadership stressed that it was essential for the organisation's ideological and political commitments "to be reflected in our daily activities" (Phaala, 1981:9). Methods of struggle and goals were linked: principles and "ideals are not only to be built after liberation, but during the struggle for it" ; and it was argued that "the nature of the struggle is going to reflect the type of society that is ... to come" (*AZASO National Newsletter*, June 1983:4; Phaala, 1982:40).

Political programme and strategy

Like its principles, the political programme and strategy that SANSCO embraced was shaped by its ideology and by structural conditions. To the racially exclusive and authoritarian political order was counterposed a non-racial democracy. In opposition to the colonial and imperialist legacy of self-determination for solely the minority white population, formalised by the "Union of South Africa" in 1910 and the declaration of South Africa as a republic in 1961, it advanced the objectives of national liberation and self-determination for black South Africans. In place of separate development and the balkanisation of South Africa, SANSCO sought an unfragmented country and a unitary South African state. Critical of bourgeois power and rejecting any "Africanisation" of exploitation, it was committed to the establishment of "people's power".

However, its political commitments extended beyond a non-racial democracy and political transformation, to include revolutionary social transformation. The stress on the creation of a society "free of exploitation ... in which harmony among people will prevail", on the social emancipation of the working class, and on the necessity of working class leadership of the liberation struggle, signalled an explicit commitment to

229

socialism. Frequently, in public meetings and workshops, reference was made to "people's power" and the creation of a "true democracy", and the two concepts were elaborated in a way that meant that they essentially served as synonyms for democratic socialism. A "true democracy" was said to be a society in which the major means of production were socialised, and the "people", particularly workers, exercised hegemony over and within the economic, political and social institutions and processes of society.

The commitment to socialism becomes even clearer when one considers how SANSCO conceptualised the Freedom Charter and how it dealt with the relationship between national liberation and socialism, both being issues that provoked considerable debate within liberation organisations. SANSCO formally adopted the Freedom Charter as its political manifesto in 1983, the AZASO *National Newsletter* proclaiming it as "the programme of minimum demands to which we commit ourselves". However, its commitment to the Freedom Charter was already evident in late 1981 when it endorsed a resolution at the anti-South African Indian Council Conference that described the Freedom Charter as "a universal document containing our minimum demands", and providing "a framework within which all struggles today are conducted".

The phrase "minimum demands" requires some discussion. The precise character of the Freedom Charter was a matter of considerable debate. In some quarters, the document was criticised as a bourgeois manifesto, which ultimately safeguarded capitalism in South Africa. In other quarters, and often in response to the above criticism, the document tended to be presented as a manifesto that guaranteed a socialist future in South Africa. SANSCO's own position was to reject both these interpretations of the Freedom Charter. Instead, its view was that the Freedom Charter was neither a bourgeois document nor as a socialist manifesto, but rather best understood as a revolutionary national-democratic programme. To the extent that the programme incorporated most working class demands as well as those of other classes experiencing national and racial oppression, the Charter was seen a positive response to the problem of racial and national oppression. Moreover, although the Freedom Charter did not proclaim socialism as the goal, and its immediate objects were a non-racial democracy and a national democratic state, it was seen as generally anti-capitalist in orientation. It not only did not retard socialist transformation but, indeed, provided a foundation for such a transformation.

The assertion that the Freedom Charter represented its "minimum demands" sought to draw attention to the fact that SANSCO had certain demands and goals that went beyond those embodied in the Charter. These demands sought to build on and extend the freedoms and rights contained in the Freedom Charter and related to the transformation of South African society along socialist lines. However, there was also an emphatic insistence that while manifestos were important in articulating a vision, they guaranteed, on their own, nothing. It was stressed that, ultimately, the precise outcome of the national liberation struggle would be determined by mass organisation and actual struggles, and the extent to which working class leadership and hegemony were exercised within the mass movement.

Turning to political strategy, South African realities were viewed as necessitating a "particular format" of struggle (Phaala, 1981:9), one referred to as the "National Democratic struggle" (*AZASO National Newsletter*, 1985:2). The thesis was that conditions in South Africa not only made imperative, but also favoured, the construction of a non-racial multi-class alliance under working class leadership. The Freedom Charter in turn was seen as providing an excellent basis for such an alliance. The term "national" went beyond simply a geographic connotation. It defined the content of the liberation struggle as anti-imperialist; denoted the task of mobilising and uniting all the black oppressed and white democrats in political action, and the need, through political struggle, to lay the basis for the emergence of a single South African nation and culture. The term "democratic", on the other hand, referred to both the goal of the liberation struggle – a democratic social order based on universal franchise – and the necessity for democratic participation, decision-making and practice in the conduct of the liberation struggle.

If SANSCO was committed to socialism, but also adhered to the Freedom Charter, and conceptualised the struggle in South Africa as, in the first place, a "national liberation" struggle rather than as a purely socialist struggle, how did it relate the national and class dimensions of the South African struggle? SANSCO was adamant in its rejection of bourgeois nationalism, and the "type of petit bourgeois leadership which wants to maintain itself, such that with the success of the struggle they can be the ones who can climb the political ladder" (Phaala, 1982:37). Its viewpoint in this regard dovetailed with similar assertions by the ANC. The ANC recognised the dangers of bourgeois nationalism. It understood that a movement founded on such a nationalist outlook would be hard pressed to redress the inequities and injustice of colonialism and apartheid. Thus the latter's *Strategy and Tactics* stated that

Our nationalism must not be confused with chauvinism or narrow nationalism of a previous epoch. It must not be confused with the classical drive of an elitist group among the oppressed people to gain ascendancy so that they can replace the oppressor in the exploitation of the mass ... (quoted by Innes and Flegg, 1978:2).

However, the ANC sought to be, and was, a political home for a wide spectrum of anti-apartheid forces, ranging from communists to liberals, whereas an explicit socialist commitment would have constricted its social base. Thus, it remained a national liberation movement committed to a project of national democracy. Still, it did hold out the possibility, under particular conditions, "of a speedy progression from formal liberation to genuine and lasting emancipation" and suggested that this was

made more real by the existence in our country of a large and growing working class whose class consciousness complements national consciousness ... (*Strategy and Tactics*, quoted by Innes and Flegg, 1978:2).

This perspective of the ANC — that of a first stage of national democracy — followed under favourable conditions, by a second stage of socialism, came to be referred to as the "two-stage theory" of revolution.

Within SANSCO, there was no adherence to the so-called "two-stage theory" of revolution, if this implied that the struggle for national liberation and for socialism were distinct and consecutive stages. Statements around the necessity to develop and assert working class leadership, and to ensure that the content and methods of struggle were related to political objectives, pointed to a rejection of any rigid two-stage theory of revolution. Indeed, there was strong agreement with the view of Ruth First that:

The national and the class struggle are not part of some natural order of succession, but take place coterminously ... It is because national demands cannot be met under capitalism that the proletariat is the essential leader of the SA revolution, and the struggle for national liberation, given this political leadership – which has, I agree, to be asserted – will at the same time be part of the struggle for socialism (First, 1978:98).

Moreover, the contention of Joe Slovo, a leading member of the ANC and general-secretary of the SACP, that

[t]here is no Chinese wall between the stages of our revolution ... [W]e are not saying that the problem of social emancipation is something that will be postponed until we have some vague form of people's power (1983:87)

was strongly supported by SANSCO members and also widely cited. Slovo argued that the ultimate outcome of the South African struggle would be strongly conditioned by the class forces that were hegemonic during the national liberation struggle. For this reason it was essential to convince workers that

... in the long run, racism cannot be overthrown without the destruction of its foundation, which is capitalism. We cannot postpone the spreading of these ideas until we have achieved the so-called first stage of revolutionary advance. They must be spread now (ibid.).

Within SANSCO it was socialist ideas that were hegemonic, and these were spread among other students and filtered into other popular organisations. If the spread of socialist ideas was combined with an emphasis also on national liberation, and popularisation of the Freedom Charter, SANSCO could have well claimed that far from being inconsistent, it was guided by Lenin. Another popular figure among SANSCO activists, Lenin had insisted that the revolutionary struggle against capitalism had to be coupled with a "revolutionary programme ... on all democratic demands: a republic ... equal rights for women ... etc.", and that "the social revolution is not a single battle, but a period" (quoted by Innes and Flegg, 1978:3-4).

With respect to the forms of opposition to racial and class domination, SANSCO was of the view that these needed to be shaped by the acknowledgement that the apartheid ruling class would not "voluntarily relinquish [its] privileged position". While it accepted the need for a flexibility in tactics it refused, however, to countenance operating within separate development political institutions, and asserted that "no government-created institution will ever be instrumental in ushering in total liberation" (SANSCO Policy Document, Appendix 2). In view of the above, an extraparliamentary opposition movement was defined as the only viable vehicle of resistance. Concomitantly, it was stressed that opposition and struggle should not be restricted to the political sphere or confined to only political issues. Instead, all arenas of society – the workplace, residential townships, education and health institutions, places of religious worship and sport – had to be transformed into sites and fronts of opposition and struggle around political issues and issues specific to particular institutions. For the "waging of a disciplined, protracted struggle against all aspects of oppression" a "strategy of mass organisation" was argued to be "the most important weapon" (Phaala, 1983a:4; 1983b:12). Organisation building and the forging of unity among oppressed people was viewed a dynamic process. Thus, it was stated that "it is through mass mobilisation and the taking up of day to day problems that people experience struggle, and organisation and unity is built" (*AZASO National Newsletter*, June 1983:4).

Education and the role of students

According to a SANSCO official, the education system was not "separate from political and economic structures in society, but "materially interwoven into the wider social totality" (quoted in Anon, *Africa Perspective*, 24, 1984:71). Education in South Africa served "the important function of ensuring the continued existence of society itself". More specifically, education was seen as performing three roles. First was the training of students in numeracy and literacy. Second was the socialisation of individuals whereby they "absorb the values, norms ... of society such as obedience, passivity, hierarchy, racism, etc."; and third, the allocation of individuals into different occupational and social roles. The effect of apartheid education was to "subjugate and subordinate the oppressed majority" and to "perpetuate white prosperity and supremacy" (*ibid.*)

A report commissioned by the World University Service and the Association of University Teachers stated with respect to SANSCO that "the ... leadership is well aware of the dangers of an elitist education and the reformist role assigned to a black middle class by the white regime" (WUS/AUT, 1986:10). According to Phaala, state strategy in the education arena during the 1980s was constituted by the "the carrot and stick method of co-option coupled with repression" (Phaala, 1981:10). Co-option referred to the attempt by the state to win the support of "a more significant number of people from the ranks of the oppressed" (ibid.). Two important elements identified in the co-option strategy were "privilege" and "ideology". The former was related to the "increasing trend towards the modernisation of the existing racial universities and colleges", a process viewed as attempting to accustom higher education students "to a privileged life" so that they could be more "easily lured into joining the machinery of control" (Phaala, 1983a:4-5). "Ideology" was seen as the mode through which black higher education students would be inculcated with notions of superiority relative to other blacks, and beliefs that "class divisions of society ... are ... natural and inevitable" (ibid.). Black higher education students were, then, seen as an important target group of the efforts of state and capital to "strengthen the already existing black middle class" and to obtain "agents for effecting an institutionalised class division" (ibid.). Moreover, it was among higher education students too that the ruling class was searching for "allies to help control the voteless and exploited black majority" (Phaala, 1981:10).

In view of this perceived strategy of the state and capital, it was stressed that black students needed to develop a clear understanding of their specific position in the process of ongoing political conflict in South Africa. Two choices were said to be open to black students: "to be part of the oppressive system or part of the oppressed majority" (Phaala, 1983a:5). Those opting to identify with the oppressed majority were in turn confronted by two further choices. The first was an alliance "of convenience" between students and the black petit bourgeoisie and, more broadly, with black workers and the poor, based on the realisation of students "that without the involvement of the masses" apartheid cannot be eradicated (Phaala, 1982:35). Here, students would be simply striving "to eradicate the barriers which prevent them from climbing the ladder of social division" (Phaala, 1981:10). Such an "opportunistic alliance where the petit bourgeoisie uses the masses as a ladder of climbing to the top" was firmly rejected by SANSCO.

A second choice available to students, and the path favoured by SANSCO, was where students "throw their lot behind the efforts of the large majority of exploited black workers to eradicate inequality in all respects" (ibid.). Such an alliance between the black petit bourgeoisie and black working class would not seek to blur the class contradictions among the black population, and here the black petit bourgeoisie would play a facilitative role in which the "masses learn through struggle to take their destiny into their own hands" (ibid.). In this scenario, the role of students would be to turn the privileges granted them "into instruments strengthening the struggle for democracy", and furthering "the workers struggle" (ibid.).

It was SANSCO's view that "there is much students can do. Historically students have played a vital role in catalysing and strengthening the struggle ... " (AZASO National Newsletter, June 1983:3). With specific reference to the government's constitutional proposals of 1982, it was argued that

[a]s intellectuals, students can grasp and understand much better the inadequacies and injustices inherent in the proposals and how they will affect the lives of the people. It is our responsibility to our people ... to enlighten them with the knowledge we have and to practically assist their organisations in fighting the proposals and the daily influence of the state propaganda machine (ibid.).

Student involvement in political and popular struggles was also motivated by drawing attention to their link to the education struggle. Moseneke, the 1983-84 president put it in the following way:

We are a student organisation and our primary site of struggle is education. We, however, know that our demand for a non-racial and democratic education system will never be met in this unjust order. This therefore, necessitates our consistent participation in the broader struggle of our people at all times.

Still, although SANSCO emphasised the reasons necessitating student participation in political, popular and worker struggles, an exclusive concentration on issues related to political power and the state to the detriment of a focus on education issues was regarded as "misleading" (AZASO National Newsletter, June 1983:4; Phaala, 1982:35).

An important thesis was that the struggle around education could make a distinctive contribution towards the establishment of a democratic society (SANSCO Policy Document, Appendix 2). The education arena was defined as an important site of struggle, and it was stated that

as much as all fronts of the struggle should work together, it is also important each front of struggle should know where its priorities lie and we being primarily a student movement, have got a responsibility to challenge the education system (Phaala, 1982:41).

This identification of the education sphere as its principal field of operation, and of its role as essentially challenging the apartheid higher education system, was to powerfully condition its activities. If SANSCO's political commitments were reflected by its adoption of the Freedom Charter and by its official colours of black, green and gold (the colours of the ANC), its emphasis on challenging apartheid education was highlighted by its official slogan "Education towards democracy". The commitment to mobilisation and action around education was also exemplified by the various organisational themes − such as "Education towards a democratic Society (1982), "Organising for people's education" (1984 and 1985), "Student action for people's education" (1986 and 1987), and "Organise, consolidate and advance towards people's education" (1988 and 1989) − that were adopted by SANSCO. According to a student newspaper, the themes sought to direct "students to concentrate on understanding and challenging the workings of apartheid education".

At a strategic level, SANSCO sought not to focus only on immediate education grievances and issues and to be purely reactive in the sense of simply protesting apartheid education. Instead, it also sought to be proactive. Democratic student representation in the form of autonomous SRCs at institutions was an important strategic objective. SRCs, however, were not seen only as providing students with a voice, but also as an integral moment of the democratisation of education institutions. There was also a strong concern to begin formulating a democratic alternative to apartheid education and it was for this reason that a mass campaign to formulate an Education Charter was launched by SANSCO.

SANSCO had strong views around whose interests a future education system ought to primarily serve. It advanced the notion of "people's education", conceived as

[a]n education system that is non-racial and democratic and geared to serve the needs of the working people of South Africa. Not the needs of the Apartheid government and the capitalist class, but the needs of those who produce the wealth of this country but do not enjoy the fruits of their own labour (AZASO, 1984a).

The theme of people's education was to be embraced more widely and also given greater content through the National Education Crisis Committee (NECC), an umbrella formation established in 1986 by scores of national, regional and local education-based organisations. Since it was a founder member of the NECC and identified with the objectives and strategies of the NECC it is necessary to briefly focus on the core themes of the NECC, so as to get a more complete picture of SANSCO's education commitments.

In the first place, the NECC was an attempt to secure a return to school of thousands of secondary school students who were involved in a long and debilitating boycott of education institutions during late 1984-85, often under the slogan "liberation first, education later". Apart from contributing to an erosion of the culture of learning and teaching, the boycott also effectively removed students from their institutional bases and weakened organised action on their part. However, while students were urged to return to school there was no notion that education institutions and education ought to no longer be a terrain of struggle. Instead, the return to schools was coupled with the formulation of new objectives and strategy and tactics of education struggle within an overall theme of "people's education for people's power".

On the one hand the "people's education for people's power" theme was a decisive rejection of the "liberation first, education later" slogan and the notion, implicit in the slogan, that national liberation was imminent. On the other hand, it marked the "shift of oppositional strategy in education from simple boycott to the construction of alternatives", and from "protest to challenge" (Muller, 1987:18, 27). As an alternative to apartheid education, people's education was seen as an education

which serves the people as a whole, which liberates, which puts people in command of their lives and which is determined by and accountable to the people (Wolpe and Unterhalter, 1991:10).

238

A NECC resolution further defined people's education as one that, among other things,

enables the oppressed to understand the evils of the apartheid system and prepares them for participation in a non-racial democratic system; eliminates capitalist norms of competition, individualism and stunted intellectual development, and replaces it with one that encourages collective input and participation by all, as well as stimulating critical thinking and analysis; eliminates illiteracy, ignorance and the exploitation of one person by another; equips and trains all sectors of our people to participate actively and creatively in the struggle to attain people's power ... ; enables workers to resist exploitation and oppression at the work place (quoted in Nkomo, 1990:425).

This was not seen as the last word on the meaning and content of people's education. As Muller writes, the term "process", which "connotes practical grassroots democracy and an emphasis on evolving the strategy and content of peoples education in the process of mass participation" (1987:24), aptly described people's education at this point.

People's education was also seen as a means of concretely challenging the apartheid state's control of education. The conjoining of education with people's power signalled the intention of the people's education movement to contest the form and content of education and to attempt to wrest control of institutions from the government and to transform them from within. The NECC believed that education could contribute to the political formation and preparation of people for participation in the realisation of people's power. Thus, there was a commitment to begin to construct people's education and democratic education structures and practices in, and as part of, the process of the struggle against the apartheid social order. However, it was acknowledged that "people's education can only finally be won when we have won the struggle for people's power" (Sisulu, 1986:107).

Many of the core ideas of the movement for people's education were, clearly, already present within SANSCO. However, there was not a strict identity between SANSCO's views on people's education and those of the NECC. For example, around the question of whose interest people's education should serve, the NECC's formulation was that it should advance the interests of "the people", understood as those groups who stood in an antagonistic relation to the state. SANSCO sought people's education to specifically advance the interests of workers. Still, the NECC did contribute decisively to sharpening the questions of the content and purpose of education. Through its attempt to introduce alternative "people's education" materials into schools, it helped bring to the fore issues related to curriculum, and learning and teaching processes and methods. Moreover, the NECC demand for parent-teacher-student associations to be constituted as the organs of democratic school governance also posed the question of the popular control of education and the political accountability of institutions. Finally, the NECC gave the notion of people's education a considerably wider profile in South Africa and created a more favourable environment for SANSCO's own struggles for people's education within higher education institutions.

8

"Creative Organisers" rather than "Powerful Speakers": Education as a Site of Struggle

Having analysed SANSCO's ideology and politics, I now examine particular aspects of its organisation. Specifically, I focus on its structure and membership, its modes of recruitment and education and training of its members, its organisational culture, and the conditions that shaped its activities. These issues are considered in relation to two distinct periods. The *first period* is the years 1979 to 1986, which were generally characterised by reform initiatives on the part of the apartheid state and by an upsurge in political opposition and mass action on the part of the dominated classes and strata. Organisational issues during this period are, in turn, discussed in relation to two phases of SANSCO's life. The first phase tracks the organisation between its formation in late 1979 and mid-1981 when it moved from a commitment to Black Consciousness towards a Congress movement perspective on struggle. The second phase covers the period mid-1981 to mid-1986, when it established a strong organisational presence at higher educational institutions.

The *second period* encompasses the year's mid-1986 to early 1990, which were characterised by states of emergency and extremely repressive political conditions, which only ended with the government's liberalisation measures of February 1990. Issues around organisation are posed in relation to the severe state repression experienced by SANSCO and other mass organisations – repression that involved not only the occupation of some campuses by the army and police and the detention of activists, but also, from February 1988, a *de facto* proscription of SANSCO.

Although I cover certain of SANSCO's activities and initiatives in this chapter, and leave others to the next chapter dealing with "mobilisation and collective action", there are no hard boundaries between many of the activities discussed. Thus, SANSCO's initiatives around education and training and women students which I deal with as a feature of its organisation can also be considered to be forms of collective action. Conversely, the Education Charter campaign that I cover under "mobilisation and collective action" can, of course, also be seen as aspects of overall organisational activity. Finally, in this chapter my analysis and evaluation of SANSCO's organisation is of a specific and limited nature. A more detailed and general assessment of issues related to SANSCO's organisational character is left to Chapter 10.

Organisation and Activities, 1979 to 1981

In line with BC doctrine, membership of SANSCO was restricted to black higher education students. There was much debate around the form that local-level organisation on the campuses should take. One position was that affiliation to SANSO by Student Representative Councils (SRCs) should be the ideal. Opponents of this position argued that SRCs were an attempt by the university authorities to control the student body. The rejoinder to this was that SRCs had been affiliates of SASO, and that at some campuses SRCs were largely autonomous and an outcome of mass student struggles. The debate was eventually resolved with the decision that "branches independent of SRCs be formed on the campuses" and that SRC members should join SANSCO as individual members of branches.[8.1]

Between late 1979 and mid-1981, SANSCO made little headway in establishing an organisational infrastructure on campuses. Yet the period April 1980 to mid-1981 was characterised by widespread mass student, worker and civic struggles and political campaigns, conditions which should have facilitated the building of an infrastructure on the campuses. However, for a number of reasons SANSCO was unable to mobilise students or to tap into this mobilisation and translate it into organisation.

First, the conflict that emerged in early 1980 between the SANSCO leadership and AZAPO was debilitating for the SANSCO officials and the fledgling organisation. Criticism of the AZAPO action meant that the "the next thing that happened is we were kicked out of the offices" (interview with Nkoane, 1995). Moreover, the effective ending of the relationship with AZAPO also denied SANSCO vital financial and material support and resources, which hindered its activities during 1980.

Second, and a more serious problem, was that student activists already committed to the Congress movement stood aloof from SANSCO. Such activists were hegemonic or influential in the SRCs at the universities of Durban-Westville (UDW), Western Cape (UWC) and Natal Medical School (UNMS), in the Black Student Societies (BSS) at the universities of Natal (Pietermaritzburg), Witwatersrand (Wits) and Rhodes, and in various other local campus-based organisations at the different higher education institutions. According to the Wits Black Students' Society the lesson of the 1980 student boycott was the "need to establish strong organisations and to elaborate a precise theory (i.e. the ideas in terms of which we understand the nature of our society and how to overcome oppression)"[8.2] – the kind of theory it was felt that SANSCO lacked. One of the tasks of the Interim Committee (IC) established at SANSCO's launch was to convene a more representative follow-up conference during 1980. Owing to a ban on all political meetings the conference could not be held. However, given the attitude of the Congress students it is likely that this conference would have been no more representatives than the inaugural one.

A number of meetings were held by SANSCO in early 1980 in Soweto, on its own, or jointly with COSAS and AZAPO. These were directed at introducing SANSCO to students, at discussing problems in education and generating parent support in resolving student educational grievances, and at pledging support for civic struggles as part of the programmatic commitment to involvement in community issues.[8.3] Such meetings, while they may have popularised SANSCO and won it some members, contributed little to mobilising and organising its constituency on the campuses and, in general, there was stagnation at an organisational level. Individual members of SANSCO were active in the 1980 boycotts at the universities of Fort Hare, the North (UNIN) and elsewhere that expressed solidarity with the secondary school student boycott. However, it was only at UNIN that a formal branch of SANSCO existed. One SANSCO activity at UNIN was the setting up of political reading and discussion groups

> because we realised that a number of activists were not reading and we wanted to make it easier for them to read so that they could be able to get engaged in debates. So there was an effort to try and have discussion groups and then what we'd do is try and organise literature, particularly banned literature because it used to be very appealing to people ... (interview with Nkoane, 3 August 1995).

The participation of SANSCO in the anti-Republic Day campaign of 1981 provided it with a greater and national public profile. Moreover, its participation also began to attract the interest of Congress student activists. For many of the Congress students SANSCO, however weak, was a reality. Some of them had participated in a meeting organised at the end of 1980 by the SANSCO Interim Committee (IC) to exchange ideas. It had become clear that many of the IC members were in fact supporters of the Congress movement and that the real difference lay around strategy. Phaala acknowledged the view of the IC that, in the aftermath of the banning of Black Consciousness organisations in 1977, what needed "to be done was to show the state that we are not afraid" (Phaala, 1983b:2). IC members supportive of the Congress movement treated SANSCO as a *fait accompli* and were of the view that that it's future direction and content had to be fought for from within.

With the public movement of the SANSCO leadership towards the Congress movement there was a softening of attitude towards the organisation on the part of those Congress activists outside SANSCO. More immediately, the strong appeal by Nkoane to Phaala and others to attend the first congress in July 1981 posed the question of how they should respond and also formally relate to SANSCO. The lawyer and underground ANC activist Griffiths Mxenge, assassinated in 1981, urged Phaala and other Durban-based activists to attend the congress.[8.4] A grouping from UNMS and UDW did, Phaala describing himself as not a member or delegate but as a "reluctant supporter.[8.5]

Between 1979 and mid-1981 SANSCO existed largely in name. On the eve of its first national congress it was organisationally weak, numbering within its ranks only one branch, and a few score individuals – predominantly male university students. It lacked any substantial organisational base within higher education institutions and was thus largely marginal to student political activity. Moreover, the tendency for SANSCO to concentrate on macro-political and township-based civic issues and to put its energies into township-based activities meant that the mobilisation and organisation of black students on the campuses was largely spearheaded by formations led by Congress activists outside of SANSCO.

Organisation: Structure and Membership, 1981 to 1986

Structure, infrastructure and membership

SANSCO's infrastructure at the campus level was constituted by a "branch". Individual affiliation to SANSCO was not permitted and those seeking membership had to belong to a branch, which had to consist of at least ten members to qualify for affiliation to SANSCO. No specific provision was made for *en masse* affiliation via SRCs. In practice, however, some campuses did affiliate *en masse* via their respective SRCs, although branch structures were also established on such campuses to co-ordinate the day-to-day work of SANSCO. On campuses where SANSCO had just begun to organise, aspirant members and supporters constituted a SANSCO "working group" as a vehicle for organisational activities. Such working groups generally participated in all SANSCO activities and policy- and decision-making forums but were precluded from nominating persons for national office and from voting in elections for national office-bearers.

The "supreme policy-making organ" of SANSCO was the Annual Congress (AC) to which each branch was permitted to send three delegates. The AC elected the national executive committee (NEC). During 1981 the NEC comprised the president, vice-president, national secretary, correspondence secretary, minutes secretary, treasurer, national co-ordinator and an additional member to who were delegated special tasks. 1983 created additional positions for a project officer, publications officer and women's organiser (AZASO, *Constitution and Policy*, 1983).

245

Later, the positions of the three secretaries were merged into a single portfolio of general secretary, and a position created for an education and training officer (*ibid.*). Members seeking election to national office had to be nominated by their branches, a practice that sought to ensure that national officials enjoyed the support and confidence of their branches and that branches were not handicapped by the loss of members to national office. NEC members were all volunteers in that none were full-time paid officials.

Apart from the AC there was also an annual General Students' Council (GSC). NEC members and delegates attended the GSC from branches and, later, also from regional councils and sub-regional councils. Regional councils were created in 1983 to co-ordinate activities of branches in a particular region, while sub-regional councils were established somewhat later to alleviate co-ordination problems in large regions. By the late 1980s there were five regions: Eastern Cape, Western Cape, Natal, Orange Free State and Transvaal, with five sub-regions in the Transvaal and four in Natal (SAIRR, 1992: 56-58).

Apart from constitutional and policy changes and election of the NEC being the preserve of the AC, there was little else that distinguished the GSC from the AC. Both forums included not only delegates but also large numbers of members and aspirant members from working groups who attended as observers. Both considered reports from branches and regions and assessed the state of SANSCO. The GSC did, however, tend to be more concerned with issues such as the state of education and training within SANSCO, with reflecting on national campaigns and projects, and with discussing the state of relationships with other progressive organisations. Since the GSC was normally held during early December, it was also its specific task to define a political and organisational theme for SANSCO for the coming academic year and, in relation to overall political and educational conditions, to formulate a programme of action and to discuss strategy and tactics.

Organisation building: Campus conditions and challenges, 1981 to mid-1983

From the outset, the emphasis of the SANSCO leadership elected in 1981 was on the building of SANSCO as a mass democratic organisation. The priorities were defined as building local branches that were characterised by democratic participation and decision-making. Phaala stressed that "the only thing that will ensure our survival from attempts to divide and repress us is mass mobilisation and democratic organisation".[8.6] The secretary, Motswaledi, elaborated that "for such an organisation, we don't need powerful speakers as much as we need creative organisers", adding that it was imperative to strike a balance between mobilising around non-educational and educational issues and conditions.[8.7]

From the beginning, SANSCO was confronted by the authoritarian attitudes and repressive controls of campus authorities at black institutions. According to Phaala, this meant

> that it has been very difficult to organise on some campuses; various means have been used, on some of the campuses actually AZASO becomes an underground organisation to survive; students know they can't walk around and declare himself an AZASO member (1983a:6).

Motswaledi asserted that campus authorities were "taking over the role of the security police" and outlined various forms of "academic terrorism".[8.8] One form of control was the attempt by administrations to impose on students unacceptable SRC constitutions. Thus, at the Medical University of Southern Africa (MEDUNSA) the constitution prepared by the administration prescribed that it was duty of the SRC president to "see to it that students don't propose motions that are against the rules and regulations of the university"; that permission had to be obtained from the rector before press statements could be issued, and that no student club or society or organisation could affiliate to any organisation without the prior approval of the university.[8.9] Other forms of control were measures to prevent SANSCO leaders from speaking at campuses; prohibitions on the dissemination of newsletters and pamphlets unless these were first approved by the authorities, and the practice of deliberate scheduling of exams and tests on well-known commemorative days in an attempt to preclude student mobilisation.

Conditions at technikons and colleges were even "more difficult actually than at the universities" (Phaala, 1983a:7). While the longer duration for degree programmes at universities provided scope for activist development; the shorter period of study at colleges (sometimes only two years) meant that, no sooner had activists developed experience, they had to leave.

> It is very difficult, because there is a slow process of making
> contact, and by the time contact is made and leadership emerges,
> and there are people who are willing to help you work they are
> already leaving (ibid.).

Furthermore, according to Phaala, teacher-training colleges had the "most dictatorial administrations in the country" because of their desire to maintain tight control on the ideas of teachers and their fear of progressive ideas being taken into schools.[8,10] At technikons, apart from authoritarian controls, an additional challenge was the nature of the academic programme. Frequently, academic courses comprised a combination of a semester of academic study followed by a semester of on-the-job training with the result that continuity in branch personnel as well as branch organisation and activity was severely disrupted.

Organising on the predominantly white campuses represented two different kinds of problems. One was the responses of conservative white students to campaigns such as those demanding the release of Nelson Mandela, the cancellation of "rebel" sports tours that occurred in violation of the international sports boycott against South Africa, or protesting Republic Day. Such events occasionally led to clashes between black and conservative white students. For SANSCO the problem was more than just the intimidating conditions created by conservative white students. As Phaala put it, the "dominant problem of organisation" on white campuses was that

> in that type of situation, it becomes very easy for attitudes of racial
> hatred to develop; and a non-racial approach to the struggle is
> affected by some of the experiences which students on these
> campuses have gone through (1983a:8).

However, threats and challenges to SANSCO's growth and development on campuses did not come only from campus authorities. One challenge, at campuses like UCT and Rhodes, stemmed from the activities of students supportive of the Unity Movement, a small left-wing grouping based predominantly in the Western Cape. In terms of the Unity Movement policy of "non-collaboration" with separate development political and social institutions, student organisations at campuses were condemned as an act of collaboration with the state, and Unity Movement students campaigned against their formation. Some left-wing students, dubbed "workerists", argued that student organisations were "petit bourgeois" and that students should rather join off-campus popular organisations. Both these groups of students were also hostile to NUSAS, which was labelled a "ruling class organisation", and strongly attacked any relationship with NUSAS and its affiliate SRCs. Although these groups did not represent a major organisational threat, they did obstruct somewhat the open and unfettered mobilisation and organisation of black students.[8.11]

A second challenge came from a combination of left wing and BC-supporting students who, while not opposed to black student organisation on campuses, attacked SANSCO's commitment to the Freedom Charter and also criticised its affiliation to the UDF and alliance with NUSAS. Both groups practised "entryism" – joining a SANSCO branch or attending meetings in order to either attempt to wrest control from Congress students or to frustrate and obstruct activities. As will be seen, the failure of an alliance of such left-wing and BC students to win control of the UCT branch of SANSCO led them to form the Students of Young Azania (SOYA) association which was based in the Western Cape.

With respect to the authoritarian controls and repressive measures of campus authorities, SANSCO stressed the need to "organise around these immediate issues" since "these restrictions and intimidatory methods allowed for the creation of an ill-informed and co-opted student body".[8.12] Repression and the attempt to create a docile student body was not seen as being in contradiction with the reformist thrust of corporate capital and the state to create a black middle-class but as an integral part of the reformist agenda. Thus, SANSCO activists spearheaded campaigns for democratic and autonomous SRCs on campuses and engaged in mobilisation to defend and expand the space for student organisation. On especially repressive campuses, alternate vehicles for activism had to be utilised and/or created, "including people getting into the various allowed societies, academic societies, faculty councils, also things like religious organisations and so on" (Phaala, 1983a:6). At technikons, the problem of students alternating a semester of academic study with a semester of on-the-job training was addressed by having a branch committee for each semester. Finally, SANSCO leaders emphasised that challenges from progressive students of differing political persuasions could only be overcome through "all round mobilisation around concrete day to day and political issues and through building up strong organisation with well equipped activists".[8.13]

The continuous emphasis on building branches and membership and patient and principled organising was to be handsomely rewarded. At the 1981 congress SANSCO had consisted of just one branch. In contrast, some 300 students participated in SANSCO's second congress in July 1982, and in attendance were branches and working groups from all the black universities and white English-language campuses, and some colleges. Almost 600 delegates and observers attended the third congress in Cape Town and SANSCO claimed to have a presence at 14 university and technikon campuses and seven colleges (SAIRR, 1984:62). Students at UNMS and UDW affiliated *en masse* through their respective SRCs. Branches existed at UWC, UNIN, UNISA, MEDUNSA, UCT, Wits and the Pietermaritzburg campus of Natal University.[8.14] Working groups operated at Fort Hare, Zululand, at the Durban campus of Natal University and Rhodes, at the Mangosuthu technikon, Mapumulo theological seminary, and a number of teacher-training colleges. Regional councils were also established by mid-1983 in the Western Cape, Natal and Transvaal.

"Organising for people's education", mid-1983 to mid-1986

Notwithstanding the progress that was made around the building of an infrastructure on the campuses, Moseneke, elected president in 1983, declared himself to be not completely satisfied.

> To date we have done a lot of work at grassroots level, getting students to understand our analysis of the situation, encouraging them to read and to discuss things. But we haven't managed to achieve an effective national presence.[8.15]

To ensure an "effective national presence" branches were called on to consolidate and expand organisation and membership and to further extend organisation to new campuses. The reference to ensure that SANSCO was "effective" was also an attempt to rally activists to deal with new threats and challenges that had the potential to seriously impede progress. Phaala, in welcoming members to the congress, had emphasised that

[t]he road ahead is going to be a very turbulent one and will require maximum vigilance, determination and discipline of our members. Attempts from various quarters to frustrate our organisation at various campuses are going to gain momentum (*AZASO National Newsletter*, June 1983:1).

Already, in early 1983, there had been verbal and physical clashes between SANSCO members and supporters and student supporters of AZAPO at a number of campuses. The most serious clash, however, was at the black student residence of UNMS. The pro-AZAPO BSS at the University of Natal (Durban) alleged that its members and guests were "attacked by a mob of about 60 people armed with sjamboks, batons, pangas, iron bars and knives, led by AZASO President – Joe Phaala".[8.16] While the allegation that Phaala led the attackers was untrue, the skirmish did signal an unwelcome development in student politics. SANSCO accorded the blame for the clashes to the "entryism" and obstructionist activities of AZAPO supporters, and stated that "if this is not deliberate provocation, opportunism, destructiveness, then we don't know what else we can call it".[8.17]

AZAPO's attitude towards SANSCO was also said to contribute to tensions and clashes.

It is common knowledge that ever since AZASO decided to align itself with progressive forces ... AZAPO people have persistently regarded AZASO not just as an opponent but actually as enemy number 1. AZASO has been accused of being Marxist-Leninist, Communist, ANC fronts etc. At all times our organisation has tried to avoid confrontation but AZAPO people have persistently pushed our members to the final limits of their patience and tolerance – and this has of late led to outbreaks of violent confrontations.[8.18]

SANSCO called on its members to exercise restraint in the face of "provocation and opportunism". However, between 1984 and 1986 there continued to be occasional clashes between SANSCO members and BC supporters (SAIRR, 1985:698; 1986:405).

In July 1983, BC students eventually launched the Azanian Students' Movement (AZASM). Whereas the campus activities of BC supporters had previously been characterised by spoiling tactics and purely criticism and opposition, the formation of AZASM meant that SANSCO was now confronted by an organisational challenge for membership and hegemony on campuses. According to the first president of AZASM, the rationale for its formation was that

Black Consciousness faithfuls found themselves politically homeless ... after the up to then BC AZASO abandoned the BC ideology for something "more contemporary" ... This act constituted an inexcusable abrogation of responsibility to the legacy of SASO (Johnson, 1988:111, quoting AZASM publication, *Awake Black Student* [March 1985]).

A concomitant challenge came from yet another new formation, the Students of Young Azania (SOYA), which was confined to the Western Cape. The formation of both AZASM and SOYA related to their differences with SANSCO regarding political approach and strategy, and to their attempt and that of their parent groupings to win a base among higher education students.

AZASM's strategy of claiming to represent the SASO tradition in order to facilitate its mobilisation of students had been expected by the SANSCO leadership. On the one hand, the SANSCO leadership saw no purpose in becoming embroiled around the question of which organisation was the "true" successor of SASO. It was believed that claims to SASO's legacy would not confer any advantage, and that the ultimate determinant of success or failure would be day-to-day organisational efforts. On the other hand, it was seen as necessary to neutralise the notion of an essential continuity between SASO and AZASM through two means. The first was to acknowledge SASO's contribution to the liberation struggle but to also critique its weaknesses. Second, it had to be shown that AZAPO and the post-1977 BC movement was not the political home of many past SASO and BC leaders and that, indeed, many such leaders were now part of the Congress movement.

The tactic of pointing to the political trajectory of BC leaders subsequent to the banning of SASO and BC organisations in 1977 was put into operation at the July 1983 congress of SANSCO, which coincided with AZASM's inaugural conference. To underlie its claim to be the successor of SASO, AZASM invited Pandelani Nefolovhodwe, a previous SASO president, and Strini Moodley, an ex-SASO publicity director, to address its conference. The SANSCO congress, in contrast, was addressed by the ex-SASO president Diliza Mji, "Terror" Lekota, a previous SASO organiser, and Murphy Morobe and Dan Montsisi, previous leaders of the secondary-school based South African Students' Movement. All four ex-BC leaders were now key members of the UDF (*AZASO National Student Newsletter*, November 1983).

If AZASO and SOYA represented a new challenge, hostile campus administrations remained an intractable threat. In late 1983, the SANSCO UDW branch was banned for being a political organisation, and the UDW SRC was suspended by the administration. A new feature of repression was the open collusion of campus security personnel with the security police – two students distributing pamphlets were arrested by the campus security and handed over to the security police.[8.20] At MEDUNSA, because of a hostile campus administration, SANSCO was forced to operate off-campus. At Fort Hare too, SANSCO had to function off-campus. In 1984, after establishing a presence at the University of Transkei, SANSCO was banned in the Transkei (SAIRR, 1985:21).

After a KwaZulu Legislative Assembly discussion on its activities (WUS/AUT, 1986:10), SANSCO was also banned at the University of Zululand (UNIZUL). More ominously, in October 1983, four students were brutally killed and many others injured by supporters of Gatsha Buthelezi's Inkatha Party.[8.21] SANSCO, of course, condemned Buthelezi for his participation in separate development structures, and had verbally clashed with him on a number of occasions. Immediately prior to the killings, SANSCO members at UNIZUL had been in the forefront of opposition to Buthelezi visiting the university. Buthelezi expressed no regrets over the killings but issued the threat that

> if those in AZASO have not yet learnt the errors of their ways and corrected their thinking, they will find the Inkatha lion has up to now only growled ever so softly. We have not bared our fangs and I pray ... that AZASO never makes us do so (quoted in Frederikse, 1986:157).

He also called upon his supporters: "Let us deal with them at every opportunity and let us do so with valour and honour" (ibid.). In early 1984, he issued an edict that students receiving KwaZulu bursaries had to sign a pledge of loyalty to KwaZulu and Inkatha, a move which involved SANSCO in raising funds for students.

In addition to physical attacks and killings, SANSCO members also became the target of state repression. A number of SANSCO members and supporters were detained, banned, and imprisoned for alleged ANC activities. Increasingly, the state viewed SANSCO as a front of the banned ANC. However, an especially repressive period for some campuses was ushered in by the declaration of a partial state of emergency in mid-1985. Activists at various campuses were detained and SANSCO called on its members stating that "in this climate the chief task of the day is to close our ranks; consolidate our struggles and membership" (AZASO National Student Newsletter, late 1985:2). There were also individual casualties. At the Transvaal College of Education, a student was killed by police during a campaign for an SRC. Another tragic casualty was Ngocko Ramelepe, a key SANSCO and UDF activist who had helped establish a SANSCO branch at Modjadji teacher-training college in the Northern Transvaal. Also in the forefront of efforts to form a democratic SRC at the college and, indeed, ita first president, Ramelepe was beaten to death by Lebowa bantustan police.[8.22]

With the declaration of the state of emergency, SANSCO defined the task as being

> principally to organise ourselves against this onslaught, understanding very clearly that there is no reason to be intimidated by this emergency. We have a task to organise every student and challenge apartheid ... Organise! Organise! Please organise! (AZASO National Student Newsletter, late 1985:3).

Physical repression was not the only threat. New legislation was also passed which gave councils of universities and technikons the power to exclude students without a hearing. Recognising its potential to intimidate students, SANSCO

> resolved to fight tooth and nail this Act which will academically and politically terrorise students from challenging wrongs which are deliberately created by these authorities (ibid.:4).

While the various repressive measures did make SANSCO's existence on many campuses extremely tenuous, they did not entirely prevent it from operating on campuses, and new issues were also provided around which to organise.

Despite the increasing repression, the process of growth of branches and expansion to new campuses continued. On many campuses activists innovated new ways of functioning and SANSCO operated through various front organisations – for example, at Fort Hare hostel committees were established as vehicles for meetings and activities. On many campuses various clubs and societies began to come increasingly under the hegemony of SANSCO activists – from the debating and drama societies and college choir at the Cape College of Education to sports and house committees at UNMS.[8.23] The previous working groups at Natal University (Durban), Rhodes, Zululand and Fort Hare all achieved branch status. There was also a penetration of some teacher-training colleges in the rural areas of the Cape and branches were formed at the Northern Transvaal and Mangosuthu technikons. SRC elections at UWC also brought into office an SRC that was strongly pro-SANSCO.[8.24]

At the end of 1983, it was noted that

1983 has been a year of growth and a year of lessons. Co-ordination and communication between the campuses has improved, organisation has been consolidated on existing AZASO campuses and the student organisation has expanded into new ones. The importance of strong organisational structure has been highlighted by the onslaught on the student movement from both university administrations and the state.[8.25]

The third GSC of SANSCO in December 1983 saw the adoption of a new theme, "Organising for people's education", to replace the previous theme of "education towards democracy". Two reasons were advanced for the change in theme. First, it was felt that while 1983 had seen high levels of mobilisation and widespread popularisation of SANSCO, there was a need to go beyond just mobilisation: "We must draw more students into AZASO and get them committed to working on a day to day basis in building AZASO. Without strong organisation we will never win our freedom" (AZASO, 1984). Second, the new theme was also an attempt to direct student mobilisation and organisational actions towards a greater engagement around the form and content of education and relations in education as contrasted with issues related to state and political power. The new theme also dovetailed with the greater emphasis that SANSCO sought to give during 1984 to its campaign to formulate an Education Charter (see Chapter 9).

SANSCO continued to expand during 1984-85. By mid-1984 the mood of the organisation was distinctly buoyant. It was claimed that many battles were won in early 1984 and that

[w]e have achieved this only through our organised strength. This strength is increasing with the large numbers of techs and training colleges joining AZASO. The AZASO approach is a practical one which ensures that we are consistently engaging the enemy in struggle. Our honesty and dedication is ensuring the rapid growth of AZASO. The 1984 congress will certainly be bigger than the 1983 one (AZASO, June 1984).

The 1984 congress in Soweto was considerably larger, bringing together "700 students from 34 universities, technikons and colleges". The new SANSCO president, Simpiwe Mguduso, stated that SANSCO "has expanded to all corners of the country",[8.26] and noted that "there is a greater preparedness among students to take up issues, even on repressive campuses such as Fort Hare".[8.27] Significant inroads were made into teacher-training colleges in Natal, the Southern Cape and Western Cape. Furthermore, students at institutions in the "independent" bantustans like the Transkei and Venda were becoming incorporated into SANSCO. The expansion and growing influence of SANSCO was not confined to an increase in the number of affiliated branches and working groups. SRCs at UNIN and UWC and at the M L Sultan Technikon were also dominated by SANSCO members and supporters. Nonetheless, technikons and colleges were targeted for still greater organisational efforts.[8.28]

The 1985 congress, on the eve of the declaration of a state of emergency, was attended by some 600 members from 52 campuses. Priority continued to be accorded to campaigning for and building democratic organisation and SRCs. At the same time there was renewed stress on improving the participation of women in SANSCO. During the three years since the low level of women's involvement in SANSCO was first identified by members at the 1982 congress as a problem, initiatives such as the creation of a women's organiser portfolio on the national executive and the establishment of a women's committee had yielded no significant improvement in participation (see also below). There was also a continued emphasis on organising in the colleges and technikons. Colleges were considered to be "strategically placed in the communities" and since many of them were located in rural areas, expansion of SANSCO into these was regarded as having the potential to contribute to resistance in "the rural areas and outlying places which we know are so important in our struggle".[8.29] A presence in colleges was also seen as part of the process of challenging the use of teachers as propagators of apartheid ideology. Finally, there was a commitment to also helping form youth organisations in townships around campuses where SANSCO had a presence.

The state of emergency disrupted SANSCO's activities and, according to Ramokgopa,

> [s]ome student organisations couldn't operate at all. Our major campaigns, such as the Education Charter campaign, were severely affected — our national programme had to be drastically changed.[8.30]

The "short term response" of SANSCO was to mobilise students against the state of emergency while the organisational challenge was defined as "to bring back the level of organisation that existed before the state of emergency". Strong local organisation in the form of SRCs and branches were viewed as "as being very important because if we become strong at the local level we will be able to absorb this heavy blow".[8.31] Although communication and co-ordination between the SANSCO national executive and local SANSCO structures, and between local structures themselves, was hampered, the establishment of SRCs and new working groups continued unabated. Numerous colleges in the Lebowa bantustan were incorporated into SANSCO's fold, and representatives of student formations at these colleges pledged to campaign for democratic SRCs, to promote the National Education Union of South Africa, a non-racial progressive teacher organisation with whom SANSCO had a close relationship, and to isolate a Transvaal-based conservative African teachers' organisation.[8.32] New working groups were also "set up at Bellville Technikon, Rand College, in Oudtshoorn and at Bechet College, Durban".[8.33] Thus, by the end of 1985, and despite many of its activists and members being in hiding and detention, SANSCO was not only organisationally intact but also growing. At a GSC in December 1985 the new theme of "student action for people's education" was adopted, a signal of SANSCO's confidence in its organisational infrastructure and capacity to mobilise in pursuit of its educational goals.

If the expected repression from the side of campus authorities and the state did materialise and was generally withstood, the challenge for membership and hegemony on campuses from AZASM and SOYA failed to materialise. Although these formations did establish a presence on some campuses they posed no serious threat to SANSCO's growth and expansion and did not limit SANSCO's influence on the student constituency. SOYA was restricted to a small presence at UCT. AZASM, while it enjoyed a presence among secondary school students in some areas, was less successful at higher education campuses. Where AZASM did attempt to challenge SANSCO's hegemony, through contesting elections to SRCs and black student societies, SANSCO members and supporters were generally able to achieve complete control of such bodies or secure comfortable majorities. Thus, for example, during a referendum among black students held by the Black Students Movement (BSM) at Rhodes in late 1983, students "voted overwhelmingly to affiliate to AZASO rather than to the black consciousness oriented ... AZASM" (SAIRR, 1984:464).

In summary, SANSCO's organisational development during the period 1981 to early 1986 was conditioned by authoritarian and repressive measures on the part of many campus administrations and the state. However, despite the difficult conditions and challenges from other progressive student groupings, SANSCO was able to grow in member-ship, establish a strong presence at the universities and also expand into a number of technikons and teacher training colleges. The theme of "student action for people's education" reflected SANSCO's satisfaction with its organisational achievements and signalled its intention to harness its organisation to campaign more vigorously around relations internal to higher education.

Organisation under National States of Emergency, 1986 to 1990

Between mid-1986 and early 1990, SANSCO was to confront its severest challenge as the apartheid government imposed successive national states of emergency. The state of emergency introduced in mid-1985 achieved only limited success in dampening mass popular resistance, and the declaration of a state of emergency on 12 June 1986, and its annual re-imposition until 1990, signalled the determination of the state to re-impose control.

The effects of the new conditions were felt almost immediately. Four months into the state of emergency, a SANSCO spokesperson reported that "administrations have been conniving with police, or else they are taking advantage of the state of emergency to make life unbearable for students" (*Weekly Mail*, 8 October 1986). A report commissioned by the World University Service and British Association of University Teachers summed up conditions and confirmed the close relationship between campus administrations and state authorities:

Some of the black campuses exist in a state of almost constant conflict and siege. The students enrolled at most of the black campuses have been confronted by a rigidly authoritarian approach to dissent. University administrators have collaborated fully with the state authorities in dealing with incidents on their campuses. Security forces are often called onto campus when incidents occur (WUS/AUT, 1989:10).

Administrations also utilised the state of emergency to deal with SANSCO members and supporters. Thus, 277 students were expelled from UNIZUL in 1987, and a further 44 in 1989, the latter being reinstated only after appeals by a delegation comprising students, parents and prominent community leaders (SAIRR, 1992:56-8).

The state of emergency impacted on SANSCO in various ways. A number of SANSCO activists were detained for varying periods while others were forced into hiding and a life on the run. At a number of campuses, activists were not able to attend classes, live in the residences or participate in student political activity because of the presence of security police in the guise of students and police raids on residences. A Wits activist asserted that "this total onslaught on BSS and SANSCO should be seen against the background of the state's systematic campaign of repression" (*New Nation*, 4 June 1987). Police spies were another hazard, a UCT student confessing in 1987 that he was in the pay of security police who had instructed him to monitor and report on SANSCO, and especially on its internal workings and any "divisions which could be used by the state to destroy" it.[8.34]

One immediate effect of the state of emergency was that the annual congress had to be postponed. With some institutions under siege by the army and police, it was felt that the congress "would not have been adequately representative"[8.35] Of course, branches and activists already had some experience of operating under emergency conditions, and arrangements were made for the sixth congress to be held in secret in December 1986. Even this congress "did not turn out to be what we expected. Key activists were in detention at the time".[8.36] Although, for security reasons, the congress was attended by only 190 members, some 72 branches were represented. As a response to the repressive conditions and the ongoing crisis in education, one decision of the congress was for SANSCO "to embark on an intensive campaign to consolidate our branches and to form strong parent committees which will deal specifically with the crisis at local level".[8.37]

The sixth congress was especially notable for the decision to change the name of the organisation from the Azanian Students Organisation (AZASO) to the South African National Students Congress (SANSCO). Having lived with the name "AZASO" for over five years, and having continuously insisted that the organisation should be primarily judged by its approach, what accounted for the organisers' changing the name six months into a national state of emergency? Debate around the name "AZASO" had been ongoing since 1981, and its retention had been a "tactical decision". In the early 1980s the non-racial approach was new and untested among students, and in order to not confuse them the issue of nomenclature was shelved and the organisation concentrated on organisation-building. However, by the mid-1980s there was a hardening of the ideological and political divide between the Congress and BC movements. "Azania" was the name by which BC adherents referred to South Africa and was thus strongly identified with BC organisations. Its retention by Congress students thus led to constant debates between SANSCO members and other Congress activists who urged their student comrades to be more "ideologically pure". Thus, to bring its ideology and politics and its name into alignment and leave no doubts about its political affiliations, the name SANSCO was adopted. It was also asserted that the name of South Africa would be "decided upon by the people of this country and not a few excitable and well-read intellectuals".[8.38]

The timing of the name change also had to do with the conviction that the Congress movement was hegemonic on campuses. As Johnson writes in an essay on youth politics in the mid-1980s:

> One of the most striking characteristics was the overwhelming dominance of the Charterist groupings. Not only in youth structures ... but also in the student- and pupil-led organisations, the Congress tradition held sway. An indicator of this trend was a decision by AZASO ... to drop the anomalous "Azania" from its title in December 1986 (1988:140-141).

Elsewhere, Johnson elaborates on the significance and meaning of the name change:

> The significance of the decision to change AZASO's name does not lie in any alteration of the organisation's ideology, structure, approach — or, indeed, prominent personnel. The content of the organisation will not change at all. Rather the change reflects a high level of organisational confidence, somewhat surprisingly, given the harshness of the state of emergency. For AZASO to risk losing the media and membership notoriety of a well-marketed trademark in favour of ideological consistency is, amongst other things, and indication that the organisation believes that it has so far outstripped its rivals (like AZASM) that it need not be concerned about their exploiting this period of change and uncertainty amongst rank-and-file supporters.[8.39]

Indeed, it was SANSCO's view that AZASM's influence on campuses was negligible and that it no longer represented any threat to SANSCO's hegemony within higher education.

The effects on SANSCO of the first eighteen months of the state of emergency were revealed by a newsletter published soon after SANSCO's seventh congress in December 1987, and in a newspaper interview given to the *New Nation* by James Maseko, the SANSCO publicity secretary. According to the newsletter, whereas "during the period 1983 to 1985 our organisation was in a fairly strong position", the state of emergency

> had a material effect on our organisations. SANSCO has not escaped this onslaught. Branches at Turfloop, Fort Hare and Ngoye have been virtually destroyed. At colleges we operate under extremely repressive conditions and this has retarded the qualitative development of organisation (*SANSCO National Newsletter*, 1st quarter 1988).

Furthermore, activists were detained, communication and co-ordination with various branches was disrupted, and important advances made in organising colleges in the Northern Transvaal collapsed. Although the seventh congress was attended by 276 members SANSCO was

> only able to count 62 branches, 10 less than our 1986 congress. We also have the situation where many of our branches, while still in existence, have been weakened significantly. In this sense we openly admit that the state of emergency has materially affected our organisation.[8.40]

Still, one success was that SANSCO was able to establish itself at three institutions in the Orange Free State (OFS), and constitute the OFS as a new region (*SANSCO National Newsletter*, 1st quarter 1988: 5). Moreover, Maseko was of the view that the state of emergency was a time of "learning". Although SANSCO had "made mistakes"

> we have also been able to pick ourselves up. While we may be weaker than before the emergency was declared, we are a lot more mature politically. The emergency also exposed the weaknesses that existed in our ranks. We were, as a result, forced to confront these weaknesses and we have overcome them to a certain extent. But we are under no illusions that we have a long way to go.[8.41]

One of the "mistakes" alluded to concerned the lack of attention to formulating strategy and tactics appropriate to organising at colleges. In this regard it was stressed that

[i]t has long been emphasised that our strategy and tactics are shaped not only by theory, but also by the material conditions obtaining in any context of our political operation (*SANSCO National Newsletter*, 1st quarter 1988:12).

Regret was also expressed for the impression that SANSCO catered only for university students and once again the need to concentrate on colleges and technikons, and for regional and national leaders to emerge from these institutions was emphasised. There was a pledge to continue fighting repression on campuses and state attempts "to crush opposition at educational institutions".[8.42]

The theme adopted for 1988 was "organise, consolidate and advance towards people's education" (SAIRR, 1988:183). The new theme was an attempt to adjust to the realities of the state of emergency that confronted SANSCO. Maseko contrasted the new theme with the previous one of "Student action for people's education" which had been adopted in 1985 when SANSCO felt itself to be organisationally strong and poised to expand into new institutions. Consequently, SANSCO was able to

talk of student action without concerning ourselves with deep questions of organisation and consolidation – not because they were not important but because they already existed in most cases.[8.43]

The new theme was

a realisation of the effects of the emergency – it has disorganised, weakened and in some ways rolled back the gains we have made. It is therefore only after we have reorganised branches that have collapsed, organise the unorganised and consolidate the stronger structures that we can effectively talk of advances.[8.44]

It was pointed out that while SANSCO had a presence on 62 campuses there were well over 100 higher education institutions in South Africa and thus much work to be done to incorporate students into SANSCO and the struggle for democracy.

Whereas during the initial twenty months of the state of emergency SANSCO was subject only to the general restrictions imposed under the state of emergency, this situation was to dramatically change on 24 February 1988. Together with the United Democratic Front, the National Education Crisis Committee, and another 14 organisations, SANSCO was effectively banned under new emergency regulations. The regulations outlawed almost all activities. Only administrative functions related to the keeping of books and records, the obtaining of legal advice and the taking of judicial steps, and activities permitted by government, were allowed. In a profile of the 17 banned organisations the *Weekly Mail* noted that "SANSCO is the dominant organisation at university and college campuses ... Its membership, difficult to estimate reliably, certainly ran to several thousand".[8.45] In December 1988, the SANSCO affiliates at Rhodes and at Wits were also proscribed under the new regulations and there were police raids on the offices of SANSCO and the SRC at UWC (SAIRR, 1989:300; *Weekly Mail*, 2 December 1988).

With the banning of SANSCO, activists operated through ad-hoc formations and new structures – thus, at Wits a Black Students Interim Committee was established and at UCT a Black Students Society (SAIRR, 1990:874). Notwithstanding the state of emergency and the banning of popular organisations, from mid-1988 popular forces were again resurgent. Once again students on campuses were mobilised in support of campaigns and actions. When a "defiance campaign" was launched in late 1989 to defy, amongst other things, restrictions on organisations, SANSCO and its branches and affiliates publicly declared themselves "unbanned". The extensive mass mobilisation of the 1988-89 period provided the opportunity to revive and revitalise branches and overall organisation.

Having declared itself unbanned, SANSCO proceeded to convene its eighth congress in December 1989, and to celebrate its tenth anniversary at the University of Western Cape. SANSCO was said to comprise 77 branches and 5 regions (SAIRR, 1992:56-58). The keynote speaker at the congress was Ahmed Kathrada, one of the ANC leaders released in October 1989, in what was to become a process leading to the unbanning of the ANC and the release of Nelson Mandela. Kathrada praised SANSCO's contribution to the democratic struggle but also questioned whether SANSCO, given its racial composition, could claim to be a truly non-racial organisation and raised the possibility of a merger with NUSAS (personal notes, December 1989). At about the same time, Andrew Mlangeni, another recently released ANC leader, issued a more forthright challenge to the NUSAS congress: namely, for NUSAS and SANSCO to form one organisation (*Weekly Mail*, 15 December 1989).

The outcome of these challenges to SANSCO and NUSAS was that both organisations adopted resolutions to look into the question of a merger. However, within months SANSCO was to be confronted with other crucial questions. On 2 February 1990, President de Klerk announced the lifting of the ban on the ANC, the SACP, and numerous other exiled organisations, and an end to restrictions on internal popular formations such as the UDF and SANSCO. Soon afterwards, Nelson Mandela was released from prison unconditionally and multiparty negotiations around a new constitution and elections for a democratic government began. The new conditions gave rise to questions and debates about the future role of SANSCO, including its relationship to the ANC and other mass popular formations.

Organisation: Issues, Processes and Culture

Having tracked the contours of SANSCO's organisational growth, I want to now discuss a number of issues related to SANSCO's organisational functioning and general culture.

Organisation building and organisational reproduction

Methods and techniques of student recruitment varied according to conditions on campuses. Where SANSCO was faced with hostile administrations and repressive conditions, the norm tended to be selective person-to-person recruitment. Individual recruitment took the form of visiting students in their rooms in residences or arranging to meet students who expressed an interest in SANSCO, or appeared regularly to attend SANSCO activities. While the building of membership was seen as an ongoing day-to-day task of all SANSCO activists, there were sometimes also concerted recruitment drives. Thus, a newsletter made mention of a recruitment drive by the SANSCO branch at UDW which netted over 30 new members (*AZASO National Newsletter*, June 1983).

Other means of recruiting members included beginning of year student orientation programmes, public seminars and workshops, campaigns and mass meetings and media in the form of SANSCO newsletters and occasional flyers and pamphlets. Thus, a *Getting to know AZASO* pamphlet produced for the 1983 student orientation period informed students that the formation of student organisations related to problems of students around day-to-day issues. The pamphlet added,

[s]imilarly there are some problems that are common to all students throughout the country. For us to handle these problems effectively we need to have a forum which we can use to share ideas and experiences, and to develop an approach to these problems. AZASO as a national student organisation acts as such a forum (*Getting to know AZASO*, pamphlet, 1983d).

In similar vein, an orientation period issue of the Wits BSS newsletter *Challenge*, apart from welcoming black students to Wits, also urged them to use their knowledge and skills to further the struggle for democracy and to participate in BSS and other popular organisations (*Challenge*, "Orientation '84"). For some students, membership of SANSCO represented their first involvement in popular organisation. Other students had previous experience through membership of the secondary-school based COSAS, youth organisations and civic and women's organisations. The contact of SANSCO activists with popular organisations and the UDF also yielded names of members of such formations who were potential recruits for SANSCO.

Generally, SANSCO encouraged mass affiliation through SRCs, one advantage of SRC affiliation being access to SRC resources and a larger financial contribution to SANSCO's national coffers. This practice however had its critics who argued that mass affiliation represented a largely paper membership and provided no indication of SANSCO's real organised strength on a campus. As a compromise, but also to ensure that the state of SANSCO on a campus was not entirely tied to the standing of the SRC, on campuses where there was mass affiliation autonomous SANSCO branches were also established to complement SRC activities. However, the relationship between SRC-affiliated campuses or SRCs which were strongly pro-SANSCO and local SANSCO branches was not always smooth, the essential problem usually being an appropriate division of labour between the SRC and the branch with respect to campaigns, meetings and programmes.

The relationship between the SANSCO national executive and local SANSCO branches and working groups was generally harmonious. On the one hand, this was the result of the strong participation of local SANSCO formations in annual congresses and GSCs, the key national policy- and decision-making forums. As noted, these forums were large gatherings comprising both delegates from branches and substantial numbers of members as observers. The congress was viewed as providing

the opportunity for people from various branches of our organisation to know each other, understand each other's common problems, differences in conditions and ways and means through which we are advancing the struggle. Congress provides a forum for national assessment of the progress or stagnation of our organisation (AZASO, 1983c:3-4).

Furthermore, its purpose was to achieve "clarity among comrades about all issues relating to the challenges facing the democratic movement ... Out of ensuing discussions emerge national principles, policy, strategies and tactics" (ibid.). Democratic participation and involvement of branches and members in policy formulation and decision-making conferred local formations with a sense of ownership of the priorities, strategies and tactics that were adopted. This contributed to a situation where the national executive played essentially a guiding and co-ordinating role, providing local formations with a large degree of autonomy around forms of organisation and activities related to local conditions.

However, two other factors conditioned the relationship between the national executive and local formations and had the effect of conferring considerable autonomy to local formations. First, the same commitment to participation and democratic decision-making that resulted in large national congresses and GSCs meant that the national executive was generally strongly respectful of local-level decision-making. Second, there was also the factor of limited finances. SANSCO's income was extremely limited. Although membership fees were levied, income from this source was irregular, small, and often utilised by branches themselves. Fund-raising through the sale of T-shirts and cultural activities only raised modest amounts of funds. What external funds did come SANSCO's way, mainly from the South African Council of Churches and intermittently from European church bodies, was either largely consumed by national gatherings or earmarked for specific projects. Often, small donations in cash or kind from traders were crucial to the holding of local and national workshops.

The lack of finance meant that many activities such as a proposed .national annual leadership-training forum and regular national publications could not be activated (see below). More significantly, SANSCO was unable to afford central or regional offices and to employ full-time staff and had to rely on facilities and resources of branches and the volunteering of time by officials who were usually also full-time students. In this context, even had a SANSCO national executive sought to be more directive and interventionist in the affairs of local formations, the person-power and resources for such a mode of operation were simply not available. Of course, and as was recognised, one means of funding some full-time officials would have been to eliminate the GSC and/or to severely limit the size of congresses and GSCs (AZASO, 1983c:3). However, this trade-off, which would have limited the participation of branch members in policy formulation, planning and decision-making, was seen as unacceptable, reflecting the strong commitment to membership involvement and democratic decision-making within SANSCO.

SANSCO: Internal composition and institutional and geographical spread

To protect members from repression, no membership cards were issued and no formal membership lists were kept. Consequently, the active membership of SANSCO is difficult to estimate. It is likely that active membership was about 1 000 students in 1983, expanded to a few thousand in the mid-1980s, and reached a peak of about 5 000 in the late 1980s. While there was strong emphasis on building SANSCO as a mass organisation and SANSCO was able to mobilise large numbers of students with relative ease, the consolidation of mass mobilisation and the translation of popular support into permanent organisation proved more difficult and represented an ongoing challenge. The key problem experienced was that while students were willing to participate in protest meetings and even militant forms of mass action, they were reluctant to become organisationally active. Indeed, a very small minority of students, although strong in their support for SANSCO and always in the van of

268

mass action, positively shunned organisational participation, preferring militant action to the grind of organisation-building.

Although SANSCO developed a national presence, and throughout the 1980s the general organisational trend was one of expansion into new campuses and new areas of South Africa, there were certain features to its organisational spread. Initially, SANSCO was essentially an organisation of university students. Only in the mid-1980s did the strategic importance of colleges begin to be realised and was serious attention paid to organising at colleges and also technikons. Still, whereas by the late 1980s almost all the university and technikon campuses were incorporated into SANSCO, only a small proportion of teacher-training colleges had SANSCO branches or working groups. Given that the majority of teacher-training colleges were located in the rural areas of bantustans, this meant that SANSCO also had a greater presence in large cities and the more urbanised areas of the bantustans and that its presence in the rural areas of both "white" South Africa and the bantustans was limited.

One other key feature of SANSCO's membership composition was that, throughout the 1980s, members were predominantly male and women were severely underrepresented in relation to the gender composition of the student body. At the 1982 congress this was recognised as a serious weakness and there was a lengthy discussion around how to address the problem. The outcome was that an interim committee was established to identify issues specifically affecting women students around which they could be mobilised and organised, and also generally to investigate ways of drawing women into SANSCO. Informal surveys conducted at various campuses identified the key problem to be socialisation processes within the family and educational system. A member of the Womens' Group of the Wits BSS expressed the problem in the following way:

> We see the lack of involvement of women students as largely due to the fact that women have been socialised into particular roles and have been forced to accept their subservient position in society as natural.[8.46]

In 1983 the portfolio of Women's Organiser was created on the SANSCO national executive, and in April 1984 a national SANSCO women's conference was held. A document argued that "black women in

South Africa suffer a triple oppression, i.e. race, class and sex" (AZASO Women's Working Programme, April 1984). As a result there was a need to "organise women as an oppressed sector around issues that directly affect them and to link this to the National Democratic Struggle" (ibid.). The reason for organising women students was that

the content of the educational system and the way it is organised perpetuates sexism. Women have to be organised to challenge these specific problems. Because sexism cannot be eradicated from our society without fundamental change, women students need to be organised to play a role in the National Democratic Struggle (ibid.).

Activists were urged to

understand the constituency we are dealing with. There are certain problems that hinder the effective participation of women students in struggle. Our methods must take cognisance of these facts and we must work from the level at which students are (ibid.).

It was stressed that the methods used to organise women had to ensure "that we raise awareness, involve the maximum number of women and strengthen organisation" (ibid.). The strategy opted for was to establish women's sections within SANSCO branches which could provide forums for women to develop confidence and leadership skills, help them to assert themselves within SANSCO, and could organise women so that their representation could increase and SANSCO could also be strengthened.

SANSCO branches commemorated National Women's Day (August 9) annually, regularly focused on the role of women in the national liberation struggle in South Africa and elsewhere, and arranged seminars around sexism and feminism. However, throughout the 1980s little progress was made in establishing women's sections within SANSCO branches and drawing women into SANSCO. According to a SANSCO publication, at the 1987 congress

not one region could report a favourable state of affairs, and it became clear that this is one area of our organisation that needs serious and consistent attention ... The congress took the attitude that this failure in the organisation of women should be shouldered by the whole organisation and not women comrades alone (SANSCO, 1989: 1-2).

The 1987 congress developed a programme of action which included the production of a newsletter with a specific focus on women, branch workshops on the women's question, the popularisation of branch womens' sub-committees, meeting of national and regional women's organisers, mobilisation of women around sport and culture and the heightening of political education on issues related to women *(ibid.)*.

During 1988-89 some gains were registered. The participation of women in the Western Cape region was said to be

> very impressive. In most campuses women's groups existed and ... there was also very good regional co-ordination ... In Natal also people were at least able to meet at a regional level and co-ordinate issues ... In the Transvaal some gains have been made in certain campuses where in the past there were no women's structures but the level of participation is still very poor without regional co-ordination (SANSCO, 1989:4).

A number of factors were identified that hindered progress in organising women. First, there was "still a lack of seriousness amongst comrades in addressing the issue of women" *(ibid.)* and blame was put on the lack of political education around the women's question and the lack of political understanding around the importance of the liberation of women. Second, many of the decisions of the 1987 congress were not implemented by many branches, with the result that "practically, the issue of women still remains the problem of the few women in the organisation with very little or no assistance from the rest of the branch" *(ibid.)*.

The fact that the organisation of women became a "problem of the few women in the organisation" placed a special burden on women activists. According to a female activist

> people who were in the full-time women's sector were often very heavily committed to organising students more generally. Those of us who had dual responsibilities often experienced a tension and very often found ourselves neglecting the women's specific issues (interview with Africa, 1995).

A final problem was that of finance. No budgets were provided for organising women and financial problems also meant that regional programmes had to be cancelled and a newsletter for women could not be produced (SANSCO, 1989:4-5). However, it was acknowledged that there may also have been a lack of understanding of the "diverse character of the body of women students" (interview with Africa, 1995). According to Africa,

> I ... have a feeling that perhaps we may have missed the point, missed the issues which affected women students because ... we didn't understand the complexity of our sector of women students (*ibid.*).

Moreover, it was also conceded that the approach of women activists could also have been a problem.

> It may also have had to do ... with the fact that in our youth and enthusiasm we may have projected in a way which was not very attractive to other women, being seen as loud and too assertive and aggressive may have scared women away from organisation (*ibid.*).

In summary, the structural problem of patriarchy and sexism, a possibly flawed understanding of the women's sector of the student body, a lack of organisational commitment, and possible weaknesses in strategies and tactics combined to ensure that SANSCO remained a predominately male organisation.

Ideological and political education

Political education within SANSCO was conducted at branch level as well as at national level through numerous designated education sessions at the annual congresses and General Students Councils (GSCs). At branch level, seminars and workshops were common mechanisms for political education. Such forums were used to induct new students into SANSCO through presentations and discussions around the history of SANSCO, its ideological and political orientation, organisational approach, and principles, policies and programme. Beyond this, seminars and workshops were used to develop among students a knowledge and understanding of theoretical, historical and contemporary issues. Thus, seminars spanned a wide range of topics which included capitalism, colonialism, neo-colonialism, and imperialism; education under capitalism and socialism;

trade unions and popular resistance; women's oppression, and liberation struggles in countries such as Cuba, Nicaragua, El Salvador, and Mozambique.

Of course, there was also coverage of issues pertaining to South Africa: South African political economy, class, racial and gender domination in South Africa, the character of the South African liberation struggle, and the history of political resistance. When required, seminars and workshops were also organised around issues of immediate political concern – for example the government's 1982 constitutional proposals and the implications of the "independence" of the Ciskei bantustan. While some seminars and workshops were deemed internal education and restricted to SANSCO members, others were advertised publicly. The public forums, apart from keeping students informed and raising their political awareness, were also used to recruit members. Education sessions were presented by SANSCO officials as well as by guest speakers from political and popular organisations and trade unions. However, the form of education sessions was not confined to papers and oral presentations. Tape-slide shows, videos and films were also utilised. To expand the knowledge of SANSCO activists and also provide material for education sessions, readers and dossiers were occasionally compiled and distributed to branches. There was also generally much circulation of political literature, including banned literature, to enhance SANSCO members' theoretical and political development. Occasionally, reading groups comprising new and old members were created for reading and discussing literature.

A regular feature of annual congresses and GSCs was numerous education sessions explicitly devoted to theoretical and political questions and to issues that had a bearing on political strategy and tactics. Presenters were usually key SANSCO intellectuals, as well as leading intellectuals from political and popular organisations and trade unions. A constant topic was an analysis of the "state of the nation" which examined conditions and developments in the economic, political and social spheres, initiatives of capital and the state, the trajectory and dynamics of mass anti-apartheid actions, and the state of popular organisations. This topic, apart from having an educational dimension, was also crucial to the formulation of the SANSCO theme and its strategy and tactics. Another regular topic was the character of South African society and the national democratic struggle, while the roles of particular social groups and organisations in the national democratic struggle also received consistent attention. Since the Freedom Charter served as SANSCO's political manifesto, a number of topics related to it received ongoing attention. Finally, education in South Africa, the role of students, and the history of the student movement and student organisations in South Africa was another consistent subject of national gatherings.

With reference to organisational skills, there was no formal or explicit training provided around meeting procedures and the chairing of meetings, general administrative and financial matters, and planning programmes, meetings and campaigns. Some members were organisationally highly skilled, as a consequence of previous membership of school-based organisations and/or concomitant membership of other popular organisations. Neophyte members generally developed skills by learning "on the job", through immersion in the day-to-day activities of SANSCO and with skilled members and older SANSCO activists serving as exemplars. The development of skills and confidence was also promoted by members being attached to branch sub-committees and the decentralisation and delegation of tasks to such sub-committees. While there was generally a spirit of "each one, teach one" (slogan of the school-based COSAS), much depended on the initiative of individual members.

One field in which there were attempts to ensure some formal training was the production of print media such as banners, placards, posters, calendars, newsletters, pamphlets, T-shirts and badges. Media training was usually organised by members already possessing skills and/or by popular media organisations such as the NUSAS-linked South African Students' Press Union, and regionally-based community newspapers to which some SANSCO branches were affiliated. The attempt to ensure that media skills were developed among members was related to the extensive use which SANSCO branches and national organisation made of print media.

First, print media were used to advertise seminars, programmes and meetings and thus had an informational function. Second, they were used to popularise SANSCO, the UDF and the Congress movement, jailed and exiled political leaders, and to express SANSCO and student demands. Third, they were utilised for mobilising students in support of planned educational and political actions and campaigns, and for harnessing student support for SANSCO candidates contesting SRC elections. Fourth, media also played a role in attempts to recruit students into SANSCO. Finally, print media also served an educational purpose, being used to raise the awareness and consciousness of students. The organisational newsletter played all these roles as well as serving to keep SANSCO members informed of developments on various campuses. However, because of a lack of finance the newsletter was produced irregularly. Newsletters, banners, T-shirts, and badges and calendars were composed in the distinct black, green and gold colours associated with the ANC, and thus explicitly symbolised SANSCO's political allegiances.

Despite the time and energy devoted to political education, successive national executive committees of SANSCO emphasised the need for greater efforts in this field. A proposal that an annual national leadership training forum be instituted failed to materialise because of a lack of finance. At the 1987 congress, a decision was taken to establish political education units at all levels of SANSCO. However, in 1989 it was noted that such units "never really [got] off the ground and presently as an organisation we cannot talk of a functional political education unit" (SANSCO, 1989:5). Nonetheless, overall, education and training was sufficient to ensure the continued functioning, organisational reproduction, and even expansion of SANSCO, and continuity in its ideology and programme. Moreover, organisational reproduction and ideological continuity was also ensured by the continuous entry into SANSCO of students who had belonged to COSAS, and by members initially schooled within popular Congress organisations.

Finally, the collective singing of "freedom songs" and the performance of the "toyi toyi", a militant "dance", in which participants imitated the actions of guerrilla fighters, were important informal means of political socialisation. Songs, melodic and rhythmic, sung with gusto and different kinds of movements and expressions contributed to making SANSCO gatherings lively and even exhilarating occasions. However, beyond the vibrant mood that singing and the "toyi toyi" gave to events, they also facilitated bonding between members from different campuses and areas and regions and fostered feelings of solidarity and a sense of belonging to SANSCO. Songs continuously changed in relation to political conditions, and often expressed commitments to particular political goals and strategies that could not be acknowledged in formal speeches.

9

People's Education and People's Power: Mobilisation and Collective Action

I n this chapter my concerns are with SANSCO's mobilisation of students and its collective actions, and especially the form and content of mobilisation and collective action, during two distinct periods. The first covers the years 1979 to 1986, during which various political reforms were instituted by the apartheid state and there was an intensification of political resistance by the dominated classes. The second period covers the years mid-1986 to early 1990 when a countrywide state of emergency was imposed by the apartheid government in an attempt to smother opposition and destroy popular organisations. Although for purposes of analysis and presentation I make a distinction between struggles around education issues and those around political issues, all SANSCO's collective actions should be treated as, ultimately, "political" activities of different forms.

Mobilisation and Collective Action, 1979 to mid-1981

During this period SANSCO existed largely in name and lacked an organisational infrastructure that could mobilise students and spearhead mass action. According to Nkoane, we did not take up education issues. What we tended to do was take up community issues, assisting workers, for instance, to form trade unions, getting involved in local communities in terms of health matters and other issues (Interview, August 1995).

Indeed, the first public meeting of SANSCO was held in Soweto around civic issues, at which Nkoane called upon students to identify themselves with the overall struggle in SA. He said that students could do this in many ways, one of which was to join hands with their parents in fighting increases in bus fares and rents (SAIRR, 1981:542).

Criticism was also levelled at the expulsion of students from black universities.

After the break with AZAPO there was close co-operation with COSAS, with meetings held to formulate a joint approach to issues (SAIRR, 1981:543). With the detention of key COSAS officials in 1980, SANSCO activists helped to keep COSAS afloat and assisted with attempts to build SRCs and a COSAS infrastructure in schools. There was also some popularisation of the Freedom Charter through its distribution at public meetings and at schools.

At the University of the North, the only institution at which SANSCO had an organisational base, activists mobilised students around a campaign for an SRC which was eventually formed in 1981. The branch also initiated a boycott of graduation ceremonies, a boycott and disruption of the twenty-first anniversary celebrations of the North, and campaigned for the disaffiliation of the college football team from a multiracial sport association. However, it was only through its participation in the anti-Republic Day campaign of early 1981 that SANSCO began to achieve a national public profile and attempted to mobilise students on a large scale.

Mobilisation and Collective Action, 1981 to 1986

Struggles around education

SANSCO mobilised black students and initiated collective actions around a wide variety of education grievances, problems and issues.

Authoritarian controls and repression

First, there was mobilisation and collective action[9.1] around the authoritarian and repressive behaviour of higher education administrations. One issue which provoked perennial conflict was the refusal of some administrations to permit autonomous SRCs, their suspension and banning of SRCs and student organisations like SANSCO, and the imposition of various controls on student activities. As a result, throughout the 1981 to 1986 period SANSCO spearheaded various forms of actions ranging from marches, to demonstrations and lecture boycotts, either to advance or defend the right of students to autonomous organisations, and to protest curbs on student activities.

During the early 1980s struggles around SRCs were mainly confined to the universities and technikons. From the mid-1980s, however, campaigns for SRCs also spread to teacher-training colleges as SANSCO began to target these institutions for organisation. The Transvaal College of Education provides a good example of the process of struggle around student demands for an SRC. The initial demands for an SRC were greeted by the authorities with the attempt to foist on students an SRC with extremely limited autonomy. With the initiation by students of a lecture boycott to press home their demand, the police were summoned by the administration. In an attack by the police on students, one student was killed. The anger and solidarity generated by this event was dramatically captured by a student leader when referring to an attempt by the rector to address students: "Just as he was about to speak, like a volcano all our frustrations, disaffections and grievances erupted in one voice saying "WE WANT AN SRC" (AZASO, 1984c, emphasis in original).

The police were frequently summoned by campus authorities during student protests. Clashes between students and the police, arrests and detentions of students, and the occasional occupation of campuses by the police and/or army tended to trigger a new wave of student mobilisation and action. Thus, in 1986 one of the demands of students at colleges in the Lebowa bantustan was for the removal of the army which had occupied one of the colleges following student protests around the banning of COSAS and other issues.[9.2]

Another cause of student action was the practice of many campus authorities to quell student activism by expelling, suspending, and refusing to register student activists and students participating in protest actions. The usual response of SANSCO was to mobilise in defence of students on the basis of the slogan "An injury to one is an injury to all" (AZASO, 1984a). Thus, in mid-1983 the expulsion of eight students from the Mabopane East technikon resulted in a lecture boycott and the eventual expulsion of the entire student body of about 1 000 students.[9.3] The practice of expelling and refusing students readmission intensified during the state of emergency of 1985-1986. About 100 students were refused readmission at Fort Hare for being "agitators", while a similar number were refused enrolment at the University of Zululand. Both cases provoked widespread student mobilisation and protest actions. On various occasions, parent committees were established to negotiate with campus authorities around the readmission of students.

The paternalistic and parochial policy of teacher colleges of expelling students who were pregnant was another source of student action. Thus, the expulsion in 1983 of five Transvaal College of Education students resulted in a solidarity lecture boycott by 600 students. From the mid-1980s, as students at colleges began to mobilise around democratic SRCs, one frequent additional demand was for the scrapping of the policy of expelling pregnant students.

There was also periodic collective action on various campuses around the repressive role played by campus security personnel and the collusion of the authorities with state security agencies. For example, in 1984, following a pledge by the University of Transkei rector to uproot all "politicians" from campus, four students were requested to report to the academic registrar's office and thereafter escorted to the offices of the state security police. The subsequent detention of the students led to intense conflict, with clashes with police and various confrontations throughout 1984 (SAIRR, 1985:700).

Finally, students did not engage in collective actions solely around their own particular grievances, but also participated in solidarity actions with students on other campuses and at schools. Often, the action was local in scope as in the case of University of Western Cape (UWC) students who in mid-1983 participated in a one-day solidarity boycott in support of local secondary school students.[9.4] Sometimes, however, solidarity actions took on a national dimension as when SANSCO declared 30 May 1984 as a "Day of National Solidarity" with students involved in conflicts with administrations on various campuses. On this occasion, students were mobilised countrywide, and they engaged in various forms of protest action (AZASO, 1984b). Similarly, following a SANSCO call, there were also national protests when COSAS was banned by the government in September 1985.

Academic conditions and issues

Dissatisfaction with academic conditions and grievances around specific academic issues was a second source of student collective action. At Durban-Westville (UDW) in 1984 there was a lecture boycott to protest the alleged incompetence of a lecturer in Human Physiology. At UWC during the same year, students boycotted lectures for a week to demand that the library's opening hours be extended and that the practice of having to pay for lecture notes be terminated (*AZASO National Newsletter*, June 1984). Also during 1984, at the University of Natal Medical School the focus of student action was dissatisfaction with new rules, a high failure rate during the previous year and academic exclusions. Students enrolled the support of parents as well as the National Medical and Dental Association, a progressive professional body, and formed a crisis committee to deal with their grievances (AZASO, 1984d). Finally, there were occasional protests around academics accused of unfairly failing students, and around examination time-tables.

During the early 1980s, with increasing black student enrolment and militancy at the white English-language universities, the government introduced a Bill proposing a quota on black enrolments at such institutions. SANSCO linked with NUSAS to protest the government's "quota Bill" and called on university authorities to refuse to implement a quota system. The response of the university authorities was to argue the need for institutional autonomy and the right of universities to decide whom to register and teach. While some SANSCO branches engaged in joint actions with the university authorities, staff and white students, to protest the quota Bill, their specific responses extended beyond proclamations of university autonomy. Thus, during a joint demonstration at Natal University, SANSCO highlighted the Freedom Charter clause "The doors of learning shall be opened", so as to link opposition to the quota Bill to the general demand for an end to racially segregated education and to apartheid laws and institutional practices that denied blacks equality of access and opportunity. At Rhodes, the SANSCO affiliate invited the vice-chancellor to a debate on the institutions' admission policies and argued that a policy based solely on the criterion of academic merit disadvantaged black applicants.[9.5] The problem of a policy that only took academic merit into account was well expressed by a student leader:

> while race is completely unacceptable as a criterion by which to admit students, "academic merit" in the South African context, is not an objective criterion either. The unequal education system and unequal access to wealth and resources in our society enormously limits the number of black students who will have access to university education. There is no such thing as freedom of opportunity in South Africa. [9.6]

The outcome of the protest against the quota Bill was a government decision that a quota would not be applied but that black student numbers would be monitored and the quota would remain as an option (SAIRR, 1984:463).

Racism on campuses

A fourth cause of collective action was the racism that black students experienced on campuses. At the predominantly white Rhodes, an anonymous pamphlet accused black students of "drunkenness, harassment of white women students, attempted rapes, spreading venereal disease" and other misdemeanours (SAIRR, 1983:517). As a result, there was a student march on the administration to demand action against the authors of the pamphlet. The racist attitudes of certain staff also provoked student action. During 1985, the Soweto College was closed following a lecture boycott demanding the expulsion of two allegedly racist lecturers. At the University of Venda there were student actions demanding the expulsion of an academic who allegedly called students "baboons". At UWC there was a lengthy lecture boycott by dentistry students demanding the removal of an academic accused of racist behaviour and a concomitant solidarity boycott by students from other faculties. The boycott ended when the university authorities determined that the academic was not suited to the institution.

Physical conditions

Physical conditions on campuses was another issue which triggered intermittent student action. In the first place, there was action around the shortage of residential accommodation for students, the practice of racially segregating of residences at the white English-language universities and the denial of residential accommodation to African students at UDW. Such struggles were sparked by increasing enrolments at black universities which stretched the ability of some institutions to accommodate students in residences, the increasing registration of African students at UDW and UWC, and the expansion of black student enrolments at the white English-language universities.

Examples of accommodation struggles are student actions at UWC, UCT and UDW in 1984. At UWC, students used marches, demonstrations and squatting in residences to pressurise the administration to address the shortage of residential accommodation.[9.7] At UCT, the shortage of accommodation for black students was linked to protesting the university authorities' acquiescence to an apartheid law which prohibited black students from being accommodated with white students and meant that black students were housed at a separate residence, in an African township. Mobilisation was spearheaded by an ad hoc committee comprising SANSCO, SOYA, and individual black students, and actions included the pitching of a squatter shelter in front of the main hall at UCT. The protests, which generated considerable support from black and white students, eventually resulted in all the UCT residences being opened to black students. Racialist residential practices were also challenged at UDW where African students were prohibited from living in the residences. The form of action employed here was the collection of 2 500 signatures for a petition that called for residences to be opened to all.

There were sporadic demonstrations and food and lecture boycotts around the cost and quality of food in cafeterias and residences. At UDW, a two-week boycott of cafeteria food which was said to be high in price but low in quality and of limited variety was organised in 1982 by the SANSCO-affiliated SRC. In 1984, there were meal and/or class boycotts around "tasteless, unpalatable and even rotten food" at various institutions in the Transvaal. A SANSCO newsletter provided a tongue-in-cheek sketch of the context:

> Students are subjected to a total onslaught: if the cops are not bashing or detaining us, then the admins. try to victimise us. The one aspect of the attack that has escaped any analysis, any national

protest, any unequivocal condemnation is the total onslaught on our diet. Students at Mabopane Tech, Medunsa and Wits recently decided enough is enough. They will no longer tolerate being attacked by admins. most lethal weapon – res. food (*AZASO National Newsletter*, June 1984).

The frustrations sometimes generated by grievances associated with physical conditions, and the way that a tardy response from a campus authority escalated conflict, were dramatically illustrated at Fort Hare. There, in August 1982, continuous electricity failures in the residences led to a mass lecture boycott, a refusal to write tests and to students venting their anger on lamps in the well-lit "Freedom Square" courtyard. During the ongoing confrontations, 1 500 students were expelled, the SRC disbanded, and all meetings were banned.

The campaign for an education charter

One important national campaign initiated by SANSCO related to the formulation of an education charter (EC). The idea of an EC emerged at SANSCO's December 1981 GSC which was devoted to the theme of "Education towards Democracy", and in coming years issues to do with goals, processes and participants were further developed. Within SANSCO it was felt that

[m]uch confusion exists over the type of education system South Africans wish to have. Although the Freedom Charter does lay down certain broad principles for education, we need to amplify this more concretely.[9.8]

It was suggested that an Education Charter Campaign (ECC) should explore the education demands set out in the Freedom Charter ... to give them greater content. The doors of learning and culture shall be opened to all; that is still our demand. Now the question we must ask is what specific demands in the long and short term will help us force those doors open.[9.9]

It was also argued that students needed to be "mobilised in the realisation of a common set of goals", and that in view of state reforms "it becomes necessary for us to have a Charter of ... demands against which we can compare the reforms".[9.10] SANSCO believed that an ECC had the potential to popularise and strengthen the organisation, and enhance its quality through research into education and through organisers developing organisational and technical skills related to the campaign.

The "declaration" that served as a framework for the ECC pledged participants to

a campaign for an Education Charter that will embody the short-term, medium-term and long-term demands for a non-racial, free and compulsory education for all in a united and democratic South Africa based on the will of the people. [9.11]

The objectives of the ECC were wide-ranging and comprised a combination of substantive and procedural goals. First, the sponsors of the ECC – SANSCO, in alliance with COSAS, NUSAS and the National Education Union of South Africa (NEUSA), a teacher organisation – aimed to produce a document that would serve both as "a guideline for a future education system in a democratic South Africa that will satisfy the needs of all the people", and a guide to "student struggles in years to come". [9.12] However, the EC was not conceived as a product purely of the intellect. The EC, it was emphasised, had to be "a product of struggle". [9.13] As the 1984-85 SANSCO president, Mguduso, put it: "People don't just sit and close their eyes for a few minutes and think what should they write down. Their demands are produced in the arena of what they are fighting for". [9.14] Moreover, it was felt that the EC had to embody not only demands articulated in contemporary education struggles, but also those raised in past struggles such as "the 1953 campaign against Bantu education, 1976 student revolt, [and] 1980 schools boycott", [9.15] while the ECC itself was to "provide a concrete channel for student grievances". [9.16]

Second, there were specific procedural goals in that the ECC was intended to "collect the demands of the people regarding education through a process of widespread consultation"[9.17] and the objective was "to reach and mobilise as many sectors of the community as possible round the issue of education (bearing in mind that education affects all sectors of society)". [9.18] SANSCO was wary of the EC "being the product of a handful of intellectuals". [9.19] Recognising the centrality of students in the education sphere, Phaala stressed that

[t]he only way to develop an alternative in education in South Africa is to involve students in formulating an education charter.

The process will inevitably be as important as the charter itself – if not of more value.[9.20]

However, the ECC was not viewed as involving only students. Since education was seen as affecting "all sectors of society" and defined broadly to include pre-school learning and adult education and training, the ECC was conceived of as a mass popular campaign involving trade unions, and women's, youth, civic and other popular organisations.

Third, in a context in which the majority of South Africans were denied the opportunity to participate in determining education goals and policy, the ECC was also viewed as providing an opportunity to participate in formulating an alternative to apartheid education. The importance of mass involvement was well put by the 1984-85 SANSCO president, as follows:

The Education Charter must involve as many people as possible if it is to have any meaning. Any document drawn up by a handful of intellectuals cannot possibly be of value. It will not raise our people's consciousness and build their different organisations which is what the ECC sets out to do.[9.21]

The reference to the raising of consciousness signalled SANSCO's view that the ECC should extend beyond merely a concern with the collection of education demands. Instead, the ECC should also help "to clarify the role of education in apartheid South Africa and the role of a progressive education system",[9.22] through seminars, workshops and conferences.

Finally, the reference of the SANSCO president to organisation-building highlighted an organisational objective of the ECC. It was hoped that mobilisation around the EC would be translated into expanded membership for the "non-racial student alliance" (SANSCO, COSAS and NUSAS) and other fraternal formations such as the Young Christian Students and NEUSA. Thus, the ECC Declaration also posited as aims:

to build student unity and strengthen the non-racial student alliance; to build and strengthen the organisations involved in the campaign; to build unity between students and parents, workers, teachers and members of the community. [9.23]

The ECC was viewed as spanning a number of phases. To begin with, there were to be consultations with trade unions and other popular organisations to harness support for the initiative. Thereafter, the ECC was to be publicised and popularised and local, regional and national structures were to be established to co-ordinate the campaign. During this phase there were to also be workshops, seminars and debates around education issues. The actual collection of demands was to constitute the third phase of the ECC. During a fourth phase, demands were to be collated and consolidated into a draft EC and there was to be discussion of the draft EC within local and regional ECC committees and within organisations. Finally, a national conference was to adopt the Education Charter.

By any measure, the ECC was both an ambitious and a massive undertaking. During the consultative phase it became apparent that while trade unions and popular organisations were sympathetic to the ECC, immediate, active and full participation could not be expected from these formations. A special joint session of SANSCO and COSAS in December 1982 acknowledged that the alternative commitments of other organisations, as well as material and human resources, had not been adequately taken into account in the conceptualisation of the ECC. Moreover, SANSCO and COSAS were themselves preoccupied with establishing a strong organisational infrastructure. In view of these factors, the ECC began to be conceived as a long-term campaign and one that needed to be creatively inserted into ongoing struggles around education. [9.24]

During 1983 little progress was made around the ECC, partly because of the embroilment of SANSCO and COSAS in various other education issues and political struggles, and partly because of a lack of person-power and financial resources. However, there was some popularisation of the ECC during the SANSCO/COSAS focus week on the 30th anniversary of the Bantu Education Act, and a few ECC committees existed at schools and at campuses. Still, at the end of 1983 SANSCO felt itself to be ready to take up the ECC more resolutely and the theme "organising for a people's education" was adopted to provide focus for the ECC. By the end of 1984, the ECC was formally launched in the Eastern Cape, Natal and Transvaal with backing from many trade unions and popular organisations. In July 1985 the ECC was launched in the Orange Free State at a meeting of 6000 students, workers and youth, and with support from local trade unions, youth organisations, and parent formations.[9.25] Thereafter, a national co-ordinating committee was established.

Despite some progress in 1985, the target date of early 1986 for the production of the EC proved impossible to meet. The ECC failed to become generalised countrywide and in late 1985 it was commented that "it is of note that the progress of the Education Charter Campaign is not impressive" (*AZASO National Newsletter*, late 1985:8). Activists reported a "lack of organisational skills, resources and finances" as major problems in the campaign".[9.26] Further problems were the declaration of a partial state of emergency in July 1985, the banning of COSAS two months later and intensified state repression in the face of escalating mass popular resistance. As an ECC publication put it:

> The initial period of the state of emergency was most devastating to us as we had not as yet learned to operate in those difficult conditions. We cannot deny that this was a blow to our organisations and their programmes.[9.27]

In the light of these difficulties participants were called on to utilise 1986 to, as conditions required, establish, consolidate and advance the ECC. Demands for the EC were to be submitted to the national co-ordinating committee by December 1986 and the target date for the national adoption of the EC was put back to 1987.[9.28]

However, the ECC was once again disrupted by the new and countrywide state of emergency which was declared in June 1986 and remained in effect for four years. Even before the state of emergency was declared, there began to be a state crackdown on mass activities and a planned ECC rally in Soweto was banned and the crowd was dispersed by the police (*The Citizen*, 6 May 1986). Still, there was some progress in particular areas. The *Cape Town Education Charter News* of November 1986 commented that

> the Education Charter is moving towards completion with the last stage of the campaign – the national collection of demands for a future education in our country. In the Western Cape region, as in the Johannesburg area, demands have begun to pour in from schools, colleges and universities.

The ECC was now linked to the "people's education for people's power" theme of the National Education Crisis Committee (NECC), the newsletter stating "let us use the Education Charter Campaign as a programme for a People's Education" (*ibid.*).

The statement that the ECC was "moving towards completion" was far-fetched. Many of the procedural goals of the ECC with respect to mass participation had yet to be fully realised, and an EC produced in contradiction with many of the commitments of the campaign would have been of questionable value. Still, in early 1987 a circular noting the demands collected until the end of January 1987 was distributed to local and regional ECC committees. The available demands (i.e. the collected demands) were listed under some eight categories that included rights related to education, curriculum, methods of education, and rights related to student organisation.[9.29] It is likely that the circular was more to motivate activists and not a serious draft EC. During 1987 the responsibility for spearheading the ECC was handed over to the NECC. However, although the ECC was spoken about intermittently in the NECC, it never became a priority issue, and as a result the ECC was never concluded, and the EC was never formulated.

While a campaign to collate demands that were articulated during education struggles and produce an EC to guide the deracialisation, democratisation and transformation of education was an important and timely initiative it was, ultimately, too massive an undertaking for SANSCO and its allied student and teacher organisations. The ECC called for the kind of intense, single-minded campaigning that was never possible, given the many other issues that required the attention of student and teacher activists. Moreover, the ECC also demanded a level of human, financial, and organisational resources that was never available to its sponsoring organisations. Finally, the ECC had to be undertaken under conditions in which SANSCO and its allies often had to struggle, in the face of authoritarian controls and repressive actions, simply to survive and maintain a presence at education institutions, never mind engage in major proactive campaigns.

Political mobilisation and actions

Although SANSCO emphasised that student activism should be geared towards contesting education issues, it did not refrain from taking up issues related to broader social and political conditions in South Africa. Consequently, students were mobilised and collective actions were undertaken around a range of social and political issues.

Apartheid political institutions

First, there was consistent student action in opposition to race-based political institutions established in terms of the framework of separate development, and to the balkanisation of South Africa through the bantustan policy. Thus, during late 1981, SANSCO participated in a campaign which mobilised Indians to boycott elections for the South African Indian Council, as well as in the Ciskei anti-independence campaign which mobilised opposition to the proclamation of Ciskei as an "independent" state and to the entire system of bantustans. SANSCO's specific contribution was to mobilise student opposition on campuses through mass meetings and placard demonstrations, and to channel activists to assist political and popular organisations and trade unions in campaign activities in black townships. During both campaigns, SANSCO joined other Congress movement formations in calling for a unitary, non-racial democracy based on the Freedom Charter.

A second political issue around which SANSCO mobilised students was in rejection of the government's 1982 constitutional proposals for a new tricameral parliament incorporating Indian and coloureds. The UCT branch of SANSCO summed up the proposals

> as an attempt to further extend racial oppression and capitalist exploitation. The proposals ... try to divide the oppressed and destroy the unity that has been forged in struggle over the past few years (AZASO UCT, 1983).

The UCT branch also noted that "the proposals ... .do not end racist education", and stressed that "as oppressed students we have a long, proud and militant history of resistance to racist education and to apartheid as a whole. AZASO is committed to continuing this tradition of resistance" (*ibid.*). In rejecting the proposals and the entrenchment of racist education, the Education Charter campaign was highlighted and students were called upon to "formulate our own education demands" (*ibid.*). Protest meetings were held on campuses to educate students around the dangers represented by the proposals and to mobilise students in active opposition. Concomitantly, SANSCO activists lent assistance to township-based initiatives to reject the constitutional proposals. Thus, a civic leader in the Johannesburg area, when asked "where is the support coming from in terms of people who are actually going out and organising and assisting?", replied that "initially support came from mostly the radical young people ... from various organisations like ... COSAS, AZASO".[9.30]

In January 1983, when a broad front was proposed to oppose the government's constitutional proposals, SANSCO was the first national organisation to endorse the idea. In a joint statement with COSAS, SANSCO expressed its support for the United Democratic Front (UDF) and called on

all democrats to commit themselves to this initiative against apartheid exploitation and oppression. Unity is essential to fight the proposals. Such unity must emerge from our common commitment to a non-racial democratic South Africa. Unity becomes real only when we act together.[9.31]

However, while both organisations were committed to a broad alliance and united action around the constitutional proposals, they also re-affirmed their "commitment to the Freedom Charter as a basis for the future South Africa" (ibid.). SANSCO played a vital role in popularising and rallying support for the UDF at higher education institutions. It also channelled members and supporters towards activities related to the public launches of the regional UDFs and the national UDF. Furthermore, hundreds of SANSCO members and supporters worked in black townships alongside members of other UDF affiliates to mobilise support for the UDF and establish grassroots structures. During the million-signature campaign of the UDF in 1984, one of the instruments to mobilise mass rejection of the constitutional proposals, there was a similar involvement by SANSCO on campuses and in black townships.

Finally, during the period immediately prior to elections to the new tricameral parliament in August 1984, SANSCO made a joint call with COSAS for a "fortnight of protest". Political and education struggle was linked through a call on students to also protest the deteriorating conditions and endemic conflict in secondary schools. It was stated that "a massive stayaway from the polls must be the objective of every democrat", and students were urged to take part in "mass demonstra-tions", to boycott classes and hold "mass rallies", to "focus on racist education" and to be actively involved in mass mobilisation in the black townships (AZASO, 1984e). The response to the call was tremendous. Despite a

> wave of repression around the election period, students withstood threats of suspensions, school closures and tough police action ... [and] almost one million students from South African schools, universities, technikons and training colleges boycotted classes countrywide.[9.32]

Through its contribution on the campuses and to a broad popular front, SANSCO helped to ensure that Indian and coloured political parties entered the new tricameral parliaments with minimal support amongst these national groups.

Apartheid personnel and "collaborators"

Popular resentment of government officials and black politicians operating within separate development political institutions was a third source of student mobilisation. In March 1981, an address by a government minister at Wits was disrupted by 300 black students. According to Brewer,

> [t]he disruption of the speech marked a new development, for it saw the emergence of a well-organized, articulate, and powerful group of black students on a white campus. They organized themselves into the Black Student's Society, and similar societies exist on other white university campuses (1986:87).

In May 1982 the invitation by the Fort Hare authorities to the Chief Minister of Ciskei to attend a graduation ceremony was greeted by mass student protests which resulted in police shooting two students, detaining twenty-five, and arresting 1 500 others. These actions led, in turn, to a boycott of classes. SANSCO's response was a call on higher education students to participate in a "National Day of Solidarity" with their Fort Hare colleagues. University administrations were also pressurised to urge the Fort Hare authorities to address student grievances.

Student protests were also engendered by the visit of F. W. de Klerk, then Minister of Education, and the visit by South African Indian Council members to the Springfield teacher-training college in Durban. Police were summoned to deal with the student protests and the college was closed by the rector on the grounds that he would "not tolerate political involvement by students at the college".[9.33] Although the protests at the Springfield college were not organised by SANSCO, the organisation immediately pledged support for the student actions and offered to assist in consolidating student mobilisation into longer-term organisation.[9.34]

A particular target of SANSCO was Gatsha Buthelezi, president of the ethnic Zulu movement, Inkatha, and chief minister of the KwaZulu bantustan. Buthelezi was intensely disliked by SANSCO for his participation in the bantustan system and his use of bantustan institutions to engage in ethnic mobilisation, for his pro-capitalist and pro-Western sentiments, and for his criticism of the exiled liberation movement's strategy of armed struggle. The presence of Buthelezi at a university usually sparked student demonstrations and attempts to disrupt his visit. At UCT, students prevented him from addressing a meeting. At the University of Natal, a walk-out was organised during a speech by him and derogatory slogans and songs were chanted, actions which resulted in his aides attacking students with sticks and truncheons (SAIRR, 1984:472). Of course (as noted earlier), SANSCO's most bitter clashes with Buthelezi were at the University of Zululand, where he was chancellor (SAIRR, 1984:474-75).

Collective action against bantustan politicians signalled the rejection by most students of their claims to black political leadership and of separate development political institutions. One feature of the conflict with bantustan leaders was that there was an acknowledgement that in some areas such leaders had been able to establish sizeable support bases. In the light of this, a distinction was drawn between the bantustan leaders and their rank-and-file followers. Thus, even in the aftermath of the brutal Inkatha attack on students at Zululand, the public response of SANSCO urged students as follows:

> We must have sympathy for rank and file Inkatha members. These are our people, misled by Gatsha and Inkatha for their purposes. Our ranks are always open to them to join us (Moseneke, quoted in Frederikse, 1986:157).

State repression

The banning, detention and imprisonment of student activists, and generally state repression, was a further issue around which there was student mobilisation. In late 1982, the detention of two female University of the North SANSCO activists under the Terrorism Act led to a six-day lecture boycott and the subsequent closure of the university for ten days. The detentions generated particular student hostility because of the assistance provided by white campus security staff to the security police. Mass meetings, co-ordinated by the SRC, were held daily to formulate plans of action and for report-backs. Student actions received the support of the Black Academics Staff Association which, although rejecting an SRC call for a strike, provided other forms of assistance, including collecting money for legal representation for the detained students.[9.35]

Collective action was also undertaken around the killing by police of political detainees, and the assassination of radical political activists. In September 1984, a former University of Transkei (UNITRA) SRC leader, Batandwa Ndondo, was killed by police. Both the killing and the refusal of the UNITRA authorities to permit a commemoration service for Ndondo gave rise to demonstrations. The killing in late 1985 of a SANSCO activist and political detainee by Lebowa bantustan police also sparked extensive protests. Finally, protest and commemoration meetings and demonstrations were routinely organised around the murder of anti-apartheid activists within South Africa and abroad. Thus, the brutal killing in 1982 of Griffiths Mxenge, a Durban attorney and underground ANC member who counselled Congress student activists to attend the first congress of SANSCO, and also provided financial support to SANSCO; and the murder, three years later, of his partner, Victoria Mxenge, resulted in lecture boycotts and memorial services on a number of campuses (AZASO National Newsletter, late 1985).

One important campaign around state repression spearheaded by SANSCO was to secure the repeal of the death penalty served on six ANC guerrillas. Beyond the immediate objective of securing the repeal of the death penalty, the "Save the Six" campaign was used by SANSCO to draw attention to the nature of social conflict in South Africa and the historical development of the armed struggle. A SANSCO pamphlet argued that the "six young men are the product of an oppressive, exploitative and unjust society, and their actions must be seen in this context" (AZASO Western Cape Region, 1983:2). It also emphasised that "the death penalty will never serve as a deterrent to people committed to

... a united, non-racial and democratic South Africa"(*ibid.*). SANSCO challenged the state's labelling of the guerrillas as "terrorists", highlighted their claims of torture in detention, and proclaimed that the six, even though found guilty of high treason were, "in the eyes of their people, heroes, if executed, martyrs" (*ibid.*).

For the "Save the Six" campaign, thousands of stickers and pamphlets were produced to mobilise opposition to the death penalty. Mass meetings were organised on campuses and in townships, some in conjunction with political organisations and church bodies. The meetings provided a platform for family members of the six guerrillas to appeal for the repeal of the death penalty and to explain the circumstances that had led them to take up arms. On the eve of the executions, numerous all-night vigils were organised which included poetry reading and education sessions. On the day of the actual executions of three of the guerrillas, protest meetings and commemoration services were held on various campuses, and students in Durban staged a march through the city centre, as did Fort Hare students in Alice. Three of the guerrillas eventually had their death penalties commuted to life imprisonment and, with wide support for the "Save the Six" campaign on the campuses and the attendance of hundreds of township residents at the all-night vigils and mass meetings, the campaign was interpreted by SANSCO as a considerable success.

Finally, state repression in the form of the state of emergency declared in mid-1985 also stimulated mass action on the part of students. On numerous campuses there were lecture boycotts and placard demonstrations. In Cape Town, there were attempted marches on Pollsmoor prison – where Nelson Mandela and other ANC leaders were imprisoned – by UCT and UWC students and staff, college and school students, and township residents. Banners and placards called for an end to the state of emergency and for the release of Mandela and all political prisoners. For the first time, black students at a white Afrikaans-medium university participated in mass action when University of Stellenbosch students attempted to march through the town of Stellenbosch to protest against the state of emergency (SAIRR, 1986:406).

International issues

On various occasions there was also collective action around international political issues. During 1982, a meeting was organised by the Wits SANSCO affiliate to express solidarity with Palestinians and the Palestine Liberation Organisation. The meeting triggered the outrage of Jewish students and led to physical clashes between black and Jewish students and the suspension of 12 students (SAIRR, 1983:516). On another occasion there was a demonstration at the American consulate in Johannesburg to highlight SANSCO's opposition to the Reagan administration's policy of "constructive engagement" with the apartheid government. Finally, a special target of SANSCO was meetings organised by conservative student bodies at the white English-language campuses which featured representatives of political movements which had a close relationship with the South African government. Such meetings were constantly disrupted, as was the case at Wits in early 1986 when students prevented a member of the Angolan UNITA party from addressing a gathering of the Student Moderate Alliance.[9.36]

Commemorations of historical events

Significant episodes related to political oppression and resistance in South Africa were a regular source of student mobilisation and collective action. Events such as the massacre of anti-pass demonstrators at Sharpeville in 1960, the ANC's Defiance Campaign of 1952, the Soweto Uprising of 1976, the Congress of the People at which the Freedom Charter was adopted in 1955, and specifically designated days such as National Detainees' Day, International Workers' Day, and National Women's Day, were all routinely commemorated.

Commemorations took the form of one-off mass meetings, or focus weeks which included mass meetings, seminars, photo displays, videos and films, and were accompanied by publications and pamphlets. Commemorations were intended to achieve a number of objectives. The first was to educate students about the history and nature of South African society, and around resistance to racial, class and gender domination in South Africa. A second goal was to strengthen among students anti-state and anti-apartheid sentiments, and to motivate them to join popular organisations and to actively participate in political struggle. Frequently, prominent political leaders were invited to address commemorations, both as a means of attracting students to meetings but also to persuade them to participate in the struggle. Thus, Gretta Ncapai of the Federation of South African Women reminded Wits students; "The Defiance Campaign was a stepping stone to bringing about a democratic, just society. It is in this spirit that students must continue".[9.37]

A third objective of commemorations was to popularise and win support for SANSCO, the Congress movement (including organisations such as the ANC and the SACP) and for the Freedom Charter. Thus, in 1982, SANSCO utilised the fifteenth anniversary of the death of Chief Albert Luthuli, a former president of the ANC and the first South African to be awarded the Nobel peace prize, to popularise the history of the ANC and the Freedom Charter. Fourth, commemorations were also used to popularise exiled, imprisoned and banned political leaders. In this regard, there were also intermittent campaigns for the release of Nelson Mandela and all political prisoners. Fifth, commemorations also provided an opportunity to reinforce student mobilisation around state reforms and repression and popular anti-apartheid campaigns. Thus, a joint SANSCO-NUSAS Sharpeville massacre meeting at the University of Cape Town in 1984 was used to attack the Nkomati peace accord between South Africa and Mozambique and to condemn the absence of peace and justice within South Africa. A final objective of commemorations was to, of course, recruit students into SANSCO.

"Community" action and worker support

One of SANSCO's aims was to "organise students so that they could play a more meaningful role in the community in general" (Appendix 2 hereto). SANSCO believed that because students had relatively more free time on their hands, were less constrained by family commitments, and were more mobile, they could render useful support to popular organisations (*AZASO National Newsletter*, June 1983:3). Consequently, on various occasions students were mobilised to participate in campaigns and activities of popular township-based organisations and trade unions — around transport and rent struggles, housing conditions and evictions, consumer boycotts, and opposition to African local authority bodies. In regions where community newspapers were produced by popular organisations, SANSCO members participated in producing and selling these. Thus, in Cape Town, a regular activity of the UCT SANSCO branch was to sell the community newspaper *Grassroots* at bus and train stations.

Relations with popular organisations were essentially confined to those organisations supportive of the Congress movement, ideological and political differences precluding relations with BC and other progressive organisations. While SANSCO provided support to popular organisations, the latter also contributed towards strengthening SANSCO branches by encouraging their student members to join SANSCO and to participate in campus-based activities. Moreover, on various occasions civic formations and church organisations assisted in the formation of parent committees when students were suspended or expelled from, or refused registration at, higher education institutions. Such committees exerted pressure on university authorities to re-admit students, negotiated on behalf of students, and sometimes initiated legal action to secure the re-admission of students.

The relationship between the UDF and SANSCO in some regions was not always smooth. On some occasions the UDF was criticised for its campaigns placing too many demands on student activists and for not providing assistance to the Education Charter campaign. It was also argued that UDF campaigns and activities diverted SANSCO from its own activities and programmes. Finally, it was suggested that the media focus on the UDF's Declaration, which articulated the Front's principles, objectives and aspirations, had the effect of diverting attention away from the Freedom Charter. The UDF response was that nothing prohibited SANSCO from promoting the Freedom Charter on UDF platforms and at UDF meetings. It was also argued that it was SANSCO's responsibility to define the nature of its role within, and contribution to, the UDF. Moreover, it was pointed out that UDF campaigns and popular mobilisation had the potential to facilitate the work of SANSCO on campuses and to provide new recruits and supporters. It was SANSCO's task, however, to translate such support into organised membership.

While there were meetings between SANSCO and the UDF to address SANSCO's concerns, tensions, albeit submerged, remained. The tensions had much to do with the inability of local and regional SANSCO structures to clearly define the nature of their participation within the UDF. Certainly, in the context of the strategic alliance that the UDF represented, there was scope for SANSCO to make explicit its ideological commitments and popularise the Freedom Charter, and to also assert more radical political positions. However, for various reasons this did not occur. In some cases, there was a lack of consistent attendance at UDF forums on the part of SANSCO delegates. In other cases, SANSCO delegates were not able to participate fully in debates around campaigns and strategies because the branches they represented failed to discuss issues on the UDF agenda and delegates lacked a mandate. No doubt, on occasions, SANSCO activists were also intimidated by political "heavyweights" from other organisations and lacked the confidence to participate fully. However, notwithstanding the problematic relationship between some SANSCO and UDF regional structures, SANSCO remained fully committed to the UDF.

With respect to worker issues, there was regular participation by SANSCO in International Worker Day activities, through meetings on campuses, to which unionists were invited to address students, and meetings in townships. There was also involvement in consumer boycotts initiated by unions. Thus, during the boycott of Wilson-Rowntree products, SANSCO popularised the boycott on campuses and collected funds for striking workers. Support was also provided to campus workers engaged in disputes with the university management, and at UCT the process of organising workers into a progressive union was initiated by a SANSCO activist.

Mobilisation and Collective Action, 1986 to 1990

In this section, I now examine student mobilisation and collective action in relation to the conditions of intense repression experienced by SANSCO and other mass organisations. Two considerations guide the contents of this section. First, since I have already sketched the education and political issues around which students were mobilised and collective actions were undertaken between 1981 and early 1986, there is little purpose in simply providing further examples of mobilisation and actions around these issues. I confine myself here to discussing only new or distinct issues around which student education and political mobilisation occurred.

Second, I discuss how the activities of the security forces in townships and the stifling of dissent gave rise to new challenges for SANSCO.

Education issues and struggles

One key feature of this period was the strong repression experienced by students at the University of the North (UNIN). Following student protests in mid-1986 and the arrest of some 200 students, the campus was occupied by the army and police, and students were subjected to a curfew, restrictions on movement, and various forms of intimidation. Despite this, there were intermittent protests around the army and police occupation, the detention of students, and the demand for a new SRC. In early 1989, a mass meeting resolved to demand the resignation of a white academic who was also a local town councillor and member of the Conservative Party, called on the administration to re-admit students excluded on academic grounds, and renewed the demand for the withdrawal of the army from the campus (*The Star*, 14 March 1989). On 21 March 1989, the anniversary of the Sharpeville massacre, there was a lecture boycott. On numerous campuses, there were solidarity actions with UNIN students. SANSCO also persuaded the heads of the white English-language universities and UWC to voice their concern at the situation at UNIN (*UWC Campus Bulletin*, 16 March 1987).

During this period there was a general intensification of efforts to increase pressure on and further isolate the apartheid government through sanctions, disinvestment, and a sports, cultural, and academic boycott. SANSCO committed itself to a total academic boycott that would prevent visits by foreign academics to South Africa, as well as overseas academic excursions by South Africans. In general, given the extent of contact between South African and overseas institutions and academics, and problems related to monitoring visits, there was little success in the implementation of the boycott. Still, there was at least one success, though the significance of the victory lay less in the visit of a well-known foreign academic being interrupted as much as in the public debate that the incident provoked around the academic boycott.

Had the Irish academic Conor Cruise O'Brien visited UCT without any public pronouncements on the academic boycott, as in the case of many academics visiting South Africa, his sojourn might well have gone unnoticed. O'Brien, however, publicly declared in a national newspaper, "I am happy to break it" (quoted by WUS/AUT, 1989:10). This provoked SANSCO to retaliate; his presence was described as a "provocation", and it was stated that "his statements were deliberately constructed to ridicule the oppressed people of South Africa in their efforts to isolate South Africa from the international community" (ibid.). SANSCO mobilised students to disrupt O'Brien's lectures and to defuse the situation the university authorities requested him to cancel his lectures.

In a lengthy reply in a daily newspaper to what it described as a "vitriolic campaign" against it by the liberal media and various groups for its disruption of O'Brien's lectures, SANSCO's defence was to argue that that the academic boycott campaign was linked to the overall liberation struggle. It was stated that "the academic boycott is only one tactic within a broader struggle"[9.38] and had to be seen as part of the strategy to isolate the apartheid government internationally in the sphere of education. Foreign academics who visited South Africa and South African academics going abroad were said to contribute little to the struggle against apartheid or towards the achievement of a democratic education. SANSCO also rejected the charge of destroying academic freedom, and alleged that its critics were silent when academic freedom was constantly violated at black institutions.

The SANSCO response enquired why its critics sought to "isolate only one "freedom" among so many others", asserted that no freedom was possible under apartheid, and added that "to tell us to respect some mythical "academic freedom" is tantamount to telling us to accept our oppression".[9.39] With reference to UCT it was argued that

[t]o talk of academic freedom at UCT as if it is an island in an ocean of apartheid is hypocrisy. UCT has all the characteristics of racism that we find in our society. Very few black students and lecturers are admitted there. From top to bottom the institution is a racist ivory tower which only serves the interests of those who monopolise wealth in this country.[9.40]

Finally, the article acknowledged the work and support of individual academics for the democratic movement, but called on UCT to commit itself as an institution to the anti-apartheid struggle.

The criticism of academics and of UCT are both points that need greater discussion. Throughout the 1980s, small numbers of black and white academics were either active members of popular organisations or sympathisers and supporters of the democratic movement. SANSCO activists generally had good relations with such academics and utilised them as resource-persons, speakers, and advisers around particular issues. On some campuses there were also small progressive non-racial or black academic staff associations and there were working relations with such bodies. A national progressive and non-racial formation of university staff, the Union of Democratic University Staff Associations, only came into being towards the end of the 1980s. Thus, for much of the 1980s, and had SANSCO been so inclined, there was little scope for major joint campaigns with academic staff around education issues. On the whole, campuses were dominated by liberal and conservative academics. The general passivity of liberal academics and their adherence to symbolic forms of protest meant that they were generally scorned by SANSCO activists and labelled as "ivory tower" academics. Racists among the conservative academics were, of course, targets of SANSCO campaigns which demanded their removal from campuses. These conditions, then, gave SANSCO little reason to hold back from a commitment to a total academic boycott.

There was, of course, also little about higher education institutions that endeared them to SANSCO. The authoritarian and repressive nature of administrations at black institutions meant that relations between SANSCO and these administrations were perpetually conflictual. The liberal authorities at white English-language universities, in contrast, were considerably more accommodating of student organisations like SANSCO and student political activity. However, SANSCO was of the view that the white institutions played a crucial role in contributing, through research and teaching, to the reproduction of the apartheid social order. The organisation was also well aware that the white English-language institutions were accorded a key role in the reform agenda of creating a black middle class. Also of concern to SANSCO was the close relationship between corporate capital and these institutions, and the strong representation of big business on their governing structures.

It was for these reasons that the SANSCO article on the academic boycott referred to UCT as serving "the interests of those who monopolise wealth in this country". For the same reasons, an article entitled "UCT not a people's university", called for governance structures at UCT to be radically changed so as to become more representative of and accountable to a wider constituency, and for the curriculum to be changed so as to address the real needs of South Africa (*Cape Town Education Charter News*, November 1986). At Rhodes, one of SANSCO's demands during a sit-in in 1987 was for representation on the university senate (SAIRR, 1988:186). Finally, for the above reasons, too, it was recognised that a special challenge to SANSCO branches on the white campuses was to interrupt initiatives attempting to produce malleable black graduates and to ensure that black students were not co-opted into support of reformist political solutions.

Although repression during the state of emergency was relatively successful in immobilising many township-based popular organisations and dampening the previous conditions of open rebellion, the campuses remained islands of protest and opposition. The all-white parliamentary elections of May 1987 provided a focus point for mass mobilisation and action on a number of campuses and led to the closure of UCT, Wits, UWC and UDW. With SANSCO making effective use of its organisational base on the campuses for continuing protest actions, the government responded by warning university administrations to either act against campus protests or face cuts in their revenues from state subsidies.

In a meeting with university heads, F.W. de Klerk, then Minister of National Education, warned that the state subsidy to universities would in future be conditional on the continuation of teaching and research; the prevention of unlawful and wrongful intimidation of students and staff; an end to unlawful gatherings, class and exam boycotts; students being prevented from using supplies, buildings and equipment for promoting the aims of unlawful organisations and promoting consumer boycotts, strikes, and civil disobedience; and on students being prohibited from printing and publishing material contravening the Internal Security Act. In short, university heads were required to impose state of emergency conditions on campuses and to assist in crushing student protest and dissent. Councils of universities were required to also inform the relevant minister in writing of all incidents, to describe the nature of the incidents, and the steps taken in response (WUS/AUT, 1989:12-13).

These regulations came into effect on 19 October 1987, the tenth anniversary of the banning of SASO. At the same time, a new law was passed that gave councils of universities and technikons permission to cancel the registration of students who refused to attend classes. The regulations led to protests, and were, in effect, immediately defied, both by students and some staff, and also by a number of institutions. There were university assemblies of students, academics, administrators and workers, and protest marches at UWC and at all the white English-language universities bar Rhodes.[9.41] The regulations were also challenged legally and, in a rare display of independence on the part of the judiciary, were ruled by the Supreme Court to be unlawful.

Political struggles

Significant during this period were the expressions of dissent on some campuses in the bantustans. Thus, at the University of Bophuthatswana, the ousting of the president, Mangope, during a brief coup was greeted with open rejoicing and a student take-over of the campus. When the coup was ended with South African assistance, students were evicted from residences and the campus closed indefinitely. At the University of Venda and surrounding colleges, there were student boycotts in late 1988 as part of a worker stayaway, with demands including the scrapping of the Venda administration and Venda's status as a bantustan.

During the late 1980s, in the face of the repressive action directed at the United Democratic Front (UDF) and popular organisations, the political lead increasingly began to be taken by organised workers and the Congress of South African Trade Unions (COSATU). Using the relative protection afforded to it by its pivotal position in the economic arena, COSATU launched a number of stayaways related both to immediate worker issues and to general political demands. A three-day general strike in June 1988 around the Labour Relations Bill and in commemoration of the Soweto uprising, which was the "biggest national stayaway in the country's history" (Price, 1991:267), saw extensive mobilisation of higher education students.

The year 1989 was a turning point with respect to political relations between the state and popular forces, as popular organisations once again embarked on a number of campaigns, and rolled back the relative success of the state in dampening political opposition through successive states of emergency. There were student actions in March 1989 during a stayaway to commemorate the anniversary of the Sharpeville massacre. A mass hunger strike by political detainees demanding immediate release from prison fuelled popular and student mobilisation and action. Fearing that the deaths of hunger strikers could intensify mass political action and stimulate further international isolation, the government released the vast majority of detainees. Finally, the murder of the Wits academic and UDF activist David Webster, in May 1989, led to the further escalation of mass action in both townships and on campuses and a new mood of defiance. At a memorial service at Wits attended by 5 000 people, ANC flags were unfurled (*Weekly Mail*, 12 May 1989).

Harnessing the new mood, in August 1989 the UDF and COSATU launched, under the umbrella of the Mass Democratic Movement (MDM), a "defiance campaign". A spokesperson for the MDM defined it as

> that political movement which unites the broadest masses of the oppressed people from all classes and strata, together with white democrats, in action around a programme of securing the transfer of political and economic power to the democratic majority of the people (*Weekly Mail*, 4 August 1989).

The MDM defined its object as a united, non-racial and democratic South Africa and saw its organisational task as rebuilding the mass popular formations that were smashed by the state of emergency, and strengthening those organisations that were still intact (*ibid.*).The most significant elements of the defiance campaign were a defiance of restriction orders on individuals and organisations, and a mass refusal to obey segregation laws and to accept segregated institutions and facilities such as public hospitals, schools, swimming pools and beaches. The campaign culminated in a week of mass action in early September, including a national stayaway to coincide with elections to the tricameral parliament.

Students at UWC and from Western Cape secondary schools were the first to engage in mass actions within the framework of the defiance campaign. Soon afterwards, defiance campaigns were launched at various campuses and mass meetings were held to declare SANSCO and its branches and affiliates "unbanned". As part of the defiance theme, SANSCO officials met with the ANC in Tanzania and participated in celebrations marking the tenth anniversary of the ANC's Solomon Mahlangu Freedom College.

On 6 September 1989, the defiance campaign reached its peak with a stayaway involving some three million people. Students participated through lecture boycotts and various other forms of protest. Mass action, however, continued. Police repression of protests and killings of demonstrators in Cape Town triggered a mass march of 35 000 through the city centre and provided the catalyst for similar marches in other cities and towns. As in the mid-1980s, support for the ANC and SACP was once again openly expressed through flags and posters. In October 1989, when veteran ANC leaders were suddenly released from prison, there were huge – effectively ANC and SACP – gatherings to welcome them. The mass action of 1988/89 culminated in the government unbanning of the ANC, SACP and other organisations in February 1990 and in the lifting of restrictions on popular organisations, including SANSCO.

10

The Character, Role and Significance of SANSCO

I t is now possible to interpret the character, role and significance of SANSCO. For this purpose, I draw on the previous chapters, which discussed SANSCO's ideology and politics, its organisation, the mobilisation of students and collective actions. I also draw on the description and analysis of the political, social and higher education conditions in Chapter 6. Finally, the interpretation of SANSCO's character, role and significance is framed and guided by the conceptual framework advanced in Chapter 1.

There is virtually no secondary literature on SANSCO. The only commentary on the organisation, conducted as part of an examination of popular politics during the late 1970s and early 1980s, is that by J.D. Brewer in his *After Soweto: An Unfinished Journey* (1986). Although, as I will argue, Brewer's interpretation of SANSCO is highly simplistic and characterised by many contradictory, and even astounding, assertions, and thus is seriously flawed, it nonetheless provides a useful starting-point for my interpretation of SANSCO.

The Character of SANSCO

In his concluding chapter, Brewer describes SANSCO as a "radicalised Black Consciousness" organisation. He writes that

during 1981 COSAS and AZASO changed their position on negotiation with Whites. They now support the idea of racial inclusiveness and of consultation with Whites of all political persuasions (Brewer, 1986:425).

According to Brewer, SANSCO was "willing to consult with Whites in order to act as a political surrogate of the ANC" (*ibid.*), thus enabling SANSCO to "reap the benefits of [the ANC's] legitimacy". Moreover, this tactic opened up to SANSCO the possibility of "mobilisation on a mass scale ... " (*ibid.*).

Brewer's analysis is misleading on a number of counts. First, the characterisation of SANSCO as a "radicalised *Black Consciousness*" (emphasis added) organisation is inaccurate and, since no reasons are provided for this attribution, it is, indeed, incomprehensible. The category "radicalised BC" only makes sense with reference to those organisations which continued to employ both racially exclusive methods of organisation *and* a racially exclusive approach to political struggle, if at the same time they also sought to incorporate into BC doctrine concerns related to social class and working class leadership of the liberation struggle. In these terms, the Azanian People's Organisation (AZAPO) and the exiled Black Consciousness Movement of Azania could be regarded as "radicalised BC" formations. The political trajectory and development of SANSCO, however, were altogether different.

With respect to SANSCO's political character, two periods can be identified. First, there was an initial BC phase, which covered the period from SANSCO's inception in November 1979 to its first national congress in July 1981. During this short phase SANSCO was closely linked with AZAPO, and also formally committed to BC. Moreover, it modelled itself on SASO and conceived of its role as essentially identical to that which SASO had previously played. Three reasons can be advanced for this argument. First, the haste with which SANSCO was formed, and the absence of broad consultation and intensive deliberations with local student formations on campuses, meant that there was little critical engagement around the goals, programme and strategies that should be adopted by a new national student formation, let alone the desirability and/or feasibility of a new national formation. Second, the initial practices of SANSCO confirm that there was no critical reflection around what the SANSCO preamble termed "the traditional role of black students in the community";[10.1] that is to say, the role that students had played under SASO. Finally, in seeking to promote black students as a "vanguard in the struggle for liberation", SANSCO explicitly assumed for students, and for itself, the kind of leading role that SASO had played. [10.2]

SASO, however, had operated during a period when a political vacuum had arisen following the smashing of the liberation movements, and under these conditions it took on the challenge of re-kindling internal radical political opposition to apartheid, and, indeed, spearheaded such opposition. The immediate post-Soweto conjuncture and political terrain was, in contrast, very different in nature, characterised as it was by the existence of a number of national, regional and local anti-apartheid formations, by intense debates among activists around resistance ideology, politics, strategy and tactics, and the beginning of a bifurcation in radical opposition politics into BC and Congress movement camps.

Yet, there was a singular failure by the founders of SANSCO to define critically the role of a national student formation in relation to these new political conditions. Instead, abstracting the role played by SASO from the historically specific conditions under which it operated, SANSCO elevated, universalised and ossified SASO's particular role into the "traditional role" of students. The close links between the founders of SANSCO and AZAPO also did not facilitate any re-conceptualisation and re-definition of the role of students and SANSCO. At the inaugural conference, Nkondo, the AZAPO president, argued that students "should direct their energy persistently to conscientising the masses, particularly the workers". [10.3] However, since all blacks were defined as workers, this did not represent any more specific definition of SANSCO's role and confirmed that what was required was simply the kind of efforts that SASO had engaged in to politicise non-student blacks.

The encouragement of these conceptions within SANSCO cannot be accounted for by any simplistic reference to the "logic" of BC. Nkondo himself had been an ANC member during the 1950s and, as later events showed, remained committed to the Congress movement. Moreover, among the founders of SANSCO were not only BC adherents but also some who claimed allegiance to the ANC, made possible by the fact that at this juncture there was no major gulf between the BC and Congress movements, and organisations were not yet indelibly marked as BC or Congress. Be that as it may, SANSCO's uncritical appropriation of SASO's role, its failure to pose anew questions of political orientation and to redefine its role all had the consequence of limiting its appeal and efficacy and rendering it ineffective. Indeed, when SANSCO was launched, COSAS, trade unions and civic organisations had already come into existence without waiting for black higher education students to play their "traditional role" or for SANSCO to act as a "vanguard".

The essential continuity with the pre-1976 BC and SASO tradition meant that far from being a *"radicalised* BC" organisation, SANSCO began, *contra* Brewer, as very much a "traditional" BC formation. However, the political identity of SANSCO was not static. In the eighteen months following its establishment it underwent a profound change in ideology and politics. It broke with a racially exclusive approach (if not with a racially exclusive organisation) to political struggle and embraced non-racialism in political conduct. It adopted an explicit, and essentially Marxist, race-class analysis of South African conditions, implicitly committed itself to the Freedom Charter and to socialist transformation in South Africa, and publicly aligned itself with the Congress movement. That SANSCO was "radicalised" is not in doubt. What has to be treated with scepticism, however, is Brewer's characterisation of SANSCO as a "radicalised *Black Consciousness*" (emphasis added) organisation. The qualitative transformation in ideology and politics that SANSCO underwent rendered it singularly distinct from "radicalised BC" organisations like AZAPO and makes Brewer's categorisation of it in these terms inexplicable. Clearly, Brewer has a poor understanding of the nature of the internal changes in ideology and politics that were occurring within various anti-apartheid organisations during the late 1970s and early 1980s and is thus unable to comprehend the real nature of SANSCO.

A second assertion of Brewer is that SANSCO was essentially an opportunist organisation that readily sacrificed its previous BC principles and its autonomy so as to be able to capitalise on the mass appeal of the ANC. If this was indeed the case, there is a failure on his part to exemplify to what distinct, and different, ends SANSCO sought to galvanise those that it allegedly mobilised on the back of the ANC and which did not accord with the ANC's own policies and project of national liberation. Here, it is again obvious that Brewer has little comprehension of the fluidity and complexities of radical and black opposition politics in South Africa during the late 1970s and early 1980s. Moreover, he also lacks an understanding of the specific conditions under – and the processes through – which SANSCO broke with BC and embraced the Congress movement.

The ideological and political re-orientation of SANSCO was not a one-off event but a process to which there were a number of contributory factors. Specifically, there was the split with AZAPO, and the actions of SANSCO's own Congress-oriented leaders to build close relations with Congress movement formations. More generally, the growing hegemony of the Congress movement within radical opposition politics in South Africa, the increasing popularity of the ANC, the Release Mandela campaign and mass student struggles of 1980, and the hegemonic position of student activists supportive of the Congress movement on various campuses also encouraged the re-orientation. However, other conjunctural conditions were also decisive and an analysis of these helps to place in context the specific and general developments that led SANSCO to become part of the Congress movement, and also makes clear that the re-orientation of SANSCO, far from being an opportunist move, was occasioned by changing ideological and political dispositions on the part of its student activists.

One of the issues that concerned the Spanish scholar Maravall in his research on the Spanish student movement was how to account for the re-emergence of political dissent among students during the period of the Franco dictatorship (Maravall, 1978). In the South African case, SASO had, of course, inaugurated independent political activity and organisation among black higher education students and, two years after its suppression, SANSCO was formed to continue this tradition. Thus, there was only a short period of discontinuity in national organisation among black higher education students. Consequently, of special interest is not so much the revival of dissent as much as the particular ideological and political content of the dissent expressed by a formation like SANSCO. Although this was not Maravall's specific concern, his overall analysis is nonetheless suggestive and his explanation for the revival of political activity among Spanish students provides useful pointers.

According to Maravall, a number of factors were responsible for the re-emergence of political dissent among students. First was the circulation of political literature, magazines and foreign books. Second was the activity of underground movements. Third was the activity (legal and semi-legal) of political activists. Finally, the moments of "deviant political socialisation" and direct political experience were also important contributing factors (Maravall, 1978:100-02; 166-67). All the moments advanced by Maravall to account for the revival of the Spanish student movement proved to be important influences in SANSCO's reorientation.

To begin with, the factor of literature: this can be considered under a number of subheadings. In the first place, the political literature of the ANC and SACP began to be more widely available from the late 1970s onwards. Such literature was crucial in providing an alternative and more theoretically informed perspective than that of BC, in stressing the relevance of the Freedom Charter, and in illuminating issues of political strategy and tactics. Articles on the history of political resistance and the liberation movements in South Africa enabled readers to place BC and SASO's role in historical perspective. While ANC-SACP literature was usually read individually, it was often referred to in discussions among activists, and there were cases when such literature served as a basis for collective discussion and debates. The conviction and imprisonment in 1980 of two Rhodes University students for possessing ANC literature and organising reading groups was only one example of a more widespread phenomenon (interview with Pillay, 1987).

Second, the radical literature on the 1976-77 uprising, including Hirson's *Year of Fire, Year of Ash* (1979) and Brickhill and Brooks's *Whirlwind before the Storm* (1980), was influential in highlighting the weaknesses and limitations of BC and student political activism, and in pointing students to explore other political options. The theoretical and political debates in the pages of the *Review of African Political Economy* (*ROAPE*) also generated considerable debate around political direction and strategy (*ROAPE*, 11, 1978). Concomitantly, the writings of radical and Marxist intellectuals challenging the liberal school of South African historiography opened up new ways of analysing South African realities. In this connection the works of Legassick, Wolpe, Johnstone and others were important departures from the traditional academic literature with its emphasis on race. [10.4] Radical books about the Soweto uprising, and journals like *ROAPE* and others that carried the writings of the "revisionist" school of South African historiography, were generally freely available in the libraries of the white English-language universities. Through black student activists at these institutions, such literature made its way to activists at other black campuses and in the townships.

During the late 1970s the literature of Marx, Engels, Lenin, and Western Marxists, already available in the libraries of the white English-language universities, also began to be sold at select bookshops. These writers were quickly purchased, or "appropriated", by political activists, photocopied and shared. Lenin's *What is to be Done* was highly popular for its discussion of political strategy and became influential in shaping political practice. Simultaneously, works on the revolutions in Cuba and Vietnam, and books on, and by, Fidel Castro and Che Guevara and Ho chi Min, and African revolutionaries like Amilcar Cabral and Samora Machel, were also more easily available. Machel, in particular, was tremendously important in re-orientating the politics of many activists, including some of the new leaders of SANSCO. As noted, it was a long statement of Machel's on "People's Power" that formed the basis of the SANSCO policy document. Moreover, Machel's "The liberation of women is a fundamental necessity of the revolution" was also important in the development of a greater concern around the "women's question".

Finally, no consideration of the role played by literature is complete without mention of two Johannesburg-based publications, *Work in Progress*, and *Africa Perspective*, and the publications of NUSAS. Theoretical articles on capitalism and expositions on Marxist concepts in *Work in Progress* provided student activists with some of the tools for an alternative class-based conceptualisation of South Africa, while excellent coverage of socio-economic and political issues spanning various fields and geographic regions kept students in touch with local, regional and national developments. At the same time, NUSAS dossiers on the revolutions in Angola and Mozambique, and various booklets on political resistance and state strategies helped broaden and deepen the political understanding of student activists.

At different moments, to a lesser or greater degree, and in different ways, all of the literature discussed above was important in shaping the ideology and politics of the SANSCO leadership. Some literature, especially that of the liberation movements was not necessarily widely or always easily available and tended to circulate among small numbers of political activists. However, most, if not all, SANSCO leaders enjoyed varying degrees of access to this literature, and were familiar with much or at least some of it. Still, Fawthrop, in writing about the ideology of the Western student movement, has argued that

[a]lthough the movement is inspired by men such as Marcuse, Che, Trotsky, Mao and others, it is more than something built upon revolutionary books. The ideology of a live movement can only be understood in the context of the experience and development of its members (Fawthrop, 1969:56).

In other words, the factor of the availability of political literature is, on its own, insufficient to explain the transformation that SANSCO underwent. The other factors identified by Maravall also need to be explored.

As in Spain, a political underground movement existed in South Africa and, after the mid-1970s, the ANC began to establish a more extensive infrastructure within the country. Members of the ANC underground were active in promoting and facilitating the formation of various organisations, and were often themselves active in mass organisations, and in this way influenced the ideology and political direction of student activists and the emerging mass organisations. The knowledge that the vast majority of the 4 000 people who left South Africa in the wake of the 1976 uprising had linked up with the ANC rather than any other exiled liberation movement, and that many leading exiled BC activists had also joined the ANC, enhanced the prestige of the ANC among political activists within the country. So, too, did the increasing armed activities of the ANC's military wing, Umkhonto we Sizwe (MK). The experiences of Mozambique, Angola, and Zimbabwe, and of the 1976 uprising itself, suggested to many activists that armed struggle was an indispensable component of revolutionary struggle in South Africa. MK activities, growing in effectiveness and frequently linked to popular struggles, contributed to expanding the political influence of the ANC.

With regard to the legal and semi-legal activity of political activists, during and after 1976, numerous old ANC and SACP stalwarts took on more prominent and public profiles. In different parts of the country they both initiated and helped guide the development of local civic and women's organisations and trade unions. Such older activists, together with the BC members who embraced the Congress movement, also functioned as political tutors, mentors, advisers and counsellors and thus played a vital role in the political schooling of the new generation of activists. It was such people, and frequently their families and political associates of old, as well as parents who had been involved in anti-apartheid politics in the past, who also came to provide a "deviant political socialisation" for some black student activists. One student commented to Frederikse, "I can say that I heard about those true leaders from my parents, because we had some political books at home which I used to read" (quoted in Frederikse, 1986:15). Another said that she learnt about politics "from talking to ... knowledgeable people who can inform us about the situation we are living in, and what can be done about it" (*ibid.*).

Finally, and perhaps most crucial, were the direct and immediate experiences of the student activists who steered SANSCO into the fold of the Congress movement. In the first instance, the uprising of 1976 had a decisive impact on them. Most, it is certain, would identify with the student who told Frederikse the following:

> The thing that made me politically minded was the influence I got from 1976 ... In fact, June 16th was the day I started to have an interest in political activity in this country (quoted by Frederikse, 1986:15).

For most SANSCO activists of the late 1970s and early 1980s period, 1976 marked the beginning of their road to student and political activism. All, in any event, cut and/or sharpened their political teeth in school and campus-based student formations and in the educational and political campaigns of the 1976 to 1981 period, although some also had experiences of activism in the fields of civic and youth organisation and sports. Apart from those student activists who were from the very beginning inducted into Congress movement politics, the initial political orientations of other student activists varied from adherence to BC, to support of the PAC, as well as loyalty to small left-wing groupings based largely in the Western Cape. However, political allegiances to non-Congress organisations were not cast in stone. During the 1977 to 1981 period, many activists were engaged in re-thinking, re-assessing and re-defining their ideological, political and organisational commitments and loyalties and thus it was not surprising that over a period such activists made their way into the Congress movement.

All these factors were pivotal in orienting and re-directing the ideology and politics of SANSCO activists towards a race-class analysis of South Africa, non-racialism in practice, and a commitment to the Freedom Charter and socialism. The "coalescence" with the Congress movement was, then, the outcome of SANSCO activists embracing ideological and political dispositions that were associated with the ANC rather than, as Brewer suggests, the result of any adroit and opportunist move. Moreover, if SANSCO's identification with the ANC did facilitate "mobilisation on a mass scale", it was towards common − if not totally identical ends − rather than any different goals related to SANSCO being a "radicalised BC" organisation − a categorisation that, as I have already indicated, makes no sense applied to SANSCO.

Finally, the most astounding of Brewer's assertions is that SANSCO was not only willing to negotiate "with Whites" but also supported "the idea of ... "consultation with Whites of all political persuasion" (1986:425), and implies that this related to SANSCO's commitment to "the idea of racial inclusiveness" and was also "in order to act as a political surrogate of the ANC" (ibid.). Given the control by whites of state apparatuses and the predominance of whites in positions of authority at higher education institutions, SANSCO's commitment to a strategy of mass mobilisation and organisation around the immediate educational and political concerns of students necessarily entailed "negotiation with Whites" for the redress of grievances and addressing of concerns. Indeed, negotiations with those in positions of authority was a concomitant of any strategy of effective mass mobilisation around day-to-day problems. There was also nothing exceptional in SANSCO's willingness in this regard − SASO had also negotiated with the white administrators of the black universities around student expulsions, suspensions and so forth.

However, there is a world of difference between a preparedness to negotiate in the interests of one's constituency and support for "consultation with Whites of all political persuasion". Even if SANSCO stressed the importance of political work within the "enemy" camp in order to erode the apartheid support base and win new recruits for the democratic movement, this is still a far cry from supporting "consultation with Whites of all political persuasions". As I noted in Chapter 9, SANSCO's political relations and network did not stretch much beyond the Congress movement. Co-operation and consultation with other progressive political organisations were extremely limited. Relations with political parties and politicians participating in separate development institutions were antagonistic and non-existent. Thus, the claim that SANSCO supported "consultation" with all whites, including, by implication, conservatives and neo-fascists is, frankly, incomprehensible. Brewer provides no evidence to support his claim. It may be that he regards support for consultation with all whites as a necessary corollary of "the idea of racial inclusiveness". Yet precisely why a policy of consultation with whites of all political persuasions should derive from a commitment to non-racialism in practice is left unstated and, indeed, Brewer would be hard-pressed to demonstrate any necessary relationship between them.

If there was no predisposition to consult with all whites, there was, of course, a principled commitment to non-racialism in practice, and it is in this regard that "the idea of racial inclusiveness" takes on its real meaning. A pamphlet stated that SANSCO "developed a non-racial, democratic approach because this is the type of society we want. Our approach reflects an objective" (AZASO, 1983d). The commitment to non-racialism in practice was manifested in numerous ways, but especially through SANSCO's alliance with the predominantly white NUSAS. The relationship with NUSAS came in for strong criticism from BC and other left-wing student activists who charged that it was a ruling class organisation, which sought to divert the national liberation struggle from a radical outcome. SANSCO's response was that

[i]n any struggle we have to draw a line between those organisations that fall into the progressive camp and those which fall in the reactionary camp ... .[T]his line has to be redrawn from time to time. We judge whether an organisation is reactionary or progressive by its political orientation and practice. [10.5]

Since NUSAS adopted consistently radical positions on political and educational issues, it was defined as a progressive formation. Moreover, to the extent that it weaned white students away from conservative and liberal politics and contributed to creating divisions within the ruling bloc, it had to be encouraged. However, SANSCO was only too aware that beyond the NUSAS leadership was a constituency that included conservative and liberal students. Hence, its relationship with NUSAS was regarded as a strategic rather than principled alliance.

SANSCO leaders stressed that non-racialism had to be forged in the process of struggle and united action and also had to be visible. Well-intended suggestions that the relationship with NUSAS should be ended in the name of "black unity", elicited the stock response that

[o]ur organisation is organising against a particular system [and] towards a particular goal and therefore we have to avoid anything which will become detrimental to the particular goal (Phaala, 1983a:13).

It was also argued that there was a danger of creating a "a monster which we cannot control" if initially SANSCO were to say "we are organising to fight whites" and then later to declare that "no, we are actually fighting the system" (ibid.).

Often, the plea for black unity was advanced by students who were interested in becoming politically and organisationally active but were yet to align themselves to any political movement, or were attracted to SANSCO but concerned and confused about its relationship with NUSAS and the accommodation of whites in Congress-movement political formations and struggles. SANSCO activists were encouraged to address the concerns of such students with great sensitivity and patience for they were in much the same situation as the Reverend Gqiba was in the early 1970s:

I had no political direction then, I just had hatred for the white man – until I met this old man, one of the greatest trade unionists of our times ... That hatred needed some kind of a guidance, and it was through him that the right politics was instilled in me ... After that I stopped hating the white man just because he happened to be white. Loza taught me that is a starting point – it's a process ... . Being anti-white is a stage which I feel each and every individual should go through, but it's not an end in itself. We have to overcome it (quoted in Frederikse, 1990:128). [10.6]

The organisation understood that although the fundamental problem in South Africa was the structures of class and racial domination rather than whites *per se*, racial oppression was bound to engender among many students" anti-white sentiments. Consequently, the policy was

[w]e should not reject such students because superficially conflict in SA does play itself out along black-white lines. Such students are often BC in ideas though not in political commitment. They must be introduced to progressive analysis and thinking and won over to the progressive democratic cause.[10.7]

Activists were urged to treat "anti-white slogans" as "primitive manifestations of political awareness", and to make it their responsibility to

make sure that the primitive type of political awareness [was] translated into positive political action whereby the masses can ultimately identify the actual enemy, which is exploitation of man by man (Phaala, 1982:38).

The organisational challenge was to accommodate both "primitive political consciousness and create the necessary structure which will make it possible for the political understanding of the masses to develop" (*ibid.*).

On a few occasions misgivings were also expressed by branch activists about SANSCO's relationship with NUSAS. The concern was that the relationship slowed the pace of student recruitment and it was argued that it was tactically legitimate to end the relationship or for relations to be limited to the non-public and leadership levels. However, such activists were usually persuaded against SANSCO adopting such a path. The majority of activists viewed dissociation from NUSAS as far more than a tactical shift and as a violation of non-racialism in practice. It was also felt that while an end to the relationship with NUSAS could result in more rapid recruitment, it also had the potential to create turmoil within SANSCO around its commitments to non-racialism, the Congress movement and the Freedom Charter.

Consequently, the organisation of students on a principled basis that ensured that SANSCO's ideological and political orientation remained intact, even if this meant a slower pace of membership growth, was favoured. What this illustrates is that SANSCO sought not to be a general student organisation that encompassed various political tendencies, but a student political organisation with a distinct and definite ideological and political character. Here, SANSCO was at one with Lenin. It turned its back on "ideological indifference", did not gloss over the differences in the student body but sought to "explain [them] as widely as possible and to embody [them] in a political organisation", and was also of the view that "only on the basis of a perfectly definite programme can and should one work among" students (Lenin, 1961d:43;50-53).

Despite its commitment to non-racialism in practice, SANSCO, of course, remained an exclusively black student organisation. This was due to strategic considerations related to the particular experiences and problems of black students and justified on the grounds that strategies and tactics were shaped not simply by principles and goals but also by structural conditions and the nature of the terrain on which mobilisation and organisation occurred. This approach, an adherence to principles coupled with a flexibility in strategy and tactics, was also manifested in other ways: in the tactical alliances that were forged with university authorities around the government's "quota bill"; and in the coalition with a wide range of organisations around the 1982 constitutional proposals. It was especially evident, however, in the tactically astute decision to retain the name "AZASO" and to only change to "SANSCO" when the organisation was well rooted on campuses and politically hegemonic among students.

The point has been reached where it is now appropriate to conclude my engagement with Brewer and go on to other aspects of SANSCO's character. As I have shown, there is little evidence to support Brewer's various assertions about SANSCO. In any event, he ought to be well aware of the hollowness of some of the claims he makes in the conclusion to his book since they are at distinct odds with his comments in an earlier chapter. There, he acknowledges that within South Africa the previous "perfunctory genuflections in the direction of the ANC have been replaced by a greater political loyalty to its policies, practices and personnel" (Brewer, 1986:265). He also recognises that

> today's statements do not come from younger students merely because they wish to legitimise their own position or because they recognise the ANC's past relevance. They arise out of a new ideological agreement with the ANC (ibid.).

Yet, and this is an especially curious feature of his treatment of SANSCO, for some reason this more insightful and accurate conception of the basis of SANSCO's commitment to the Congress movement is overturned in the concluding chapter. Why this is the case need not detain us here. However, to the extent that the concluding chapter of a book represents an author's final thoughts, Brewer's characterisation of SANSCO and his account of its transition from BC to the Congress movement must be regarded as seriously flawed.

The nature of SANSCO's ideology and politics leaves no doubts about its revolutionary character. Its conceptualisation of South African society in terms of an analytical framework of racial capitalism emphasised that black oppression was rooted in both racial and national domination and class exploitation. Its goal of people's power embodied both a commitment to national liberation and the fundamental transformation of South Africa along socialist lines. While it advanced the Freedom Charter as the basis for the transformation of South Africa, it stressed that this manifesto represented its minimum demands – the implication being that its own commitments extended beyond the national democracy envisaged by the Freedom Charter and included the construction of a democratic socialist order.

There was also within SANSCO much reference to "true democracy". On the one hand, the concept was used to argue the limits of political rights and freedoms, a vote every five years and representative democracy, although it was recognised that in the South African context the winning of democratic rights and institutions would be an important achievement. On the other hand, it represented a call for political rights to be supplemented by various forms of economic and social rights, and for democracy within the political sphere to be complemented by popular democratic control of economic and social institutions. That is to say, liberation was understood in terms of conferring rights on social groups such as workers, teachers and students, to participate in decision-making around issues that impinged on their lives. This is similar to the contention of the Italian theorist of democracy, Bobbio, that

> [n]owdays, if an indicator of democratic progress is needed it cannot be provided by the number of people who have the right to vote, but the number of contexts outside politics where the right to vote is exercised (1987:56).

In other words,

the criterion for judging the state of democratisation achieved in a given country should no longer be to establish "who" votes, but "where" they can vote; ... how many more spaces there are where citizens can exercise the right to vote (*ibid.*). [10.8]

SANSCO's analysis of education provided a further indication of its essentially revolutionary constitution. The structure and form and content of education was related to capitalist social relations and apartheid education was conceived of as an essential element in the reproduction of race, class and gender domination in South Africa. On these grounds, the mid-1970s demand for equal education gave way to the call for people's education, an education which was to contribute to social transformation and was oriented towards primarily serving the social interests of workers. Educational demands were conjoined with broader economic, political and social demands since it was held that people's education was, ultimately, only possible with the achievement of people's power. Still, education was defined as an important arena of ideological and political struggle and victories and advances in this sphere were seen as an integral part of building a democratic educational system and a democratic social and political order.

Finally, in its political and educational work among students, SANSCO confined itself to developing an understanding of the conditions that gave rise to the liberation movements" strategy of armed struggle. Understandably, there were no explicit statements of support for or promotion of the armed struggle, but there was strong tacit support. And on occasions this was not so tacit. According to Mguduso, some activists would insist in

public meetings, [that] you must all go out and join Umkhonto ... [and] in the 1985 conference there had to be an intervention from the NEC to explain that because of legal constraints there are certain things that we agree with but we cannot say so publicly (Interview, 1995).

The revolutionary nature of SANSCO was also reflected by its strategic predispositions. Whereas during the first eighteen months a key feature was a distinct lack of organisational focus, after mid-1981 a strong and consistent characteristic was the emphasis on mass mobilisation, democratic organisation and the development of a mass base on the campuses. On the one hand, a mass approach to educational and political struggle was conditioned by the reality of authoritarian campus administrations and an authoritarian political regime. It was recognised that only "mass mobilisation and democratic organisation" would "ensure our survival from attempts to divide and repress us". [10.9] Moreover, it was also understood that united mass action spearheaded by a strong organisation was a necessary condition if students were to realise their educational and political demands. Hence the assertion of a SANSCO secretary that "we don"t need powerful speakers as much as we need creative organisers". [10.10]

On the other hand, the stress on mass mobilisation and organisation and mass action was also conditioned by ideology – a conviction that the active and conscious participation of workers, students and other strata was a necessary condition of any meaningful social transformation. It was this belief that led SANSCO to stress that an Education Charter produced solely by intellectuals would be of limited value, and to place great emphasis on the procedural dimensions of the Education Charter campaign. This included a stress on mass involvement in the campaign, the insistence that the ECC had to contribute to the quantitative growth and qualitative development of its sponsoring organisations, and that it had to strengthen ties between SANSCO and other popular organisations. Indeed, part of the reason why the ECC was never concluded was that SANSCO refused to compromise on the EC being a product of mass participation. Democratic, participatory processes, then, were considered to be as important as substantive outcomes and products.

The strategic predispositions of SANSCO, and especially the stress on building mass organisation, coupled with a sober understanding of the repressive potential of the apartheid state, combined to ensure that SANSCO was characterised by a strategically and tactically calculating temperament and that there was little of the voluntarism and spontaneity that had characterised SASO. The "SANSCO approach" referred to in Chapter 7 included the schooling of activists to rigorously analyse conjunctural conditions in the political and educational spheres prior to the launch of collective action. Indeed, it was in terms of such analysis that SANSCO's themes such as "organising for people's education" and "student action for people's education" were formulated to give focus to its educational, political and organisational activities.

SANSCO's strategically and tactically calculating nature was best reflected by its campaign for the repeal of the death sentences on six ANC guerrillas. In some quarters the campaign was criticised as ill-conceived and "adventurist". SANSCO's view, however, was that the campaign was both politically necessary and strategically opportune. Though fully aware that the campaign could expose it to severe state repression it was felt essential to develop a political understanding of armed resistance and also to counter the state's labelling of guerrillas as "terrorists". Moreover, the campaign was also seen as a means of testing the political response of students and other social groups to the ANC's armed activities. During the early 1980s there was no national political organisation to spearhead the campaign countrywide, and SANSCO's view was that popular organisations had to be protected from the severe repression that such a campaign could unleash. Higher education institutions were seen as providing a measure of political protection, and as a result SANSCO took the initiative to spearhead the campaign nationally.

The ideas, views and conceptions of SANSCO, and the so-called "SANSCO approach", gave the organisation its particular "cognitive identity" (Eyerman and Jamison, 1991). The discourse of SANSCO was, in the first place, the outcome of the engagement of its "organisation intellectuals" with various kinds of radical political literature. Second, it also stemmed from contact between key SANSCO activists and underground ANC activists, and other political activists involved in legal and semi-legal organisations. Finally, it was also the result of the deviant political socialisation and direct political experience of the "organisation intellectuals". To be sure, the political literature that was read, the advice and counsel of activists, and the direct political experiences were mediated and critically interpreted by SANSCO intellectuals and thus SANSCO's discourse was not ready-made but was socially constructed. Moreover, and to their credit, the "organisation intellectuals" advanced the important thesis that education was a site of struggle, and introduced the notion of people's education.

Yet, when SANSCO's ideology and politics are considered in their entirety, there was little that was particularly novel or innovative about the overall "cognitive praxis" and knowledge production of SANSCO intellectuals. That is to say, ideas and conceptions were by and large culled from various sources and, if adroitly synthesised into a general ideological and political discourse, represented no really original and distinctive thinking. Indeed, the output of SANSCO's intellectuals in the form of essays and articles around theoretical and contemporary political and educational issues was extremely limited. In part, this can be accounted for by the nature of the 1980s political terrain: numerous theoretical and political journals and scores of seasoned Congress movement intellectuals existed to elaborate and articulate ideological, political and strategic perspectives, thus sparing SANSCO intellectuals from this kind of activity. On the other hand, while within SANSCO there was a concern with theoretical and ideological issues, there was not a fixation with such matters. In a sense, ideology and politics were regarded in instrumental terms and the real pre-occupation was with mass mobilisation, organisation and collective action.

Still, given SANSCO's emphasis on education as a site of ideological and political struggle, one would have expected that — especially around education — there would have been a greater attention to knowledge production. Indeed, one of the objects of the Education Charter campaign was to develop a greater understanding regarding education; and, despite the view that the Education Charter needed to be a product of struggle and the masses, there was ample scope for SANSCO intellectuals to initiate or produce discussion papers and articles to facilitate critical engagement around educational questions. No initiatives, however, were taken in this regard.

There was also a curious theoretical incongruence in the way that SANSCO conceptualised education, that went unnoticed. Under the influence of Marxist reproduction theorists of education, such as Althusser (1971) and Bowles and Gintis (1976), education was seen as an instrument of the reproduction of capitalist relations of production, and educational policies were viewed as unproblematically serving the functional needs of capital and its allied social forces. Educational reforms were interpreted as simply securing the reproduction of apartheid society through new means (Wolpe and Unterhalter, 1991:5-6). Concomitantly, as I have indicated, education was also defined as a site of struggle. However, this dualism at the theoretical level was not overcome.

The recognition of education as a contested terrain did not lead to any re-conceptualisation of the functionalist argument that allocated to education an essentially reproductive role. And despite the intense conflicts around education, education policies and reforms were not interpreted as the outcome of political contestations but instead seen as flowing simply from the needs of capital and the state. Put another way, there was a curious lack of recognition of the efficacy of student struggles and SANSCO's own part in them. While the need to struggle for reforms was acknowledged, state reforms were only understood in terms of reproducing racial domination and capitalism, rather than as necessitated by student and popular struggles and as creating new, and possibly more favourable, conditions for struggle.

If education was viewed as reproducing society, later, in terms of the slogan "peoples education for people's power", education also came to be seen a mechanism of social transformation. However, the historically specific conditions under which education could contribute to under-mining, modifying or transforming the racial and capitalist social order were never the object of detailed and rigorous analysis. Such an analysis would have revealed that the transformative potential of education was crucially dependent on conditions in the political, economic and other social spheres, and contingent on radical restructuring in these arenas. It was taken as a given, not incorrectly, that educational transformation was only possible in a free and democratic South Africa. However, it was also blithely assumed that a transformed education system in a democratic South Africa would also guarantee a transformative role for education and there was no recognition that transformation *in* education was not a sufficient condition for a contribution to social transformation *through* education.

SANSCO's inattention to theoretical questions was coupled, during the late 1980s, with a sceptical attitude towards the production of knowledge that was not directly functional in the sense of serving the immediate needs of popular organisations and the liberation struggle. Progressive academics who maintained a distance from popular organisa-tions, or whose writing was either critical of one or other aspect of liberation organisations, or whose work did not appear to be in any way connected to immediate political issues, were condemned as ivory tower academics. As a result, SANSCO activists were to draw the charge of being anti-intellectual. Indeed, there tended to be a gulf between many progressive academics and researchers on the one hand and activists on the other, and a relationship of animosity and mutual distrust. On the one hand, the intolerance and impatience among activists with certain progressive academics was not unrelated to the intense repression of the late 1980s and the exigencies of both survival and continuing to engage in mass action. On the other hand, there was also an absence of serious thinking around the purposes of radical intellectual production, around questions of the autonomy and accountability of intellectuals, and a general lack of appreciation of the intellectual labour of progressive academics and a refusal to acknowledge such labour as a form of activism.

Thus, Jakes Gerwel, Rector of the University of Western Cape was moved to point out that "good intellectual work entails hard work of a special type. It is as difficult, if not more difficult, than organising door to door work, street committees and mass rallies" (Gerwel, 1990:3). The demand of activists for research that was directly functional in nature, for "relevant" research, drew the response from a left-wing intellectual and trade unionist that " ... if political organisations made all the decisions we would have little pure science, no economic theory, no philosophy, and very little history" (Lewis, 1989:68).

The hostility towards progressive academics who raised important questions about the theoretical, policy and strategic postulates of liberation organisations betrayed an unawareness of the critical function of intellectuals. For, as Wolpe has argued,

> if the role of research and writing is to be restricted entirely to providing the materials for and confirmation of already defined policies, then this is to reduce research to a purely ideological function and to deny any autonomy or value to intellectual work and hence to the critical yet essential function of such work (Wolpe, 1985:74).

In other words, it was short-sighted of activists to expect progressive academics to be the ideological and political functionaries of the liberation movement and simply to accept without question the positions of the liberation organisations. Buci-Glucksmann has suggested that for Gramsci, an intellectual of whom SANSCO activists would have approved, "philosophy must produce knowledge for politics, without cutting itself off from the objective and scientific investigation of the world" (1980:15). If SANSCO activists had seriously reflected on the question of the autonomy of intellectuals, and if they had been serious about academics contributing to political struggle, the rationale for such an approach might have been appreciated. For if research is not approached in the manner that Gramsci suggests, the knowledge production of progressive academics would become trapped in a situation in which, as in the case of Stalinism, "philosophy becomes a mere political instrument, never producing any knowledge for politics since it is already a political ideology" (Buci-Glucksmann, 1980:15).

Enough has been said about the ideological, political and strategic aspects of SANSCO's character. To conclude this section, I now want to consider certain features of SANSCO that relate more to its internal organisation and structure.

Throughout the 1980s there was much emphasis on building SANSCO as a mass organisation. However, precisely what was meant by "mass" was never spelt out. I have suggested that at its peak the membership of SANSCO possibly numbered some 5 000. Thus, if SANSCO sought to be a "mass" organisation in the sense of incorporating the majority of higher education students as members, then relative to the size of the higher education student body SANSCO was by no stretch of the imagination a mass formation. In terms of such a definition, SANSCO was essentially a respectably large organisation constituted, in the main, by committed activists. However, if "mass" denoted the desire to construct an effective organisation with popular support among a significant number of students, then to a large extent SANSCO achieved this objective.

SANSCO members and other progressive student activists constituted a tiny fraction of the overall student body and, in Hamilton's (1968) terms, were the "militants". Within the "militant" bloc, SANSCO members predominated. A small percentage of the student body, though larger than the "militants", comprised "non-participants" who for a variety of reasons refrained from any kind of political involvement altogether. The vast majority of students were "sympathisers" who, in the main, politically identified with SANSCO and its allied formations such as the UDF and participated in its campaigns and activities. The "militants" and "sympathisers" together constituted the higher education black student movement. The majority support for SANSCO among both these groups meant that SANSCO was the politically hegemonic organisation among black higher education students and organisationally hegemonic within the black student movement.

SANSCO's position within the student body can also be approached using Lenin's more fine-grained and politically grounded categories (Lenin, 1961). In terms of this framework, five groupings can be identified within the black student body – Congress movement supporters, Black Consciousness supporters, adherents of other smaller progressive groupings, "indifferents" and "reactionaries".[10,11] "Reactionaries" were a very small component of the black student body, and their size and the fact that they generally kept their political allegiances private meant that they did not represent any challenge to SANSCO. "Indifferents", as the term implies, stood aloof from student political activity and were no threat to SANSCO. Of the politically aligned groupings, Congress movement supporters were by far the dominant group. Of course, not all supporters of the Congress movement were members of SANSCO. Many students identified with SANSCO without joining the organisation. A smaller number of students preferred being active in other campus organisations or non-campus youth, women's, religious and civic organisations, though they usually helped with important campaigns and projects. Moreover, the identification with the Congress movement was not always necessarily the direct result of SANSCO's activities – students were also won through the township-based campaigns of the UDF and the general mushrooming of support for the ANC. This facilitated the hegemony of SANSCO, if it at the same time made it more difficult for formations like AZASM and SOYA to have much of an impact on the campuses.

With respect to institutional presence, SANSCO was predominantly located at universities and technikons and had a limited presence at teacher-training colleges. Colleges were of strategic importance for two reasons. First, their location in the rural areas of bantustans provided the possibility of student activists contributing to the political activation of rural communities. Second, college students represented the future generation of school teachers and their political mobilisation and involvement in campaigns such as that around the Education Charter could have had a positive effect on the attempts to build people's education in schools. The strategic significance of teacher-training colleges was belatedly recognised, and though efforts were made expand into colleges, only a small number were represented within SANSCO. However, the existence of over one hundred colleges, their geographical spread and location, their administrative control by bantustan governments and the extremely authoritarian character of these institutions also meant that there were major obstacles around organising them. The fact that SANSCO mainly existed at universities and technikons meant that geographically it was concentrated in large cities and the more urbanised areas of the bantustans and had a limited presence in the rural areas.

The domination of SANSCO by university students and urban campuses was also reflected in the composition of the national executive committees (NECs) elected by various congresses. The vast majority of NEC members were from universities, and frequently from the white English-language universities and the urban campuses of the universities of Durban-Westville and Western Cape, which gave these campuses a representation at leadership level that was out of proportion to membership on the ground. Thus, in 1981, 75% of NEC members were from these campuses, in 1983 70%, and in 1987 87,5%. Moreover, all the SANSCO presidents, bar the 1984-85 president who was from the University of Zululand, came from English-language universities. The election to national office of activists from the white English-language institutions and UWC and UDW may have been influenced by considerations such as the greater facilities and material resources available at such campuses, the repressive conditions on most black campuses and ease of communication and contact. Be that as it may, the composition of the NEC gave SANSCO the image of being an organisation solely for university students, and it was not surprising that at the 1987 congress regret was expressed having given this impression.

Finally, SANSCO was a predominantly male organisation. During the late 1980s, women students constituted over 40% of university students, about 38% of technikon enrolments and over 60% of teacher-trainees (Table 3, Chapter 6). However, women members would probably have made up no more than 15% of overall members, so that in relation to the gender composition of the student body women were severely under-represented within SANSCO. This under-representation also extended to SANSCO's branch, regional and national executive structures, which essentially comprised male activists. Indeed, between 1979 and 1990, apart from the obligatory election of a woman to the portfolio of women's organiser, only one woman was ever elected to the national executive.

There was, as was noted, much concern around the lack of participation of women in SANSCO and various attempts were made to address the problem. However, genuflections to the importance of women's involvement in SANSCO aside, the mobilisation and organisation of women was generally treated by male members as the task of women activists. According to an activist, during the early 1980s there was

> something of a tension between the acceptance of the need to organise students more generally and the need to organise women. It was always at the initiative of women who were particularly concerned about women's issues that initiatives were taken. So ... whilst there was an in principle commitment, carrying the can really rested with women students within AZASO (interview with Africa, 1995).

There was little change during the late 1980s. Thus, the SANSCO women's organiser reported that

> [o]n many campuses comrades in leadership positions like the executive cannot give an account on [sic] the position of women in their campuses, because most branches are still not involved as branches in the organisation of women (SANSCO, 1989:4).

In the scheduling of activities and tasks, the organisation of women generally tended to be relegated well down the list of priorities (interview with Mguduso, May 1995). As a result, it was legitimately contended that

> [i]n SANSCO, generally the issue of women's participation in the struggle has been reduced to the level of theoretical discussions held in regions and national gatherings with little or no effort whatsoever being put into practicalising the work on the ground (SANSCO, 1989:4).

This is not to suggest that there were no obstacles around organising women. As SANSCO women activists learnt, the sexist and patriarchal nature of South African society was a real impediment to mobilising women. A SANSCO president also pointed out that in the context of the position of women in African communities, African women students needed "a very, very strong will" to participate in student politics (interview with Mguduso, 1995). It would have been a case of

> self destruction for a female just to be kicked out of a campus and to go home ... You would be ostracised by your community in African areas because they will see you as being bad. Unlike if you are a male — you are seen as a hero, people had the type of respect of some type of a local Mandela and so on ... You carry the stigma of being a failure. Far more serious socially speaking than being a male (*ibid.*).

Mguduso also suggests that within African communities dangerous activities were deemed to be men's work. However, it appears that instead of challenging such notions, male activists reinforced them, for example, by sheltering women from confrontations with the police. Thus, Mguduso states that "if the police are about to chase us with dogs we would ask females not to join us ... because we were scared they would get injured and so on" (*ibid.*). In conclusion, if there were structural problems in organising women, there was also a problem of political and organisational will.

Finally, as I noted, there was much emphasis on democratic organisation and practice. In general, SANSCO was characterised by a high degree of internal democracy, with extensive participation by branches and members in the formulation of policies and organisational strategies and in the election of national and local officials. There were regular elections to office, a periodic turnover of officials, and also a generally consultative style of leadership on the part of officials. Ample scope was usually provided for discussion and debates around ideological and political issues as well as around organisational and strategic and tactical questions. As was noted, there was also considerable emphasis on a sensitive handling of students who tended towards Black Consciousness in ideas and who were hostile to relations with white democrats and, indeed, it was such an approach that facilitated the early 1980s growth of SANSCO on campuses.

After the mid-1980s, however, there was some constriction in internal democracy with the emergence of a measure of ideological and political intolerance within the organisation. The 1987 SANSCO congress witnessed the first formal expulsion and disciplining of members. A SANSCO newsletter referred to problems in the University of Cape Town branch, and specifically to the

> continued and conscious attack of SANSCO's ideological position by some members of our organisation and the conscious efforts to undo the work of the organisation. The NUSAS-SANSCO alliance has been the target of these attacks. (*SANSCO National Newsletter*, 1988:5).

Following interviews with the members alleged to have attacked SANSCO, the congress decided to expel two students "since they are considered beyond redemption" and to bar another student from re-joining SANSCO. In addition, six more students "were reprimanded by Congress for their destructive activities" (*ibid.*). The advent of intolerance towards ideological and political questions was accompanied by a heightened intolerance towards other progressive political tendencies. At UWC, the SANSCO-dominated SRC rejected an application by the Azanian Students' Movement to affiliate to the SRC on the grounds that all affiliates had to be committed to non-racialism in practice.

The change of name from AZASO to SANSCO in 1986 and the expulsion of members were connected: both represented a shift on the part of SANSCO to become more ideologically "pure". The indisputable hegemonic position of SANSCO on campuses, and of the Congress movement within radical anti-apartheid politics, was taken as confirmation of the "correctness" of its ideology and politics. Thus, questions around ideological issues and the relationship with NUSAS began to be treated with intolerance. Moreover, with the concept "racial capitalism" that was previously used by SANSCO becoming associated with Black Conscious-ness and left-wing groups opposed to the Congress movement, there was also a greater insistence that South Africa be regarded as a "colonialism of a special type", and on members employing language and terms that were consistent with that of the Congress movement.

Mguduso confirms that on occasions the concepts and language used became the basis for inclusion and exclusion:

It's true there was ... a campaign, not so well organised, but everybody had to know that anybody who talks that language must be ostracised, must be sidelined and so on (interview, 1995).

He also confirms that there was a measure of intolerance. However, he attributes this to the intensified resistance and repression of the period and the effect of "operating in a crisis situation" (*ibid.*). According to him, in a situation in which people were "demanding freedom in their lifetimes",

there was impatience with any quarter that is trying to introduce a delaying tactic, be it in the form of people who will try to start an Inkatha branch in the university or the type of people who will try to introduce ... what appears to be sterile academic debate, that is going to delay people from knowing what their task of the day is. So there was that impatient intolerance (*ibid.*).

The "impatience" itself is said to have been bred by the anger of members who were bloodied in battles with police at black campuses. Such members felt a deep frustration with people who were perceived as "just talking, not doing anything" and were angered by "anything that delayed the process" of the liberation struggle (*ibid.*).

The Role of SANSCO

In previous chapters, I described the specific activities of SANSCO in the educational arena and the political sphere, and in relation to students and other social groups. I now want to draw together those observations so as to identify the general role played by SANSCO.

In the first place, SANSCO mobilised black students around physical, social and academic conditions at higher education institutions and around various political issues. Second, SANSCO also engaged them in direct collective mass action. These roles involved the formulation and representation of student grievances, claims and demands, the selection of targets for the addressing of demands and as objects of mass action, and the selection of forms of mobilisation and effective action. Effective leadership of student mobilisation and protests also entailed decisions of a strategic and tactical nature such as whether, in the face of repressive actions on the part of campus authorities or the police, to retreat or extend the scope of claims and demands and escalate the level of conflict. Such decisions involved, among other things, an analysis of the propensity and capacity of students for ongoing actions, and the implications of these for student unity and future mobilisation.

Student mobilisation and collective actions also involved SANSCO in the formulation of strategic goals, whether organisational, educational or political, beyond the immediate focus and aims of student mobilisation and action, and agitation around these. Thus, to the demands of teacher-trainees for an end to the policy of expelling pregnant students was frequently coupled the call for democratic SRCs; and to the protests of black students around the shortage of residential accommodation at the white English-language universities was attached the call for an end to racially segregated residences. Finally, providing effective student leadership meant developing student political consciousness and building support for programmatic goals. One way in which SANSCO did this was by connecting the immediate problems of students to broader educational and political issues. Thus, a national campaign around repression on bantustan campuses linked such repression to the authoritarian political conditions within bantustans, rejected the state strategy of bantustan independence and advanced the political demand for a unitary and democratic South Africa. The protests against the governments proposed quota on black students at white universities be used to critique segregated educational facilities and to highlight the demands of the Freedom Charter in relation to education.

For much of the time, the primary role of SANSCO was that of a detonator and catalyst of local-level mobilisation and action on campuses. However, a crucial additional role was, either on its own or in alliance with COSAS and/or NUSAS, to initiate, direct and co-ordinate national campaigns and struggles and to generalise conflicts on specific campuses and in particular geographical areas into national and countrywide struggles. This involved a definition of the educational and political issues that either impinged on black students in general or warranted a cross-campus response. Thus, for example, in May 1984, with school boycotts in Pretoria and the Eastern Cape and conflict at the University of Transkei, SANSCO linked with COSAS and NUSAS to declare 30 May as a National Day of Solidarity with boycotting students. Moreover, one response to the tricameral elections of 1984 was to call for a "fortnight of protest", while the banning of COSAS resulted in a SANSCO call for national mass protests. Thus, an important part of SANSCO's activities was to mobilise students nationally to support struggles on a particular campus, at specific campuses or secondary schools, and as a component of general anti-apartheid political resistance.

The theorist of collective action, Charles Tilly, has argued that the "repertoire" or forms of collective action available to a group is usually limited (1978:151). Traditions develop of acting in particular ways that are learned and historically specific, and change slowly. Repertoires are conditioned by a group's organisation and experience, but also by institutional conditions. SANSCO was of the view that "the sophistication of our methods of resistance must increase so we ensure victory in our struggles against racist education" (AZASO, 1984f:3). It was suggested that while the boycott as a tactic of struggle was useful, campus "authorities have developed the art of containing" it, and there was a need "to consider alternative actions suited to specific issues and individual institutions". [10.12] Certainly, other forms of action apart from the boycott were utilised, but by and large SANSCO was characterised by a largely fixed repertoire of both forms of mobilisation and collective action. Mobilisation was usually undertaken through the dissemination of printed media, person-to-person contact and mass meetings, while collective actions took the forms of petitions, sit-ins, marches, demonstrations, lecture and meal boycotts and, occasionally, destruction of property. There was little innovation in forms of collective action, and only the 'squat-in" that originated during protests around the shortage of residential accommodation at institutions can be regarded as a novel form of action.

SANSCO's role in collective action can be usefully analysed in terms of the three kinds of collective action that are identified by Tilly: namely, "competitive", "reactive", and "proactive" collective action (1978:144-47). Competitive collective action lays claim to resources also claimed by rivals and enemies. Collective action of a reactive nature is characterised by a group opposing a claim made by another group to its resources and by "group efforts to reassert claims when someone else challenges or violates them" (ibid.). Proactive collective action asserts "group claims which have not previously been exercised" (ibid.) and is the means by which a group lays claim to a resource it does not already control. The basis of the above classification of action is the "claims being asserted not ... the form of the action" (ibid.:148) or the nature of the interaction between groups.

SANSCO's role in student mobilisation and mass action encompassed all three forms of collective action. First, the terrain on which SANSCO operated was also occupied by "enemies" such as the state and corporate capital and rival student organisations. In this context, competitive collective action sought to thwart and neutralise the efforts of capital and the state to co-opt black students as part of the strategy of promoting a black middle-class, as well as to counter rival student groups and ensure the hegemony of SANSCO among students. If the mix of repression and reformist initiatives within higher education was directed at winning black students to separate development or reformist political solutions and capitalism, SANSCO's activities attempted to win them to the cause of national liberation. Whereas rival student organisations tried to convert students to Black Consciousness or other progressive ideologies, SANSCO ensured that students were won over to its political vision and in support of the Congress movement.

Second, the right of students to autonomous SRCs, to join organisations of their choice, to invite speakers onto campuses and to publish and disseminate media was won through intense student struggles. Throughout the 1980s, however, there were numerous attempts by campus authorities to impose various controls and restrictions on student activities, to undermine the autonomy of SRCs and even to prohibit student organisations. Reactive collective action on the part of SANSCO was directed at defending itself and the SRCs against attacks from campus authorities, defending the gains of previous student struggles and at asserting student claims to various rights.

Finally, throughout the 1980s considerable efforts were also put into campaigning for autonomous and democratic SRCs at institutions and into extending the scope of student rights. Such proactive collective action was, of course, not confined to the education sphere. In the political arena too, campaigns advanced demands for citizenship rights, human rights and for a non-racial democracy.

SANSCO's resources and energies were, however, not exclusively focused on student mobilisation and mass action. Efforts were also occasionally devoted to harnessing the support of parents, religious leaders and institutions, and even some academic institutions, around particular student struggles, and also to get these parties to mediate in some conflicts.

SANSCO, as has been noted, defined education as a site of struggle and its slogan, "education towards democracy", attempted to focus attention on educational issues. Specific themes such as "organising for people's education" and "student action for people's education", were intended to concentrate energies around contesting the control, structure and form and content of education. The Education Charter campaign was an attempt to move beyond a critique and protest of apartheid education and to elaborate an alternative vision for education. In reality, however, SANSCO's initiatives around contesting power relations within higher education institutions and in addressing specific academic issues were rather limited. The challenge around power relations in institutions was confined to struggles for autonomous SRCs. Even though it was noted that the "bare bones" of a democratic education included "student representation on university councils and meaningful representation of popular organisations at council level"[10.13] there was very little mobilisation around the democratic governance of institutions. Moreover, there were only isolated demands for a student voice in academic governing bodies and there were no campaigns for student participation and representation in academic faculty and departmental structures.

One campaign initiated by SANSCO was to demand of campus authorities the removal of racist academics on the grounds of their racist attitudes and the political conservatism of such academics. The intellectual and academic conservatism and authoritarian pedagogic approaches of these and many other academics, however, received scant attention. No effort was put into developing an explicit or systematic critique of academic courses and curriculum content, of prescribed academic texts and the nature of library holdings, of learning-teaching methodologies, and modes of student assessment and examination. In essence, there was a general silence around vital matters related to the academic process.

On the one hand, SANSCO could take comfort from the radical political orientation of its student constituency. To an extent, the political work of SANSCO among students and its education programmes acted as a counterweight to the authorised curriculum. However, as Gwala points out, while the political outcomes of black higher education may have been at odds with what was intended by the apartheid government, this confuses "political and academic effects" and overlooks the "destructive effect" of such education (1988:171). He argues, with some justification, that

> ... the very same politically radicalised students have no critical and analytical academic skills, and instead they unproblematically reproduce ... neo-positivist and ideologically-laden conceptions of reality. This becomes more evident in the area of social sciences (*ibid.*:172).

The failure of SANSCO to organise around the academic process meant that there was no challenge to mechanisms and practices which controlled and suppressed the "intellectual and analytical abilities of black students" (*ibid.*), and which, in turn, constructed barriers to intellectual and knowledge production by black graduates. In summary, despite talk around "organising" for, and "action" for, "people's education", there was a singular failure by SANSCO to understand the centrality of curriculum and pedagogic transformation to any project of people's education, and hence little action in this regard.

Even where conditions, such as those that existed at UWC after 1987, facilitated the building of "people's education", SANSCO's involvement in transformation processes was marginal. The appointment of a radical academic, Jakes Gerwel, as rector of UWC in 1987, and Gerwel's public commitment to transforming UWC into a radical institution with an explicit anti-apartheid, pro-democratic movement orientation created a new environment for SANSCO's activities. In a pamphlet, SANSCO stated that

> UWC has embarked on a transformation process from being an ivory tower to a People's University. In this light, the SRC has a role in democratising every section of life especially where student involvement is required (SANSCO UWC, 1987).

SANSCO was of the view that "the democratisation of our university ... further advances the struggle for non-racialism and democracy in our country", and the SRC was seen as an organ of "people's power" (*ibid.*). Students were, however, warned not to expect "changes to occur as a free gift" (*ibid.*).

The myriad changes that occurred at UWC after 1987 and SANSCO's activities on this campus is an important topic in its own right and cannot be addressed here. In general, the conditions that made possible the reorientation and transformation of the university were created by militant student struggles and the mass popular resistance of the mid-1980s. With its reorientation, UWC witnessed an influx of progressive academics, many path-breaking initiatives relating to admissions policy, academic development programmes, curriculum and teaching and learning. However, while SANSCO helped make possible a new era at UWC, its contribution to the substantive changes that occurred after 1987 was negligible. By and large, the lead was taken by progressive academics and a visionary rector. As the hegemonic organisation at UWC, there was a general failure on SANSCO's part to adjust politically and organisationally to the challenges of the new institutional conditions. In essence, it was unable to make the transition from a largely oppositional political role to one that was simultaneously critical and reconstructive, and unable to launch and actively participate in initiatives around the transformation of learning and teaching and the democratisation of UWC.

SANSCO was, of course, an integral part of the democratic movement in South Africa, and I now want to turn to the role it played in political and popular struggles. As I noted, SANSCO sought to be a student political organisation with a distinct and definite ideological and political character. This predisposition led to a general preference for relations based on a programmatic unity, rather than for a tactical unity of all progressive organisations. As a result, SANSCO took little initiative to forge working relations with radical organisations with differing ideological and political commitments, which meant that its relations were essentially confined to Congress movement organisations and its contributions in the field of popular struggles were largely within the ambit of the Congress movement.

In the first place, SANSCO supported the organisational efforts and campaigns of political and popular organisations. Thus, to take the example of the UDF, SANSCO's contributions to the UDF were fourfold. First, it popularised the UDF on campuses and won support for it among higher education students. Second, through its presence at institutions in the rural areas and in some bantustans, SANSCO helped extend mobilisation and protests around the constitutional proposals into, and contributed to building the UDF in, such areas. This was especially the case where affiliates had close links with local residents of townships. Third, SANSCO contributed the organisational skills of its activists and provided its student supporters for building the UDF and its affiliate organisations in black townships. Finally, key SANSCO leaders directly contributed to the UDF through election to UDF regional executive structures. At a more general level, SANSCO branches popularised campaigns of popular organisations, brought meetings in townships to the attention of students, and acted as a resource by printing media for popular organisations and providing transport and other services.

The extent and intensity of SANSCO's involvement in off-campus popular struggles was shaped by conditions on campuses, the proximity of black townships, the availability of transport, the state of popular organisations and the nature of the links between SANSCO branches and local popular organisations. Periods of education boycotts generally freed students to become more intensely involved in contributing to the activities of popular formations, and through campus meetings students were organised into contingents to liaise with popular organisations and to work under their auspices, and also to report back on activities. Thus, Bundy, writing about the mid-1985 period in Cape Town noted that "At the end of the first week of boycotts, UWC students began a mass meeting by hearing reports from groups of students liaising with community organisations" (1987:319). Although assistance to popular organisations was encouraged by SANSCO, students were also warned to discard attitudes of arrogance and superiority. Phaala stressed that "we must however not try to use our privileged positions ... to dominate our more deprived majority" (Phaala, 1983a:6). Instead, students were urged to show humility and respect for members of popular organisations and township residents and to "submit to the will of the majority at all times" (*ibid.*).

A second role of SANSCO was that of a detonator and catalyst of mass campaigns and resistance. On numerous occasions, mass student actions led by SANSCO, at times in consultation with fraternal organisations, were the trigger for complementary actions from the side of secondary school students and township residents. In other cases, the participation of SANSCO provided impetus to popular struggles and contributed to the broadening and deepening of such struggles. Third, SANSCO consciously popularised imprisoned and exiled ANC leaders, and the banned ANC and SACP. Indeed, many SANSCO activists perceived the organisation to be a "front" of the ANC or the higher education student-wing of the ANC.

As previously noted, Melucci draws a distinction between the "visible" and "latent" dimensions of collective action, and urges that the latent dimensions should not be ignored. As he argues, activities related to political formation and training, the diffusion of ideology and the influencing of new individuals and groups play an important role in sewing "the potential for resistance or opposition ... into the very fabric of daily life" (Melucci, 1989:70-71). In these terms, an important, and fourth, role of SANSCO was the political education of members of popular organisations through the participation of its activists in programmes hosted by these organisations. SANSCO "organisation intellectuals" were especially in demand around topics such as the nature of South African society, the national-democratic struggle and the Freedom Charter.

Furthermore, through its educational role, through its contact with members of popular organisations, and especially through the example of its relationships with NUSAS and white democrats, SANSCO disseminated the ideology and politics of non-racialism among popular organisations. As in the case of some black students, some members of popular organisations were also hostile to, or sceptical about, the participation of whites in the anti-apartheid struggle. In this regard, the experiences of SANSCO in persuading students to accept non-racialism in practice was put to good use in also convincing members of popular organisations to embrace a non-racial approach. A final role of SANSCO was that it was a source of cadres for political and popular organisations.

Student activists who received their political education and organisational training in and through SANSCO were often also active members of off-campus organisations. Moreover, many SANSCO members who either dropped out or graduated continued to be politically active as members of popular organisations, underground ANC structures and the ANC in exile.

Despite SANSCO's resolve

to identify with the liberation of the black worker and strive towards eradication of their exploitation in the labour field, [and to] seek a working policy relating directly to the struggle of the workers as conducted by the progressive trade union movement (Appendix 2 hereto),

its links with trade unions were limited. On the one hand, relations with unions was conditioned by the unions" own ideological commitments and their approach to political struggle. Thus, close links existed only with those unions which were either part of the UDF or supportive of the Congress movement and which emphasised the linkage between trade union struggles and political struggles. Links with Black Consciousness unions, and unions within the Federation of South African Trade Unions were non-existent, while those with independent unions like the Food and Canning Workers Union and the General Workers Union were loose and sporadic. On the other hand, there was no attempt by SANSCO to formulate, in conjunction with the unions, ways in which students could support their activities and workers. Though some students did conduct literacy work among workers and staff advice bureaux, which assisted workers with problems corncerning influx control, pass laws, residential rights and various other issues, SANSCO did not discuss such activities. Moreover, in the case of the organising of workers at UCT, this was the result of individual initiative on the part of a SANSCO member rather than an organisational action.

The Significance of SANSCO

SANSCO was the hegemonic organisation within the overall black higher education student movement and among black higher education students. As a national student political formation with a presence on scores of campuses, SANSCO enabled the organised participation of black higher education students in the struggle for national liberation and educational and social transformation. It provided leadership to students, broadened specific campus struggles into national struggles, and contributed to unite action by students on and across campuses. Moreover, it continued the tradition of educational institutions being arenas of political activism and militant opposition to apartheid.

The special significance of SANSCO, however, lay in its definition of education as a site of struggle, the identification of the education sphere as its principal field of operation, and the concomitant delineation of the role of students as that of primarily challenging apartheid education and democratising and transforming education. SANSCO's explication of such an approach was of twofold importance. First, understanding the limits of the political power of students, it directed students away from the notion of being the vanguard of the liberation struggle and towards seeing their role as supporting worker and popular struggles. Second, students were guided away from conceiving their role exclusively in terms of participating in struggles in the political arena around citizenship rights and state power and supporting popular struggles. Instead, students were directed to utilise their institutional location and make education the locus of their struggles and educational institutions their primary terrain of struggle. In this way, SANSCO believed that students could make a specific and distinctive contribution to the national liberation struggle.

SANSCO's formulation of such a role for students was shaped by its ideological commitments as well as by political conditions. The commitment to working-class leadership precluded any conception of students leading the national liberation struggle. More importantly, the context in which it operated was one in which political and popular organisations and trade unions were already challenging race, class and gender domination in various social spheres. It made little sense for students to duplicate the role of such organisations or to merely engage in solidarity actions. SANSCO had, following Cockburn, to "first be itself" (1969:16) if it was to make a meaningful contribution to the national liberation struggle. Apartheid education was an obvious target and the educational sphere a natural focal point of student actions.

Also of tremendous significance was the fact that SANSCO did not merely critique and challenge conditions in education but also posed the issue of a future post-apartheid education order. It recognised that a vital component of the education struggle was the need for students and allied social groups to elaborate a vision of a future education system and seriously to engage questions related to the orientation, goals, content and contours of such a system. In this regard it initiated the Education Charter Campaign (ECC), which it hoped would both generate a radical education programme and provide a framework for discussion and debates around education. The fact that the ECC was of limited success and that no Education Charter (EC) was produced does not detract from the significance of SANSCO's interventions in this area. Many of its conceptions were later taken up by the National Education Crisis Committee (NECC), of which SANSCO was a founder member and by allied education formations.

However, there were other important elements to the EC, which related to SANSCO's conceptions around the document as well as the campaign. First, the EC was understood as an aspect of the ideological and political contestation around education between popular education formations and conservative social forces and the state. Thus, its value was not seen as lying in some distant future but as immediate: as a "beacon" of the education struggle and as a "barometer against which students could measure current educational reforms".[10.14] Second, the formulation of educational goals and policies is frequently seen in technocratic terms, as the exclusive responsibility of government officials aided by expert functionaries. SANSCO, however, insisted on the participation of students, teachers, workers and other social groups in the formulation of the EC. In so doing, it in effect popularised the idea of the right of these groups to participate in education decision-making and policy formulation and also advanced the notion of a considerably more democratic education decision-making and policy formulation process.

As part of its thinking around an alternative to apartheid education, SANSCO contributed the notion of people's education. Of course, its conception of people's education was limited to the view that such an education needed to serve the interests of working people and it provided no extended definition of people's education. Nonetheless, the concept of people's education was given greater content during the late 1980s by the NECC and become a key and defining feature of the mass education movement. As noted, SANSCO also did not give much attention to the meaning of people's education in the context of higher education. However, its struggles around conditions on the campuses, its assertion of the right of students to democratic representative structures, and its call for people's universities helped create the conditions, especially at an institution like UWC, for radical initiatives around curriculum and learning and teaching and other academic and administrative aspects of institutions.

Although SANSCO was largely an organisation of university and technikon students, it did to some extent draw teacher-trainees into educational and political struggles. In this way it ensured that at least a proportion of the new generation of school teachers would have progressive political commitments, would be supportive of the educational and political actions of school students and identify with progressive teacher organisations. However, given SANSCO's relative inattention to issues concerning the academic process, and the stranglehold of "Fundamental Pedagogics" – a conservative education doctrine and approach to education – at teacher-training colleges, it is by no means certain that the progressive political orientation of neophyte teachers would have been accompanied by a progressive educational approach.

The presence of SANSCO at teacher-training colleges in rural bantustan areas, at bantustan universities, and at the white English-language campuses had certain important effects beyond that of its general role as a detonator and catalyst of black student actions. Its presence in the bantustans exemplified the opposition of students to the bantustan system and their commitment to citizenship and political rights in a unitary South Africa. Moreover, in the context of the extremely repressive conditions in the bantustans, SANSCO was able to use its institutional location to initiate and support organisation and popular actions by other social groups.

In the case of the white English-medium universities, its significance was fourfold. First, its criticism of the racial character of these institutions, of their close links with corporate capital and of their admissions policies and general culture, compelled these institutions to re-think their traditional role and to institute changes in their traditional approaches and policies. Second, the criticism of these institutions" attachment to purely symbolic forms of protest against apartheid education and white domination also led to more active and concrete responses from their side.

346

Third, SANSCO's activities brought home to white students, traditionally sheltered by segregationist laws from any real contact with blacks, the specific problems and concerns of black students. In this regard, SANSCO exposed white students to black political aspirations and the loyalty of many black people to political leaders and organisations considered by the white-controlled commercial media and white social groups to be "terrorists". For white students brought up to view imprisoned and exiled ANC leaders and organisations such as the ANC as part of the "communist onslaught" against South Africa, the political allegiances of black students were, if discomforting, also an introduction to political realities. Finally, SANSCO activities also helped illustrate the futility of political reforms whose object was continued white domination and the limits of parliamentary politics in the process of social change in South Africa. Thus, in different ways, SANSCO contributed to the strengthening of democratic commitments among white students and also contributed to building an appreciation among such students for the particular political positions adopted by NUSAS.

Although SANSCO considered an exclusive or predominant pre-occupation on the part of a student organisation with issues of state and political power to be "misleading", and to the detriment of the opportunity of students to make a distinctive contribution to the national liberation struggle, it, of course, did not shy away from explicitly political questions. It made a vital contribution to popularising a race-class analysis of South African realities, to highlighting the structural roots of domination and exploitation, and to securing an acceptance of a non-racial approach to the struggle. The lived realities of national and racial oppression and state initiatives during the 1980s to modernise political domination provided SANSCO with tremendous scope for agitation and mobilisation around political issues related to questions of state and political power. Frequently, it acted as a detonator and catalyst of political resistance. Furthermore, activists that were politically and organisationally schooled in SANSCO were later to make an important contribution to other popular organisations. With the transition to political democracy in South Africa, ex-SANSCO cadres came to occupy positions as ministers in regional governments, ANC members of parliament, key officials in the civil service, and executive officers of state agencies.

Finally, black higher education was an important instrument of the attempts of both the apartheid government and corporate capital to safeguard capitalism and prevent radical change in South Africa. Black graduates were to be a major component of the black middle class that both groups sought to promote for the purposes of fracturing black inter-class solidarity, widening the social base of adherents to the "free enterprise system" and creating an ideological and political buffer between the black working class and the ruling class. On the one hand, conditions within black higher education institutions and the unwillingness of the apartheid government, prior to February 1990, to institute reforms that acknowledged the rights of blacks to citizenship and political rights within a unitary South Africa militated against any easy achievement of reformist objectives. Indeed, the state's "total strategy" of combing reforms and repression had much the same effect that Lenin described with respect to Russia:

> More clearly than ever before, a revolutionary note rings in the students" appeals and resolutions. The policy of alternating brutal repression with Judas kisses is doing its work and revolutionising the mass of students (Lenin, 1961: Vol. 6, 81).

However, in South Africa it was not simply a case of the inadequacy of state reforms and the continuing repression. Both, in any event, were a response to the mass resistance of the dominated classes and strata. On the other hand, SANSCO was also crucial in frustrating the reformist objectives of the state and corporate capital. It persuaded students against any alliance with social forces which offered prospects of better employment opportunities and a better living standard at the expense of economic and social opportunities for all the oppressed and national liberation. It mobilised students to reject political reforms that attempted to fracture black unity and extend the apartheid social base through the co-option of Indians and coloureds into the political process while continuing to relegate Africans to the bantustans. It held out the possibility, through mass organisation, collective mass action and alliances with other oppressed social groups and white democrats, of educational and social transformation. Most important of all, it shaped the political affiliations of students in favour of the Congress movement and the outlawed ANC. In this way it contributed to the erosion of apartheid rule, to undermining attempts to restructure and modernise domination, and to creating the conditions that obliged the apartheid government to eventually lift the restrictions on exiled and banned organisations and begin to negotiate the transition to a non-racial democracy in South Africa.

Conclusion

The aims of this book were defined as the analysis and interpretation of the character, role and significance of the South African Students' Organisation (SASO) and the South African National Students' Congress (SANSCO). This, I argued, entailed an investigation of the ideology and politics of SASO and SANSCO, an examination of particular aspects of their internal structure and activities, and an analysis of their collective actions. I also argued that the analysis and interpretation of SASO and SANSCO could not be abstracted from the institutional conditions in the education and political arena and the particular historical conditions under which they operated. Consequently, in Chapters 2 and 6 I outlined the structural and conjunctural conditions which constituted the context of the activities of SASO and SANSCO respectively. Thereafter, in Chapters 3 and 4 in the case of SASO, and Chapters 7 to 9 in the case of SANSCO, I analysed the ideology and politics of the two organisations, issues related to their internal organisation and their activities in the education and political spheres. Finally, in Chapters 5 and 10, I offered my interpretation of the character, role and significance of SASO and SANSCO respectively.

I now draw together my analysis of SASO and SANSCO. In particular, I identify and discuss the similarities and differences, and continuities and discontinuities between SASO and SANSCO with respect to their ideological, political and organisational character, and their role and significance in the struggle for national liberation in South Africa. I also draw attention to certain developments in higher education student politics in the post-1990 period and offer some tentative thoughts on the trajectory of student politics in the future. Finally, I outline what I consider to be the distinctive contributions of this book.

The Character of SASO and SANSCO

If the character of both SASO and SANSCO was to be summarised in a single sentence, it would be that they were mass, black, revolutionary, national, higher education student political organisations. While such a definition does not exhaust all the key features of either, it does accurately convey the essential character of both SASO and SANSCO and it also highlights their common properties and qualities. However, the definition also obfuscates certain significant differences between the two organisations. Notwithstanding this, this summary definition provides a useful point of departure, and in discussing each of the traits common to SASO and SANSCO I also draw attention to the different meanings and connotations that they take on in relation to each of the two organisations.

SASO and SANSCO were both higher education student organisations. Membership was restricted to students in institutions of higher learning and the primary institutional location of both organisations was higher education institutions. In the case of SANSCO, throughout the 1979-1990 period its infrastructure in the form of SRCs, branches and working groups was on higher education campuses. SASO, in contrast, while it was predominantly located on campuses did operate through off-campus "locals" as a means of catering for correspondence students and circumventing the repressive actions of higher education authorities.

In the light of the conceptual conflation in the literature on student politics around categories such as "student movement", "student organisation" and "student body", it is necessary to stress that both SASO and SANSCO were specifically student *organisations*, and not student movements. A student movement, as I argued, comprises

> [t]he sum total of action and intentions of students individually, collectively and organisationally that are directed for change in the students' own circumstances and for education and wider social change (Jacks, 1975:13).

It is not reducible to a single organisation, or an extension of one or even many student organisations. However, as I also pointed out, it is often the case that a specific student organisation stands in a particular relationship to the student movement, enjoys a certain status within, and plays a certain role *vis-à-vis*, the student movement. Both SASO and SANSCO were politically and organisationally hegemonic within the black higher education student movement of their respective periods, stood at its head and provided political direction and leadership to the student body and to other student organisations.

Of course, SASO and SANSCO were not just student organisations but student *political* formations. That is to say, the interests of both organisations were not in any way parochial and restricted to purely academic or cultural issues or immediate questions of student conditions within education institutions. To employ Burawoy's definition of "politics", SASO and SANSCO were engaged in "struggles over ... relations of structured domination, struggles that take as their *objective* the quantitative or qualitative change of those relations" (1985:253, emphasis in original). Their "student politics" encompassed the education arena and relations in education as well as the political sphere and social and political relations in general. Through their concerns with student rights and the democratisation and transformation of education institutions both organisations were involved in "education politics" and in struggles around relations in education. Moreover, as a consequence of their concerns around citizenship, human, and political rights for the black oppressed, and around national liberation and social transformation in South Africa, they were also involved in "state politics" and in struggles around social and political relations in South Africa.

Finally, SASO and SANSCO were also student *political* organisations in the sense that they were characterised by distinct ideological and political positions, and the basis of affiliation to them was essentially political. SASO was a revolutionary nationalist organisation. It formulated the doctrine of Black Consciousness in terms of which "race" and racial oppression was defined as the primary problem and united political action by "blacks" (African, Indian and coloured South Africans) was to be the means for ending apartheid. Its goals were the psychological and physical liberation of black South Africans and the creation of a non-racial society. SANSCO, on the other hand, was a revolutionary socialist organisation. It employed a "race"-class analysis to define the system of racial and national domination and class exploitation, or "racial capitalism", as the essential problem of social relations in South Africa. A national democratic struggle whose constituent elements included mass mobilisation and democratic organisation, a non-racial multi-class alliance of blacks and white democrats, united mass action, and working-class leadership was to be the vehicle for political and social transformation in South Africa. SANSCO was committed to the political, economic and social rights and goals embodied in the Freedom Charter, and saw this manifesto as providing the foundation for the realisation of its own goal of socialist transformation in South Africa.

The label "revolutionary" takes on different meanings when attached to SASO and SANSCO. To the extent that SANSCO was committed to a struggle against not just racism and national oppression but also against capitalism, and stood for socialism, and its struggles had the effect of contributing to the undermining of apartheid rule, its characterisation as "revolutionary", in the Marxist sense, is warranted. SASO, of course, paid little attention to the questions of class and capitalism, and left vague the issue of the content and class character of the non-racial society to which it was committed. However, as Nolutshungu has, correctly, argued:

[t]he revolutionary significance of a political movement, whatever its class character, is not determined solely by its own internal characteristics (programmes, ideologies and organisations) but also by the nature of the political terrain and the effects of that terrain on its political practice (1982:200).

To the extent that capitalism in South Africa was inextricably tied with white political domination and SASO's object was to end this domination, and to the extent that through its actions it made a significant contribution to eroding white political hegemony, its characterisation as a "revolutionary" formation is entirely appropriate.

Although in terms of their ideological and political orientations SASO and SANSCO were considerably different, there were certain continuities. On the one hand, for a brief period and largely as a result of its birth process, SANSCO identified with Black Consciousness and, indeed, defined its role essentially in terms of continuing the traditions of SASO. On the other hand, the questions of class and capitalism to which SANSCO later came to attach considerable importance were not entirely absent in SASO. Towards the latter part of its existence, there did arise within SASO a concern with these issues and a gravitation towards a

354

Marxist analysis of South African realities which led to the accusation that the organisation was becoming "red". The founders of SANSCO, however, either chose to ignore this development or were unaware of it, and thus launched SANSCO as a virtual clone of SASO.

A more explicit continuity between SASO and SANSCO related to their exclusively black membership. Both organisations advanced strategy rather than principles as the grounds for an exclusively black membership. However, the reasoning behind the strategy was somewhat different for the two organisations. In the case of SASO, black exclusivity was formulated as an integral tenet of Black Consciousness because of a rejection of what was perceived to be white domination in the definition of the goals and strategies of anti-apartheid resistance politics. As a consequence, relations with white anti-apartheid organisations were strongly discouraged. In this context, SASO was the organisational vehicle through which black students would no longer be onlookers and on the sidelines of anti-apartheid politics and would "do things for themselves and all by themselves" (Biko, 1987:7, 15). In the case of SANSCO, an exclusively black membership was not an integral element of its doctrine. The participation of white democrats in anti-apartheid popular organisations was welcomed and, indeed, SANSCO enjoyed a close working relationship with the predominantly white National Union of South African Students'. SANSCO, however, opted to be exclusively black because it was considered that the markedly different political and social positions of black and white students in apartheid South Africa, their different lived experiences and the vastly differing conditions at black and white higher education institutions necessitated separate vehicles for the organisation of black and white students.

Both SASO and SANSCO were national organisations with national, regional and local structures and officials. However, of the two, SANSCO had a wider national presence. SASO was essentially composed of students at the black universities while SANSCO also incorporated black students at the white English-language universities and students at technikons and teacher-training colleges. Moreover, while SASO's presence was largely restricted to those areas designated as "white" South Africa, SANSCO's presence also extended to the urban and rural areas of the bantustans. In part, the differences in the geographical and institutional spread of the two organisations were related to historical conditions. During SASO's existence, there were very few black students at the white English-language universities, there was only one university in the bantustans and there were no technikons (although there were colleges of advanced technical education, their enrolment of higher education students was very small). On the other hand, SANSCO also made a special effort to establish a presence at teacher-training colleges, many of which were located in rural bantustan areas.

SASO and SANSCO were also mass organisations in the sense that they enjoyed widespread support among black higher education students and were able to mobilise and engage in collective action the bulk of the black student population. However, if a more restrictive definition of "mass" — the incorporation of the vast majority of black students as members - is employed, neither SASO or SANSCO qualify as mass organisations. In terms of this stricter definition of "mass", both organisations were essentially large organisations of politically committed activists and formally incorporated only a very small percentage of the student body. The majority of students stood in a relation of "supporters" and "sympathisers" to the two organisations.

The gender composition of SASO and SANSCO was very similar. Both were predominantly male organisations, with women constituting a tiny minority of the membership and being poorly represented in leadership positions. However, there was an important difference in the culture of the two organisations. In the case of SASO, its culture was singularly sexist, related to the absence of feminist politics during its period of existence. Not surprisingly, no special attempts were made to mobilise and organise women. SANSCO, on the other hand, operated in a period when feminism was beginning to impact within and outside popular organisations. Consequently, within SANSCO there was a greater sensitivity to feminist issues, attempts to promote an anti-sexist culture, and sexist practices considered anathema. Moreover, there were women's groups within SANSCO and the portfolio of women's organiser existed on the national executive committee.

Yet, ultimately, much of the anti-sexism of SANSCO was rhetoric, for at local levels the mobilisation and organisation of women was not given serious attention by the predominantly male membership, it seldom became an organisational priority and was generally relegated to women activists. In terms of gender representation, SANSCO's failure to incorporate larger numbers of women was more serious than that of SASO. During the latter's period of activity, and taking the universities as an example, black women comprised less than 25% of the student body. During SANSCO's period, however, black women constituted over 40% of the university black student population. This meant that not only did SANSCO not make inroads among a sizeable proportion of the university student body, but in terms of its gender composition it was considerably unrepresentative of the general student body.

Until now, my discussion of the character of SASO and SANSCO has centred around my summary definition of them as mass, black, revolutionary, national, higher education student political organisations. However, as I indicated, such a definition does not exhaust the key features of either SASO or SANSCO, and I now want to turn to other important characteristics of the two organisations.

With respect to the internal organisational culture of the two organisations, both SASO and SANSCO were generally characterised by high levels of internal democracy. There was, in the main, considerable latitude for debate and discussion, and there were annual policy conferences, a regular turnover of elected national officials and a consultative leadership style on the part of officials. SANSCO placed much emphasis on democratic organisation and democratic practice, and the internal functioning of the organisation was generally true to these commitments. There was extensive participation by members and local structures in policy- and decision-making, and extensive decentralisation of decision-making and responsibilities to local structures.

In general, there was also a sensitive and tolerant attitude on the part of SANSCO activists towards the ideological and political questions of students who were anti-white and Black Consciousness in ideas, if not in organisational loyalties. However, during the late 1980s, the space for ideological and political debates within SANSCO shrank, and the organisational culture of SANSCO became somewhat less tolerant towards critical questioning around ideological and political questions. These developments were shaped by a combination of external political conditions and an internal organisational predisposition. First, the intensified repression and the exigencies of survival bred an impatience towards any perceived pre-occupation with ideological questions. Second, there was an escalation in conflict between the Congress and Black Consciousness movements and the divide between them became solidified. In this context, critical questioning was wont to be interpreted as infidelity towards SANSCO and the Congress movement. Finally, there was also a drive by SANSCO to become more ideologically and politically "pure". This, combined with its high degree of internal political homogeneity, and its hegemonic position among students, had the effect of breeding an organisational culture that was less tolerant than during the early 1980s.

In the case of SASO, the term "democracy", and the notion of democratic practice, were notably absent from its discourse. Notwithstanding this, SASO too was characterised by an essentially democratic internal organisational culture. With respect to SASO, the leeway for expression and debate was conditioned, in part, by the fact that Black Consciousness was not a ready-made or fixed and closed system of ideas and required the continuing input of SASO members for its fuller elaboration as a doctrine. On the other hand SASO, unlike SANSCO, was not politically homogeneous. Its members were politically either loyal to one or other of the exiled liberation movements – the African National Congress and the Pan-Africanist Congress – or held no particular organisational preferences. This meant that SASO had, necessarily, to avoid any explicit and specific affiliation to one or other liberation movement. But it also meant that SASO's leaders had to work to create an internal culture that catered for and accommodated differing political loyalties and to ensure that specific loyalties were not suppressed, nor that they paralysed the organisation. In this regard, the general Black Consciousness call for black solidarity and the emphasis on black unity was, in the case of SASO, also an organisational imperative.

A key feature of SASO was also the leeway provided for spontaneous initiatives on the part of activists, resulting in myriad projects and activities in the fields of community development, culture, media, education and theology. Indeed, although SASO activists may contend that they operated very much within the "bounds of possibility" (Pityana, 1991a:202), I have argued that SASO was characterised by a distinct voluntarism. On the one hand, this voluntarism, and the indomitable spirit and courage and bravery of its activists, contributed to it surviving intense repression at the hands of campus authorities and the state. It also contributed to the innovative political and organisational features that were associated with SASO. On the other hand, the voluntarism was also a source of weakness. First, there was an underestimation of the power of the apartheid state and an exaggerated notion of what could be achieved by students. Consequently, when conditions necessitated a re-thinking of strategies and tactics, there was a tendency to continue with old methods and simply to attribute organisational problems to a lack of will and determination on the part of activists and students. Second, there was a singular absence of any prioritising of projects and initiatives in relation to strategic aims and objectives and little attention was also paid to questions of human and financial resources. As a result, many projects did not get off the ground, were poorly implemented or had eventually to be abandoned.

SANSCO, in contrast, was by temperament much more strategically calculating. In part this was due to an approach that considered thorough prior analysis of the political and education terrain, student consciousness and organisational capacities a pre-requisite for effective collective action. However, it was also related to the strong dual commitments of SANSCO to both mass mobilisation and collective action and to organisation-building. For if mass mobilisation had the potential to produce victories and generate organisational gains in the forms of increased membership and support and stronger organisation, it also held the risk of defeat, and organisational costs in the forms of weakened support among students, repressive actions against the organisation and members, and weakened organisation. In practice, as activists were well aware, there was no straight line from collective action to organisational growth and, indeed, occasionally an intractable tension between the dual commitments of SANSCO. Consequently, this disciplined activists to assess seriously the political and organisational costs and risks attached to collective actions, the possible gains, and to also give attention to questions of trade-offs between gains and costs.

The characterisation of SASO as voluntarist and SANSCO as strategically calculating is not at all to suggest that SASO activists were, therefore, naive in their approach. The overriding priority of SASO was to infuse blacks with a sense of self-worth and a positive identity and to break through the fear, apathy and acquiescence that was a feature of the late 1960s and to re-kindle political opposition to apartheid. Given this exigency, and the confidence that SASO felt because of the strong support it enjoyed among students, it is understandable that myriad projects and initiatives were encouraged and launched, either with an over-estimation of the available labour-power, expertise and organisational capacities or without too much attention to such issues. Moreover, if mistakes were made they also have to be understood in relation to the historical conditions under which SASO operated. For SASO activists were a generation that was obliged entirely to make its own way in the political world. They ventured into uncharted territory with no examples or experiences to draw on or exemplars to guide them. SANSCO activists, on the other hand, operated under considerably less stringent conditions. They inherited the greater political space for oppositional activities and the revival of anti-apartheid politics that was bequeathed by SASO and the BC movement. Their milieu was also one in which, in the light of the Soweto uprising and the experiences of the BC movement, crucial questions of theory, ideology, political strategy and tactics were widely and vigorously debated. Thus, SANSCO activists had both the experiences and lessons of the SASO period to draw on and a plethora of organisations and seasoned activists, including former SASO leaders, to advise and guide them and to generally facilitate their political development and activities.

The very differing conditions that confronted SASO and SANSCO were especially reflected by the "cognitive praxis" of the intellectuals of the two organisations. The experience of the founders of SASO was one of white domination and black marginalisation within NUSAS and white liberal hegemony over the definition of the goals and strategies and tactics of anti-apartheid politics. To redress this situation, SASO's intellectuals argued for the need for blacks to assert themselves as the key and central force in anti-apartheid politics and to do things *for* themselves and *by* themselves. This, of course, also extended to the production of ideas. In this regard they formulated, over a period of time, the doctrine of Black Consciousness with its tenets of black self-reliance, exclusive black organisation, black pride and solidarity and the psychological liberation of blacks from feelings of inferiority engendered by an ideology of white supremacy. If aspects of the discourse of Black Consciousness were idealist and inchoate, the doctrine was, overall, unquestionably novel, innovative and path-breaking. Equally significant, it reflected intellectual and knowledge production by young blacks whom apartheid education had failed to render intellectually sterile.

If conditions during the late 1960s and early 1970s obliged SASO intellectuals to put considerable effort into the development of an intellectual framework and to engage in intellectual production, the conditions under which SANSCO intellectuals operated largely spared them such formative efforts. Indeed, the founders of SANSCO contributed nothing in the way of new ideas and were content to appropriate, rather uncritically, the conceptions and praxis of SASO. The existence of fraternal formations like progressive trade unions, political and popular organisations and active underground structures of the ANC, and the wide availability of political and academic literature by left-wing intellectuals enabled SANSCO intellectuals who assumed leadership in 1981 simply to distil their core ideas and notions from these various sources and to synthesise an ideological and political framework. Later, of course, there was the distinct contribution by SANSCO intellectuals of the notion of education as a site of struggle which had important consequences for the organisation's focus and activities. However, beyond this, albeit an important conception, there was little else that was particularly original with respect to the ideological and political discourse of SANSCO. Moreover, unlike in the case of SASO intellectuals, there was little intellectual production by SANSCO intellectuals.

The Role of SASO and SANSCO

SASO and SANSCO mobilised students in struggles around apartheid education and racial and class domination. However, the focus of the activities of the two organisations and the terrain on which their activities were primarily concentrated was somewhat different. In the case of SASO, its activities among students were little concerned with addressing specific education issues. Instead, and in line with the theme of being black before being students, SASO education, media and community development projects sought to immerse black students in activities among black communities and within black townships. Projects and initiatives were geared towards overcoming the psychological oppression of blacks, towards breaking the fear and apathy that militated against their involvement in political opposition to apartheid, and towards building black solidarity through the development of a positive black identity.

SASO's focus and involvement in black townships was shaped by the dearth of political and township-based popular organisations during the period 1968 and 1977. To address the absence of radical organisations among blacks and to extend community development projects within townships, SASO was instrumental in establishing the Black People's Convention and youth and cultural organisations, and the Black Community Programme. Indeed, it gave birth to the Black Consciousness movement, stood at the head of the movement, and assumed the responsibility of being the vanguard of internal black political opposition to apartheid.

SANSCO also subscribed to the notion of black students being oppressed before being students. However, between 1979 and 1990 numerous political and popular organisations existed which mobilised blacks around a range of political and socio-economic issues. Under these particular conditions it was recognised that an exclusively political focus and orientation towards issues pertaining to conditions of life in townships was "misleading". Instead, SANSCO's trajectory was similar to the one recommended by Cockburn who had argued, in the aftermath of the 1968 student uprisings, that, once the student movement had committed itself to a revolutionary alliance with workers, its role should not be conceived of as external to revolutionary politics and simple solidarity with workers. Rather, the student movement, if it was to make an effective contribution to revolutionary struggle, had to "first be itself" and "to explore the specific contribution it can itself make to the general revolutionary cause" (Cockburn, 1969:15;16).

SANSCO sought to "first be itself" by building a mass student base and attempted to make a distinctive contribution to the democratic struggle in South Africa by defining the education sphere as its primary terrain of struggle, and the democratisation and transformation of higher education institutions as its principal objective. In contrast to SASO, then, although SANSCO did participate in the formation of youth and political organisations and did engage in township-based struggles, these were very much secondary activities to the primary ones of building a mass student organisation and contesting apartheid education. Moreover, unlike SASO, SANSCO did not play a vanguard role in relation to the anti-apartheid movement or political and popular struggles, instead playing the role of supporting popular formations and struggles.

There were two reasons for this. First, its ideological commitments led it to accord vanguard status to the black working class and to define for students a supportive and subsidiary role. Second, politically, organisations like the ANC and the South African Communist Party, and to a lesser extent the Congress of South African Trade Unions and the United Democratic Front, were recognised as the vanguard of the national liberation struggle. However, in the context of national liberation politics in the 1980s, even if SANSCO had defined itself as the vanguard, its prospects of being accorded and playing such a role were highly remote. It would have been considered an anachronism by oppressed social classes and strata and progressive political and popular organisations and would have found few followers.

However, if SANSCO did devote greater attention to the education sphere, and took up a wider range of education issues than SASO, in practice it shared in common with SASO an important omission. This was a neglect of certain crucial education issues. Certainly, the idealist conceptions of SASO around the "black university" and SANSCO's notions of "people's education", as well as other utterances of the two organisations, did pose the important questions about the governance of institutions, and curriculum and learning and teaching. However, in reality, both organisations were characterised by only minimal consistent and proactive engagement around these issues.

A further role of SASO and SANSCO was that they functioned as detonators and catalysts of collective action by other dominated social groups. The role of SASO in establishing a number of Black Consciousness formations has already been noted. More generally, the political and education activities and media of SASO also contributed to independent actions on the part of black school students and youth and radical cultural production. SASO was, of course, a central actor in organising the pro-FRELIMO demonstrations of 1974 and also helped create the climate for the June 1976 Soweto uprising. In the aftermath of the Soweto uprising and the 1980 student boycotts, the detonative and catalytic power of students was well understood by SANSCO and popular organisations. Consequently, on its own initiative, or on the suggestion of popular organisations, or in consultation with popular organisations, on numerous occasions, SANSCO initiated student actions in a conscious attempt to stimulate resistance by other social groups and to extend the base of popular resistance. Finally, on various occasions, both SASO and SANSCO also mobilised black parents, professionals and religious groupings in support of student actions and to mediate conflicts with campus authorities.

SANSCO functioned as a detonator and catalyst of popular struggles much more frequently than SASO. Furthermore, student actions under SANSCO activated a considerably wider range of social groupings and larger numbers of people than was the case with SASO. This contrast is accounted for by the different strategic goals of the two organisations and also the very different political conditions under which they operated. In the first place, during SASO's time there were no black mass radical political and popular organisations and there was a general fear of engaging in political actions. SASO's objective was to develop an anti-apartheid political consciousness and black solidarity through low-key education and community development activities. In terms of this, high-profile mass mobilisation and collective actions and confrontation with the state were generally not considered opportune. Moreover, the fact that SASO did not have deep roots within black townships and the concomitant dearth of popular formations made it unlikely that mass action on its part would have triggered complementary action by other oppressed social groups.

SANSCO, in comparison, operated alongside an enormous number of political and popular organisations and under conditions of a general upsurge in political opposition to racial and class domination. It was strongly committed to mass mobilisation and action, and conceived political consciousness and unity as developing in and through struggles. Thus, the apartheid government's political restructuring, political repression and conditions in education were all seized upon to detonate and catalyse popular resistance among oppressed social groups other than black higher education students. However, the fact that there were usually positive responses from other social groups and that resistance did become generalised also owed much to the existence of trade unions, professional associations and popular organisations in black townships and in schools.

Significance of SASO and SANSCO

SASO, formed in 1968, was the first national black higher education student political organisation in South Africa. During the nine years of its existence it established a tradition of independent national organisation among black higher education students, and the practice of the organised political involvement of such students. SANSCO, formed in 1979, two years after the banning of SASO, continued this tradition for some twelve years until its merger with NUSAS in 1991. For a variety of reasons, including political repression, independent and national student political organisations usually tend to be short-lived. SASO and SANSCO not only survived for considerable periods, but also did so under conditions of an authoritarian and repressive political order. This, in itself, was a major achievement by both organisations. But more significantly, SASO and SANSCO constituted black higher education students as an organised, independent social force within the overall movement for national liberation in South Africa and ensured their organised participation in popular struggles against apartheid education and racial and class domination.

The existence of SASO and SANSCO and their organisation, mobilisation and politicisation of students had a number of important consequences for the struggle for education and social transformation in South Africa. First, through their location at higher education institutions, SASO and SANSCO opened up a new front of opposition and resistance to apartheid and turned higher education institutions into sites of struggle. Second, on some occasions the collective actions spearheaded by SASO and SANSCO forced the apartheid state and campus authorities to engage in institutional restructuring and to introduce reforms which advanced the deracialisation and democratisation of institutions and also created more favourable conditions for student organisation and political opposition.

Third, the 1960s and 1970s were the heyday of the apartheid state's separate development and bantustan strategy. In terms of this strategy, black higher education students were to be groomed to provide the high-level and middle-level personpower for black economic and social institutions and the separate development bureaucracy. In the aftermath of the Soweto uprising and during the 1980s, on the other hand, the emphasis of corporate capital and reformist elements within the state was on creating a black middle class which would be supportive of capitalism and act as a buffer between the ruling class and a black working class inspired by revolutionary political goals. The political co-option of black higher education students, socially destined to be salaried professionals and middle class in terms of their location in the class structure, was crucial to the success of this new strategy of black embourgeoisement.

However, during both the 1970s and 1980s neither corporate capital nor the state were able to pursue their strategic objectives at will and their interventions were mediated and contested by SASO and SANSCO, who were hostile to their goals. On the one hand, and using as an indicator the mass support they enjoyed among students, both organisations generally thwarted the attempt politically to co-opt students and extend the social base of the ruling classes. On the other hand, SASO and SANSCO also won students over to a radical project of national liberation and to seeing their futures as inextricably tied to that of other dominated social classes and strata.

Finally, SASO and SANSCO functioned as schools of political formation and contributed seasoned cadres to political and popular organisations and the exiled liberation movements. Both organisations gave much attention to the political education and organisational training of activists, though in the case of SASO such education and training was more formalised and institutionalised through "formation schools". However, without doubt, the actual cut and thrust of organisational activities, popular mobilisation and engagement in collective actions would have provided some of the richest education experiences for activists. SASO activists played leading roles in the numerous Black Consciousness organisations that SASO helped spawn. Later, they figured prominently in post-1976 political and popular organisations associated with both the Black Consciousness and Congress movements. SANSCO

activists were often also simultaneously key cadres of popular organisations and members of underground structures of the ANC. On leaving
higher education, many SANSCO activists continued to be involved in
anti-apartheid formations. Today, activists who received their political
education and training essentially in SASO and SANSCO occupy
important positions in the ANC, government and various institutions of
civil society.

Over and above the significance for the national liberation struggle
that they shared in common, SASO and SANSCO also made certain
contributions that were of distinct significance. To begin with SASO, an
important contribution was its rejection of the appellation "non-white"
and its positive identification of Africans, Indians and coloureds as "black".
Granted, the term "black" as a means of self-identity was not widely
adopted outside of student, youth and professional circles, and may have
obfuscated differing material interests among these national groups related
to their differential location in the apartheid social hierarchy. Still, it was
notable for its attempt to draw attention to the common experience of
racial oppression and political domination by Africans, Indians and
coloureds and to forge solidarity between, and united action by, all
oppressed national groups. During the 1980s there was an attempt by the
state to subvert the original meaning of the term "black" when, as one
means of fracturing the growing unified action of all oppressed groups, it
was adopted to refer exclusively to Africans. In this context, and as part of
the ideological contestation between popular forces and the apartheid
state, the democratic movement and SANSCO continued to employ the
term "black", emphasising, however, the original meaning given to the
term by SASO.

Of the utmost significance was SASO's reversal of the political silence
of the late 1960s and early 1970s that had been occasioned by the banning
of the national liberation movements and its rekindling of resistance to
apartheid. Its establishment, and the various organisations it helped launch,
reconstituted the terrain of legal, internal and organised radical opposition
to apartheid. Moreover, it, and the Black Consciousness movement in
general, provided an alternative mode of political involvement to the
collaboration politics of separate development institutions and the exile

and underground politics associated with the banned liberation movements.

Equally significant was SASO's intellectual production, the cultural production it inspired and promoted, the pride and assertiveness that it developed among its followers, its articulate spokespersons, and the courageous, combative and defiant spirit that was personified by its leaders. All of this created a new milieu and mood of opposition and challenge to apartheid and helped produce the subjective conditions for the countrywide rebellion of 1976/1977, better known as the Soweto uprising. That rebellion, in turn, fundamentally altered political relations between the dominant and dominated classes, obliged the apartheid state to engage in comprehensive restructuring to ensure continued racial and class domination, and created new and more propitious conditions for struggle by the dominated classes. Moreover, thousands of participants in the rebellion who fled the country swelled the ranks of the exiled liberation movements and contributed to their revitalisation.

The distinct significance of SANSCO lay in its definition of education as a site of struggle, its concentration on developing the higher education sphere as a front of the national liberation struggle and its attempt to ensure that education transformation was an integral moment of any project of political and social transformation. Through the Education Charter campaign it posed the question of a future education system, and emphasised the need to construct an education vision and programme as part of any overall vision and programme of political and social liberation. In its insistence on the participation of students and other social groups in the formulation of the principles, goals and form and content of a future education, it popularised the notion of, and paved the way for, democratic and accountable policy-making processes around education. On various campuses, the collective actions led by SANSCO created the conditions for institutional transformation, even if as an organisation it was unable to make the transition from a politics of critique and opposition to a politics of reconstruction and transformation.

Given the centrality of teachers in any project of education transformation, the efforts of SANSCO around organising and mobilising at teacher-training colleges were of twofold importance. First, it enabled the dissemination of ideas around people's education, including notions of democratic school governance and the involvement of parents and students in education decision-making. Second, it built among a section of the future generation of school teachers a commitment to radical education change and to becoming the carriers of ideas around people's education into schools. In the specific case of the white English-language universities the presence of SANSCO ensured that these institutions were not spared the education and political conflicts that characterised black institutions. Collective actions there forced authorities to accelerate the deracialisation of these institutions, to reconsider goals and priorities that were historically shaped by a tradition of serving privileged white students and the political and economic interests of corporate capital, and to restructure various aspects of institutional culture and practices.

The specific significance of SANSCO was, however, not restricted to the education arena. More than most popular organisations, SANSCO, through its campaigns, media and icons, contributed to popularising, and winning loyalty to and support for, the banned ANC, its imprisoned and exiled leadership, and its political programme and strategies. Furthermore, through its affiliates at campuses in rural areas, SANSCO also helped to build organisations among rural people, draw them into the struggle and extend the terrain of anti-apartheid resistance. Finally, during periods of extreme state repression when mass opposition through political and township-based popular organisations was more difficult, SANSCO acted as a substitute and assumed the responsibility of keeping visible and alive mass public resistance to apartheid. In this regard, the strong presence of SANSCO at the white English-language universities was especially important. Relative to black campuses, these institutions provided greater space for student organisation and mobilisation and the expression of political dissent, and SANSCO was able to effectively exploit this for the purpose of collective action.

Overall, SASO was, perhaps, of greater and wider political significance than SANSCO. It made a pivotal and profound contribution to ending the apathy, fear and political acquiescence bred by state repression, to the regeneration and rejuvenation of radical anti-apartheid political opposition during the 1970s, and to the creation of the conditions for the emergence of mass popular resistance during the 1980s. The absence of internal radical political and popular organisations, eliminated by state repression

369

of the early and mid-1960s, meant that its contributions took on special importance and were also considerably more visible and unambiguous. The nature of its significance, was, of course, strongly shaped by the historical and political conditions under which it operated.

SANSCO, on the other hand, operated under rather different historical and political conditions. It was simply one of many popular radical organisations during the 1980s and did not occupy the central position in the political sphere that SASO had previously. Its contributions in the political arena, although important, were somewhat less distinct and also more diffuse than those of SASO. However, there was nothing indistinct about SANSCO's contribution in the education sphere and to the struggle for education transformation. If its preoccupation with the education terrain meant that its impact was relatively narrower and more localised, it was also precisely this that ensured that with respect to the struggle for education transformation it was of far greater significance than SASO.

It is clear that the character, role and significance of both SASO and of SANSCO take on real meaning, and can only be understood, in the context of the interplay between three elements: the respective ideological, political and organisational dispositions of the two organisations, the social structure and the historical, political, social and education conditions that constituted the wider and immediate terrain of the two organisations, and the substantive activities and effects of SASO and SANSCO on this terrain. However, ideology, politics, strategies and activities are themselves shaped by social structure and historical conditions, even if they may contribute to the modification of social relations and conditions. To the extent that all three elements, in combination and together, are the determinants of the character, role and significance of an organisation, a change in one or more of these elements necessarily has implications for the character, role and significance of any organisation.

This is clearly evident in student politics during the post-February 1990 period. While it is not possible, short of a detailed analysis of the kind that was conducted for SASO and SANSCO, to speak with any authority on the character, role and significance of student organisations after 1990, it is possible to signal certain developments. On the one hand, the tradition of organised activism by black students represented by

SASO and SANSCO continued during the February 1990 to April 1994 period of political liberalisation and negotiations leading to the first democratic elections, and has continued in the past three years of South Africa's first democratically elected government. On the other hand, important changes have occurred in the politics and activities of SANSCO, occasioned by the new political conditions and debates around state-civil society-social movements relations provoked by the collapse of (so-called) communism in the Soviet Union and Eastern Europe.

In the first place, unlike the youth and women's organisations which became part of the ANC, SANSCO defined itself as an autonomous organisation of civil society. In this regard, while it pledged its support for the ANC and the new ANC-led government, it also voiced its intention of primarily serving student interests and of adopting a critical position *vis-à-vis* the ANC and the new government. Second, in September 1991, after investigating the desirability of a radical higher education student organisation that was non-racial in composition, SANSCO merged with NUSAS to form the South African Students' Congress (SASCO). Third, SANSCO's activities and later those of SASCO began to be focused considerably more around policy issues relating to higher education, the reconstruction and transformation of higher education, and the institutional transformation of universities, technikons and teacher-training colleges and student conditions. To an extent, the almost exclusive concentration on education and student issues led to a weakening of concerns with the interests of other previously oppressed social classes and groups, concerns of a broader political nature and relations with popular organisations. In the commitments and concerns of SASO and SANSCO there was a distinctively moral and selfless strain that put at the forefront rights and opportunities for – and the liberation of – all the oppressed. It may be that, in contrast with the previous "we" generation of black higher education students, what is now emerging in South Africa is a new "me" generation of students.

The generally poor knowledge among student activists about past student politics and organisations suggests that each generation seems destined to have to learn on its own the lessons already learnt by activists who were involved in previous student struggles and organisations. Of course, since SASO and SANSCO operated under particular historical conditions, there are limits to what they can contribute to the education of future generations of student activists. The new political conditions of post-apartheid South Africa mean new priorities and challenges and possibly a student politics that is new in both form and content. Yet, especially to the extent that post-apartheid student organisations seek to embrace a commitment not just to democratic education, but also to political and social emancipation, a knowledge of the character, role and significance of SASO and SANSCO, and their strengths and weaknesses, could be immensely instructive.

It is appropriate to conclude by indicating what I consider to be the contributions of this book. First, it advances a conceptual framework which I believe is of considerable value for the analysis of student organisations, and student movements and politics in general. The virtues of the framework are fourfold. In the first place, whereas the international literature on student politics gives little attention to a clear definition of concepts such as "student organisation", "student movement", "student body" and "student politics" itself, and is generally conceptually sloppy, the book delineates these various concepts and their interrelations. In this way it hopefully promotes a conceptually more rigorous approach to the field of student politics.

Second is the emphasis on not abstracting organisations from historical conditions and "circumstances directly encountered, given and transmitted from the past", and the insistence that any balanced analysis and interpretation of student organisations must take into account the actual terrain on which organisations operate. A failure in this regard may lead to imputing characteristics to organisations that are unwarranted and misleading, and also to a flawed understanding of their role and significance. Third is the argument that an organisation's character and significance cannot be read from an examination simply of its ideological and political dispositions and its membership, but this examination must also incorporate an analysis of its practices and effects on the terrain on which it moved. Such an analysis, as I have shown, may require a re-thinking of the character and significance attributed to an organisation on the basis of an investigation solely of its internal elements.

Finally, the borrowing from social movement theorists extends the analysis of student organisations in new and fertile ways. The notion that formations should be seen as "action *systems*" and that it is important to focus on the "latency" phases of organisations and on the "latent" dimensions of collective actions steers one to consider the internal structures, processes and relations of organisations and leads to the analysis of not just the ideological and political character of organisations but also their organisational character. Such an analysis may also reveal the cultural, expressive and symbolic elements of organisations which might otherwise be ignored, but which need to enter into the interpretation of the character, role and significance of organisations. The view that discourses of organisations are "social constructions" and the product of "cognitive praxis" on the part of organisation intellectuals helps to pose questions about the determinants of discourses, their processes of development and the mechanics of their dissemination. The answers to these questions have, of course, a bearing on the issues of the role, character and significance of an organisation.

Turning to the core of the book, with respect to SANSCO there exists only one extremely brief and, I have argued, highly flawed analysis which covers its early years. Thus, the description, analysis and interpretation of SANSCO herein is entirely original and for this reason considerably more space has been accorded to SANSCO. No doubt, quite different interpretations of SANSCO are possible and some ex-SANSCO activists may be displeased with the interpretation that is advanced by this book. To the extent that the book provokes responses and stimulates debate and especially writing this is only to be welcomed since there is a dearth of discussion and literature around student politics in South Africa.

There is, of course, a more extensive literature around SASO. In relation to this literature and to SASO the distinct contributions of this book are fivefold. First, somewhat surprisingly, no scholars have really focused on or interrogated SASO's views on education and universities and its activities in the education arena. Moreover, there has been no detailed investigation of SASO's internal structure and processes, its institutional spread and the composition of its membership. Thus, it is for the first time that both these issues are the object of investigation and critical analysis. The book reveals the idealist conceptions of SASO around education and its inattention to issues of curriculum and learning and teaching in higher education, and argues that, consequently, the political significance of SASO far outweighed its significance in the arena of higher education.

Third, whereas other scholars have tended to take the doctrine of Black Consciousness as a given, this book has been concerned with tracing its development and elaboration and also with identifying its political and social determinants. This has helped to reveal both the shaping of SASO's doctrine by structural and conjunctural conditions as well as the social construction of the doctrine through the "cognitive praxis" of SASO intellectuals. This has, in turn, enabled a better understanding of the character and significance of SASO. Fourth, analyses of SASO have interpreted it primarily in political terms and its discourse has tended to be viewed as essentially instrumental. By drawing on social movement theory, the book demonstrates that seeing SASO in purely political and instrumental terms obfuscates the important cultural, expressive and symbolic moments of the organisation.

Fifth, to date there has been no sustained and explicit engagement with Hirson's highly influential interpretation of SASO as an essentially reformist organisation of no major political significance. The book rejects, on various grounds that include a critique of Hirson's problematic, this characterisation of SASO. Instead it argues that SASO was a revolutionary nationalist student political organisation that played a vital and crucial political role during a period of political apathy, fear and acquiescence on the part of the oppressed and that it was of tremendous significance in the struggle for national liberation in South Africa.

The non-existence of any detailed examination of SANSCO has meant that there has also been no comparative analysis of SASO and SANSCO. Consequently, the analysis of the similarities and differences and continuities and discontinuities between SASO and SANSCO and assessment of their respective contributions under particular historical conditions to education and social transformation in South Africa is a further original and distinct contribution of this book.

Finally, some aspects of the character and role of SASO and SANSCO are identical to those of student organisations and movements in other social formations. This might be accounted for by shared ideological predispositions and/or the experience of similar historical circumstances such as "race" inequality, imperialist domination, political authoritarianism, suppression of political movements and the like. Yet, the character and role of SASO and SANSCO and especially their significance have been shown to be related, ultimately, to distinctive structural and conjunctural conditions. The book thus reveals not only the "the vital influence of diverse national conditions" (Emmerson, 1968:391-92), but also the constraints and possibilities of different historical conjunctures within a single social formation.

Appendix 1

SASO Policy Manifesto

SOUTH AFRICAN STUDENTS' ORGANISATION
TARA ROAD, WENTWORTH, DURBAN

Telegrams: P.O. Box 23,
Telephone: Austerville
                                                             Natal

SASO POLICY MANIFESTO

1   SASO is a Black Student Organisation working for the liberation of the Black man first from psychological oppression by themselves through inferiority complex and secondly from physical oppression accruing out of living in a White racist society.

2   We define Black People as those who are by law or tradition, politically, economically and socially discriminated against as a group in the South African society and identifying themselves as a unit in the struggle towards the realization of their aspirations.

3   SASO believes:

(a) South Africa is a country in which both Black and White live and shall continue to live together,

(b) That the Whiteman must be made aware that one is either part of the solution or part of the problem,

(c) That, in this context, because of the privileges accorded to them by legislation and because of their continual maintenance of an oppressive regime, Whites have defined themselves as part of the problem,

(d) That, therefore, we believe that in all matters relating to the struggle towards realizing our aspirations, Whites must be excluded,

(e) That this attitude must not be interpreted by Blacks to imply "anti-Whiteism" but merely a more positive way of attaining a normal situation in South Africa,

(f) That in pursuit of this direction, therefore, personal contact with Whites, though it should not be legislated against, must be discouraged, especially where it tends to militate against the beliefs we hold dear.

4 (a) SASO upholds the concept of Black Consciousness and the drive towards black awareness as the most logical and significant means of ridding ourselves of the shackles that bind us to perpetual servitude.

(b) SASO defines Black Consciousness as follows:

    (i) BLACK CONSCIOUSNESS is an attitude of mind, a way of life.

    (ii) The basic tenet of Black Consciousness is that the Blackman must reject all value systems that seek to make him a foreigner in the country of his birth and reduce his basic dignity.

    (iii) The Blackman must build up his own value system, see himself as self-defined and not as defined by others.

    (iv) The concept of Black Consciousness implies the awareness by the Black people of the power they wield as a group, both economically and politically and hence group cohesion and solidarity are important facets of Black Consciousness.

    (v) BLACK CONSCIOUSNESS will always be enhanced by the totality of involvement of the oppressed people, hence the message of Black Consciousness has to be spread to reach all sections of the Black community.

(c) SASO accepts the premise that before the Black people should join the open society, they should first close their ranks, to form themselves into a solid group to oppose the definite racism that is meted out by the White society, to work out their direction clearly and bargain form a position of strength. SASO believes that a truly open society can only be achieved by Blacks.

5   SASO believes that the concept of integration can never be realized in an atmosphere of suspicion and mistrust. Integration does not mean an assimilation of Blacks into an already established set of norms drawn up and motivated by white society. Integration implies free participation by individuals in a given society and proportionate contribution to the joint culture of the society by all constituent groups.

Following this definition, therefore, SASO believes that integration does not need to be enforced or worked for, Integration follows automatically when the doors to prejudice are closed through the attainment of a just and free society.

6   SASO believes that all groups allegedly working for "Integration" in South Africa ... and here we note in particular the Progressive Party and other Liberal institutions ... are not working for the kind of integration that would be acceptable to the Black man. Their attempts are directed merely at relaxing certain oppressive legislation and to allow Blacks into a white-type society.

Appendix 2

SANSCO Constitution and Policy Document

SANSCO

South African National Students Congress
Constitution and Policy

PREAMBLE

Whereas we the Black students of South Africa, realising that we are members of an oppressed community before we are students, and committing ourselves to non-racial democratic society free of exploitation and national oppression, in which harmony among people will prevail, find it necessary to articulate the aspirations of the oppressed people in a united and organised manner are therefore determined.

1. To organise students so that they could take up their demands for a relevant role in society.
2. To also organise students so that they could play a more meaningful role in the community in general.

We therefore resolve to found a national students' organisation.

SECTION 1

Name

The name of the organisation shall be the South African National Students Congress hereinafter referred to as SANSCO.

SECTION 2

Membership

Membership shall be open to all students in all institutions of higher learning and training and as decided by the GSC. Associate membership conferred to organisations by GSC.

SECTION 3

Aims and Objectives

1. To unite students of South Africa.
2. To take up demands of students in South Africa.
3. To be the national and international voice of the student community in South Africa.
4. To forge links with all relevant organisations concerned with the liberation of oppressed and exploited people in South Africa.
5. To identify with the liberation of the black worker and strive towards the eradication of their exploitation in the labour field.
6. To strive for the eradication of exploitation in our society.

7 To strive for a relevant and non-racial education.

POLICY

The main guide to SANSCO policy is a resolution which was drawn from discussion at the 1st AZASO conference in July, 1981. The resolution reads as follows:

We at the AZASO conference, learning from the struggles of oppressed people in the world against oppression, pertinently in Angola, Mozambique and Zimbabwe, and realising that they have fought against the system and not against individual Portuguese colonialists of white Rhodesians and noting Samaro Machel's statement of racism and capitalist exploitation. "We always say that we are struggling against the exploitation of man by man of which Portuguese colonialism is today the principle expression in our country ... There are nationalists — some naively, because they do not have a developed class consciousness and others because they are involved in exploitation — who think that the purpose of our struggle should be a struggle between black power and white power, whereas for us the struggle is between the power of exploiters and people's power. A black state of rich and powerful men in which the minority decides and imposes its will would be the continuation in a new form of the situation against which we are struggling".

We wish to dispel the myth that all blacks are workers, whilst we confirm that black workers in South Africa are the most exploited and therefore the vanguard in the national struggle for democracy.

We therefore resolve that:

1 AZASO urges the oppressed community to take cognisance of the above and support those who have already taken this position to confirm that we are struggling against the system and not individual whites.

2 We must seek a working policy relating directly to the struggle of the workers as conducted by progressive trade union movement.

3 Since the success of our struggle depends upon effective mobilisation of all people committed to democracy, we call for genuine unity of the oppressed against the oppressive system.

EDUCATION

1 SANSCO regards the present form of education as a kind of education that prepares black people to be the tools of the system and obedient followers, and a kind of education that aims at dividing black people firstly into racial and ethnic units and secondly into classes which go seek to make us ineffective as a force against the present system.

2 SANSCO condemns the presence of uniformed gun-toting servicemen in black institutions of learning and regards this with the contempt it deserves, as we view this as an attempt to subjugate and intimidate black students into inaction so as to render them important in the struggle for democracy.

3 SANSCO believes that students have the right to organise themselves and demand a relevant education but always realising that the goal of a just education system can only be achieved in a democratic society and that the education struggle will contribute to the establishment of a democratic society.

SPORT

SANSCO rejects multi-racial sport as we view this as being meant to exploit the presence of black players in these multi-racial sporting organisations in order to gain international recognition. We endorse the call by several organisations which has also been taken up by the United Nations Committee against Apartheid to have racist South Africa isolated from international sporting, cultural and economic activity. We urge all international sportsmen, artists, musicians and other personalities to avoid being used as mercenaries of apartheid. We also call upon all peace-loving South Africans to stop supporting all sporting and cultural activities which involve international artists for this can only perpetuate our oppression by giving credibility to these mercenaries of apartheid.

DIALOGUE, NATIONAL

SANSCO believes in discussing points of mutual interests, establishing and maintaining working relations with organisations inside the country, whose principles and policies are not in conflict with those of SANSCO.

INTERNATIONAL

SANSCO fully recognises the need for dialogue with genuinely progressive organisations on the international front, as long as such dialogue shall be based on the principle of mutual respect.

GOVERNMENT-CREATED INSTITUTIONS

SANSCO views with scepticism all government-created bodies and believes that the oppression cannot voluntarily relinquish his privileged position and therefore asserts that no governmental-created institution will ever be instrumental in ushering in total liberation. SANSCO regards all government created institutions as the apartheid system's strategy to delay our struggle for a democratic society.

FOREIGN INVESTMENTS

SANSCO rejects the practice of foreign investment in South Africa and views this as operative in sustaining the apartheid exploitation system of South Africa and in furthering the super-exploitation of black workers. If progressive organisations are offered facilities by these multinational companies they should only be accepted if there are no strings attached.

Endnotes

Introduction

1   The fact that one and the same organisation has gone by two names – the Azanian Students' Organisation (AZASO) between 1979 and early December 1986, and the South African National Students' Congress (SANSCO) after early December 1986 – has presented the dilemma of how to refer to the organisation. One option was to refer to the organisation as AZASO/SANSCO but this proved to be clumsy. Another option was to refer to the organisation by the name that it actually went by. In terms of this, the organisation would have been called AZASO until early December 1986 and, thereafter, SANSCO. However, this proved to be difficult because of the essentially thematic rather than chronological nature of the book. I have thus opted for calling the organisation by the single name of SANSCO. As will be seen, the change in name in 1986 signalled no major change in the ideology and politics and activities of the organisation. While I refer to AZASO as SANSCO, when quoting I have however retained the references to "AZASO", and have also cited documents and pamphlets of the organisation by the relevant name.

2   From Crisis to Stability to Crisis: The Apartheid Social Order and Black Higher Education, 1960 to 1976-77

2.1   For our purposes, racism, racialism, capitalism and patriarchy as the essential features of social structure in South Africa can be taken as essential givens for the entire period that is the concern of this book. This is not to suggest their inter-relationship was unchanging – a point made later.

2.2   Indeed, between 1956 (enactment of the Industrial Conciliation Act which enabled the establishment of industrial tribunals, one of whose duties was to prevent blacks from doing tasks traditionally performed by whites) and 1971, only 27 job-reservation determinations, affecting 3% of the labour force, were promulgated. Furthermore, exemptions were also granted from these determinations.

2.3   Most of the SASO leaders were born in the immediate post-1945 period and were in their early to mid-twenties. While there are no statistics for this period, in 1986, 53,3% of black students at the universities of Fort Hare, the North and Zululand were 25 years and older, and 30,0% were aged between 21 and 24 years (DET, 1987:347).

3 SASO: The Ideology and Politics of Black Consciousness

3.1 See Pogrund (1990), and especially Burchell (1986) and Beard (1972) for descriptions of student and SRC activities at Fort Hare.

3.2 Biko's "objection to NUSAS was fourfold: it was doing nothing, it repeated the same old liberal dogma, within NUSAS itself black and white formed separate opposed camps" (Nolutshungu, 1982:167), and the nature of NUSAS placed limitations on the mobilisation and organisation of black students.

3.3 According to Pityana, the idea of a black organisation began to take shape within Biko after he attended the NUSAS conference in mid-1968. Immediately after the NUSAS conference he had visited Pityana and shared with him the idea of an exclusively black student organisation. Thereafter, Biko and Pityana both attended the UCM meeting (Wilson, 1991:23-24).

4 "SASO on the Attack": Organisation, Mobilisation and Collective Action

4.1 The title of a SASO publication of early 1973.

4.2 The UNIN rector was J.C Boshoff, a previous under secretary for bantu education; the chancellor was W.E. Eiselen, the architect of bantu education.

4.3 *Cape Times*, 10 July 1973.

5 The Character, Role and Significance of SASO, 1968 to 1977

5.1 This literature acknowledges the central position of SASO within the overall BC movement, and thus its general conclusions about the BC movement can also be seen as a commentary on SASO.

5.2 Lodge supports this reading of Hirson. He writes that, for Hirson, the "historical importance" of SASO and the BC movement "one is led to conclude, was an essentially negative one" (1983:331). Moreover, he suggests that, Hirson, appears to be saying that

In as much as it was influential at all, with its lack of resistance strategy and its sociological obfuscation, the movement helped to immobilise and confuse a group which might have provided the experienced leadership so badly needed during the course of the uprising (Lodge, 1983:330).

5.3 This assertion is supported by recourse to another political analyst's appraisal of Malcom X. The latter is described as speaking "for nothing but his rage, for no proposal, no plan, no program, just a sheer outpouring of anger and pain" (Howe, cited by Hirson, 1979:298).

5.4 Hirson's treatment of the student activists on the one hand and workers on the other is revealing. He is greatly excited by the worker strikes of 1973, although he acknowledges that the consciousness of these workers was confined to "economic and trade union demands". Still, this kind of consciousness, as Hirson is aware, may be a platform for the development of a class and revolutionary consciousness. In relation to workers, then, he exercises a patience and offers no criticism for their failure to give leadership to the school students during the Soweto uprising. In contrast, his impatience with the student activists, "busy in their soul-searching and quest for "personal identity" (1979:283), as he puts it, is obvious. The possibility that there concerns with identity and the like could provide the platform, as it did, for ideological and political development in more radical ways is ignored.

8 "Creative Organisers' rather than "Powerful Speakers": Education as a Site Struggle

8.1 P. Mtinkulu, "AZASO's mammoth task ahead", *Post*, 27 November 1979.

8.2 Wits Black Students' Society, Circular, 6 August 1980.

8.3 *Post*, 15 January, 1980; *Rand Daily Mail*, 30 January 1980; *Post*, 4 February 1980; *Post*, 5 April 1980.

8.4 Mxenge was to play an important role in the early days after mid-1981 in providing financial and material support for SANSCO activities.

8.5 Notes on an address by Phaala to the 8th congress of SANSCO, December 1989.

8.6 Quoted in "Elect Mandela, say students", *SASPU Focus*, 1, 2, June/July 1982, page 4.

8.7 Motswaledi quoted in "Key to student strength is to organise and consolidate, *SASPU National*, 3, 2, August 1982.

8.8 *Ibid.*

8.9 "Struggle for SRC continues", *Eye*, June 1983.

8.10 Quoted in "Teachers in crucial place in the battle of ideology, *SASPU National*, 4, 4, October 1983:9.

8.11 AZASO 2nd GSC "Group 5: Re: Opposition groups; relationships with whites, NUSAS, and problems of black students in white universities", Durban, December 1982.

8.12 "Key to student strength is to organise and consolidate, *SASPU National*, 3, 2, August 1982.

8.13 AZASO, 2nd GSC, 1982: "Group 5: Re: Opposition groups; relationships with whites, NUSAS, and problems of black students on white universities" Durban, December 1982.

8.14 "AZASO launched on local campus", *Echo*, 19 May 1983.

8.15 J. Collinge, "Freedom Charter splits black student organisations", *The Star*, 15 July 1983, page 8.

8.16 *Ibid.*

8.17 *Ibid.*

8.18 *Ibid.*

8.19 *Ibid.*

8.20 "Westville students locked in battle with admin. over SRC", *SASPU National*, 4, 4, October 1983, page 9.

8.21 "Horror at Ngoye: 5 students murdered", SASPU National, 4,4, October 1983, page 3.

8.22 "Thousands remember Ramelepe," *SASPU National*, 6, 3, December 1985, page 7.

8.23 AZASO, 3rd GSC "Campus reports", Pietermaritzburg, December 1983. ·

8.24 "Stormy year for AZASO campuses", *SASPU National*, 4, 5, November 1983, page 8.

8.25   *Ibid.*

8.26   "AZASO gets ready for challenging year ahead", *SASPU National*, 5, 4, August 1984, page 6.

8.27   *Ibid.*

8.28   *Ibid.*

8.29   Ramokgopa, quoted in "AZASO: New Priorities", *SASPU, State of the Nation*, October/November 1985, page 20.

8.30   *Ibid.*

8.31   *Ibid.*

8.32   "Students teachers drawing the line", *SASPU National*, 7, 3, June 1986, page 9.

8.33   "Colleges have been closed but AZASO is expanding", *SASPU, State of the Nation*, October/November 1985, page 23.

8.34   G. Davis, "Students claim there's a pattern to campus incidents", *Weekly Mail*, August 14 to August 20, 1987, page 3.

8.35   Interview with SANSCO publicity secretary, James Maseko, *New Nation*, 22 December 1987.

8.36   *Ibid.*

8.37   Joshua Raboroko, "SANSCO is for a new education", *Sowetan*, 24 December 1986.

8.38   *Ibid.*

8.39   S. Johnson, "AZASO becomes SANSCO", *Weekly Mail*, 18 December 1986.

8.40   Interview with SANSCO publicity secretary, James Maseko, *New Nation*, 22 December 1987.

8.41   *Ibid.*

8.42   T. Mkhwanazi, "Students aim at colleges in 1988", Weekly Mail, 18 December to 23 December 1987, page 2.

8.43   Interview with SANSCO publicity secretary, James Maseko, *New Nation*, 22 December 1987.

8.44   *Ibid.*

8.45   "Lest we forget: What the 17 organisations did", *Weekly Mail*, February 26 to March 3, 1988.

8.46   "Women mustn't be passive", *SASPU National*, 3, 3, November 1982, page 3.

9   People's Education and People's Power: Mobilisation and Collective Action

9.1   "Mobilisation" needs to be distinguished from "collective action") Here, the former refers to means by which students were mobilised, while the latter refers to the form and content of the struggles that students were involved in.

9.2   "SADF raids Northern Transvaal colleges", *SASPU National*, June 1986, page 4.

9.3   "Boycotts spread to more schools", *The Star*, 27 July 1983.

9.4   "SRC calls for 1 day boycott of lectures", *The Argus*, 9 August 1983.

9.5   "Henderson agrees to debate, *Daily Dispatch*, 19 May 1983.

9.6   *SASPU Focus*, 3, 1, February 1984.

9.7   *SASPU National*, 4, 2, May 1983, page 2.

9.8 "Student charter will strengthen, unite and guide", *SASPU Focus*, 3, 2, November 1984, page 19.

9.9 "Summary of Commissions on the Education Charter at the AZASO Congress on 2-4 July 1982 at Hammanskraal".

9.10 The National Co-ordinating Committee, Education Charter Campaign, 1986.

9.11 *Ibid.*

9.12 *Ibid.*

9.13 *Ibid.*

9.14 Quoted in "Student charter will strengthen, unite and guide", *SASPU Focus*, 3, 2, November 1984, pages 18-19). See also "They'd prefer to close than to listen to us", *SASPU Focus*, 3, 2, November 1984, page 30.

9.15 "AZASO and COSAS inspire Education Charter campaign", *SASPU National*, September 1983.

9.16 The National Co-ordinating Committee, Education Charter Campaign, 1986.

9.17 *Ibid.*

9.18 *Ibid.*

9.19 "AZASO and COSAS inspire Education Charter campaign", *SASPU National*, September 1983.

9.20 Phaala, quoted in "Students launch blueprint", *SASPU National*, 3, 2, August 1982, page 3.

9.21 Quoted in "Student charter will strengthen, unite and guide", *SASPU Focus*, 3, 2, November 1984, pages 18-19.

9.22 The National Co-ordinating Committee, Education Charter Campaign, 1986.

9.23 *Ibid.*

9.24 "Education campaign spelt out", *SASPU National*, 4, 3, March 1983, page 5.

9.25 *SASPU, State of the Nation*, October/November 1985, page 20-21.

9.26 Cited by "Doors of learning — Demanding the key", *SASPU National*, 6, 2, June 1985, page 6.

9.27 The National Co-ordinating Committee, Education Charter Campaign, 1986.

9.28 *Ibid.*

9.29 The National Co-ordinating Committee, Education Charter Campaign, 1987.

9.30 Dr I. Mohamed, quoted in Anon, *Africa Perspective*, 23, 1983, pages 46-57.

9.31 "Students reject reform proposals", *SASPU National*, 4, 2, May 1983, page 3.

9.32 "Students stay away to keep constitution out", *SASPU National*, 5, 5, September 1984.

9.33 "Durban Indian college shut after demo", *Natal Mercury*, 7 May 1983.

9.34 "SAIC visit sparks protests", *SASPU Focus*, 2, 1, June 1983.

9.35 "The Turf gets rough as students return to class", *SASPU National*, 3, 4, November 1982, page 1.

9.36 R Becker and B Ludman, "Not even ivory towers can escape the strife", *Weekly Mail*, March 27 to April 3, 1986, page 9.

9.37 *SASPU Focus*, 1, 2, June/July 1982, page 4.

9.38 "The academic boycott: Reply from AZASO" [feature article], *The Cape Times*, 30 October 1986.

9.39   *Ibid.*

9.40   *Ibid.*

9.41   P. Sidley, "A rare unity between academics and students", *Weekly Mail*, October 30 to November 5, 1987, page 12.

10   T̶ḫe C̶ḫaracter, Role anɒ Significance of SANSCO, 1979 to 1990

10.1   P. Mtinkulu, "Azaso's mammoth task ahead", *Post*, 27 November 1979; *Rand Daily Mail*, 26 November 1979)

10.2   *Ibid.*

10.3   P. Mtinkulu, "Varsity students form new body", *Post*, 23 November 1979.

10.4   See for example, Wolpe (1972), Legassick (1974), and Johnstone, (1976).

10.5   SANSCO Second GSC, "Group 5: Re: Opposition groups; relationships with whites, NUSAS, and problems of black students on white universities", December 1982.

10.6   Loza was a worker and member of the ANC-linked South African Congress of Trade Unions who died in security-police custody in 1977.

10.7   *Ibid.*

10.8   Of course, Bobbio uses "vote" here to refer to "the most typical and common way of participating" and certainly does not reduce or "limit participation to casting a vote" (Bobbio, 1987:56).

10.9   Quoted in "Elect Mandela, say students", *SASPU Focus*, 1, 2, June/July 1982, page 4.

10.10 Motswaledi quoted in "Key to student strength is to organise and consolidate", *SASPU National*, 3, 2, August 1982.

10.11 Lenin's category of "academics" has been eliminated since there was no grouping that called for student politics to have an exclusively academic orientation.

10.12 Moseneke, quoted in *The Star*, 12 July 1984.

10.13 *Ibid.*

10.14 Phaala, quoted in "Students launch blueprint", *SASPU National*, 3, 2, August 1982, page 3.

Bibliography

Books and articles

Anonymous. (1978). Black consciousness. *Bulletin Two: A Journal of Student Critique.*

Anonymous. (1979). Our black universities: The UWC incident. *Social Review*, 4.

Anonymous. (1982). Training for capital: De Lange reports. *Work in Progress*, 21.

Anonymous. (1984). Forward with the Education Charter: Interview with Azaso activists. *Africa Perspective*, 24.

Abedian, I. (1986). Economic obstacles to black advancement. In: Smollan, R. (ed.). *Black Advancement in the South African Economy.* London: Macmillan.

Abrams, P. (1982). *Historical Sociology.* New York: Cornell University Press.

Adelman, S. (1985). Recent events in South Africa. *Capital and Class*, 26.

Alexander, N. (1991). Black Consciousness: A reactionary tendency? In: Pityana, N.B., Ramphele, M., Mpumlwana, M. & Wilson, L. (eds). *Bounds of Possibility: The Legacy of Steve Biko and Black Consciousness.* London: Zed.

Ali, T. (ed.). (1969). *New Revolutionaries: Left Opposition.* London: Peter Owen.

Altbach, P.G. (1967). Student's and politics. In: Lipset, S.M. (ed.). *Student Politics.* London: Basic Books.

Altbach, P.G. (1968). *Student Politics in Bombay.* Bombay: Asia Publishing House.

Altbach, P.G. (1989). Perspectives on student political activism. *Comparative Education*, 25(1).

Althusser, L. (1971). *Lenin and Philosophy and Other Essays.* London: New Left Books.

Balintulo, M.M. (1981). The black universities in South Africa. In: Rex, J. (ed.). Apartheid and Social Research. Paris: UNESCO.

Beale, E. (1991). The task of Fort Hare in terms of the Transkei and Ciskei: Educational policy at Fort Hare in the 1960s. *Perspectives in Education*, 12(1).

Beard, T.V.R. (1972). Background to student activities at the University of Fort Hare. In: Van der Merwe, H.V. & Welsh D. (eds). *Student Perspectives on South Africa.* Cape Town: David Philip.

Behr, A.L. (1978). *New Perspectives in South African Education.* Durban: Butterworths.

Biko, S. (1972). White racism and Black Consciousness. In: Van der Merwe, H.W. & Welsh D. (eds). *Student Perspectives on South Africa.* Cape Town: David Philip.

Biko, S. (1987). *Steve Biko: I Write What I Like.* Stubbs, A. (ed.). London: Heinemann.

Black Community Programmes. (1973). *Black Review, 1972.* Durban.

Black Community Programmes. (1974). *Black Review, 1973.* Durban.

Black Community Programmes. (1975). *Black Review, 1974/1975.* Durban.

Blumenfeld, J. (1987). Economy under siege. In: Blumenfeld, J. (ed.). *South Africa in Crisis.* Kent: Croom Helm.

Blumenfeld, J. (ed.). (1987). *South Africa in Crisis.* Kent: Croom Helm.

Bobbio, N. (1987). *The Future of Democracy: A Defence of the Rules of the Game.* London: Polity Press.

Bot, M. (1985). *Student Boycotts, 1984.* Durban: Indicator Project.

Bowles, S. and Gintis, H. (1976). *Schooling in Capitalist America: Educational Reform and the Contradictions of Economic Life.* London: Routledge & Kegan Paul.

Brewer, J.D. (1986). *After Soweto: An Unfinished Journey.* Oxford: Clarendon Press.

Brookes, E.H. (1968). *Apartheid: A Documentary Study of Modern South Africa.* London: Routledge & Kegan Paul.

Brooks, A. and Brickhill, J. (1980). *Whirlwind before the Storm: The Origins and Development of the Uprising in Soweto and the Rest of South Africa from June to December 1976.* London: International Defence and Aid Fund.

Brym, R.J. (1980). *Intellectuals and Politics.* London: George Allen & Unwin.

Buci-Glucksmann, C. (1980). *Gramsci and the State.* London: Lawrence & Wishart.

Budlender, G. (1991). Black Consciousness and the liberal tradition: Then and now. In: Pityana, N.B., Ramphele, M., Mpumlwana, M. & Wilson, L. (eds). *Bounds of Possibility: The Legacy of Steve Biko and Black Consciousness.* London: Zed Books.

Bundy, C. (1986). Schools and revolution. *New Society,* 10 January.

Bundy, C. (1987). Street sociology and pavement politics: Aspects of youth and student resistance in Cape Town. *Journal of Southern African Studies,* 13(3).

Burawoy, M. (1985). *The Politics of Production: Factory Regimes under Capitalism and Socialism.* London: Verso.

Burchell, D.E. (1986). The emergence and growth of student militancy at the University College of Fort Hare in the 1940s and 1950s. *Journal of the University of Durban-Westville,* New Series, 3.

Buthelezi, S. (1991). The emergence of Black Consciousness: An historical appraisal. In: Pityana, N.B., Ramphele, M., Mpumlwana, M. & Wilson, L. (eds). *Bounds of Possibility: The Legacy of Steve Biko and Black Consciousness.* London: Zed Books.

Carmichael, S. & Hamilton, C. (1967). *Black Power.* New York: Random House.

Carr, E.H. (1964). *What is History?* Harmondsworth: Pelican.

Catholic Institute of International Relations. (1987). *South Africa in the 1980s: Update No. 4.* London: Catholic Institute of International Relations.

Cawthra, G. (1986). *Brutal Force: The Apartheid War Machine.* London: International Defence and Aid Fund.

Cefkin, J.L. (1975). Rhodesian university student's in national politics. In: Hanna, W.J. (ed.). *University Student's and African Politics.* London: Holmes and Meier.

Chisholm, L. (1984a). Redefining skills: Black education in South Africa in the 1980s. In: Kallaway, P. (ed.). *Apartheid and education: The Education of Black South Africans.* Johannesburg: Ravan.

Chisholm, L. (1984b). Redefining skills: South African education in the 1980s. *Carnegie Conference Paper 96,* Second Carnegie Inquiry into Poverty and Development in Southern Africa.

Chisholm, L. (1986). Broadening the education base: From revolt to a search for alternatives. *Work in Progress,* 42.

Chisholm, L. and Christie, P. (1983). Restructuring in education in Moss, G. and Obery, I. (eds). *South African Review 1: Same Foundations, New Facades?* Johannesburg: Ravan.

Christie, P. (1985). *The Right to Learn: The Struggle for Education in South Africa.* Johannesburg: Ravan.

Christie, P. and Collins, C. (1984). Bantu education: Apartheid ideology and labour reproduction in Kallaway, P. (ed.). *Apartheid and Education: The Education of Black South Africans.* Johannesburg: Ravan.

Clingman, S. (ed.). (1991). *Regions and Repertoires: Topics in South African Politics and Culture.* Johannesburg: Ravan.

Cockburn, A. & Blackburn R. (eds). (1969). *Student Power: Problems Diagnosis, Action.* Middelsex: Penguin and New Left Review.

Cohen, L. and Manion, L. (1994). *Research Methods in Education.* London: Routledge.

Cohen, R. (1986). *Endgame in South Africa? The Changing Structures and Ideology of Apartheid.* London: James Currey.

Cohen, R. Muthien, Y. and Zegeye, A. (eds). (1990). *Repression and Resistance: Insider Accounts of Apartheid.* London: Hans Zell.

Davidson, C. (1969). Campaigning on the campus. In: Cockburn, A. & Blackburn R. (eds). *Student Power: Problems Diagnosis, Action.* Middelsex: Penguin and New Left Review.

Davies, J. (1984). United States foreign policy and the education of black South Africans. *Africa Perspective,* 25.

Davies, R. (1979). Capital restructuring and the modification of the racial division of labour in South Africa. *Journal of Southern African Studies,* 5(2).

Davies, R. O'Meara, D. & Dlamini, S. (1984). *The Struggle for South Africa: A Reference Guide to Movements, Organisations and Institutions.* London: Zed.

Davies, R., O'Meara, D. & Dlamini, S. [1984] (1988). *The Struggle for South Africa: A Reference Guide to Movements, Organisations and Institutions.* London: Zed, Second edition.

De Clerq, F. (1984). Education and training in the homelands: A separate development? A case study of Bophuthatswana. *Africa Perspective,* 24.

De Lange J.P. (1983). Educational changes in support of economic, social and political change. In: Van Vuuren, D.J. et al. (eds). *Change in South Africa.* Pretoria: Butterworths.

Department of Bantu Education. (1976). *Annual Report.* Pretoria: DBE.

Department of Education and Training. (1982). *Annual Report, 1982.* Pretoria: DET, RP88/ 1982.

Department of Education and Training. (1983). *Annual Report, 1983.* Pretoria: DET, RP65/ 1983.

Department of Education and Training. (1984). *Annual Report, 1984.* Pretoria: DET, RP91/ 1984.

Department of Education and Training. (1986). *Annual Report, 1985.* Pretoria: DET, RP32/ 1986.

Department of Education and Training. (1987). *Annual Report, 1986* Pretoria: DET RP42/ 1987.

Dreijmanis, J. (1988). *The Role of the South African Government in Tertiary Education.* Braamfontein: South African Institute of Race Relations.

Du Toit, D. (1981). *Capital and Labour in South Africa: Class Struggles in the 1970s.* London: Kegan Paul.

391

Ehrenreich, B. and Ehrenreich, J. (1969). *Long March, Short Spring: The Student Uprising at Home and Abroad*. New York: Modern Reader.

Emmerson, D.K. (ed.). (1968). *Student's and Politics in Developing Nations*. London: Pall Mall.

Etheridge, D. (1986). The role of the private sector in education and training. In: Smollan, R. (ed.). *Black Advancement in the South African Economy*. London: Macmillan.

.Eyerman, R. and Jamison, A. (1991). *Social Movements: A Cognitive Approach*. Pennsylvania: The Pennsylvania State University Press.

Fatton Jr. R. (1986). *Black Consciousness in South Africa: The Dialectics of Ideological Resistance to White Supremacy*. Albany: State University of New York Press.

Fawthrop, T. (1969). Towards an extra-parliamentary opposition. In: Ali, T. (ed.). *New Revolutionaries: Left Opposition*. London: Peter Owen.

Feinberg, W. (1981). On a new direction for educational history. *History of Education Quarterly*, Summer, 222-239.

Feuer, L.S. (1969). *The Conflict of Generations: The Character and Significance of Student Movements*. London: Heinemann.

File, J. (1990). Critical challenges for South African universities. In: Hartmann, N. and Scott, I. (eds). *Restructuring Tertiary Education: Academic Contributions to the Debate on Rationalisation*. Durban: Union of Democratic University Staff Associations.

Finnegan, R. (1996). Using documents. In: Sapsford, R. and Jupp, V. (ed.). *Data Collection and Analysis*. London: SAGE.

First, R. (1978). After Soweto: A response. *Review of African Political Economy*, 11:93-100, January-April.

Frankel, P. (1990). Business and politics: Towards a strategy. In: Schrire R. (ed.). *Critical Choices for South Africa; An Agenda for the 1990s*. Cape Town: Oxford University Press.

Frederikse, J. (1986). *South Africa: A Different Kind of War: From Soweto to Pretoria* London: James Currey.

Frederikse, J. (1990). *The Unbreakable Thread: Non-racialism in South Africa*. Johannesburg: Ravan.

George, M. (1986). The university and the South African liberation struggle. Twentieth Richard Feetham Memorial Lecture, University of Witwatersrand.

Gerhart, G.M. (1978). *Black Power in South Africa: The Evolution of an Ideology*. Berkeley: University of California Press.

Gerwel, J. (1987). Inaugural Address. University of Western Cape.

Gerwel, J. (1990). Policy research and the struggle to transform South Africa. Unpublished address to conference on health in Maputo, Mozambique.

Gordon, I. (1957). Report on the government's intended action to remove the Faculty of Medicine from the University of Natal. Durban. Unpublished mimeo.

Gwala, N. (1988). State control, student politics and black universities. In: Cobbet, W. and Cohen, R. (eds). *Popular Struggles in South Africa*. London: James Currey.

Halisi, C.R.D. (1991). Biko and Black Consciousness philosophy: An interpretation. In: Pityana, N.B., Ramphele, M. Mpumlwana, M., & Wilson, L. (eds). *Bounds of Possibility: The Legacy of Steve Biko and Black Consciousness*. London: Zed.

Halliday, F. (1969). Student's of the world unite. In: Cockburn, A. and Blackburn, R. (eds). *Student Power: Problems Diagnosis, Action*. Middelsex: Penguin and New Left Review.

Hamilton, W.L. (1968). Venezuela in Emmerson, D.K. (ed.). *Student's and Politics in Developing Nations*. London: Pall Mall.

Hanna, W.J. (ed.). (1975). *University Student's and African* Politics. London: Holmes & Meier.

Hartshone, K. (1986). The role of the state in education and training. In: Smollan, R. (ed.). *Black Advancement in the South African Economy.* London: Macmillan.

Hellmann, E. & Lever, H. (eds). (1979). *Race Relations in South Africa, 1929-1979.* Johannesburg: Macmillan.

Hill, C.R. (1964). *Bantustans: The Fragmentation of South Africa.* London: Oxford University Press.

Hirschmann, D. (1990). The Black Consciousness Movement in South Africa. *Journal of Modern African Studies,* 28. (1). March.

Hirson, B. (1979). *Year of Fire, Year of Ash. The Soweto Revolt: Roots of a Revolution?* London: Zed.

Hobsbawm, E.J. (1973). *Revolutionaries: Contemporary Essays.* London: Weidenfeld & Nicolson.

Horrell, M. (1963). *African Education: Some Origins and Developments until 1953.* Johannesburg: South African Institute of Race Relations.

Horrell, M. (1964). *A Decade of Bantu Education.* Johannesburg: South African Institute of Race Relations.

Horrell, M. (1968). *Bantu Education to 1968.* Johannesburg: South African Institute of Race Relations.

Human Sciences Research Council. (1976). *University Education in the Republic of South Africa.* Pretoria: HSRC.

Hyslop, J. (1986). Perspectives on Wits: A university serving the community. *Work in Progress,* 44.

Hyslop, J. (1991). Food, authority and. student riots in South African schools, 1945-1976. In: Clingman, S. (ed.). *Regions and Repertoires: Topics in South African Politics and Culture.* Johannesburg: Ravan.

Innes, D. (1983). Monopoly capitalism in South Africa. In: Moss, G. and Obery, I. (eds) *South African Review 1: Same Foundations, New Facades?* Johannesburg: Ravan.

Innes, D. (1986). Monetarism and the South African crisis. In: Moss, G. and Obery, I. (eds) *South African Review 3.* Johannesburg: Ravan.

Innes, D. and Flegg, E. (1978). Editorial. *Review of African Political Economy,* 11:1-5, January-April.

Jacks, D. (1975). Student Politics and Higher Education. London: Lawrence & Wishart.

Johnson, S. (ed.). (1988). *South Africa: No Turning Back.* Basingstoke: Macmillan.

Johnstone, F.A. (1976). *Class, Race and Gold.* London: Routledge & Kegan Paul.

Jones, G.S. (1969). The meaning of the student revolt. In: Cockburn, A. and Blackburn R. (eds). *Student Power: Problems Diagnosis, Action.* Middlesex: Penguin and New Left Review.

Kallaway, P. (1984). An introduction to the study of education for blacks in South Africa. In: Kallaway, P. (ed.). *Apartheid and Education: The Education of Black South Africans.* Johannesburg: Ravan.

Kallaway, P. (ed.). (1984). *Apartheid and Education: The Education of Black South Africans.* Johannesburg: Ravan.

Keane, J. and Mier, P. (1989). Preface in Melucci, A. *Nomads of the Present: Social Movements and Individual Needs in Contemporary Society.* Philadelphia: Temple University Press.

Keenan, J.H. (1981). Open minds and closed systems: Comments on the functions and future of the "urban" "English-speaking" university in South Africa. *Social Dynamics*, 6(2).

Kotze, D.A. (1975). *African Politics in South Africa, 1964-1974: Parties and Issues*. London: Hurst & Company.

Kraak, A. (1989). New insights into the skills shortages debate in South Africa, *Perspectives in Education*, 11(1).

Langa, B.J. (ed.) (1973). *Creativity and Black Development*. Durban: SASO Publications.

Laurence, P. (1979). Black politics in transition. In: Hellmann, E. & Lever, H. (eds). *Race Relations in South Africa, 1929-1979*. Johannesburg: Macmillan.

Legassick, M. (1974). South Africa: Capital accumulation and violence. *Economy and Society*, 3(3).

Lenin, V.I. (1947). *What is to be done*. Moscow: Progress.

Lenin, V.I. (1961a). Signs of Bankruptcy in *Collected Works*, Volume 6. London: Lawrence & Wishart.

Lenin, V.I. (1961b). Draft resolution on the attitude towards the student youth. In: *Collected Works*, Volume 6. London: Lawrence & Wishart.

Lenin, V.I. (1961c). Speech on the attitude towards the student youth. In: *Collected Works*, Volume 6. London: Lawrence & Wishart.

Lenin, V.I. (1961d). The tasks of the revolutionary youth in *Collected Works*, Volume 7. London: Lawrence & Wishart.

Lenin, V.I. (1961e). Plan of letters on tasks of the revolutionary youth in *Collected Works*, Volume 7. London: Lawrence & Wishart.

Lenin, V.I. (1963). The student movement and the present political situation in *Collected Works*, Volume 15. London: Lawrence & Wishart.

Levin, R. (1991). People's education and the struggle for democracy in South Africa. In: Unterhalter, E. *et al.* (eds). *Apartheid Education and Popular Struggles*. London: Zed.

Lewis, D. (1989). Keynote address at the UDUSA Congress, July 1989. *Transformation*, 10:64-69.

Lewis, G. (1987). *Between the Wire and the Wall: A History of South African "Coloured" Politics*. Cape Town: David Philip.

Lipset, S.M. and Altbach, P.G.(eds). (1969). *Student's and Politics*. Boston: Houghton Methlin.

Lodge, T. (1983). *Black Politics in South Africa since 1945*. Johannesburg: Ravan.

Lodge, T. & Nasson, B. (eds). (1992). *All, Here and Now: Black Politics in South Africa in the 1980s*. London: Hurst & Company.

Lonsdale, J. (ed.). (1988). *South Africa in Question*. Cambridge: University of Cambridge African Studies Centre.

Macdonald, K. and Tipton, C. (1993). Using documents. In: Gilbert, N. (ed.). *Researching Social Life*. London: SAGE.

Makalima, M.W. (1986). The making of the urban black petty bourgeoisie in South Africa, 1973 to 1983: Ideological and structural considerations. Unpublished MA dissertation, Centre for Southern African Studies, University of York.

Malherbe, E.G. (1977). *Education in South Africa, Volume 2: 1923-1975*. Johannesburg: Juta.

Mandel, E. (1969). The new vanguard. In: Ali, T. (ed.). *New Revolutionaries: Left Opposition*. London: Peter Owen.

Mangena, M. (1989). *On Your Own: Evolution of Black Consciousness in South Africa/Azania*. Braamfontein: Skotaville.

Maravall, J. (1978). *Dictatorship and Political Dissent: Workers and Student's in Franco's Spain*. London: Tavistock.

Marcum, J.A. (1982). *Education, Race and Social Change in South Africa*. London: University of California Press.

Marx, A. W. (1992). *Lessons of Struggle: South African Internal Opposition, 1960-1990*. Oxford: Oxford University Press.

Matona, T. (1992). *Student Organisation and Political Resistance in South Africa: An Analysis of the Congress of South African Student's, 1979-1985*. Dissertation submitted to the University of Cape Town in partial fulfilment of the requirements for the degree of Honours in Political Studies.

Meth, C. (1983). Class formation: Skills shortage and black advancement. In: Moss, G. and Obery, I. (eds). *South African Review 1: Same Foundations, New Facades?* Johannesburg: Ravan.

Melucci, A. (1989). *Nomads of the Present: Social Movements and Individual Needs in Contemporary Society*. Philadelphia: Temple University Press.

Meluxi, A. (1985). The symbolic challenge of contemporary movements. *Social Research*, 52(4):789-816.

Mohamed, Y. (1990). The power of consciousness: Black politics 1967-77. In: Cohen, R., Muthien, Y. & Zegeye, A. (eds). (1990). *Repression and Resistance: Insider Accounts of Apartheid*. London: Hans Zell.

Mokoape, K., Mtintso, T. & Nhlapo, W. (1991). Towards the armed struggle. In: Pityana, N.B., Ramphele, M., Mpumlwana, M. & Wilson, L. (eds). *Bounds of Possibility: The Legacy of Steve Biko and Black Consciousness*. London: Zed.

Molobi, E. (1986). People's education: Learning and teaching under a state of emergency. Twentieth Richard Feetham Memorial Lecture, University of Witwatersrand.

Molteno, F. (1987). Students take control: The 1980 boycott of coloured education in the Cape Peninsula. *British Journal of Sociology of Education*, 8(1).

Moodie, G. (1994). The state and the liberal universities in South Africa, 1948-1990. *Higher Education*, 27.

Moodley, K. (1991). The continued impact of Black Consciousness. In: Pityana, N.B., Ramphele, M., Mpumlwana, M. & Wilson, L. (eds). *Bounds of Possibility: The Legacy of Steve Biko and Black Consciousness*. London: Zed.

Morgan, N. and Hendricks, J. (1987). UWC – A long proud history of struggle, *UWC News*, 1. (4). December.

Moss, G. and Obery, I. (eds). (1983). *South African Review 1: Same Foundations, New Facades?* Johannesburg: Ravan.

Moss, G. and Obery, I. (eds). (1984). *South African Review 2*. Johannesburg: Ravan.

Moss, G. and Obery, I. (eds). (1986). *South African Review 3*. Johannesburg: Ravan.

Moss, G. and Obery, I. (eds). (1987). *South African Review 4*. Johannesburg: Ravan.

Motlhabi, M. (1984). *Black resistance to Apartheid: A Socio-ethical Analysis*. Braamfontein: Skotaville.

Muller, J. (1987). People's education and the National Education Crisis Committee. In: Moss, G. and Obery, I. (eds). *South African Review 4*. Johannesburg: Ravan.

Myr, R.O. (1968). Brazil. In: Emmerson, D.K. (ed.) *Students and Politics in Developing Nations*. London: Pall Mall.

Mzamane, M.V. (1991). The impact of Black Consciousness on culture. In: Pityana, N.B., Ramphele, M., Mpumlwana, M. & Wilson, L. (eds). *Bounds of Possibility: The Legacy of Steve Biko and Black Consciousness*. London: Zed.

Naidoo, K. (1990). The politics of student resistance in the 1980s. In: Nkomo, M. (ed.). *Pedagogy of Domination: Towards a Democratic Education in South Africa*. New Jersey: Africa World.

Nettleton, C. (1972). Racial cleavage on the student left. In: Van der Merwe, H.W. & Welsh, D. (eds). *Student Perspectives on South Africa*. Cape Town: David Philip.

Nkomo, M. (ed.). (1990). *Pedagogy of Domination: Toward a Democratic Education in South Africa*. New Jersey: Africa World Press.

Nkomo, M.O. (1981). The contradictions of Bantu education. *Harvard Educational Review*, 51(1).

Nkomo, M.O. (1984). *Student Culture and Activism in Black South African Universities: The Roots of Resistance*. Connecticut: Greenwood.

Nkomo, S. (1991). Organising women in SANSCO: Reflections on the experience of women in organisation. *Agenda*, 10.

Nkondo G.M. (ed.). (1976). *Turfloop Testimony: The Dilemma of a Black University in South Africa*. Johannesburg: Ravan.

No Sizwe. (1979). *One Azania, One Nation: The National Question in South Africa*. London: Zed Press.

Nolutshungu, S.C. (1982). *Changing South Africa: Political Considerations*. Manchester: Manchester University Press.

O' Connel, B. (1991). Education and transformation: A view from the ground. In: Unterhalter, E. *et al.* (eds). *Apartheid Education and Popular Struggles*. London: Zed.

O'Leary, J. (1986). Just words of apartheid or vehicles of change. *The Times Higher Education Supplement*, 14 November.

O' Meara, D. (1983). *Volkskapitalisme: Class, Capital and Ideology in the Development of Afrikaner Nationalism, 1934-48*. Cambridge: Cambridge University Press.

Phaala, J. (1981). The student movement in the struggle for democracy in *NUSAS Congress Speeches*, November, 1981.

Phaala, J. (1982). History of Black consciousness and the student movement, NUSAS July Festival.

Phaala, J. (1983a). Organisation and unity mean victory. In: Azanian Students' Organisation, *Education towards Democracy*.

Phaala, J. (1983b). The student movement today, NUSAS July Festival.

Phahle, R. (1982). We don't want no education. *Ufahamu*, 11(3).

Pityana, B. (1972). Power and social change in South Africa. In: Van der Merwe, H.W. and Welsh, D. (eds). *Student Perspectives on South Africa*. Cape Town: David Philip.

Pityana, N.B. (1991a). Revolution within the law. In: Pityana, N.B., Ramphele, M., Mpumlwana, M. &. Wilson, L. (eds). *Bounds of Possibility: The Legacy of Steve Biko and Black Consciousness*. London: Zed.

Pityana, N.B. (1991b). The legacy of Steve Biko. In: Pityana, N.B., Ramphele, M., Mpumlwana, M. & Wilson, L. (eds). *Bounds of Possibility: The Legacy of Steve Biko and Black Consciousness*. London: Zed.

Pityana, N.B. Ramphele, M., Mpumlwana, M. & Wilson, L. (1991). (eds). *Bounds of Possibility: The Legacy of Steve Biko and Black Consciousness.* London: Zed.

Piven, F.F. & Cloward, R.A. (1979). *Poor People's Movements: Why they Succeed, How they Fail* New York: Vintage.

Pogrund, B. (1990). *How Can Man Die Better. Sobukwe and Apartheid.* London: Peter Halban.

Poulantzas, N. (1978). *Classes in Contemporary Capitalism.* London: Verso.

Price, R.M. (1991). *The Apartheid State in Crisis: Political Transformation in South Africa, 1975-1990.* Oxford: Oxford University Press.

Ramphele, M. (1991a). Empowerment and symbols of hope: Black Consciousness and community development. In: Pityana, N.B., Ramphele, M., Mpumlwana, M. & Wilson, L. (eds). *Bounds of Possibility: The Legacy of Steve Biko and Black Consciousness.* London: Zed.

Ramphele, M. (1991b). The dynamics of gender within the Black Consciousness organisations: A personal view. In: Pityana, N.B., Ramphele, M., Mpumlwana, M. & Wilson, L. (eds). *Bounds of Possibility: The Legacy of Steve Biko and Black Consciousness.* London: Zed.

Ramphele, M. (1995). *A Life.* Cape Town: David Philip.

Rathbone, R. (1977). Student's and politics in South Africa. *Journal of Commonwealth and Comparative Politics,* 15.

Republic of South Africa. (1969). *South African Statistics, 1968.* Pretoria: Bureau of Statistics.

Republic of South Africa. (1975). *South African Statistics, 1974.* Pretoria: Department of Statistics.

Republic of South Africa. (1979). *South African Statistics, 1978.* Pretoria: Department of Statistics.

Republic of South Africa. (1983). *South African Statistics, 1982.* Pretoria: Central Statistical Services.

Republic of South Africa. (1985). *SA Digest.* Pretoria: Department of Information.

Republic of South Africa. (1985a). *SA Yearbook.* Pretoria: Department of Information.

Republic of South Africa. (1986). *SA Digest.* Pretoria: Department of Information.

Republic of South Africa. (1987). *South African Statistics, 1986.* Pretoria: Central Statistical Services.

Republic of South Africa. (1987a). *SA Digest.* Pretoria: Department of Information.

Republic of South Africa. (1990). *South African Labour Statistics, 1988/89.* Pretoria: Central Statistical Services.

Republic of South Africa. (1993). *South African Statistics, 1992.* Pretoria: Central Statistical Services.

Rootes, C.A. (1980). Student radicalism: Politics of moral protest and legitimation problems of the modern capitalist state. *Theory and Society,* 9(3).

Rose, B. and Tunmer, R. (eds). (1975). *Documents in South African Education.* Johannesburg: Donker.

Saul, J.S. and Gelb, S. (1981). *The Crisis in South Africa.* London: Zed.

Saul, J.S. and Gelb, S. (1986). *The Crisis in South Africa.* London: Zed. Second edition.

Sisulu, Z. (1986). People's education for People's Power. *Transformation,* 1:96-117.

Slovo, J. (1983). Tribute to Moses Mhabida. *African Communist,* First Quarter.

Smith, D. (1991). *The Rise of Historical Sociology.* Cambridge: Polity.

Smollan, R. (ed.). (1986). *Black Advancement in the South African Economy*. London: Macmillan.

Soares, G.A.D. (1967). The active few: Student ideology and participation in developing countries. In: Lipset, S.M. (ed.). *Student Politics*. London: Basic Books.

Sono, T. (1993). *Reflections on the Origins of Black Consciousness in South Africa*. Pretoria: HSRC.

South African Institute of Race Relations. (1950-1978). *A Survey of Race Relations in South Africa*. Johannesburg: SAIRR.

South African Institute of Race Relations. (1979). *Education for a New Era: Report of the Education Commission of the South African Institute of Race Relations*. Johannesburg: SAIRR.

South African Institute of Race Relations. (1979-1984). *Survey of Race Relations in South Africa*. Johannesburg: SAIRR.

South African Institute of Race Relations. (Issues 1985-1992). *Race Relations Survey*. Johannesburg: SAIRR.

SPM (undated). South African Student's organisation policy manifesto.

Stadler, A. (1987). *The Political Economy of Modern South Africa*. Kent: Croom Helm.

Strachan, B. (1985). *Never on our Knees: Youth in Apartheid South Africa*. London: United Nations Youth Association.

Suttner, R. and Cronin, J. (1986). *30 Years of the Freedom Charter*. Johannesburg: Ravan.

The 1961 Education Panel. (1963). *Education in South Africa: First report*. Johannesburg: Wits University Press.

Thoahlane, T. (1975). *Black Renaissance: Papers from the Black Renaissance Convention*. Johannesburg: Ravan.

Tilly, C. (1978). *From Mobilisation to Revolution*. London: Addison-Wesley.

Tosh, J. (1984). *The Pursuit of History: Aims, Methods and New Directions in the Study of Modern History*. London: Longman.

Union of South Africa. (1961). *Union Statistics for Fifty Years, 1910-1960*. Pretoria: Government Printer.

United Nations Eduational, Scientific and Cultural organization. (1967). *Apartheid: Its Effects on Education, Science, Culture and Information*. Paris: UNESCO.

Unterhalter, E. Wolpe, H., Botha, T., Badat, S,. Dlamini, T. & Khotseng, B. (eds). (1991). *Apartheid Education and Popular Struggles*. London: Zed.

Van der Merwe, H.W. and Welsh, D. (eds). (1977). *The Future of the University in Southern Africa*. Cape Town: David Philip.

Van der Merwe, H.W. and Welsh, D. (eds). (1972). *Student Perspectives on South Africa*. Cape Town: David Philip.

Van Holdt, K. (1986). The economy: Achilles heel of the new deal. In: Moss, G. and Obery, I. (eds). *South African Review 3*. Johannesburg: Ravan.

Wilson, J. (1973). *Introduction to Social Movements*. New York: Basic Books.

Wilson, L. (1991). Bantu Stephen Biko: A Life. In: Pityana, N.B., Ramphele, M., Mpumlwana, M. & Wilson, L. (eds). *Bounds of Possibility: The Legacy of Steve Biko and Black Consciousness*. London: Zed.

Woddis, J. (1972). *New Theories of Revolution: A Commentary on the Views of Frantz Fanon, Regis Debray and Herbert Marcuse*. London: Lawrence & Wishart.

Wolfson, J.G.F. (1976). *Turmoil at Turfloop: A Summary of the Reports of the Snyman and Jackson Commissions of Inquiry into the University of the North*. Johannesburg: South African Institute of Race Relations.

Wolpe, H. (1972). Capitalism and cheap labour power: From segregation to apartheid. *Economy and Society*, 1(4).

Wolpe, H. (1983). Apartheid's deepening crisis. *Marxism Today*, 27(1).

Wolpe, H. (1985). The liberation struggle and research. *Review of African Political Economy*, 32:72-78.

Wolpe, H. (1988). *Race, Class and the Apartheid State*. London: UNESCO/James Currey.

Wolpe, H. (1988a). Educational resistance. In: Lonsdale, J. (ed.). *South Africa in Question*. Cambridge: University of Cambridge African Studies Centre.

Wolpe, H. (1992). Convergence of reform and revolution. *Cooperazione*, 117:14-16.

Wolpe, H. & Unterhalter, E. (1991). Introduction: Reproduction, reform and transformation: approaches to the analysis of education in South Africa. In: Unterhalter, E. *et al.* (ed.). *Apartheid Education and Popular Struggles*. London: Zed.

World University Service. (1986). *The Doors of Learning – South African Education in Conflict*. London: World University Service.

WUS/AUT. (1986). Divided Campus – Universities in South Africa. London: World University Service and Association of University Teachers.

WUS/AUT. (1989). *South Africa's Universities*. London: World University Service and Association of University Teachers.

Documents of student organisations

Azanian Students' Organisation/ South African National Student's Congress. (AZASO/ SANCO)

Documents and pamphlets

Azanian Students' Organisation. (1981). *AZASO Policy Document.*

Azanian Students' Organisation. (1983a). *Constitution and Policy.*

Azanian Students' Organisation. (1983b). *Education towards Democracy.*

Azanian Students' Organisation. (1983c). *3rd National Congress 1983, Cape Town.*

Azanian Students' Organisation. (1983d). Getting to know AZASO.

Azanian Students' Organisation, University of Cape Town Branch. (1983). *AZASO Newsletter*, August.

Azanian Students' Organisation, Western Cape Region. (1983). Demand a stop to the execution of the six, March.

Azanian Students' Organisation. (1984a). Orientation News.

Azanian Students' Organisation, *Women's Working Programme*, April 1984.

Azanian Students' Organisation. (1984b). In Solidarity, UCT branch, May 1984.

Azanian Students' Organisation. (1984c). Forward with the democratic SRC, August.

Azanian Students' Organisation. (1984d). Natal Medical School Crisis, Western Cape,.

Azanian Students' Organisation. (1984e). Fortnight of Protest, August.

Azanian Students' Organisation. (1984f). AZASO, 4th Congress, 4-8 July 84 Soweto, Brochure. •

South African National Students' Congress, UWC. (1987). SRC Elections.

South African National Students' Congress. (1987). *Annual National Congress.*

South African National Students' Congress. (1988). *Constitution and Policy.*
South African National Students' Congress. (1989). *SANSCO Women Marching Forward.*

Newsletters

AZASO National Newsletter, June 1983.
AZASO National Newsletter, November 1983.
AZASO National Newsletter Discussion Series No. 1, March 1984.
AZASO National Newsletter: National Student Solidarity against Bantustan Repression, June 1984.
AZASO National Student Newsletter Building Unity and Growing Stronger late 1985.
SANSCO National Newsletter, 1st Quarter, 1988.

South African Students' Organisation Documents and pamphlets

South African Students' Organisation. (n.d). *Constitution and Standing Rules. (Adopted as revised and amended at the second General Students' Council, July 1971, Durban).* Durban: SASO.

South African Students' Organisation. (n.d). SASO Policy Manifesto. Durban: SASO.

South African Students' Organisation. (n.d). *Black Students' Manifesto.*

South African Students' Organisation. (1971). Minutes of the second General Students' Council held 4-10 July, 1971, University of Natal, Black Section, Alan Taylor Residence, Wentworth, Durban.

South African Students' Organisation. (1972a). *SASO 1972.* Durban: SASO.

South African Students' Organisation. (1972b). Minutes of the proceedings of the third General Students' Council of the South African Students' Organisation, St Peter's Seminary, Hammanskraal, 2-9 July 1972.

South African Students' Organisation. (1972c). National Formation School: Towards black education. December 4th-8th: Edendale Lay Ecumenical Centre, Edendale. Durban: SASO.

South African Students' Organisation. (1973a). *SASO on the Attack: An Introduction to the South African Students' Organisation 1973.* Durban: SASO.

South African Students' Organisation. (1973b). *SASO Newsletter,* 3(1), March/April. Durban: SASO.

South African Students' Organisation. (1973c). Report on the proceedings at the National Formation School held at FEDSEM, 11th-13th May, 1973.

South African Students' Organisation. (1973d). Minutes of the proceedings of the fourth General Students' Council of the South African Students' Organisation, St Peter's Seminary, Hammanskraal, 14th-22nd July 1973.

South African Students' Organisation. (1973e). Commissions presented at the fourth General Students' Council of the South African Students' Organisation, St Peter's Seminary, Hammanskraal, 14th-22nd July 1973.

South African Students' Organisation. (1973f). Composite report of the national executive to the fourth General Students' Council, St Peter's Conference Centre, Hammanskraal, 14th-22nd July 1973.

South African Students' Organisation. (1973g). Presidential address: Paper presented by acting president Henry Isaacs at fourth General Students' Council St Peter's Seminary, Hammanskraal.

South African Students' Organisation. (1974a). Minutes of the proceedings of the fifth General Students' Council of the SASO, St Peter's Seminary, Hammanskraal, 14th-19th January 1974.

South African Students' Organisation. (1974b). Reports presented at the Federal Theological Seminary, Alice, 23rd May to 26 th May, 1974.

South African Students' Organisation. (1974c). Composite executive report to the sixth General Students' Council at the Wilgespruit Conference Centre, Roodepoort, Transvaal, 30th June, 1974 to 7th July, 1974.

South African Students' Organisation. (1974d). Report of the president: Presented at the sixth General Students' Council.

South African Students' Organisation. (1974e). Minutes of the proceedings of the sixth General Students' Council of the SASO, St Ansgars Fellowship Centre, Roodepoort, 30 June – 6 July 1974.

South African Students' Organisation. (1976). SASO Day: 10th May 1976. King Williamstown: King SASO Local Branch.

South African Students' Organisation. (1977). September 1977: A tribute. Durban.

Newsletters

SASO Bulletin, 1(1), 1977.

SASO Newsletter, June, 1970.

SASO Newsletter, 2(1), March/April 1972.

SASO Newsletter, 2(3), May/June 1972.

SASO Newsletter, 2(4), September/October 1972.

SASO Newsletter, 2(5), November/December 1972.

SASO Newsletter, 3(1), March/April 1973.

SASO Newsletter, 5(1), May/June 1975.

SASO Newsletter, 5(2), July/August 1975.

SASO Newsletter, 5(3), November/December 1975.

SASO Newsletter, 6(1), March/April 1976.

Other campus/student documents

Anonymous. (1986). Cape Town Education Charter News.

Committee of 81. (1980a). From the schools to the people. Cape Town, May.

Committee of 81. (1980b). Boycott as a tactic of struggle. Cape Town, June.

Ngombane, N. (1991). A case for the independence of the student movement. Discussion article, 13 August, University of Western Cape.

The National Co-ordinating Committee, Education Charter Campaign. (1986). The Doors of Learning and Culture Shall be Opened.

The National Co-ordinating Committee, Education Charter Campaign. (1987). Circular to: All organisations – A summary of some of the demands collected in the Education Charter Campaign up to 31st January 1987.

University of Western Cape. (1987). UWC Campus Bulletin, 16 March.

University of Western Cape. (1990). Statistical Data. Office of the Registrar, Bellville, October.

Wits Black Students' Society. (1983). Circular, 6 August.

Wits Black Students' Society. (1984): Orientation '84. *Challenge* (newsletter).

Newspapers

ANC Weekly Newsbriefings. African National Congress, London

Facts and Reports: Press Cuttings on Southern Africa. Holland Committee on Southern Africa, Amsterdam

New Nation. Pretoria, South Africa

Rand Daily Mail. Johannesburg, South Africa

SASPU Focus. South African Students' Press Union, Johannesburg, South Africa

SASPU National. South African Students' Press Union, Johannesburg, South Africa

SASPU State of the Nation. South African Students' Press Union, Johannesburg, South Africa

Sunday Post. Johannesburg, South Africa

Sunday Tribune. Durban, South Africa

UDUSA News. Johannesburg, South Africa

The Cape Times. Cape Town, South Africa

The Citizen. Johannesburg, South Africa

The Star, International Airmail Weekly. Johannesburg, South Africa

The Times Higher Education Supplement. London

The Weekly Mail. Johannesburg, South Africa

Interviews

Mr Devan Pillay, SANSCO member. (London, 1987).

Mr Simpiwe Mguduso, SANSCO president, 1984-85. (Durban, May 1995).

Mr Abba Omar, SANSCO general secretary, 1982-83, SANSCO vice-president, 1983-84. (Johannesburg, July 1995).

Mr Mike Koyana, SANSCO president, 1989-91. (Cape Town, July 1995).

Mr Tiego Moseneke, SANSCO president, 1983-84. (Johannesburg, July 1995).

Mr Billy Ramokgopa, SANSCO president, 1985-87. (Johannesburg, July 1995).

Mr Tom Nkoane, SANSCO interim president, 1979-81. (Pretoria, August 1995).

Ms Sandy Africa, SANSCO member (Pretoria, August 1995).